Beyond Partnership

Strategies for Innovation

and Lean Supply

Richard Lamming

Prentice Hall

New York   London   Toronto   Sydney   Tokyo   Singapore

First published 1993 by
Prentice Hall
An imprint of
Pearson Education Limited
Edinburgh Gate
Harlow, Essex CM20 2JE,
England

Disc conversion in 10/12pt Times
by Columns Typesetters of Reading

Transferred to digital print on demand, 2002

Printed and bound by Antony Rowe Ltd, Eastbourne

Library of Congress Cataloging-in-Publication Data

Lamming, Richard.
    Beyond partnership : strategies for innovation and lean supply /
by Richard Lamming.
        p.   cm. – (Manufacturing practitioner series)
    Includes bibliographical references and index.
    ISBN 0–13–143785–2 : $35.00
    1. Automobile supplies industry—Management.   I. Title.
II. Series.
HD9710.3.A2L35   1993
629.2'068—dc20   92–38797
                                                            CIP

British Library Cataloguing in Publication Data

A catalogue record for this book is available from
the British Library

ISBN 0–13–143785–2 (pbk)

---

5   6   7   8   9   03 02 01 00 99

MPS

Beyond
Partnership

Manufacturing Practitioner Series

To my parents, John and Barbara Lamming

The car itself is now a styling concept . . . the technology is in the components.

William J. Abernathy, 1978

There is nothing more vulnerable than entrenched success.

George Romney, Head of American Motors, 1956

If two players go for a ball which then goes into touch, there's never any doubt among those players which of them touched the ball last. So, why is it that every time the ball goes into touch both players claim the throw-in for their own side? Is it because they are very, very stupid or is it because a dishonest advantage is as welcome as an honest one?

From *Professional Foul* by Tom Stoppard 1978

Contents

Acknowledgements

This book is the culmination of eight years' work. During this time many people have influenced and guided me and I am pleased to acknowledge them – my work would not have been possible without their support.

Professor Daniel Jones was a constant guide and supporter, during my early research, throughout the IMVP years, and since. His comprehensive knowledge of the automotive industry and his encouragement in the formulation of my ideas have been of the greatest value. Professor John Bessant has been a similarly vital inspiration in my work for many years. In this research, in addition to his great moral support and friendship, his experience in the field of innovation has been a prime source of guidance for me. Dr James Womack provided me with a constant friendly challenge in order to check the validity of my concepts. His vast knowledge of the industry and international perspective have been invaluable.

Thanks are also due to colleagues from the academic world: Mark Dodgson, Paddy FitzGerald, Paul Gardiner, Andrew Graves, Robert Griffith-Jones, Susan Helper, Masayoshi Ikeda, John Krafcik, John Paul MacDuffie, Dennis Marler, Toshihiro Nishiguchi, Roy Rothwell, Ann Rowbotham, Daniel Roos, Mari Sako and Anthony Sheriff.

My industrial contacts are too numerous to mention here and some need to remain anonymous for professional reasons. Thanks are due to them all. In particular I should like to thank: Jody Chatterjee (The Technology Partnership), John Griffiths (Nissan), Peter Hill (Nissan), Dietmar Kailer (ZF), HansJorg Manger (Robert Bosch GmbH), and William Raftery (MEMA – USA).

I am pleased to acknowledge the help of my father, John Lamming. His long experience in the British automotive industry provided many technical details, some of which are noted in the text by his initials, JLL.

Lastly, I must thank my wife Leigh and daughters, Louise and Rosalie, for their forbearance during the long absences, mental and physical, which this work has required: their support has been perhaps the most important of all.

Introduction

This book is about coordinating the dynamic chains of activities, responsibilities and organizations, that are needed to make complex products. The subject is variously called out-sourcing, purchasing and supply, supply chain management, logistics and materials management. Major forces are at play in the international business environment which make this subject increasingly important. These forces must be understood in order to make new plans for dealing with them.

To explore this subject, I have chosen to focus upon the situation and prospects of manufacturing companies around the world which depend to varying extents upon the automobile and its requirements for continuing business and technological development. They are not only the companies which produce the vehicles, (the 'assemblers'), but those which design, manufacture and supply the many component parts, sub-assemblies, and 'systems' which make up the modern car.

This example was chosen because the automotive industry has been the first to encounter, in a comprehensive way, the clash between an old logic of supply chain management and the new world of 'partnership' logistics introduced by the best Japanese automobile firms. This book will show that neither of these systems is right or sufficient for global adaptation in the world of the 1990s and beyond. A new concept – lean supply – will be proposed. This concept is equally relevant to every complex industry.

The structure of this book and how to use it

The book is intended for 'straight-through' reading. Alternatively, the reader may wish to refer specifically to parts of it. The following table is intended to help in this process.

Table I.1 The structure of this book and how to use it

	Chapter	Title	Subject focus	Read for reference to
Backgrounds	1	Markets and motor cars	The development of the industry and the roles of the components suppliers through 'craft', 'mass' and 'lean' production (1900–90)	Historical perspective and background to the changes now facing the industry in America, Europe and Japan Data on current Japanese international investments
Backgrounds	2	The automotive industries today	The automotive assembly and components industries, described and dimensioned	Data on size and structure of the industries Description of recent developments Key issues emerging for assemblers and suppliers
Concepts	3	Shared technical change: the nature of innovation	Concepts of innovation – some of the historical ideas and current thought	Summary of the important writers' ideas on innovation Important terminology and ideas introduced, explained and related
Concepts	4	Shared technical change: strategic collaboration	Theoretical frameworks for understanding strategic and technical collaboration	As above, but for strategic collaboration Supply chains and value chains
Concepts	5	Development of new automobiles	Combines key points of Chapters 1–4 and concludes on how innovation occurs in the industry	'Lean' product development and the customer/supplier roles within it Innovation in the context of the industry
Lean supply	6	Customer–supplier relationships	Models for understanding developments in relationships – up to partnership/Japanese levels Starts with a summary of major writers on customer/supplier relationships	Original, extensive research by author – practical tools for planning developments of supply bases and strategies Overview on theories of relationships
Lean supply	7	Lean supply	Lean supply explained Supply relationships within lean production: harnessing innovation	Original research by author – a further practical tool for deliberate development in relationships Development of the components industry
Lean supply	8	Strategies for going lean	Strategic planning for suppliers – policy implications for customers	New ideas and terminology for lean suppliers: frameworks for positioning Examples of the strategies
Lean supply	9	Beyond partnership: the implications of lean supply	Broad context for the future Implications for management and for theory	Next stages in relationships and the benefits/challenges contained within them Using the innovation ideas Relationship assessment and relationships portfolios

Background

The research upon which the book is based has been very practically oriented: over an eight-year period, 181 interviews were conducted (56 with assemblers, 109 with suppliers, and 16 with industry associations) in twelve countries throughout the world. This fresh research has built upon my own experience in purchasing in the UK automotive industry.

The theoretical models which I derived from all this research have been tested and refined by many presentations and discussions and are presented here as frameworks for strategies for component suppliers in the move towards a new paradigm in automotive manufacturing – lean production. The models contain just as many implications, however, for the customers of these suppliers – the vehicle assemblers. While it is the automotive industry which is used as a context, the findings of the research present some fundamental challenges for Purchasing and Supply in all sectors of business.

I have tried to make the book interesting, useful and relevant to managers and to researchers and students working in academic environments. I hope the reader will find the endnotes to each chapter valuable – they contain many details about the industry and the concepts as well as the necessary references to further reading. I have made the bibliography long and, I hope, comprehensive.

Where theories are included in the discussion, they are there for a practical purpose – theoretical frameworks are an essential part of strategic decision making. Where the focus is on the practical side, I have avoided the 'how to do it' style. Much of the book is about the future and the people best suited to work out how to do it are those within industry. The intended contribution and value-added of this book are the food for thought which it should provide and the frameworks to be used in making sense of the situation facing industrial organizations.

For the automotive component manufacturers ('suppliers') the economic environment has changed fundamentally in recent years and is likely to carry on changing for some while to come. Technical change, linked to market requirements and scientific or technological innovation, is presenting the vehicle manufacturers with a plethora of product opportunities – more than they can handle at once. The component suppliers, for long undervalued players in the industry, are facing demands from their automotive customers to play new technological roles – sometimes as 'partners'.

For a few suppliers this is not new: they have been leading the technological developments for a long time. Even for these expert designer/manufacturers, however, the new roles present major challenges. The scope of engineering input, of speedy development, and of product and process innovation required of them is increasing greatly, while demands for 'world class' manufacturing (excellence in quality, process control, delivery performance, etc.) alter the fundamental basis of their businesses.

This book argues that successful positioning within this reshaped industry depends upon the nature of the relationship between the supplier and its assembler customers. Since all suppliers need to deal with several assemblers at once, this relationship must not be a cosy one-to-one affair, but a much more complicated mixture of factors which builds to an effective, supportive, communication channel, without which the necessary collaboration on process and product development could not be achieved.

Objectives

The objective of the book is to analyze the customer–supplier relationships in the automotive industry, on a fully international basis, and to produce a series of models which might aid understanding and be used in practical applications to develop the relationships themselves. This analysis culminates in models of strategy for automotive components manufacturers, which contains significant implications for the purchasing policies of the vehicle assemblers.

Approach to the subject

The approach to this research was based upon many personal interviews with individuals on both 'sides' of the relationship: purchasing and engineering managers in the assemblers, and senior executives in the suppliers. As noted above, these many interviews were conducted over almost a decade in most parts of the global industry (UK, France, Germany, Belgium, Italy, Sweden, USA, Canada, Mexico, Japan, Australia and Malaysia). The interviews were backed up by several postal data collection surveys and my personal involvement (1986–90) in the International Motor Vehicle Program (IMVP) – the major, automotive industry-sponsored research programme based at the Massachusetts Institute of Technology (discussed in Appendix 1).

The breadth of research was essential because it is no longer useful to speak of national industries in understanding the automotive business. The national industries have fused to become regional, and even global, in their concerns and capabilities. The same is true for many other industries.

Theoretical context

Two key factors which underpin the development of customer–supplier relationships in this industry were observed to be technical change and collaborative strategies. Thus, the literature which this book explores is that of technological innovation and strategic collaboration.

It is important to recognize other paths which might be chosen: the political and social relations within the industry, the organization of labour, and alternative financial structures are all equally important in understanding the developments. The automotive industry has provided many fascinating cases in these areas – from

Henry Ford's ideas on payment systems and international politics, to the present day globalization of the Japanese companies and their policies.

A body of literature on supply relationships also exists and it is to this body that this book adds. I have already published some of the models developed during the research, within the context of the IMVP, and they have been tested extensively in seminars within the industry around the world. They have been quoted and used by several academic authors in papers and books and several companies have used them as the basis for discussions. The models of strategy developed in Chapter 8 were chosen in 1991 by the UK Department of Trade and Industry as a major focus for discussion in a booklet on strategic collaboration for UK automotive components suppliers (DTI, 1992).

The IMVP culminated in an immensely successful book, *The Machine that Changed the World* (Womack *et al.*, 1990) in which the chapter on supply systems included parts of my work. The book introduced the concept of 'lean' production. I hope that this new book will dovetail with that work – picking up where it left off as regards the component industry and purchasing within the assemblers.

While much is known about the innovation process, about new product development and time-based strategies, lean production is still a new, largely uncharted, area. Similarly, a great deal has been written about 'horizontal' collaboration (joint ventures between firms of similar status) but little about 'vertical' collaboration (e.g. between customers and suppliers). The key contribution of this book is to develop the latter in the context of lean production, arriving at the concept of 'lean supply'.

The book examines a process of change rather than the immediate manifestations of the change. Indeed, the change is still under way, and far from completed.

When I announced the title of this book to a sociologist friend of mine she remarked that it might be put on library shelves under 'Psychology'. I am an engineer, not a psychologist, but her jest was not far off the mark: lean supply is about a fundamental, very difficult, strategic attitudinal change – as much a challenge for the hearts and minds of manufacturers as for the technical skills their designers and managers.

RCL
Bath, September 1992

Markets and Motors Cars

1

From its origins just over 100 years ago in Germany and France, the motor vehicle has become arguably the most fundamental single influence upon modern life.[1] In both direct and indirect senses, much of the activity in modern social and working life either would not take place, or would take place in an entirely different fashion, were it not for the passenger car and the commercial vehicle. The extensive infrastructural requirements of the motor vehicle, its reliance throughout its history upon consumption of fossil fuels, and the consequent pollution caused by the internal combustion engine, have made it a target for environmental lobbies since the mid-1960s.

Throughout its life the motor car has been an object of desire and fashion. Competition has often been based upon styling as much as technical refinement, upon image as much as performance. Millions of people spend much of their time 'loving' their cars: the machine is said to have 'character'.

Since its inception, however, the basic concept of the motor vehicle itself has not changed greatly. As Altshuler *et al.* point out (1984, p. 11), it is still 'a four-wheeled, internally-powered personal transport apparatus for road use, designed to carry a driver and a few passengers.'

One could add to this that most of the engines still combust gasoline or diesel fuel, creating linear motion (in pistons) which is transferred into rotary motion (via a crankshaft) which is itself transmitted though ninety degrees once or twice before reaching the driven wheels. Most bodies are made of painted metal, all tyres are of pneumatic design with rubber casings, etc., etc. The motor vehicle remains a massive assembly of small parts – some 10 000 in an average car[2] – which are made by many different types of firm and brought together by highly visible (in the public/political sense) 'assemblers'.[3]

The development of vehicle specifications within this context has led to much sophistication and also standardization of basic components. The latter fact is the result of industry agreements on aspects of interchangeability, safety, measurement, and many other operational features. National and international agreements on standardized components did not lead to fixed designs but became the basis for component suppliers to become decoupled from assemblers as a separate, identifiable industry in their own right. Thus, while the steering gear in a modern Ford might not be interchangeable with that in a BMW, they are both designed and manufactured by the same 'steering gear supplier'. Many of the complex components which go to make up the highly differentiated vehicles are in fact standardized in their basic design. Defining where the automotive industry stops and the automotive components industry begins is a complex task and subject to factors which continually change.

While the concept of the car has remained the same, the automotive industry and its practices (in particular, the manner in which vehicles are designed, provisioned and assembled) have changed greatly over the past century and the basis of competition has altered significantly several times. In the 1980s the two major research programmes at MIT defined the 'transformations' through which the industry has passed; these are discussed below.[4]

■ Origins of the automotive industry: 'the industry of industries'[5]

Discussion of the automotive industry and its development inevitably becomes a discussion of manufacturing itself. This is because the three sets of methods, approaches and techniques of manufacturing – characterized as *paradigms*[6] and separated by what have been called *transformations* – whilst they have not started in the production of automobiles, have been most clearly developed within this industry and fundamentally linked to it throughout its life, being significantly affected by it and upsetting it in return.

From about 1880 until 1908, the dominant form of manufacture for vehicles, in common with other major products, was a system now known as 'craft' production. This was developed in Europe – with the automotive industry itself starting in Germany and France. Craft production had grown from the rich industrial experience which existed in Europe following the industrial revolution, over a century earlier, and the history of skilled manufacture, professionalized by the 'apprentice–journeyman–master' system and the guilds.

Vehicles made in the craft firms were the products of skilled craftsmen, using flexible, multi-purpose tools. The companies which made them were typically engineering firms, such as the British gas engine manufacturer, Crossley, the Swedish railway engineers, Scania, and the American firm Buick – now part of General Motors – started by the plumbing manufacturer, David Buick. The parts of each vehicle were individually and collectively unique: the modification work entailed in the process of fitting them together meant that a part or sub-assembly from one vehicle would probably not fit into the same location on another. Inevitably, the process of manufacture of parts and assembly of the vehicle took a long time but the customer had the advantage of buying a bespoke product – a wide variety of personal tastes and requirements could be satisfied through extensive involvement of the customer during the process of manufacture. As a result, only the wealthy could afford such vehicles – particularly for personal transport – and the car remained a specialist product (rather than an 'industrial' product) in Europe and North America until the end of the nineteenth century.

The firms which made these vehicles had a background in skilled operation and were naturally accustomed to subcontracting parts of the process to their own skilled craftsmen. Their subcontractors – suppliers – were firms of all sizes, also with skilled engineering workforces, which specialized in specific processes. As Womack *et al.* note:

> Most parts and much of the vehicle's design came from small machine shops. The system was coordinated by an owner-entrepreneur in direct contact with everyone involved: customers, employees and suppliers. (Womack *et al.*, 1990, p. 24)[7]

As for the assembly process – the collecting together and 'fitting' of all the components to make an entire vehicle – there were many firms in the industry. By 1906 there were hundreds of small firms in North America and Western Europe were producing vehicles using craft production methods, with almost 50 000 out of the world total of 82 000 units produced in that year coming from France and Germany (see Womack, 1988, p. 302 and Altshuler *et al.*, 1984, p. 14).

All this was to change very rapidly. In 1896 Frank Duryea, a bicycle mechanic of Springfield, Massachusetts, made thirteen cars to the same design, heralding the start of standardization in automobile manufacture in the USA (Flink, 1970, p. 25). In 1909 the annual output of the sixty-nine North American assemblers reached 123 900 vehicles[8] and by 1915 it was close to one million. By 1917 it had almost doubled again. In 1914 Henry Ford's Highland Park plant was turning out 1200 cars per day. In 1923 the number of North American assemblers had dropped to below fifty and Ford supplied 44 per cent of the world's vehicle market from his American production base. As Halberstam records:

> When he began producing the Model T, it took twelve and a half hours to make one car. His dream was to make one car every minute. It took him only twelve years to achieve that goal and five years after that, in 1925, he was making one every ten seconds. (Halberstam, 1986, p. 67)

A transformation had indeed occurred.

■ The first transformation: mass production and a large market, hungry for volume

The first transformation took place in the first decade of the twentieth century, with the development of 'Henry Ford's system' – involving both product and process innovation in a radical sense.[9] In fact, as we shall see, Ford did not invent the system but is credited with bringing together many existing ideas into one integrated approach. It was to lead to Ford's dominant position – 55 per cent of the North American market by 1921 – although its originator's incomplete vision would mean that shortly after that point, his company would lose the lead to a more imaginative marketing strategy.

The changes that Ford made in product design were driven both by the market – the need to provide 'a universal car for the common man' (rather than one which needed to be driven by a specialist chauffeur and maintained by a specialist mechanic for even the slightest adjustments) and by technology. As Womack *et al.* point out:

> Ford also benefited from recent advances in machine tools able to work
> on *prehardened* metals. The warping that occurred as machined parts
> were being hardened had been the bane of previous attempts to standardize
> parts. Once the warping problem was solved, Ford was able to develop
> innovative designs that reduced the number of parts needed and made
> these parts easy to attach. For example, Ford's four-cylinder engine block
> consisted of a single, complex casting. Competitors cast each cylinder
> separately and bolted the four together. (Womack *et al.*, 1990, p. 27)[10]

This reduction in complexity represented a cost reduction process with accompanying potential improvements in quality (by reducing the number of things which could go wrong in the assembly process) and many other benefits. Today it would be called 'design for manufacture' (reducing the complexity and number of components to make assembly simpler) or 'corner engineering' (integrating several components into one major sub-assembly or 'corner' so that the supplier may deliver one large item to the assembly line – thereby simplifying the assembly process). It can also have significant implications for the supply of parts to the assembler – fewer parts may mean fewer suppliers; larger and more sophisticated parts mean more demanding challenges (and thus opportunities for competition) for suppliers and so on. This is something which we shall meet again later; it is worth remembering that the concept is not new.

The Model T Ford, which gave the company a dominant position in the automotive industry and shifted the focus of best practice from Europe to the USA,[11] was therefore more than an innovative vehicle in itself. While it contained much in the way of new product technology, such as planetary transmission, flywheel-mounted magneto[12] and use of vanadium steel (previously unknown in North America, and imported by recruiting a British engineer to work for Ford in the USA), it represented an entirely new way of looking at manufacture – and of using subcontracting. As Abernathy (1978, pp. 22–3), and Womack *et al.* (1990, pp. 26–7) point out, the basis of mass production, as Ford was to call his system,[13] was not the famous moving production line (although this clearly played a very significant role) but the ability to specify and receive interchangeable parts – often made to drawing by an independent subcontractor – which could be fitted together simply and quickly. Chandler (1964) reminds us again that this was not Ford's idea:

> The idea of interchangeable parts as applied to a specific model of machine was standard practice long before this (1908) in some industries, but it had not been fully applied in the automobile industry; and the development of it in this industry, especially as applied to improvements in structural design, was apparently largely due to Ford.[14]

Abernathy also notes:

> High-volume, low-cost production of automobiles rests on two basic concepts: precision-made, interchangeable parts and mass production. Both of these concepts were widely applied on the bicycle industry before 1900, and the early producers of automobiles brought knowledge of these practices with them. Of the early firms, Cadillac was recognised for its expertise in precision-machined interchangeable parts and . . . the Olds Motor Works was mass producing cars in 1901, before the Ford motor company was even founded. (Abernathy, 1978, p. 22)

and '[In] 1902 . . . the Olds Motor Works . . . produced and sold 2,500 small two-cylinder cars . . . [and was] recognised as the world's first company to mass-produce cars.' Leland's Cadillac design of 1906 even won an award for the innovation of using interchangeable, standardized parts.

In a more profound sense, it may be argued that mass production began much earlier, in nineteenth-century Britain, following the ideas of Adam Smith (see Piore and Sabel (1984, pp. 23–6)).

Bessant provides a summary of further influences from which Ford's ideas grew:

> Whereas the British tradition had largely been one of 'making', it was the US industry which really laid down the basic ideas behind 'manufacturing'. One of the key forces in this were the ideas of Eli Whitney, originally introduced to carry out high volume gun manufacture in the early 1800s. These gave birth to factories such as that operated by Samuel Colt in Hartford, Connecticut in which '. . . the whole floor-space is covered with machine tools. Each portion of the firearm has its particular section . . . the first group of machines . . . is employed in chambering cylinders; the next is turning and shaping them; here another is boring barrels'. (Bessant, 1991, p. 18)

Henry Ford's own early career was entwined with machines: repairing them and using them. His first fascination was actually with watches, not cars, and it is said that he initially intended his ideas for the development of mass production to be applied to watch manufacture (Halberstam, 1986, pp. 72–4). By 1896, however, he had built one car and was working on a second. He also experimented with a racing car – the '999' whose success was to be an important influence upon him.

The transfer of ideas is neatly summed up by a quote from Nevins and Hill:

'The Ford Company was trying to make low-cost cars as reliable and as well supplied with good, cheap spare parts as a Singer Sewing Machine or the McCormick Reaper' (Nevins and Hill, 1954b, p. 348). Whatever his influences, Ford achieved a cost advantage and also the ability to remove the need for skilled labour from the process.[15]

Ford's dedication to purpose was to lead to his loss of market leadership through lack of flexibility. At his River Rouge plant, built in Detroit after World War I, the line production equipment was so inflexible that even the smallest product design change was avoided, and a new model introduction (Model A in 1927) proved almost disastrous for the firm: he lost over US $200 million during the transition year, laid off over 60 000 workers and had to scrap over 15 000 machine tools, rebuilding a further 25 000.

It would be wrong, however, to interpret his famous statement on market demand as a total lack of market sensitivity:

> In 1909 I announced one morning, without any previous warning, that in the future we were going to build only one model, that the model was going to be 'Model T', and that the chassis would be exactly the same for all cars, and I remarked 'Any customer can have a car painted any colour that he wants so long as it is black'. I cannot say that anyone agreed with me. (Ford, 1922)[16]

Chandler (1964) records, however, that as early as 1908, Ford was offering a range of styles: 'a touring car retailing at $850, a town car at $1,000, a roadster at $825, a coupe at $950, and a landaulet at $950.' There were eventually nine different styles of Model T, including a van. While these were just different body styles built upon one identical chassis and mechanicals, it is apparent that Ford did feel the need to respond to what he saw as market requirements. Another quote from Ford himself, directed to one of his senior colleagues, Charles Sorensen, relates to Ford's accidental discovery of the strength of vanadium steel, and his realization of the market potential: 'Charlie', he said, 'this means entirely new design requirements and we can get a better, lighter and cheaper car as a result of it' (Sorensen, 1956, p. 98).

The first transformation in the automotive industry was completed, however, not by Ford but by the firm which had overtaken him (in terms of market share) in 1926 – General Motors (GM).[17] The innovations in marketing which were developed in GM and the administration system devised by its third president – Alfred P. Sloan Jr (who had been recruited to GM when the components firm, Hyatt Roller Bearing Co., of which he was president, was acquired by the growing giant in 1916)[18] – were clear signs of organizational change in response to market pressure (carried out with massive financial assistance from wealthy backers: the DuPont family and J.P. Morgan).[19]

The organizational innovation which GM pioneered was twofold: the retention of autonomous operating entities (Buick, Oldsmobile, etc.) linked by communications and reporting systems which enabled such decentralized operation, and the capability to provide market variety, which sprung from this. The company was able to offer a wide range of vehicle 'marques' – the well-known names of the firms which had been absorbed into the corporation. Whilst he totally rejected the first of these ideas, Ford did follow GM to an extent, buying the Lincoln company in 1922 and later creating a new marque – Mercury.[20] Despite this, his retention of central control and often idiosyncratic personal intervention, sometimes verging on paranoia (see Halberstam, 1986, Chapter 5, especially pages 100 and 101), lost him not only his lead but also second place. Walter Chrysler's company gradually increased its share (of the North American market) to 25.4 per cent in 1937 (compared to Ford's 21.4 per cent) and 23.7 per cent in 1940 (compared to Ford's 18.9 per cent). Chrysler copied General Motors' strategy of offering 'a full line' of cars to the market, creating marques such as the low-priced Plymouth.

These strategies had their effect on the industrial geography of North America, with automotive assembly and component supply congregating in what was to become known as the 'rust belt', half a century later. Robertson and Langlois note:

> Early in its development the industry became concentrated in the East North Central states of Michigan, Ohio, and Indiana. In 1904, 53.3% of total output by value came from those states, of which approximately one-half (26.6%) originated in Michigan. A decade later, these three states accounted for 81.1% of total output, with Michigan alone accounting for 62.9% of total output. And, despite a reduction in later years, Michigan, Ohio and Indiana still accounted for 67.6% of output in 1925, with Michigan's share 51.7% of total output.
>
> Localization allowed assemblers to take advantage of external economies that flowed from concentration of suppliers. But because of high transportation costs for finished units, the structure of the industry has been compared to an hourglass, with parts from diverse suppliers funnelling into a small number of plants to make subassemblies that were then shipped to various plants around the nation for final assembly into automobiles. This was true, however, only of Ford, and later General Motors, the largest manufacturers. Other firms concentrated their activities in the East North Central States or in New York. This made it possible for them to share not only parts suppliers, but also to draw from a larger pool of skilled workers and to share information more easily. (Robertson and Langlois, 1988, pp. 9–10)[21]

Integration policies in mass production

If craft production had relied upon component parts made by independent suppliers, then the first transformation in the automotive industry represented a major upset for the industry that might have grown up to supply those parts. In 1910 Ford was still buying his bodies, wheels, radiators, engines, transmissions and chassis from outside firms (the last three from Dodge Brothers, originally 'charter' (founder) investors in the Ford Motor Company, but soon to be ousted by Ford and eventually to become part of the Chrysler Corporation). By 1915 he had brought all of this work 'in-house' – under his direct control. It is suggested by Womack *et al.* (1990), and by Chandler (1964) that this was primarily because other manufacturers (presumably still stuck ideologically in craft production thinking) were unable to match Ford's process innovation and subsequent expectation for quality. Certainly, the obtuse Henry Ford is credited with several disparaging judgements of his erstwhile suppliers.

Purchasing practices at Ford in 1907 were described by Sorensen as follows:

> Until then, the large requirements like tyres would be handled as an individual job by Mr Ford and other large items by [Mr] Couzens. Buying was on a hand-to-mouth basis, generally in quantities no larger than were actually needed for short periods. [Mr] Flanders stabilised some of this helter-skelter buying by setting production schedules of fixed monthly output. As volume increased with rising production ... Diehl [the new purchasing manager] required large suppliers to submit prices covering six and twelve month periods ... His buyers were instructed to look for at least two sources of supply and be sure of competitive bidding. Next he required each bidder to submit prices based on material, labour and overhead and even the amount of profit. Under such a system, there was no question about costs being kept down and the savings were tremendous. (Sorensen, 1956, p. 102)[22]

It is unlikely, however, that much of the information on costs and profits, etc., that Ford received was accurate, or of any strategic value, and little confidence was built up. Mistrusting his suppliers, Ford proceeded to integrate. Whatever the initial reasons for the in-sourcing of everything, this obsession with control eventually led to the ultimate in vertical integration – the River Rouge plant, opened in Detroit in 1927. In this apogee of contemporary manufacturing, Ford reached perhaps the limit of technical control and the nadir of market relatedness. As Chandler puts it:

> Here Ford produced nearly all the parts that went into the (Model) T and even made his own glass and steel. Into the Rouge poured a ceaseless stream of Ford-owned ore, coal and lumber. Every minute or so, out came a completed car. A brilliant technological achievement, the Rouge was far less impressive as a business venture. Huge capital investment brought inflexibility and high fixed costs. The whole complex was set up to build a product which was more than fifteen years old. Even small changes in design could come only at great expense. (Chandler, 1964, p. 14)

General Motors had an accidental introduction into the idea of subcontracting: as Abernathy reports:

> A fire in the Olds Motor Works in late 1901, when mass production was just beginning, destroyed the Olds's shops. Consequently a final assembly operation was organised for the first time and parts were subcontracted out to suppliers. (Abernathy, 1978, p. 23)

Ransome E. Olds, traditionally a manufacturer of gasoline engines, now bought engines from Leland and Faulconer, transmissions from the Dodge brothers and bodies from Briscoe: see Robertson and Langlois (1988).

Later, GM was to mimic Ford's policy of total vertical integration. Whereas at Ford the obsession of its founder/owner drove it unchecked towards the sclerosis of the Rouge, the committee structure of GM, introduced by Sloan in 1920, proved to be part of its salvation. In 1909 under the leadership of its founder, William Crapo Durant, GM had acquired more than twenty firms, including Buick, Cadillac and Oldsmobile, and several components companies. Durant persuaded Albert Champion, a Frenchman, to locate his factory in Flint Michigan, later absorbing him into the GM fold as the A.C. parts company. He even proposed a total merger of North American auto companies, under his control. Henry Ford avoided this with some masterful tactical play: see Chandler (1984, p. 54) and Halberstam (1986, p. 82).

Durant did not install a successful structure within GM, however, and was ousted by his bankers in 1910. He gained control again in 1915, a year before he recruited Sloan, but was sacked finally in 1919. Like Ford, Durant had created a massive organization, which he was unable to manage.

In 1921, under Sloan, the GM executive committee decided that it would not operate in component manufacture, but rely more on outside firms. The strategy was quoted as remaining only in businesses 'that relate to the construction of the car, truck, or tractor' (GM archive, quoted in Chandler (1964)). GM therefore turned more to outside suppliers, assembling a wide variety of models from the common parts thus obtained. In this way the new market leader was able to pursue Alfred Sloan's goal of 'a car for every purse and purpose'.

It is apparent, however, that a very broad interpretation of the phrase 'construction of the car, truck or tractor' and narrow definition of 'component' were employed. A glimpse at the organizational chart of General Motors in 1920 shows that the Accessories and Parts Divisions encompassed the following sub-divisions (quoted in Chandler, 1964):

Accessory Division: Hyatt Bearings Division; Remy Electric Division; Jackson Steel Products Company; Dayton Engineering Laboratory Company (DELCO); Harrison Radiator Division; Lancaster Products Company; New Departure Manufacturing Company; United Motors Service Corporation; Domestic Engineering Company; Klaxon Company; Champion Ignition Company; Novelty Incorporated Lamp Company;

Saginaw Parts Division: Saginaw Products Company; Saginaw Malleable Company; Central Foundry Company; J.C.W. Company;

Detroit Parts Division: Central Gear Company; Northway Motor Company; Central Axle Company; Central Forge Company; Canadian Products Company;

Muncie Parts Division: T.W. Warner Company; Muncie Products Company.

A summary of the parts produced by these companies (nowadays we would say 'technologies') would reveal an almost complete vehicle. Most of the firms remain today within the GM structure (some now renamed, others combined, such as New Departure Hyatt (NDH), A.C. Rochester, and Delco Remy, etc.). In the 1920s General Motors' decision to 'out-source' did not stimulate the independent component supply industry very much, as it has not on successive occasions, most recently during the 1980s. GM's perception of 'components' was evidently restricted to very basic parts.

At Ford, integration grew steadily. The first item had been radiators (1914), followed by the massive investment in basic technologies (mining and iron and steel production, glass and cardboard manufacturing, 1924–26) and carburettors (1924). The company even made tyres for a ten-year-period (1937–47).[23]

As discussed above, however, components manufacturers were distinguished from assemblers by the standardization of component specifications – Abernathy speaks of a 'progress towards a dominant design'. This applied especially to their interfaces with other parts (thread sizes, etc.) and functional expectation (e.g. steady electrical output of an alternator or generator). Thus the in-house facilities of assemblers had to align themselves not only with the particular wishes of their parent but also with the technical trends in the separate industry, of which they wished to be a part. This dilemma remains to this day and causes the subsidiaries of assemblers problems in selling to other automotive customers.

Robertson and Langlois record that:

Recognition of the value of external economies resulted in two important agreements [in the USA] in 1910 and 1915. The first, sponsored by the Society of Automotive Engineers, led to the establishment of a set of standards for parts. In the early period of the industry, most independent suppliers built to specifications laid down by the assembler. As a result, there were more than 1,600 types of steel tubing used and 800 standards of lock washers, with a similar proliferation of other components. Early attempts to set common standards had been unsuccessful, but the panic of 1910 brought a crisis among assemblers. The failure of suppliers in the panic emphasised the vulnerability of small assemblers who were not readily able to switch to other firms because of peculiarities in specifications. Led at first by Howard E. Coffin of the Hudson Motor Car Company, over the next decade the S.A.E. set detailed standards for numerous parts, in the process increasing interchangeability across firms. After standardisation, for example, the number of types of steel tubing had been reduced to 210 and the number of lock washers to 16. Throughout the initial period of standardisation, until the early 1920s, most interest was shown by the smaller firms, who had the most to gain. The larger firms, such as Ford, Studebaker, Dodge, Willys-Overland, and General Motors, tended to ignore the S.A.E. and relied instead on internally established standards. (Robertson and Langlois, 1988, p. 10)[24]

The component supply principle of mass production, whether it was overt and proud such as in the Rouge, or strategically covered up and sometimes publicly denied, such as at GM, was classic vertical integration.

International spread of mass production in the automotive industry

Ford, General Motors, and later Chrysler, took their new automotive industry paradigm around the world: to Europe – where Ford opened an assembly plant in Trafford Park, Manchester in England in 1911 – to Australia in 1925 (Ford and GM),[25] and to the Far East. Ford and GM set up 'completely knocked-down' kit assembly (CKD) operations in Japan in 1925 and 1927 respectively and, together with other foreign-owned subsidiaries, accounted for more than 95 per cent of Japanese new vehicle registrations between 1926 and 1935 (Cusumano, 1985, p. 7).

The Europeans, notwithstanding their long history of skilled, innovative labour, and attitudinal difficulties of managers (see Womack *et al.*, 1990, pp. 230–1) adopted the deskilling process of mass production and the craft companies disappeared.[26] The many famous names of European automotive engineering gradually became history, or badges owned by new conglomerate organizations. The name of Ford became commonplace, whilst General Motors' policy of acquisition, so successful in the USA, led it to use the names of its new companies: Vauxhall and Bedford in the UK, Opel in Germany, Holdens' in Australia, etc.[27]

Womack *et al.* record the visits of all the European and Japanese manufacturers (including the eponymous founders of companies still in existence today) to Ford's Highland Park plant (and later to the Rouge, etc.): 'an endless stream of industrial pilgrims began to arrive around 1911 in a flow that continued for forty years (indeed the pilgrimages ended only with the visit of Eiji Toyoda in 1950)' (Womack *et al.*, 1990, p. 231).

It appears that the first transformation in the automotive industry – from craft production to mass production – contained several fundamental shifts:

- A new manufacturing process paradigm (Ford's adoption of the interchangeable parts idea from other industries, plus the moving production line – from other automobile manufacturers).
- A new product (marketing) policy (GM's 'full line' variety concept – copied successfully by Chrysler and half-heartedly by Ford).
- A new integration/supply systems policy (vertical integration – in a variety of guises).
- A new corporate organization approach (Sloan's decentralized approach, with strong central policy making).

It was accompanied by:

- A creative crisis (recognized by Ford: the need to be able to produce high volume, low price 'universal' vehicles, with a large but inexperienced workforce).

■ Regional transfer (i.e. from the USA to Europe and the rest of the world) to overcome the trade barriers which would have arisen if the American firms had tried to manufacture only in North America and export to other regions.[28]

■ An important 'demonstrator effect' (as European, Japanese and other automotive firms copied the Ford/GM methods).

■ A lengthy catching-up period (for the imitators, during which the originators had a massive competitive advantage).

The characteristics of mass production within the automotive industry, as summarized by Womack, were:

High scale, particularly in major mechanical components produced with single-purpose machines;

Specialisation of work tasks at every level from the shop floor to the design, engineering and financial staffs;

Concentration of the industry at the assembler level into [in the USA] the familiar 'Big Three';[29]

Vertical integration of the final assembly and components manufacturing with the objective of coordinating an extremely complex process with multiyear leadtimes and enormous capital investments. (Womack, 1988, p. 303)

■ The second transformation: modification of mass production and a large market hungry for variety

The influence of the American assemblers was far reaching and fundamental. In the 1930s Europe began to adopt the American version of mass-production system (a process which accelerated after World War II). In countries where organization of labour was problematic the deskilling aspects were attractive; in others such as Germany the logic and rational approach (e.g. economies of scale) of mass production clearly appealed to the industrial engineering professional who had emerged to cope with the planning tasks of the system.[30]

Unlike North America, however, there was no one European market for which to cater. The tastes and requirements of the different countries gave rise to a vast array of vehicle types. As Altshuler *et al.* note:

In Italy, low incomes, high fuel taxes and the concentration of population in ancient cities with narrow streets and limited parking combined to channel consumer demand towards very small cars. In Sweden with its lower fuel taxes, higher incomes, less dense cities and harsh winter driving conditions, consumers desired larger, sturdier cars, even at the expense of higher purchase cost and fuel consumption. (Altshuler *et al.*, 1984, p. 21)

These differing tastes, coupled with the flow of vehicles from one country to another, the separate development of many assemblers (even after the loss of many more names in the denouement of craft production) and the protective tariffs which effectively barred North American imports from the recovering post-war continent, led to a plethora of design experiments. Altshuler *et al.* note:

Some producers favoured large engines; others experimented with very small displacements and unusual cylinder layouts. Some producers used rear engine/rear-drive arrangements, other offered front-mounted engines with rear-wheel drive, and still others concentrated on front-mounted engines with front-wheel drive. Unit bodies (monocoque) competed with chassis-on-frame designs, diesels vied with gas (petrol) engines, and a myriad of suspension systems and body types were available. (Altshuler *et al.*, 1984, p. 21)

It is doubtful whether the tariffs were necessary to discourage the importation of US-built cars. For one thing, the Big Three American producers all had thriving European subsidiaries building European-designed vehicles; for another, as Altshuler *et al.* put it, 'The North American producers had standardized on a large, 6 or 8 cylinder front engine/rear drive, gasoline-fuelled, chassis on frame design, which they were intent upon producing in the highest possible volumes' (Altshuler *et al.*, 1984, p. 21). The American cars were clearly totally unsuitable for any market other than North America (with a very few exceptions, such as the Middle East). Apart from their physical size and opulent, sometimes garish (to European eyes) style, their fuel consumption was unacceptable anywhere except in the low-fuel-price USA, fascinated as it was by what Veblen in 1899 had dubbed 'conspicuous consumption'.

While the tariffs caused restriction in trade across the Atlantic, the European producers suffered from a lack of economies of scale: each national market was small and little opportunity was taken for joint venturing across boundaries. When tariffs were removed in the 1950s and 1960s, the Europeans found fruitful markets in North America for their 'different' small cars. Exports of European cars to North America grew steadily, from just 0.3 per cent of the market in 1950 to 10.5 per cent in 1970, with cars such as the Volkswagen 'Beetle' capturing not only market share, but also the all-important lifestyle image.

The Europeans, who had modified mass production, now had the opportunity to gain economies of scale and to consolidate their progress in product innovation. CKD kit assembly operations were set up in developing countries – where the smaller European cars were more suitable than the American 'gas-guzzlers' and genuine assembly plants were added with Volkswagen, for example, eventually establishing two plants in North America (Westmoreland in the USA and Puebla, Mexico).

The Europeans also managed to establish successful market penetration in the

USA with 'specialist' or luxury cars which were large by European standards but small compared to the Detroit designs. Domestically produced prestige cars were relatively inexpensive in the USA and the prospect of being seen to spend a great deal of money on an exotic European sports or luxury model appealed to the affluent American society characters. So it was the likes of Jaguar, Mercedes Benz, Porsche, BMW, Saab, Volvo, Rover and Ferrari who found buyers in plenty across the Atlantic. This situation remained virtually unchecked (the indigenous luxury cars such as Cadillac and Lincoln, and the Corvette sports model were much less expensive) so that by the early 1980s in the USA the US $20 000-plus luxury/specialist car sector was dominated by the European manufacturers, with no American car, other than customized limousines, in evidence.

Components supply and the second transformation

The European component suppliers had their origins in the highly skilled craft-based companies which played such a vital role in the automotive industry in its earliest years. Much of the technology which had been embodied in them remained and was utilized in the technological expansion during the second transformation in the automobile industry. In some cases, they had a 'natural' propensity for 'systems' thinking, having been involved in such projects as airships (Zahnradfabrik Friedrichshafen), control systems (Robert Bosch) and military vehicles (GKN).

Such firms had remained and the industry was characterized by a large number of companies, both unaligned (i.e. not dependent upon a specific assembler) and wholly owned subsidiaries. Few fell between these two positions, i.e. assemblers did not favour taking minority equity stakes in suppliers. Mass production ideas had permeated the European firms sufficiently to give rise to extensive in-house component manufacture, with some assemblers approaching GM/Ford levels of vertical integration. National identity played a large role, however (not surprisingly, considering the political events occurring in Europe during the first half of the century), and these, more than company-specific issues, tended to determine roles. In the Federal Republic of Germany, for example, the immensely influential industry association – the VDA – served to bind German assemblers and suppliers together. Much of the product technology produced in the large German component suppliers was reserved first for the German assemblers – a practice referred to (by non-German firms) as 'top-drawer' technology (implying that German assemblers would get first pick of new ideas).

The independent component suppliers in Europe had not suffered as much, in creativity terms, as their American counterparts from mass production, and the second transformation of the industry at large benefited from their innovative capacity to support their assembler firms. For example, front-wheel drive, whilst it was a technical reality during the 1940s at Citroën, was transformed into a widespread basis for traction delivery by the development of the constant velocity joint by the UK firm GKN over a decade later.

Response to the second transformation from the mass producers

The second transformation led to an industrial paradigm which was summarized by Womack as follows:

Intermediate scale, balancing economies of scale against the need for truly differentiated products with different physical attributes and images. The Europeans discovered that selling prices can fall faster than production costs if production is pushed to a level where a product is perceived as a 'commodity';

Intermediate levels of concentration at the assembler level, which consists in the 1980s of six high-volume producers [in Europe] (including GM and Ford) and another half-dozen luxury- and performance car producers;

Lower levels of vertical integration, coupled with a technologically sophisticated components industry. (Womack, 1988, p. 304)

The impacts of the second transformation upon the American producers were not as fundamental as those wrought in the European industry by mass production, but the competitive threats did give rise to new model strategies and some corporate strategy moves.

The mass producers in North America responded to the European influx of small cars with small cars of their own (some of which represented the early days of collaborative ventures with Far Eastern partners). Some of these were unsuccessful, both technically and in market terms (e.g. the Chevrolet Corvair). As Abernathy reports, however, there was initially cause for hope in Detroit: 'The Big Three's compact-sized cars, introduced for 1960, checked the first foreign invasion, and by 1962 the market share for all imports fell to less than 5%' (Abernathy, 1978, p. 38). The Europeans countered with a broader range of alternative exotic cars (again led by the VW Beetle) from the Rover 2000 to the Mercedes Benz top line models.

Abernathy continues:

The second import invasion was more serious. With Volkswagen in the lead, the market share of imports started back up in 1964, reaching 9% of the market by 1967. Despite the introduction of subcompacts like the Vega and Pinto in the early 1970s, the tide was not halted.' (Abernathy, 1978, p. 38)

GM began to talk again of out-sourcing more of its component requirements – of encouraging more input from independents – and of making in-house subsidiaries compete, both technologically and commercially, with them. The assembler had realized the significance of the bought-in cost element in the vehicle and the degree to which its component divisions had drifted from competitive positions; in short, GM was paying far too much for its components, as a result of its integration policy. The exercise was not taken very seriously by GM's component divisions, however, and little actual out-sourcing occurred.

15

Table 1.1 Vertical integration comparisons: US Big
Three assemblers, 1947–65

	Value-added as a percentage of sales value		
	GM	Ford	Chrysler
1947	47.0	37.0	28.8
1950	51.5	38.4	30.6
1955	50.0	41.3	35.3
1960	48.6	47.1	31.9
1965	52.2	40.4	37.3

Source: Crandall (1968, p. 82), quoted in this form by Abernathy
(1978, p. 37).

For the component suppliers in Europe and North America, however, the second transformation did not represent a major watershed. Vertical integration, with fiercely adversarial out-sourcing, remained the norm for automotive assemblers, as mass production developed. This is shown by Table 1.1.[31]

■ The third transformation: origins of flexible mass production: 'lean' production and a tiny market, hungry for variety

At the time when the European small cars were landing in North America, creating new niches and causing the American producers to reconsider product strategies, the first Japanese cars to be imported to the USA were being considered in California. After 1955 the American producers' joint share of their own market began to decline (from its peak of 95 per cent in that year) as the import of European vehicles began to bite. In 1957 Nissan displayed two cars and a van at the Los Angeles Automobile Show. In 1958, as Nissan began a serious import campaign in the USA, two Nissan cars entered the nineteen-day, 10 000 miles trans-Australia rally. One of them won and the other finished well up in the field. This was an omen with a profound precedent: over fifty years before, the win by Barney Oldfield in the young Henry Ford's '999' racer had encouraged its constructor to start his own auto business (Abernathy, 1978, p. 12).

The principles of the production system which had enabled this achievement (ten years before, Japan's manufacturing capacity had been in ruins) are attributed not to Nissan, but to Eiji Toyoda[32] and Taiichi Ohno, of Toyota. It was a production system, however, that, like mass production before it, affected not simply one company but an entire national industry, and subsequently it was to spread globally. The Japanese had been making vehicles since the 1930s but events in the industry following World War II signified a new paradigm shift in automobile production.

The situation which gave rise to this is summarized by Womack *et al.* as follows:

The domestic market was tiny and demanded a wide range of vehicles;

The native Japanese workforce ... was no longer willing to be treated as a variable cost or as interchangeable parts;

The war-ravaged Japanese economy was starved for capital and foreign exchange, meaning that massive purchases of the latest Western production technology were quite impossible;

The outside world was full of huge motor vehicle producers who were anxious to establish operations in Japan and ready to defend their established markets against Japanese exports. (Womack *et al.*, 1990, pp. 49–50)

The Japanese government severely restricted foreign investment in the industry, giving the national firms a breathing space for catching up with the best practice mass producers. A further intention of the Japanese Ministry of International Trade and Industry (MITI) – to force the twelve car firms to coordinate their product offerings for economies of scale – was thwarted by the 'disobedience' of the firms themselves, which began to develop full lines of vehicles. Honda, arguably the most progressive of the Japanese assemblers in terms of global activity, was told by MITI not to enter the car market (Horsley and Buckley, 1990, p. 158). This general defiance of the wishes of MITI probably saved Japan from mass production and secured, with its emphasis on market-driven product variety, the country's long-term growth and position in the world industry.

MITI's policies clearly helped the Japanese car manufacturers in a general sense, however. Horsley and Buckley note that:

During and right after the Occupation, foreign car makes were unopposed in the Japanese market in price and quality. To help the home industry MITI imposed a 40% tariff on all imported vehicles, cutting the proportion of imports (including commercial vehicles) from two-fifths in 1951 to less than 10 percent in 1955. ... The growing clamour from overseas led to Japan's cutting its tariffs on finished cars and then removing them altogether in the 1970s. By then, though, Japanese cars had a reputation for reliability and good value. Foreign makes were kept to a share of around 1 percent of the Japanese market between 1960 and 1980. (Horsley and Buckley, 1990, p. 157)

It was not simply a question of a protected industry which led to the Japanese success. Led by Taiichi Ohno, the visionary head of production engineering for Toyota, Japanese firms realized that mass production – now some fifty years old – was ill matched to the product differentiation which was emerging as fundamental market feature (something that the American producers began to observe late in the 1950s, after years of pseudo-differentiation – the 'this year's model' syndrome – as their domestic market share began to fall). It was this realization, coupled with the economic situation in Japan after the war, which provided the context for the innovative thinking which led to the third transformation – lean production.[33]

Like the previous two transformations, lean production encompassed a new production paradigm, a corporate strategy model and an integration model.

The production paradigm, as described by Womack *et al.* (1990), includes the just-in-time concepts pioneered by Ohno, including the many specific techniques explained in *Toyota Production System* (Monden, 1983) such as *kaizen, andon, heijunka, negare,* and the removal of *muda, mura* and *muri*[34] coupled with quality management techniques developed in Japan by the American advisers sent there after the war, such as W.E. Deming and Joseph Juran. Application of such concepts in the West has been essentially tactical in nature, however, despite the common use of the word 'philosophy' in connection with them. The essence of lean production is the irreversible installation of such principles as the fundamentals of a manufacturing strategy. The lean producer assumes the benefits of just-in-time, total quality, total employee involvement, etc., and builds a global strategy on that basis. This is fundamentally different from grafting a new technique, e.g. just-in-time delivery, on to an otherwise traditional mass production system. The work of Krafcik and MacDuffie (1989) shows that lean producers have been able to re-create such strategies in overseas plants (i.e. North America), whilst mass producers have not met with success in adopting a piecemeal approach.

The IMVP revealed the results of the lean approach, some forty years after its inception, in massive differentials between lean and mass production. The mass producers were in most cases requiring twice as much effort to complete the same activities (see Chapter 2). Of particular interest was the measured difference between lean and mass production in terms of essentially unnecessary features, such as rework (rectification) areas. Using Toyota as an example, Womack *et al.* report:

> Today, [1989] Toyota assembly plants have practically no rework areas and
> perform almost no rework. By contrast ... a number of current day mass
> production plants devote 20 percent of plant area and 25 percent of their total
> hours of effort to fixing mistakes.... Toyota's vehicles have among the
> lowest number of defects of any in the world, comparable to the very best of
> the German luxury car producers, who devote many hours of assembly
> plant effort to rectification. (Womack *et al.*, 1990, p. 57).

The lean paradigm extends to product development and design, with lean producers requiring half the time (in terms of elapsed time for new product introduction and also human effort – engineering hours) taken by mass producers (see Chapter 5).

The lean production corporate strategy model is based upon global operation, in the three principal regions of North and South America, West and East Europe, and Asia (including Australia) with full autonomy in each region. Womack *et al.* conclude that lean producers will be forced to develop self-reliance in each region. This means development and design as well as manufacture of an entire range of vehicles in each region, with the ability to trade products (vehicles and/or component systems) between regions – possibly to fill niches in markets. No automobile producer has yet achieved a fully lean organization, however, and Womack *et al.* suggest that not all the Japanese have realized the full implications of what is required.

There is some evidence of the development of a lean production global scenario. The Accord station wagon was developed by Honda in the USA and shipped (in right- and left-hand drive versions) to Europe in 1991 in volumes planned to increase to 10 000 by 1995. Honda plans a total US export level of 70 000 units per year in 1995, to eighteen countries. In 1991 the company was exporting over 13 000 units a year from the USA to Japan, including the Accord coupé, partly designed in the USA and assembled exclusively in Ohio, which is sold as a prestige car in Japan. Toyota began exporting American-made, right-hand drive Camry Wagon estate cars from Georgetown Kentucky to Japan in September 1992, at planned annual volumes of 8000. Nissan sold almost 2000 UK-produced Primeras in Japan in 1992 and announced plans to start exporting a new small station wagon from its new Mexican plant to Japan in 1993. Mitsubishi sent 500 American and Australian station wagons to Japan in 1992 while Mazda sold almost 2000 Ford-badged cars there in the same year.[35]

Mitsubishi's plans for 1993 included exporting 5000 vehicles from Australia to Europe, 90 per cent of which would be left-hand drive.

Ford followed a similar strategy in the late 1980s, with the Scorpio and Sierra XR4i, both engineered and built in Germany and sold in the USA under the specially invented 'Merkur' marque. Success was very limited, leading some commentators to accuse Ford of half-heartedness. Daimler Benz have had more success for some time in adding extras to a car which sells as an inexpensive taxi in its home country, managing to present it as a prestige model in the USA (and elsewhere, including other European countries) at over twice the showroom price.

All the major Japanese assemblers have technical centres in North America and Europe (see Tables 1.2 and 1.3) and it is clear that this aspect of the full-scale lean production scenario predicted by Womack *et al.* (1990) is developing already. The acceptance of Honda in North America (the Honda Accord was the best selling American-built car in 1989, 1990 and 1991) shows the lean organization strategy in practice. Womack *et al.* argue that the final step relies on human resource policies, including non-Japanese main board directors for Honda.

It will be some time before this global scenario is complete. Honda, for example, will not be able to design and develop a totally new platform (basis for a vehicle) in North America until 1999, whilst Toyota and Nissan are still in the early implementation stages of such a capability. Similar scenarios are even further off in Europe.

The role of suppliers in lean production

The integration policy of lean production also differs greatly from mass production. The vertical integration principle, which began as an approach to optimizing value chains (see Chapter 4) in fact resulted in many inefficiencies in

Table 1.2 Japanese automakers' North American R&D centres

Name of company	Headquarters (*division offices*)	Current (planned) employees	Current/ (planned) functions[a]
Honda R&D North America Inc.	Torrance, CA (*Marysville, OH; Denver, CO; Toronto, Ont; California City, CA*)	330 (500)	1–7 (–)
Isuzu Technical Center of America Inc.	Los Angeles, CA (*Detroit, MI*)	80 (150)	1,3,4 (2,5,6,7)
Mazda R&D of North America Inc.	Irvine, CA (*Flat Rock, MI; Ann Arbor, MI*)	167 (230)	1–5 (6)
Mitsubishi Motors America Inc.	Detroit, MI (*Ann Arbor, MI; Los Angeles, CA; Normal, IL; New York, NY; Washington, DC; Bridgeport, NJ*)	96 (150)	1,3,4 (5,6)
Nissan R&D Inc.	Plymouth, MI (*Ann Arbor, MI; Washington, DC; Los Angeles, CA; Stanfield, AZ*)	393 (600)	1–7 (–)
Toyota Technical Center Inc.	Ann Arbor, MI (*Detroit, MI; Los Angeles, CA; Lexington, KY; San Francisco, CA; Phoenix, AZ*)	206 (650)	1–4 (5–7)

Note: [a]Function key:
(1) technical support for procurement of parts for local production;
(2) evaluation of parts; (3) evaluation of vehicles; (4) styling and general design; (5) parts design;
(6) vehicle design; (7) prototype production.
Source: JAMA (1991b).

the interfaces between component supplier and vehicle producer. This was evidenced by the survey of subsidiary suppliers conducted by General Motors in the USA in the mid–1980s, in which GM companies were reportedly as much as 50 per cent more expensive than independent suppliers.[36]

Since lean production originated in Japan, it is perhaps to be expected that some of its characteristics were profoundly affected by the Japanese business context and the post-war situation. Whereas cultural arguments about attitudes to work and use of operators' problem-solving skills may be discounted, the configuration of Japanese customer–supplier relationships is the clear result of what happened in Japan in the 1950s, although the story is not the same for each vehicle assembler.

In the 1920s the Japanese operations of General Motors and Ford were supplied by complete kits sent from the USA. The few Japanese vehicle producers also imported any parts which they did not make themselves. The two leading American mass producers began to subcontract some parts manufacture during the 1930s, encouraged by tariffs introduced in 1931 and other political pressures. Not surprisingly, the technology was geared to American standards.[37]

Table 1.3 Japanese transplant activity in Europe[a]

name of company	Location and status	Products (local content)	Annual capacity	Employees	Total investment (£ million)
Nissan Motor Mfg UK Ltd	Tyne & Wear, UK Sole entry Established April 1984	Bluebird, 1990 Primera, 1990 Micra, 1992 (80%)	100 000 units (300 000 in 1993) (500 000 in 1995)	3600	600
Honda of the UK Manu-fact'g	Swindon, UK Sole entry[b] Established Feb 1985	Honda Accord from 1992 n/a	50 000 cars in 1993 100 000 cars in 1995 70 000 engines in 1995	2000 in 1995	370
IBC Vehicles Ltd (Isuzu/GM)	Luton, UK GM 50% Isuzu 40% Established Sept 1987	Fargo light van Frontera, sports 4WD from 1991 (80%)	70 000 units	2000	34
Toyota Motor Mfg UK	Derby, UK and Deeside, UK Sole entry Established Dec 1989	Carina saloon, engines (60% from 1993, 80% from 1995)	31 000 in 1993 (planned 100 000 by 1995 200 000 by 1997) 75% for export	400 in 1991 (planned: 3300)	700 in Derby 140 in Deeside
Toyota joint production with VW	Hanover, Germany From Jan 1989	Toyota: Hilux VW: Taro n/a	15 000	n/a	n/a
Nissan Motor Iberica SA	Barcelona, Spain Nissan 67.6% Local 32.4% Established June 1987	Safari, Vanette, trucks, engines n/a	67 200 units	6870	n/a
Salvador Caetano IMVT SA	Ovar, Portugal Toyota 27% Local 73% Established 1946	Dyna, Hiace Hilux, Land Cruiser from Oct 1986 n/a	12 000 units	n/a	n/a

Notes: [a] In addition to the plants listed here, Honda has an R&D centre in Germany, Nissan in the UK, Spain and Belgium, and Toyota in Belgium. In July 1992, VW and Suzuki announced joint venture plans to develop a mini-car for assembly in Spain, in VW's subsidiary, SEAT.
[b] Honda of the UK Ltd is owned 4.1 per cent by Honda, 75.91 per cent by Honda of Europe and 20 per cent by British Aerospace PLC.
Source: JAMA (1991a).

21

The number of suppliers in Japan in 1930 was 30. By 1938 this had increased to 136. During this period the Japanese government required automotive components suppliers to register themselves as such and instigated a scheme of subsidies to encourage improvements in quality, etc.[38]

Initially, Toyota had built a supply base in the way one might expect in a developing country. Cusumano describes the situation in 1931–33:

> During 1931 they [Toyota] bought and tested foreign engine components while surveying local firms that might be able to copy the parts. Then, in 1932, Kiichiro [Toyoda] purchased a Chevrolet engine after deciding that this would be easier to produce than a Ford engine, and in October 1933 had the automobile department of Toyoda Automatic Loom acquire a new Chevrolet car and begin disassembling it to analyse the pieces. The department also placed orders with Japan GM for various replacement components, although in November Kiichiro [Toyoda] and Suda [Takatoshi] visited parts makers between Osaka and Tokyo to line up potential suppliers ... Suda ... ordered malleable cast iron parts from Tobata Casting as well as iron and steel components from Hachiman Steel and Sumitomo Metals. They obtained some of the other components from suppliers in the Nagoya area but had to import the body, frame, and chassis from the United States. (Cusumano, 1985, p. 64)

Interestingly, Tobata Casting was the firm from which Toyota's great rival, Nissan would be formed in 1934. In 1937 Tobata Casting merged with Hitachi, now one of Nissan's most significant suppliers, and considerably larger (in employment terms) than Nissan Motor itself. Nissan and Hitachi are both part of the IBJ *keiretsu*.[39]

By 1934, Cusumano records that:

> Toyoda Automatic Loom obtained chassis components and other parts that were difficult to manufacture, such as gears, directly from General Motors, but fabricated the cylinder head and blocks, housings and transmission cases in house. While Kiichiro [Toyoda] had trouble buying the proper suspension parts and decided to make these, he managed to order electrical parts, spark plugs, and hydraulic brakes, tires, batteries, radiators, wheels, springs, pistons, gaskets, and related components from Japanese firms that produced imitations of American equipment. (Cusumano, 1985, p. 65–6)

Cusumano goes on to record that Toyota found too many defects in the parts which it bought in from these imitator subcontractors, especially in electrical parts, and attributed the failure of the 1935 car to this:

> The experience convinced Koiichiro to manufacture more parts and materials in-house. Until production equipment was ready in 1936, he imported the electrical components that failed in the first vehicle, but the factory that he eventually established became Nippondenso in 1949. (Cusumano, 1985, p. 66)

Toyota thus went through a similar experience to that of Henry Ford –

dissatisfaction with subcontractors brought about an in-sourcing exercise. There were no long-lasting, trusting relationships between customers and suppliers at this time in Japan: technology and quality were both very weak: see Nishiguchi (1989, pp. 81–8). The component companies that Toyota created as a part of this in-sourcing, however, did not fall under the ownership style of their parent in the same way as Ford or GM's divisions: Japan had not adopted the mass production style of deskilling the upstream operations in the assembly process and the supply chain.

Purchasing was becoming established in Japan at the time: in Toyota between 1937 and 1939, and at Nissan between 1937 and 1940. In both cases the function became a department, rather than a section or subsection (of production) – a significant upgrade. Mazda followed, establishing a purchasing department in 1943. At the same time, the supplier groups began to emerge, led by Toyota's *kyoryokukai* in 1939 (which was renamed as *kyohokai* in 1943) which initially consisted of twenty suppliers. In setting up the group, Toyota anticipated the Japanese government's Rationalization Outline by over a year.

Nissan, which had its origins in the components industry – in Tobata Casting – also began by adopting the American idea of vertical integration for similar reasons to Toyota. After World War II, however, both companies and the other vehicle producers began to change this part of their operations and to rely on suppliers over which they had little or no direct financial control. As Nishiguchi points out:

> [In the 1930s] Toyota motor vehicles' local content increased whereas in-house manufacturing did not. Toyota's reliance on purchasing also increased. In November 1936 when a mere 200 Toyota motor vehicles were produced, 51% of the manufacturing cost per vehicle [was] accounted for by purchased parts. In 1939, when twelve thousand units were manufactured, a Toyota motor vehicle consisted of 66% purchased components, excluding raw materials. Including raw materials, then, purchased components and materials accounted for well over 70% or even 80% of the manufacturing cost at Toyota when it began to produce in large quantities. (Nishiguchi, 1989, p. 58)

The Rationalization Outline of the Machinery, Iron and Steel Industries issued by the Ministry of Commerce and Industry (later renamed the Ministry for Munitions, and subsequently, the Ministry for International Trade and Industry – MITI) in 1940 set about forming a tightly knit subcontracting structure in Japan. This pruned the weaker suppliers and strengthened the successful firms. (For a comprehensive discussion see Nishiguchi, 1993, pp. 73–81.)

At this time the relationships strategies which have subsequently proved so valuable for Japan, were formed. Nishiguchi (1989) records the following decisions by Kiichiro Toyoda in 1940. At a time when purchased materials and components represented between 70 and 80 per cent of Toyota's manufacturing costs, its founder and vice-president decided to bring more work in house, in order to control costs better. Having differentiated between in-house, quasi-in-house (components made in Toyota subsidiaries) and purchased components, he published a policy statement (which would be rigidly enforced) on purchasing, dividing it into three parts:

(a) General Purchasing: Components of this type can be made by and bought-in from any factories. These can be manufactured by commonplace facilities. Therefore these subcontractors may be switched as necessary.

(b) Special Purchasing: The manufacturer of components of this type requires a certain degree of facilities and our teaching. We specifically allocate the manufacture of these components to factories with which we have close capital or financial ties. We regard them [as] Toyota's special subcontracting factories. Therefore, prototypes and items for study purposes should preferably be ordered from them. Only in unavoidable cases can these things be ordered from (a).

(c) Special Factory Purchasing: The manufacture of extremely special components of this type requires distinctively special facilities. We, therefore, will consider establishing close capital and financial ties with those with such facilities in the future. (*Toyota Jidosha 30 Nen Shi* (*A 30 Year History of Toyota Motors*), Toyota Motor Corporation, 1967, translated and quoted in Nishiguchi (1989, pp. 59–60)

Toyota's policy anticipated the Japanese government's plan by three years. In 1943 the Minister responsible for Commerce and Industry (MCI) stated:

MCI positively plans to make 'child' factories dedicated to 'parent' firms and 'grandchild' factories to 'child' firms. 'Child' and 'grandchild' factories must stop manufacturing finished products and must manufacture components primarily for their parent factories. 'Parents' and 'children' must share labour management, materials, and capital.'[40]

The post-Meiji revolution (1870) industrial organization in Japan had revolved around the big groupings, known as *zaibatsu*. The American administration in Japan after World War II ruled that these groups should be disbanded, and they were. The new structures which emerged were known as *keiretsu*: groups of firms without single leader companies (which had been the power bases to which the Americans had objected so strongly).

The formation of the *keiretsu* is well described by Womack *et al.*:

The Japanese companies initially were financed almost entirely by loans supplied by the big Tokyo banks and guaranteed by the American government. Since companies had only these loans and their physical assets their capital was very modest. As the economy took off and many companies became profitable, they began to worry about being bought up by foreigners. They also distrusted the arm's-length stock market as the primary means of generating equity, because they couldn't imagine a system in which there was no reciprocal obligation.

To address these concerns, the growing companies of the 1950s and 1960s hit upon the idea of selling equity to each other, often with no cash

changing hands. So each member of the pre-war groups, and some newcomers
as well, joined the new *keiretsu* in which the equity went round in a circle . . .
Their stocks traded in small volumes on the highly volatile Tokyo stock
market, but the stock that really counted was not for sale. (Womack *et al.*,
1990, pp. 194–5)[41]

Imai (1989) provides an illuminating account of developments in Japan at this
time (and for some time before). He refers to the corporate forms which emerged
as 'fuzzy' – not clearly defined within the supply chain – and stresses the
importance of the sharing of information between firms.

As a part of this phenomenon, following the success of the Rationalization
Outline in 1940 and the early group formation (e.g. at Toyota in 1939) the vehicle
producers developed their supplier relationships. Whilst the original Toyota
grouping included cooperation and mutual benefit in its statement of intent,
relationships were not formed in a naive manner. Cusumano quotes Okumura
Shoji, an assistant general manager of Nissan's production planning department in
the 1950s, who notes three reasons why his firm chose to de-integrate vertically:
'to avoid the capital expenditures necessary to produce a wider variety of
components in large quantities; to reduce risk by maintaining low factory capacity
in case sales for the industry slumped; and to take advantage of the wage scales in
smaller firms' (Cusumano, 1985, p. 244).

During the 1950s the process of development in the supply industry, driven by
the vehicle assemblers and MITI, gave rise to impressive improvements in
productivity.

In the early 1960s, more than 70% of the 314 manufacturers of automobile
components in Japan had less than 500 employees although 84 companies that
had 500 or more workers accounted for 75% of parts production by value.
Productivity at these larger firms in particular rose throughout the 1950s and
1960s as they received direct assistance from Nissan, Toyota, and other
Japanese automakers, in addition to foreign companies such as Robert Bosch
and the Bendix Group (American). Higher productivity then made it possible
for the Japanese automakers to demand price reductions from all their
suppliers of around 10 percent a year during the late 1950s and 1960s.
(Cusumano 1985, p. 245)

This historical development is of fundamental relevance to the lean production
paradigm. Firstly, here was a protected industry into which massive aid was
provided by competitors, customers (the assemblers) and government. Secondly,
the regimented approach to industry policy in Japan meant that the number of
companies was known precisely (it never has been in Europe or North America)
and decisions on development could thus be made objectively. Thirdly, the
peculiar ownership pattern gave a stability to the industry seldom provided by
Anglo-Saxon capitalist economies (or, for that matter, the centrally planned
economies). Fourthly, the sector was developed consciously in the light of the
limitations of the American system (Taiichi Ohno, a regular visitor to the USA at

this time, must have wondered why the Americans persisted with their inefficient vertical integration model). Finally, and most crucially, there was a constant and universal environmental pressure to increase productivity and quality simultaneously. The automotive component suppliers in North America and Europe at the time would have taken a dim view of a request to reduce prices annually by 10 per cent!

It can thus be seen that lean production in the automotive industry, as major an upset to established thinking in the 1980s as mass production had been seventy years before, grew from a set of historical circumstances, a creative crisis and the ashes of a previous paradigm. The need to combine high volume, high quality, low cost and high worker motivation all at once could not have been satisfied by mass production or craft production.

For the component suppliers, a crucial factor was the help of the assemblers in setting up their businesses to run under the lean paradigm. Such firms were developed *ab initio* in this manner, installing the principles in virgin territory. In the 1990s Western mass producers are aware of the need for this collaboration but all such efforts face the double challenge of removing old ideas before installing lean principles.[42]

The control exerted over smaller *keiretsu*[43] members by the leading firms has sometimes been seen as very close to vertical integration, in terms of policy making and apparently unequal treatment. The much-publicized case of the American businessman, T. Boone Pickens, provides food for thought. In the 1980s, having bought 26.4 per cent of the shares in the largest Japanese manufacturer of car lights, Koito, Pickens became the largest shareholder (Toyota had 19 per cent). He was unable, however, after prolonged legal battles, to secure a single seat on the board of directors. Koito's position as a member of the Toyota group effectively excluded the American investor, who eventually announced the sale of his stake: it was apparent that the Japanese firms were not willing to internationalize the groupings.[44]

Another example of the limitations of the *keiretsu* system is provided by the extraordinarily public display of discontent by a senior Japanese industry executive, Mr Tetsuya Tsukatani, who is ex-chairman of Japan's largest manufacturer of rear-view mirrors and second largest producer of lights, Ichikoh. Ichikoh is an independent manufacturer, with shares held by a variety of companies, including Nissan (20.5 per cent), Toyota (6.3 per cent) and Isuzu (3.0 per cent).[45] In response to intense pressure from Nissan to become a part of their *keiretsu* (his rejection of which eventually led to his removal from the board), Mr Tsukatani is quoted as saying:

> Independence is important for the workers' morale. Once you are a *keiretsu*
> member, you simply become another Nissan factory. In order to provide
> good service for other customers in the U.S., you have to be independent. If
> Nissan controls Ichickoh, it will hurt competition. (*The Financial Times*,
> 15 May 1991)

The implication of Tsukatani's statement (which was in the form of a publicized written appeal to President Bush – a remarkable departure from Japanese practice of restraint) was that Ichikoh had to remain outside the Nissan group in order to conduct business (from its North American transplants) with the US assemblers.

The significant point here is not that the Japanese assemblers wish to prevent their suppliers from dealing with Western customers, but that they appear to wish to control such dealing themselves, as a *keiretsu* affair – something the globalizing suppliers may not be able to accept. The Japanese realize that Western assemblers have not traditionally required extensive information exchange with their suppliers and so there may be opportunities for component manufacturers to reap higher financial returns from such business. As long as the technology involved is not leading edge, it therefore suits a Japanese assembler for its suppliers to deal with American and Western automotive firms – a situation which might be seen cynically as the Western customer subsidizing the Japanese (if the supplier's margins from sales to Western firms are higher, those back home can be lower).[46] The supplier, meanwhile, may wish to form a more technological, comprehensive relationship with its new Western customers – something of which the 'parent' assembler might disapprove.

It is perhaps not surprising that there have been painful experiences in the transfer of lean ideas from Japan to the West. The process challenges both the close integration of Japanese assemblers and their *keiretsu*, and the established practices of the mass producers. It is apparent that the Japanese model of supplier relations, as practised in Japan, will need development in order to function globally – part of the total lean production approach. This is discussed further in Chapter 7.

The mass producers face lean production

The impact of lean production on mass producers has been immense. In North America, the arrival of the Japanese producers during the early 1980s[47] with so-called 'transplant'[48] operations has not only shown the latent dissatisfaction which had built up in the American consumer for the products of the Big Three, but also demonstrated clearly that lean production is transferable to non-Japanese workforces. The successes[49] of such plants as the New United Motor Manufacturing Industry (NUMMI) joint venture between General Motors and Toyota, utilizing an existing but defunct GM plant in Fremont California,[50] or the Honda plant in Marysville, Ohio, or the Ford (Mazda) plant in Hermosillo, Mexico,[51] among others, indicate that lean production is not necessarily a cultural phenomenon confined to Japan.[52] By 1992 65 per cent of Honda cars sold in North America were made there, and the company was exporting to eight countries, including Japan. The extent of Japanese transplant investment in the USA is shown in Tables 1.2 and 1.4. While the Japanese assembly plants in the USA are spread across several states, there is a clear preference for R&D centres in a few main locations, as shown in Table 1.2.

The IMVP data also indicate that Europe, as yet hardly affected by Japanese

Table 1.4 Japanese automakers' local production in the USA, 1990–91

Name of company	Location and status (announced)	Products (local content)[b]	Annual capacity	Employees	Total investment (US $ million)
Honda of America Manu-fact'g[a]	Marysville, E. Liberty and Anna, OH Sole entry Feb 1978	Accord, Civic, Engine parts (75%)	510 000 cars 500 000 engines	10 000	2200
Nissan Motor Mfg Corp. USA	Smyrna, TN Sole entry July 1980	Sentra, one-ton truck, engines (70%)	250 000 units (450 000 in 1992)	4000	776[c]
Mazda Motor Mfg (USA) Corp.	Flat Rock, MI Sole entry Jan 1985	Mazda MX-6 and 626 Ford: Probe (75%)	240 000 units	3500	550
Diamond Star Motors Corp. (Mit-subishi)	Blooming-ton–Normal, IL Joint venture 50/50 Chrysler[d] Oct 1985	Mitsubishi: Eclipse/ Mirage Chrysler: Plymouth Laser Eagle Talon Eagle Summit (60%)	240 000 units	3000	600
New United Motor Mfg Inc. (Toyota)	Fremont, CA Joint venture GM 50/50 1984	Toyota: Corolla and small truck, GM: Geo Prizm (60%)	200 000 units (300 000 in 1992)	3100	800 (1100 in 1991)
Toyota Motor Mfg[a] USA Inc.	Georgetown, KY Sole entry Jan 1986	Camry, engines and axles (75%)	200 000 cars 400 000 in 1993 300 000 engines	3500 (over 5000 in 1993)	1100 (2000 by 1993)
Subaru–Isuzu Automo-tive	Lafayette, IN Joint venture Mar 1987	Fuji: Legacy Isuzu: truck (65%)	160 000 units	1900	500
Total			1 800 000 units	29 000	6326

Notes: [a] Honda, Toyota and Suzuki also have plants in Canada: see JAMA (1991a).
[b] Local content figures are publicly stated but are calculated in various ways, i.e. they are 'fickle' data.
[c] Nissan's investment was almost certainly much higher than this quoted figure.
[d] Diamond Star is now 100 per cent owned by Mitsubishi.
Sources: JAMA (1991a and 1991b).

transplants (in comparison with North America), is also still suffering from the inefficiencies of mass production. Once again, as in North America, it may be expected that the 'demonstrator effect' of lean competitors close at hand will result, as it has for American producers, in improvements.[53] Japanese transplant investment in Europe is shown in Table 1.3.

This is the situation faced by today's automotive industry. Since the publication of *The Machine that Changed the World*, the dissemination of the lean production ideas within the industry has been comprehensive and rapid. The problems of implementation (and learning) are still daunting for most firms.

■ Mass production and vertical integration versus lean production

The vertical integration developed by Ford and Sloan served the mass production industry well during the years when the market accepted what it was offered. The divisionalized structure of the American Big Three, copied to some extent in Europe, as we have seen, provided control over the value-added and technological expertise. It appears that this model of vertical integration does not work in lean production, and yet the Japanese industry *keiretsu* system appears to be very similar in many ways. What is the difference, and why does vertical integration, Japanese style, appear to work, while the American version is in decline? To answer this question we must understand the structure of the international industry today.

In the next chapter, we shall see how the present day automotive assembly industry and components industry are organized and explore the nature of the challenges they face from the need to become lean. At the end of Chapter 2 a contrast will be drawn between the Japanese and American versions of vertical integration.

■ Notes

1. The development of the industry from its origins to the present is described and explained in excellent clarity by the writings, principally of James Womack and Daniel Jones, in two major books: *The Future of the Automobile* (Altshuler *et al.*,1984) and *The Machine that Changed the World* (Womack *et al.*, 1990). Much of the substance of this chapter is based upon these two books, which were the final reports of two major research programmes conducted at MIT during the 1980s. The first programme was entitled The Future of the Automobile (1980–84), the second was the International Motor Vehicle Program (IMVP) (1986–90). Details of these programmes are provided in Appendix 1.
2. Henry Ford wrote in 1922: 'A Ford car contains about five thousand parts – that is

counting screws, nuts and all' (Ford, 1922). The figure of 10 000 is a commonly used estimate in 1990 (see for example, Womack *et al.*, 1991, p. 138).

3. The term 'assembler' is used to denote the company which builds the vehicle from the component parts. This terminology has become standard practice in the industry. It should not be inferred that the role of such firms is limited to the assembly of the vehicle in a literal sense: design, development and sometimes component manufacture, retailing, etc., come under the auspices of the assembler. It is also true that some assemblers subcontract the assembly process to suppliers. Toyota, for example, carries out less than half of its own Japanese vehicle assembly: it has seven subcontractor assemblers – Toyoda Auto Body, Toyoda Automatic Loom Works, Gifu Auto Body, Daihatsu, Hino, Araco and Kanto Auto Body. This concept is discussed in Chapter 9.

4. These transformations are described in *The Future of the Automobile* (Altshuler *et al.*, 1984) and again, in a developed sense, in *The Machine that Changed the World* (Womack *et al.*, 1990). The account given here is abstracted mainly from a synthesis of these descriptions (separated as they were by six years and the perspectives gained from the IMVP) and a further piece by Womack in Mowery (1988, Chapter 9).

5. This expression was coined by Peter Drucker (1946).

6. As Bessant (1991, p. 8) explains, the term 'paradigm' is now commonly used in the sense defined by Kuhn (1962), i.e. 'a dominant pattern which influences thinking across a broad front'. The idea of 'paradigm shifts' follows from this. Dosi (1982) develops the concept further, within the field of innovation, introducing the idea of 'trajectories'. This is discussed in Chapter 3.

7. In the UK, for example, such firms as Clyno, and Swift were almost pure assemblers – making almost none of the parts of their vehicles. Many engine manufacturers were in existence in Europe before World War II to provide the power units for such assemblers (JLL).

8. Figures in this paragraph (including US Federal Trade Commission data) are taken from Abernathy (1978, p. 18), Womack *et al.* (1990, p. 37) and Chandler (1964).

9. The first transformation itself may be further dissected. Thomas (1977, pp. 6–8) identifies four 'eras' within the period: 'invention' (pre–1900); 'product development' (1900–08); 'rapid expansion' (1900–18); and 'replacement demand' (1918–29).

10. To be more precise, the separate cylinders were more usually not bolted to one another but to the crankcase, which thus formed the main strength member of the engine assembly, keeping the cylinders in place (JLL).

11. By the mid-1920s, American firms were producing more than 85 per cent of the world's vehicles and accounted for over 70 per cent of world export of motor vehicles (Womack, 1988, p. 303).

12. Ford's flywheel-mounted generator is usually referred to as a magneto but was technically an alternator, since it developed low tension, not high tension voltage. The high tension for the sparking plugs was created from this output via a set of 'trembler coils' mounted below the dashboard. The design of the alternator was doubly innovative: the radially mounted magnets were a soft 'V' shape and formed a part of the engine lubrication system. Each 'bucket' magnet passed through a sump of oil at the bottom of its rotation (i.e. on the perimeter of the flywheel) and carried the oil upwards, disgorging into an oilway at the top of the engine (JLL).

13. Defined by Ford for *Encyclopedia Britanica*, 1926: see Womack *et al.* (1990, p. 26).

14. Hounshell (1984) claims that Chandler was wrong in his conclusion. He argues that what Ford achieved (that Leland and the others did not) was the introduction of machines capable of consistent production of repeatable parts with very fine tolerances, so that no 'fitting' was necessary. This ensured real interchangeability. Leland managed this on the Cadillac in 1906 by carefully hand fitting each part against a blueprint so that when the cars were finally assembled the parts did indeed fit. However, this method was highly labour intensive in the steps prior to final assembly.

15. Using the data from Hounshell (1984) (originally taken from observations made by

journalists Arnold and Faurote in 1915) Womack *et al.* (1990, p. 29) calculate that the time required for assembling major components into a vehicle was reduced by 88 per cent by Ford's introduction of mass production methods in 1913–14. They go on to point out that this improvement was largely due to the moving production line: other features of mass production, such as interchangeable parts and division of labour were already evident in 'late craft production' at Ford. Arnold and Faurote's results are more commonly quoted as an improvement of 8:1 in effort requirement after the introduction of mass production (see Abernathy, 1978, p. 24). Abernathy calculates a reduction in labour requirement to build a car (including all activities, not just final assembly) from between 1260 and 4664 man hours (small to large cars) in 1912 to 100 man hours in 1976.

16. Ford's own words from *My Life and Work* (1922). It should be borne in mind that Ford was still using wooden bodies. They took a long time to prepare and dry, making provision of a variety of colours very time consuming and costly. The introduction of pyroxlin paint by Dupont in 1923 and the switch to steel bodies (requiring a fundamental change in automobile assembly techniques) enabled the assemblers to offer a choice of colours (Chandler, 1964).

17. In 1923 Ford had 50.4 per cent of the US market, and GM had 20.8 per cent. In 1926 Ford had to close down to effect the model change. GM took the lead in market share and Ford never regained it (Abernathy, 1978, pp. 29 and 32).

18. GM still practises the interchange of top managers between vehicle and parts divisions. For example in August 1991, Paul Tosch, successful chairman and managing director of the UK assembler subsidiary, Vauxhall, was moved to Detroit to run the Harrison components (radiators) division. Tosch was replaced by William Ebbert, formerly director of business operations for GM's parts division: Automotive Components Group (ACG) in Troy, Michigan.

19. As Chandler points out, corporations the size of GM were still a relatively new phenomenon, and financing systems for such enormous projects were still in an experimental state.

20. The same strategy can be identified in Ford's purchase of the small but significant British specialist assembler, Jaguar, in 1989.

21. Robertson and Langlois quote as their sources Seltzer (1928, p. 82) and Hurley (1959, pp. 1–14).

22. The reference to 'hand-to-mouth' buying is just one of several instances within the accounts of Ford's techniques which remind the modern reader of just-in-time approaches, attributed to the Japanese, almost half a century later. In Ford's UK tractor factory in 1936, work in progress was kept to about two hours' worth. The tractor, unencumbered by glazing, upholstery and complicated electrics was an ideal case for total integration – almost everything was made on one site (JLL).

23. For a fully documented account, see Abernathy (1978), Tables 5.7 and 6.8.

24. Robertson and Langlois quote as their sources Epstein (1928, pp. 41–3 and 236–9) and Seltzer (1928, pp. 44–5).

25. Ford had a presence in Australia since 1908 through their agent, Tarrant. Tarrant had been the first Australian auto manufacturer (1900–07). Uhlenbruch (1986) records that Ford's Australian plants were set up by Ford of Canada. This was because Australia's protection laws gave Most Favoured Nation status to countries within the British Commonwealth.

26. To some extent this was connected to Ford's policy on payment. In 1936, for example, an assembly worker at Ford's Dagenham plant in the UK would receive one shilling and nine pence (£0.09) per hour, and a floor sweeper, one shilling and seven pence. A skilled fitter anywhere else in the area would usually receive only one shilling (£0.05) an hour (JLL).

27. A blend of nationalism and protectionism was rife then as now in France and Italy. Both Ford and GM were prevented by the Italian government from setting up plants in

that country – such was the influence of Fiat. Ford had more success in France, with a plant in Strasbourg (and others since); GM failed to negotiate successfully with the French government. In the early 1990s the European move to compete against Japanese firms by protectionist measures has been led by the French and Italians.

28. Altshuler *et al.* report that during the depression years Europe remained protected by high import tariffs against American imports. 'No European manufacturer seems to have been able to produce an automobile, even in the most modern manufacturing complex, at a cost comparable to those of the Ford and GM operations in Detroit': see Altshuler *et al.* (1984, p. 18), for a full discussion of tariffs.

29. Whilst not as polarized as the USA, Europe tended towards concentration also, with national champions emerging within the heterogeneous continent: Fiat in Italy, Renault, Peugeot and Citroën in France (with the latter two combining in 1980), Volkswagen, Daimler Benz and BMW in Germany, and British Leyland in the UK. The last example was the first to fall from national champion status, in the troubled industrial times in the UK in the 1970s and 1980s.

30. Craft production appeared to remain at the heart of German manufacturing, however. For a good discussion on this process of dissemination see Piore and Sable (1984).

31. Vertical integration figures are always fickle data. In this case, the source has used sales value as the denominator in the calculation. If cost of sales were used the integration figures would be a more meaningful measure of policies in place. The implications of Chrysler's lower integration figures are discussed further in Chapter 5. For an interesting discussion on vertical integration calculations see Robertson and Langlois (1988), Monteverde and Teece (1982b, pp. 206–13), Katz (1977, pp. 14–15) and White (1971, pp. 77–9).

32. The role of Kiichiro Toyoda, founder of Toyota Motor Corporation, is recognized by Womack *et al.* (1990) in a footnote. He was amongst the visitors to Detroit in 1929 and is credited with conceiving ideas such as just-in-time. The system was not implemented in pre-war Japan, however.

33. The term 'lean' was applied to this system by the IMVP in 1990 following the observation and measurements undertaken during the research programme (1986–90). It was applied because the system Toyoda and Ohno invented apparently uses significantly less of every resource than mass production or craft production: it operates with a bare minimum of everything: labour, materials, organizational complexity, space, etc. – much less than is required by mass production. It originated from a discussion between two researchers, John Krafcik and Andrew Graves. Graves had extensive experience in motor racing where the practice of reducing the specification of every part to a bare minimum – sometimes until it broke in operation, requiring a small increase in specification – was called 'lean'. Comparison with the concept of removing bodily fat to reach fighting weight is appropriate. Initial signs are that the term 'lean' has been well accepted generally in the industry and will spread to other manufacturing and even non-manufacturing sectors, rather in the same way that 'mass' did.

34. Specific concepts such as these are not dealt with in detail here. The Monden book provides an excellent explanation. Other references include Bessant (1991), Schonberger (1982, 1987), Voss (1987), Voss and Robinson (1987) and Ikeda *et al.* (1988).

35. Various sources, including *The Financial Times*, 17 July 1992.

36. Inevitably such data are extremely sensitive and GM did not reveal details to the public. The author's industry interviews at the time were used as the basis for this estimate. The figure has never been seriously denied by GM interviewees.

37. Ford and GM were subsequently forced to cease operations in Japan in 1939 due to 'disadvantageous measures such as a ceiling on production, increased import duties, and revised foreign exchanges' (Nishiguchi, 1990, pp. 57–8, note 16). In 1936 Toyota and Nissan became the first licensed Japanese automobile manufacturers, under the

Motor Vehicle Manufacturing Business Act (May 1936), followed by Isuzu and Mazda (formerly a machine tool manufacturer (Toyo Kogyo) but soon to become the leading maker of popular three-wheeled vehicles).

38. Data on the history of the Japanese industry, unless otherwise stated, are taken from the definitive historical account contained in Michael Cusumano's book *The Japanese Automobile Industry* (1985). Nishiguchi (1989, pp. 49–53) notes the crucial influence of World War II (including the Manchurian campaign) upon subcontracting in Japan. The number of suppliers increased greatly, matching the rise in demand for munitions.

39. IBJ (Industrial Bank of Japan) is not one of the six big Japanese groups but counts, along with Tokai, as one of the big eight *Kigyo Shudan* (horizontally connected groups: the other (big six) are DKB, Fuyo, Mitsubishi, Mitsui, Sanwa, Sumitomo). Before World War II, Nissan itself was one of the ten big *zaibatsu* groups which effectively controlled the Japanese economy (Toyota was not). For the definitive account of the groupings in Japan see Dodwell (1990b).

40. From *Nippon Sangyo Keizai* (*Japanese Industry and Economy*), 8 July 1943, quoted in Fujita (1965) *Nihon Sangyou Kozo to Chuso Kigyo* (*Japanese Industrial Structure and Small Business*), pp. 186–7, translated and quoted in Nishiguchi (1989, p. 80).

41. Nishiguchi (1989, p. 74) notes that the implementation of the *keiretsu* had been started by the Japanese government's Implementation Outline of Rationalization in 1944. Horsley and Buckley (1990, pp. 48–9) point out that the American plan did not work: the *zaibatsu* were effectively reborn in the form of *keiretsu*. 'In the 1970s and 1980s, the firms within the *keiretsu* groupings were in control of a quarter of the Japanese economy: the same proportion as the *zaibatsu* controlled in the pre-war period.'

42. For a discussion on 'unlearning' see Dodgson (1991b).

43. Whilst *keiretsu* is used here the argument is also relevant to the *kyoryokukai* groupings.

44. Pickens bought his shares in March 1989 from the Japanese property developer, Azabu, which held 33 per cent of Koito. The head of Azabu, Kitaro Watanabe, had built up the holding intending to 'greenmail' Toyota or Koito (coerce them into buying the shares from him). When the greenmail failed, Watanabe sold the shares to Pickens. When Pickens failed to get a seat on the Koito board, he sold them back to Watanabe in June 1991. In August 1991 it was announced that Azabu would sell the whole of its stake to a Swedish company, Carlsson Investment Management, apparently at a significant loss. Koito was quoted as being 'very surprised' at this second deal – never having heard of Carlsson. On the one hand, the plotting behind Watanabe's activity (much more significant than Pickens's) is typical of Western capitalism; on the other, the response of the Japanese firms (Toyota and Koito) shows the perceived importance of responsibility with ownership within the lean system.

45. Figures from Dodwell (1990a). It is interesting to note that the previous edition of the Dodwell directory (1986) showed the shares to be Nissan (22.4 per cent), Toyota (8.6 per cent) and Isuzu (4.1 per cent).

46. Nippondenso, for example, has about 40 per cent of its sales outside Toyota and derives a high proportion of its profits from this business.

47. Honda's car assembly plant at Marysville opened in 1982, following the commissioning of company's motorcycle plant on the same site in 1979.

48. It should be noted that this term is not liked by the Japanese inward investors, because of the double implication of simple transference of practices and imposition of principles. This dislike may be seen as a feature of the lean production paradigm: global presence requires local adaptation and integration. See Womack *et al.* (1990, Chapter 8 and also Ohmae (1990).

49. This was measured by IMVP: see Figure 2.1. For a full explanation, see Krafcik (1986) as well as Womack *et al.* (1990).

50. The GM Fremont plant had been closed in 1982. The NUMMI deal was done in 1984 and the plant reopened towards the end of that year.

51. While it is not strictly a *macquila* (free trade zone) plant, Hermosillo benefits from many Mexican government special provisions, due the size of Ford's investment.
52. It is perhaps too early in the development of the lean production concept to draw conclusions about its transferability, despite the positive evidence referenced here. Dankbar (1990, p. 18) suggests a series of European cultural factors which might provide significant barriers to lean production. See also Graves, (1991, pp. 22–30).
53. Results of the IMVP assembly plant survey indicated that the American/Japanese joint venture assembly plants in North America were 'leaner' than their traditional (mass production) counterparts. In some cases the American plants themselves had learned the lean messages over the period of the IMVP (1986–90). See Womack *et al.* (1990, pp. 85–6).

2 | The Automotive Industries Today

The industrial activity in the automotive industry today may be characterized as the application of a mixture of new and old ideas to a mature product in the context of a rapidly changing set of market requirements. On the one hand, there is the commonly held view that 'cars all look the same, nowadays'. This factor is leading to adoption of new practices in the retailing of vehicles – an expected feature of a mature market. On the other, there is a need to develop so-called 'zero-emission vehicles' (required by law by the end of the 1990s in California), totally recyclable vehicles (encouraging, for example, the substitution of aluminium for steel) and a multitude of high-technology systems for safety, comfort, navigation and maintenance, etc. In fact, the automotive market is rapidly moving towards a niche structure.

In manufacturing terms, the IMVP data identified best practice in assembly (measured in terms of the effort required to build a standardized vehicle[1] and the number of customer-reported quality defects) as a Japanese achievement, up to now (Womack et al., 1990, p. 85) but not a Japanese prerogative. As we shall see, Western assemblers are learning to adopt lean practices in order to compete. Before considering this in more depth, a general view of the forecast demand pattern for the industry is useful.

The total number of vehicles assembled throughout the world is forecast to rise over the next five years. In 1990 the total was over 35 million cars, divided between the regions and assemblers as shown in Table 2.1. Long-term prospects for the industry are seen by the UK consultancy, Euromotor, as very good, with massive growth foreseen in the developing countries. By 2010 the report predicts world automotive sales of 74.7 million per annum, compared with the 1990 total of 49.3 million, including commercial vehicles. Noting that in 1990 Western markets accounted for 79 per cent of all vehicle sales and 76 per cent of the world vehicle fleet, for only 15 per cent of the world population, Euromotor (1991b) forecasts that by 2010 more than a third of world sales will be in what are now developing countries – a rise of over 300 per cent since 1960. In more established markets, it is forecast that sales of cars will increase by 40 per cent and commercial vehicles by 62 per cent by 2010.

Table 2.1 World passenger car assembly, 1989–96: sales and production (thousand units)[a]

	1989	1990	1991	1992	1993	1994	1996
Sales							
World total	35 377	35 469	34 202	34 649	36 746	38 143	40 464
Western Europe	13 415	13 249	13 526	13 391	13 584	14 100	15 022
USA	9 867	9 295	8 373	8 695	9 805	10 032	10 047
Japan	4 404	5 102	4 868	4 674	4 814	4 970	5 215
South Korea	500	604	745	836	919	993	1 132
Rest of world	7 191	7 219	6 690	7 053	7 624	8 048	9 048
Production							
World total	35 628	35 867	34 266	34 958	37 053	38 339	40 745
Western Europe	13 701	13 587	13 103	13 179	13 815	14 266	15 171
USA	6 967	6 298	5 733	6 238	6 702	6 798	7 051
Japan	9 052	9 947	9 753	9 618	9 882	10 005	10 243
South Korea	860	943	1 128	1 268	1 429	1 551	1 681
Rest of world	5 048	5 092	4 549	4 655	5 225	5 719	6 599

Note: [a] 1989, 1990 and 1991 are actual figures; 1992–96 are forecasts.
Source: DRI Europe (1992).

Forecasts by the industry analysts, Data Research International/McGraw Hill show an expected increase in annual passenger cars build worldwide of 19 per cent between 1991 and 1996, concentrated mostly in the USA (23 per cent increase in production), Europe (16 per cent) and non-traditional countries (45 per cent); the increase in Japan is seen as only 5 per cent over the period. A large part of these forecast increases is expected to result from Japanese transplant investment, in Europe and elsewhere, coming on stream during this period. Table 2.2 gives the estimates for the EC. These data are drawn from EC estimates which forecast the total Japanese transplant share of EC sales of passenger cars and light vehicles as 10 per cent by 1998. The complete EC forecast is shown in Table 2.3.

In addition, the European assemblers and General Motors have begun major investments in Eastern Europe: GM and Volkswagen in the eastern part of Germany, Fiat, Peugeot and GM in Poland, Volkswagen in Czechoslovakia, GM in Hungary and Fiat in Yugoslavia. In April 1991 Suzuki announced plans to become the first Japanese assembler operating in Eastern Europe, with a 40 per cent stake in the Hungarian industry, an enterprise called Magyar–Suzuki. (Suzuki was also the first Japanese firm to assemble cars in India – at the Maruti joint venture, in the early 1980s – and has been established in Pakistan for some years.) In July 1992 Peugeot signed an agreement with its Egyptian distributor to assemble 10 000 cars a year in Egypt.[2] In the same year, Peugeot had announced plans to assemble its 405 model in Argentina. Egypt has also attracted assembly investment from GM (commercial vehicles, and cars from 1993) and Chrysler (military jeeps), with Suzuki (minivans and trucks, from 1994) and Hyundai negotiating for local assembly accords.

Meanwhile, GM and Ford continue to produce cars in Europe, Australia and other parts of the world. The tendency for assemblers to enter into international

Table 2.2 Japanese automotive sales and production in the EC (thousand units)

	Total EC (12) market (cars)	Total Japanese sales in EC (12)	Japanese cars produced in EC
1987	11 187	1065	0
1988	11 745	1078	57
1989	12 261	1109	81
1990	12 154	1219	76
1991	12 580	1371	120
1992	12 440	1368	145
1993	12 582	1510	301
1994	13 034	1607	385
1996	13 878	1735	700
1999	15 100	2430	1200[a]

Note: [a] Other estimates have put 'transplant' output as high as two million units per year (including light trucks) by 1999.

Source: Actual/estimated data from DRI/McGraw Hill (*The Financial Times*, 2 August 1991) following EC/Japan agreement on limits during transition period 1991–99. Updated, June 1992 (*The Financial Times*, 8 June 1992).

collaborations means that a car built in Korea could be a North American product (e.g. the Ford Festiva, built by Kia) designed in Japan (by Mazda, as the 121)[3]. GM employed this strategy, without much success, in the 1980s with the Pontiac LeMans, designed in Germany (e.g. Pontiac LeMans – basically an Opel Kadett) and built in Korea by Daewoo. Both the LeMans and the Festiva were very small cars.

Thus it may be seen that regional production figures may not be interpreted as output from firms of any particular national ownership: the automotive industry has become international. There are still regional differences, however, connected to the position of the assembler along the path from mass production to lean production. The IMVP data show these clearly, when measured vehicle-assembly efforts are compared, as shown in Figure 2.1.

IMVP data on Japanese plants in Newly Industrializing Countries (NICs) suggest that it is reasonable to expect the new Japanese transplants to be established with lean principles: it is less clear how the European assemblers will organize the East European plants. Levels of integration also vary, although all assemblers state publicly that they intend to out-source more of the value-added in the vehicle. Current levels are shown in Table 2.4.

It is difficult to be exact or entirely satisfactory when discussing levels of integration, and practically impossible to prove figures right or wrong. The ranges given in Table 2.4 are from data provided personally by senior purchasing interviewees within the assemblers. The North American figures compare well with those quoted in a report by the independent Washington DC based Economic Policy Institute which estimated integration at GM at 70 per cent, Ford at 50 per cent and Chrysler at 30 per cent.[4] Levels for specific models vary, necessitating the use of averages. Definition of 'subsidiary' is also a point for debate: the Japanese suppliers are not wholly owned but some would argue their position is the same in practice as the integrated suppliers within, say, GM. In Europe, various public figures have been used. Renault spends FFr50 billion a year on components and records this as 60 per cent of its manufacturing costs. Audi,

Table 2.3 Japanese imports and transplant sales as proportions of total sales in EC, 1989–99[a]

Markets	1989 actual	1998 forecast	1998 % share	1999 forecast
France total	**2 667 000**	**2 850 000**	**100.0**	**2 850 000**
Japanese imports		162 000	5.7	150 000
Japanese transplants		155 000	5.4	
Total Japanese share	3.0%	317 000	11.1	
Italy total	**2 519 000**	**2 600 000**	**100.0**	**2 600 000**
Japanese imports		148 000	5.7	138 000
Japanese transplants		142 000	5.4	
Total Japanese share	2.0%	290 000	11.1	
Spain total	**1 376 000**	**1 475 000**	**100.0**	**1 475 000**
Japanese imports		84 000	5.7	79 000
Japanese transplants		196 000	13.3	
Total Japanese share	3.0%	280 000	19.0	
Portugal total	**252 000**	**275 000**	**100.0**	**275 000**
Japanese imports		23 000	8.4	23 000
Japanese transplants		35 000	12.7	
Total Japanese share	14.0%	58 000	21.0	
UK total	**2 600 000**	**2 700 000**	**100.0**	**2 700 000**
Japanese imports		189 000	7.0	
Japanese transplants		594 000	22.0	
Total Japanese share	11.0%	783 000	29.0	
Restricted markets total	**9 414 000**	**9 900 000**	**100.0**	
Japanese imports		608 000	6.1	
Japanese transplants		1 122 000	11.3	
Total Japanese share	5.5%	1 728 000	17.5	
Unrestricted markets total	**4 531 000**	**5 200 000**	**100.0**	
Japanese imports		714 000	13.7	
Japanese transplants		378 000	7.3	
Total Japanese share	17.4%	1 092 000	21.0	
Total EC	**13 946 000**	**15 100 000**	**100.0**	**15 100 000**
Japanese imports	1 237 000	1 320 000	8.7	1 230 000
Japanese transplants		1 500 000	10.0	1 200 000
Total Japanese share	**9.4%**	**2 820 000**	**18.7**	**16.1%**

Note: [a] Includes light commercial vehicles under five tonnes gross vehicle weight (which accounts for differences between Tables 2.2 and 2.3).
Source: EC projections, September 1990 and EC monitoring targets (1999) July 1991. Quoted in *The Financial Times*, 26 September 1991.

meanwhile, claims to have reduced integration to 20 per cent, while other German manufacturers plan similar levels at their new East German plants. The three regional ranges in Table 2.4 illustrate a difference in practice, which is discussed later.

In 1991, the BCG/PRS (BCG 1991) report on the European components industry calculated integration levels at European and Japanese assemblers, based upon added value as a percentage of sales. These data are shown in Table 2.5. They suggest that the degree to which value is added in the assemblers' component divisions varies greatly. This is in fact a function of how these

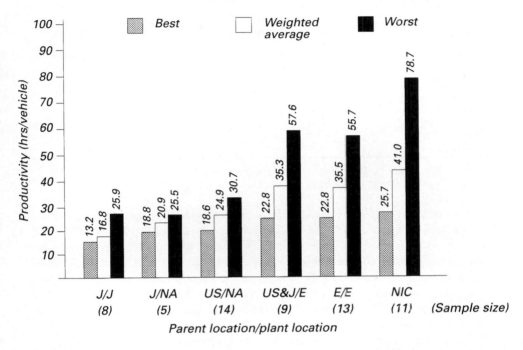

Note: [a] Volume producers only: the American Big Three, Fiat, PSA, Renault, Volkswagen in Europe and all of the companies from Japan. J/J = Japanese-owned plants in Japan; J/NA = Japanese-owned plants in USA/ Canada, including joint venture plants with American firms; US/NA = American-owned plants in USA/ Canada; US&J/E = American- and Japanese-owned plants in Europe; E/E = European-owned plants in Europe; NIC = plants in newly industrializing countries (Mexico, Brazil, Taiwan, and Korea).

Source: Womack *et al.* (1990, Figure 4.3, p. 85).

Figure 2.1 Regional comparison of assembly plant efficiency[a]

manufacturing activities are viewed by the assembler. Volkswagen, for example, professes to have no component divisions but actually makes many of its own components (steering gear, constant velocity joints, etc.), i.e. it chooses not to

Table 2.4 Levels of integration in vehicle assemblers

Region	Level of Integration (%)
USA/Canada	30–70
Europe	30–65
Japan	17–30

Note: Level of integration is defined as value-added within the assembly plant, plus value of parts bought in from wholly owned subsidiaries or off-site facilities. Sample = 3 USA/Canada, 9 Europe, 3 Japan.

Since the ranges are based upon a small number of companies, no average figure should be imputed. See discussion in text for comment.

Source: Author's research.

Table 2.5 Integration levels of European assemblers

Assembler	Value added as a percentage of sales	Value added/sales percentage including component divisions
Fiat	36	51
Volkswagen	60	60
Renault	55	60
Ford	40	55
General Motors	40	65
Daimler Benz	50	51
Peugeot	45	53

Source: *The Competitive Challenge Facing the European Automotive Components Industry* 1991, Boston Consulting Group, p. 11.

differentiate between component manufacture and vehicle assembly for purposes of integration levels. It remains relatively highly integrated (at 60 per cent). Fiat appears to have taken the opposite path, separating out its component activities and forming a new company to conduct the business. This firm, Magneti Marelli, has succeeded in establishing its own identity. Currently Fiat holds 61 per cent of Magneti Marelli shares but there may be plans for this holding to be reduced. For practical purposes, it is the figure in the right-hand column that should be taken as the level of integration.

Competition is increasing rapidly for established vehicle assemblers. In response, all the major firms have formed international alliances in order to access new regions and new techniques. For some, such collaborative ventures are seen as a route to survival (i.e. against new competition from expanding lean assemblers).

For example, the 800 saloon launched by Volvo in mid–1991 was seen as the last time such a project would be undertaken by the Swedish company on its own. Its strategic alliance with the French, state-owned Renault would become the basis of all future product strategy and plans were made for Volvo's two experimental production plants, Kalmar and Uddevalla, to be closed. In April 1990 the two firms set up a jointly owned (50/50) research subsidiary in France and began to exchange senior staff. One influential industry commentator (Euromotor 1991b) publicly advised that a total takeover of Volvo by Renault was the only way in which either firm would be able to compete in the long term. The outgoing Renault Chairman, Mr Raymond Levy, said in May 1992 that a full merger was possible, but not the only way forward. In October 1990 the two firms began to merge their component-buying activities and had achieved a 15 per cent commonality by mid-1992, when a full purchasing merger was announced (with an 80 per cent commonality target). Similar mergers of sales, quality and technical research were also under way at this time.

Womack *et al.* (1990) suggest that collaborating with a lean producer is a necessity for mass producers changing their organizations. For the Japanese, collaboration with indigenous assemblers has sometimes been used as a means of gaining acceptance. In Europe, for example, Honda's collaboration with Rover, which involved the development of entirely new models together for several years before the stage of equity exchange was reached in 1989, enabled the Japanese company to become accepted as part of the UK industry. The Toyota–GM joint venture in the USA, NUMMI, performed a similar function for Toyota. Ohmae (1990) refers to this process as 'insiderization' – gaining local acceptance through gentle insinuation.

NUMMI also showed for the first time that lean practice was transferable. Womack *et al.* (1990, pp. 82–3) describe this in detail. The data in Table 2.6, measured by the IMVP, illustrate the degree to which the learning process worked.

The number of companies producing motor vehicles has steadily declined in Europe since the early days when there were hundreds of small craft firms. In the USA, the Big Three (Ford, General Motors and Chrysler) remain the only indigenous assemblers, each represented in the marketplace by a collection of brand names. In Japan, the industry is split into large firms – Toyota, Nissan, Mitsubishi, Honda and Mazda (Toyo Kyogo) – and smaller firms – Suzuki, Daihatsu, Subaru (Fuji Heavy Industries) and Isuzu.

In Europe, the various shake outs have left six volume producers, including GM and Ford; the others are Volkswagen, Fiat, Peugeot and Renault. All these firms except Fiat have plants in several EC countries, including strong assembly industries in Belgium and Spain.[5] The 'specialist' firms are predominantly German: Mercedes Benz (part of the giant Daimler–Benz organization), BMW and Porsche. Several other smaller volume firms are now part of these majors: Jaguar and Aston Martin are owned by Ford, Lotus is part of GM and Ferrari and Alfa Romeo are subsumed within Fiat. Earlier mergers left Lancia within the Fiat fold, Citroën as a part of Peugeot, and Audi and Seat as parts of Volkswagen (which was later to absorb Skoda).

Saab Automobile is a 50:50 joint venture (1989) between GM and Saab–Scania; Volvo, as discussed above, is now cross-linked to Renault (20 per cent equity swap). Volvo Nederlands (30 per cent Volvo, 70 per cent Dutch government) is to become an equal holding three-way collaboration between the existing partners and Mitsubishi, depending upon approval by the EC.

In Britain Rover is 20 per cent owned by Honda, 80 per cent by British Aerospace and represents the last major British holding in the automotive industry. Producing a mix of cars which compete with the volume firms, but on the basis of lower overall output than some of the specialists, Rover is dependent upon Honda

Table 2.6 The transfer of lean production through a joint venture: General Motors Framingham versus Toyota Takaoka versus NUMMI Fremont, 1987[a]

	Framingham	Takaoka	NUMMI
Assembly hours per car	31	16	19
Assembly defects per 100 cars	135	45	45
Assembly space per car*	8.1	4.8	7.0
Inventories of parts (average)	2 weeks	2 hours	2 days

Notes: [a] Framingham was chosen by the IMVP as a worst-case mass production plant (it is now closed); Takaoka is a lean plant (but not a new one – it was opened in 1966); NUMMI is the Toyota–GM joint venture (New United Motor Manufacturing Inc.) which uses an existing GM workforce and factory in California, and Toyota organization principles (lean production).
* Assembly space per car is square feet per vehicle per year, corrected for vehicle size.
Source: IMVP World Assembly Plant Survey in Womack *et al.* (1990, Figure 4.2, p. 83).

for technical input, but has bullish plans to reposition itself within the specialist market.

Thus the automotive industry may be seen as follows:

■ Concentrated: a small number of firms assembling cars.
■ Subject to rapidly changing market technical requirements.
■ Highly competitive – on the bases of price and product differentiation.

■ The automotive components industry today

From earlier discussion of developments in the three principal regions in the automotive industry – North America, Western Europe and Japan – we can see three different types of evolution in the components industries. Currently these differences are disappearing as firms from all regions seek international presence and technological strength through growth.

In Europe small and large firms exist in each major country (UK, Germany, France and Italy) with Robert Bosch GmbH dominating the scene. Reflecting their roots in engineering, craft manufacture and medium-variety mass production, the companies show a sound technological base (see Chapter 5) and a high degree of dependency upon the automotive industry. They have some experience in international operation and the larger players are currently expanding within Europe (especially into the UK and Spain, to be near the Japanese transplants setting up in those countries) and further afield, sometimes through collaboration.

In North America the very large firms in the components industry usually have a major presence in other, non-automotive markets: indeed, automotive business often represents a small part of their sales turnover. This reflects the high degree of vertical integration traditionally practised in this region. The large firms have become international, especially in terms of European operations, and have also entered into international collaboration.

In Japan the major component firms are often highly automotive dependent, reflecting the way in which subcontracting has become a vital part of the Japanese economy and the close links which have been built up between assemblers and suppliers. Many have only recently made their first moves overseas, often by direct investment in new plants in North America and also by joint venturing, now seen in Europe. Some of the very large, multi-market Japanese corporations are also major players in the automotive industry, with most of their business, like their American counterparts, in non-automotive markets. This is illustrated in Table 2.7.

There are significant regional differences in the relationship between assemblers and components suppliers, in terms of their profitability, as measured by the Boston Consulting Group in their report to the European Commission (1991): see Figure 2.2. As BCG remark:

> In Japan the levels and direction of profits move together, whilst they are dissimilar and diverging in the US and Europe. This suggests a high degree of cooperation between component manufacturers and their suppliers in

Table 2.7 Worldwide corporate and automotive sales of selected component manufacturers, 1988–90 (US$ billion)

| | Europe 1988 | | | USA 1989 | | | Japan 1989 | |
	Auto	Corp.		Auto	Corp.		Auto	Corp.
Bosch	8.1	15.6	Allied Signal	3.9	11.9	Nippon denso	8.5	8.6
Valeo	2.9	2.9	TRW	3.4	7.3	Aisin Seiki	2.9	3.1
Magneti Marelli	2.7	2.7	ITT	2.6	20.0	Hitachi Sisakusho	2.2	24.9
ZF	2.4	2.9	UTC	1.9	19.5	Yazaki	2.0	2.7
Lucas	2.2	3.7	Eaton	1.9	3.7	Sumitomo Electric	1.4	4.7
GKN	2.2	4.3	Johnson Controls	1.3	3.7	Aisin A.W.	1.3	1.3

Note: figures include domestic and foreign business and aftermarket sales. See Tables 2.10, 2.14, 2.18 for longer lists.
Source: Author's interviews 1988–89, and various published data.

Japan. Improvements in performance are pursued together and gains and reductions in profitability seem to be shared. The philosophy of *unmei kyodotai* ('shared destiny') is reflected in the concrete sharing of operating and financial gains.

In contrast, in Europe and the US vehicle producers are consistently more profitable than component suppliers. This may reflect the relative bargaining strength of the OEMs [assemblers] relative to a fragmented supplier base and purchasing strategies aimed to a large extent at obtaining low prices. (BCG, 1991, pp. 22–3)

The reduction in Japanese return on net assets is attributed by BCG to the strengthening yen over the period (coupled with the increasing dependency on export sales). The report concludes that:

profitability [in Japan] is known to have recovered in 1989–90 to similar levels to those in the EC. This implies that the Japanese industry was passing on its gains in competitiveness (in terms of labour productivity and stockturns) in competitive pricing and investments in expansion abroad.

The gains referred to are shown in Figures 2.3 and 2.4.

The European automotive components industry

The difficulty in categorizing an automotive components supplier is shown by my own conclusion from data also examined by BCG. The figures are shown in Tables 2.8 and 2.9. Both estimates use similar sources. The definition of a components supplier is, however, not straightforward. The differentiation between major and minor companies was an attempt on my part to qualify the count: the terms are based upon the views of interviewees. 'Minor suppliers' does not, however, include every company whose product in some way ends up on a

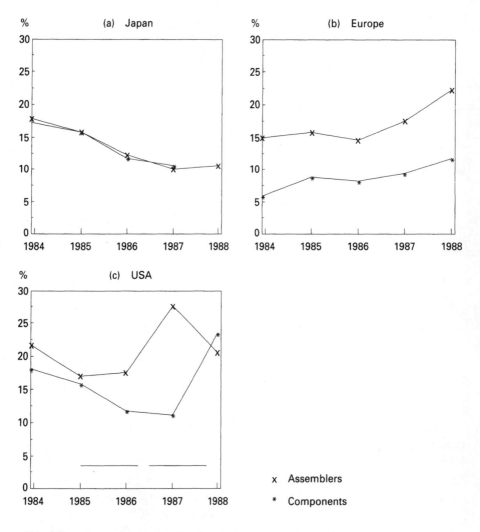

Note: [a] Figures are weighted average returns for profit before interest and tax as a percentage of net assets.

Source: Boston Consulting Group *The Competitive Challenge Facing The European Automotive Components Industry*, January 1991: Executive Summary, p. 22.

Figure 2.2 Comparison of return on net assets: Japanese, US and European assemblers and component firms, 1984–88[a]

vehicle: one estimate using this criterion put the number of automotive firms in West Germany alone as 30 000.[6]

It is clear that, which ever way they are counted, there are a great many firms in the components industry in Europe. The BCG (1991) report estimates the employment total in the industry to be 950 000 (EC12, 1990) or 2.6 per cent of total EC employment. Despite this number, business is strongly concentrated in the

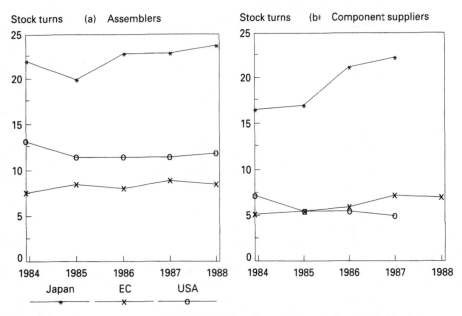

Source: Boston Consulting Group *The Competitive Challenge Facing The European Automotive Components Industry*, January 1991: Executive Summary, p. 21.

Figure 2.3 Comparisons of stock turnover: assemblers and suppliers in Japan, the EC and the USA

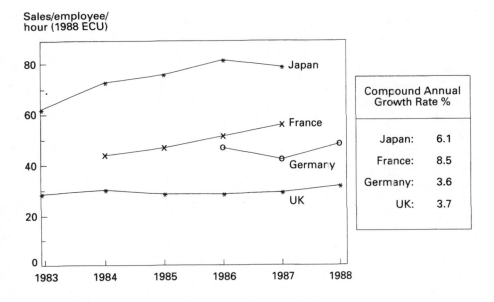

Source: BCG (1991, p. 20).

Figure 2.4 Comparisons of labour productivity in the autocomponents industry: Japan, the EC and the USA

Table 2.8 Estimated number of components suppliers in
Western Europe (1)

	Major	Minor
West Germany	450	5000
France	400	1500
UK	300	1500
Italy	250	1000
Spain	50	500
Others	50	500
Total	1500	10 000

Source: Lamming (1989a), p. 13.

Table 2.9 Estimated number of components suppliers in
Western Europe (2)

Italy	1000
West Germany	600
Spain	450
France	400
UK	350
Others	446
Total	3246

Source: BCG (1991).

top few companies. Table 2.10 is based upon the author's own research surveys, modified to include data gathered in the BCG survey and the EIU special reports, 1989 and 1991. Components production in independent suppliers in 1988 was estimated by BCG as shown in Table 2.11.

It is apparent from the above data and other estimates that the European automotive components industry is very concentrated. The total value of the European components industry output in 1988 was estimated by BCG (1991) at ECU78.5 billion, or US$95.5 billion.[7] The top twenty-five components suppliers have an estimated joint share of approximately 40 per cent of the market.[8] If the internal spend on components by the assemblers is removed from the demand side, this proportion rises to 45 per cent. The top five countries (Germany, France, Italy, Spain and the UK) account for 95 per cent of the production, value-added and consumption. BCG comment on these figures as follows:

> Germany's importance within the EC autocomponent industry is even greater than in vehicles: it accounts for 35% of vehicle production but 39% of component production, and 44% of value added, given the generally greater technological content of German production. These figures exclude the impact of German unification which has clearly further enhanced Germany's dominance. (BCG, 1991, p. 3)[9]

Japanese component suppliers have been building a presence in the European industry for almost forty years. In most cases the initial step was a technology link

Table 2.10 The major suppliers active in the European automotive components industry[a]

Company	Nationality of ownership	Automotive sales 1990 (US$ million)	Automotive % of total sales	Total sales 1990 (US$ million)	Automotive sales 1987 (US$ million)
Bosch	German	10 756	50.5	21 301	8 663
Philips	Dutch	4 793	14.5	32 996	3 786
Valeo	French	3 936	100.0	3 936	2 063
Magneti Marelli	Italian	3 370	100.0	3 370	2 038
ZF	German	3 112	75.0	4 149	1 942
GKN	British	2 750	55.0	4 999	1 803
Lucas	British	2 448	58.0	4 220	1 989
ACG–GM	American	2 400	100.0	2 400	1 997
ITT Teves	American	1 807	9.0	20 000	1 306
BTR	British	1 804	13.9	12 983	820
Allied Signal	American	1 770	14.3	12 343	2 341
TRW	American	1 770	21.7	8 169	1 200
Saint-Gobain	French	1 616	12.0	13 467	771
T&N	British	1 496	62.0	2 413	1 080
Pilkington	British	1 262	27.0	4 675	956
Mahle	German	1 248	90.0	1 386	861
SKF	Swedish	1 226	28.0	4 379	1 779
VDO	German	1 222	83.4	1 466	859
BBA	British	1 215	51.3	2 367	928
Siemens	German	1 163	2.9	40 397	600
Hella	German	1 139	76.8	1 482	600
Freudenberg	German	1 029	36.0	2 858	607
Epeda B Faure	French	1 008	62.8	1 605	655
Behr	German	935	95.0	990	770

Note: [a] Sales figures do not apply purely to Europe but include exports and non-European production. Automotive sales figures include original equipment and after-market sales, and exclude raw materials for use by assemblers (metals, plastics, paints and coatings, consumables, etc.) and tyre manufacturers (since they are predominantly after market). Note that ACG–GM and Magneti Marelli are owned respectively by GM and Fiat. The component divisions of, say, Ford are not identified as a separate entity in this way.

Source: Various, including (EIU 1989, 1991), updated by author's interviews.

Table 2.11 European automotive components production estimates: production, value-added and consumption by country: independent suppliers only

Country	Production 1988		Value-added 1988		Consumption 1988	
	ECU billion	%	ECU billion	%	ECU billion	%
Germany	30.6	39.0	14.5	44.3	23.5	33.1
France	16.9	21.5	5.7	17.3	15.2	21.5
Italy	11.1	14.1	4.5	13.7	9.2	13.0
Spain	8.8	11.2	3.6	10.9	9.3	13.1
UK	8.2	10.5	3.3	10.2	9.1	12.8
Others	2.9	3.6	1.3	3.5	4.6	6.4
Total	78.5	100.0	32.7	100.0	70.9	100.0

Source: BCG (1991).

(e.g. licensing agreement) followed by a physical presence. Some examples are given below:[10]

- Nippondenso and Bosch began a technology exchange in 1953; the relationship remains.
- Smiths Industries and Kanto Seiko signed a technology cooperation agreement in 1964 for the manufacture of speedometer cables, an area from which Smiths wished to withdraw.
- NTN Corporation started a technology licensing agreement with GKN Hardy Spicer for the Bisfield type constant velocity joint in 1963. In 1964 NTN Bearings–GKN Ltd – a manufacturing company – was established in the UK.
- Kasai Kogyo Co. began a technology agreement with Gerb. Happich (sun visors) in 1964.
- Tachi-S Co., a manufacturer of seats, formed a technology assistance agreement with Slumberland Group in 1969.
- Nippondenso and IMI have had several technical agreements in force since 1969.

An overview of Japanese component suppliers' activities in Europe is given in Table 2.12.

A listing of these manufacturing investments is contained in Appendix 2. A further listing of Japanese component firms non-manufacturing investments and presence in Europe is contained in Appendix 3.

The UK has attracted the lion's share of inward investment from component

Table 2.12 Analysis of Japanese component supplier positions in Europe (manufacturing investments only, summer 1990)

Location of manufacturer			By OEM alliance		
	No.	% of total		No.	% of total
UK	13	45	Independent	18	62
Germany	3	10	Nissan	6	21
France	4	14	Toyota	4	14
Spain	3	10	Honda	1	3
Others	6	21	Total	29	100
Total	29	100			

Equity investment			By component type		
	No.	% of total		No.	% of total
100%	10	36	Engine cooling	5	17
> 50%	6	21	Electrical	9	31
50%	4	14	Suspension/brake	5	17
< 50%	8	15	Tyre/rubber	5	17
Total	28[a]	100	Exterior trim	2	7
			Body	2	7
			Others	1	4
			Total	29	100

Note: [a] One unknown.

Source: Technomic Consultants International (1990).

suppliers, apparently as a result of the Japanese assemblers' decisions to locate here. Some Japanese supplier ventures predate these decisions, however (examples from Chatterjee, 1991):

- NSK Bearings Europe, a subsidiary of Nippon Seiko was set up in 1974 and now employs 344 people in the manufacture of bearings.
- Bridgestone Tyre UK, a manufacturing joint venture between Bridgestone (51 per cent) and C.Itoh (49 per cent), was established in 1972.
- Bearings manufacturer Minebea established NMB Ltd in 1971.
- Nachi (UK) is a joint venture between Nachi–Fujikoshi and Nissho Iwai (60 per cent/40 per cent) with thirteen employees established in 1971.
- Aisin Seiki UK Research Laboratory was set up for R&D in automotive components in 1983.
- Clarion Shoji (UK) Ltd, a subsidiary of Clarion Co., was established in 1980. It employs sixty people in the manufacture of car audio equipment.
- Merlin Ariels Ltd, part of Nihon Antenna Co., was set up in 1976 to manufacture antennae and cables.

Whilst earlier technical liaisons involved the flow of technology from Europe to Japan (and some still do, e.g. the licensing of cable loom technology by Rists Wire and Cable to Kyoritsu Hiparts Co.), more recent joint ventures have sometimes reversed the direction. In some cases the technology is only licensed to the joint venture firm, not 'given'. The following are examples:

- Eften–Rose, a venture between Wagon Industrial and Tri-Wall (a Japanese cardboard manufacturer, half owned by Honshu Paper) makes car roof linings, using technology licensed to the joint venture company by Tri-Wall.
- Unipart and Yotaku-Giken have a joint venture making catalytic converters in the UK, with technology licensed to the joint venture by the Japanese partner.

There is an important difference between this type of collaboration and that in which the technology is vested in the joint venture firm by one of the partners.[11] A listing of forty-four cases of technical liaison between Japanese and British components firms is contained in Appendix 4.

The year 1990 saw the advent of the Japanese supplier association concept – the *kyoryokukai* – in Europe. Work in the UK automotive industry, by the Welsh Development Agency (WDA) (Hines, 1992) applied the concepts, in the light of successes in the area by the Japanese camera manufacturer, Canon, in France. Llanelli Radiator Ltd, an established UK company now owned by Calsonic (Nissan group), was approached by the WDA to be the head of an association. Early indications are that the experiment has worked and that others will follow; a similar club is to be set up amongst Toyota's Welsh suppliers for its engine plant in Deeside. Other forms of club are emerging – Nissan has initiated several in the north-east of England, to encourage dialogue and cooperation between suppliers and customers.

Japanese suppliers have been quick to take advantage of exit strategies of European firms. For example, Lucas Automotive has a very successful joint venture with Sumitomo, making wiring harnesses for Honda and Toyota at the old Smiths Industries factory in Ystradgynlais in Wales, but has sold its instrumentation business in South Wales to Nippon Seiki. The sale of Llanelli Radiators by Rover to Calsonic was a similar case (i.e. exit strategy). Calsonic, a Nissan group company, subsequently sited its Technical Research and Development for Europe centre in the UK. Further examples are provided by the acquisition of IMI (Marston) Radiators by Nippondenso as part of the IMI restructuring, and Takata's 80 per cent stake in General Motors's seat belt and electronic components plant in Belfast.

In some cases, two or more Japanese firms have used strategic partnerships to form joint ventures in Europe. Examples include the following:

- DHK (UK) Ltd, a springs manufacturer formed by Daido Kogyo Co. (70 per cent) and Hayami Spring Manufacturing Co. (30 per cent).
- Nissan Yamato Engineering Ltd, which is owned by Daiwa Kogyo (20 per cent) and Nissan Motor Manufacturing UK Ltd (80 per cent).
- SP Tyres UK Ltd, owned by Sumitomo Rubber Industries (81 per cent), Sumitomo Electric Industries (7 per cent), Ohtsu Tyre and Rubber Co. Ltd (6 per cent) and other (6 per cent).

Lastly, Japanese firms have entered into European-based joint ventures with non-European suppliers. Examples include the following:

- Ikeda Bussan–Hoover company (Japan–USA), seat suppliers to Nissan.
- Reydel–Kasai, a collaboration of Reydel from the USA and Kasai Kogyo (door casings and trim).
- ACK controls: Acco Controls (USA) (51 per cent), Chuo Spring (35 per cent) and Kokoku Steel Wire (14 per cent) (control cables).

It is clear that the Japanese component firms intend to establish a significant presence in Europe, as they have in the USA. It is probable that they will employ the lessons they have learned in the USA and take a 'softly softly' approach. Some observers suggest that the Japanese assemblers are discouraging their suppliers from setting up in Europe (e.g. EIU, 1992 and *The Financial Times*, 23 July 1992) whilst others feel that further expansion may be expected, including 'second-tier' suppliers and toolmakers, etc.

American firms have played a major role in the European components industry for a long time. In some cases (e.g. TRW, Bendix, Motorola) they have become a 'natural' part of the industry, in the same way that their Detroit-based customers have done. In other cases, acquisition of a European firm has itself resulted in the American parent's automotive strength (e.g. the case of ITT, which would be much less significant in the automotive industry without its European acquisition, Alfred Teves).

The North American automotive components industry

The three national industries within the North American region – Canadian, US and Mexican – differ in their characters. For the purposes of this discussion, however, the first two may be considered together.

The Mexican autoparts industry services Chrysler, Ford, GM, Volkswagen and Nissan, all of which assemble passenger cars and engines in the country,[12] and four truck manufacturers. There is a preponderance of US-owned companies, but several strong Mexican firms exist, the largest five having sales of over US$100 million (1988). The estimated total number of suppliers in Mexico is 400, although at least a quarter of these are very small, general subcontractors. A more commonly used figure is therefore 300 firms. Out of a national original equipment components market of some US$3 billion per year (including heavy trucks) about half is placed with Mexican suppliers, the remainder coming from the USA, Canada, Europe, Brazil and Japan. When automobiles and light trucks only are considered, the domestic suppliers account for only 45 per cent of the US$2.8 billion market.[13]

Mexico is heavily influenced by the industrial pattern in the USA. There is also a clear German influence with the presence of Volkswagen (cars) and Daimler Benz (trucks, and cars from 1993),[14] major firms such as Robert Bosch, and family-owned suppliers started by German and Austrian expatriates in the 1950s. Suppliers are apparently becoming influenced by Japanese practices, led directly by the requirements of Nissan Mexicana, and indirectly via the American and German assemblers.

The NAFTA (North American Free Trade Agreement) agreements currently being negotiated by the three North American countries will clearly have an effect upon autoparts business, although the specific impacts are unclear as yet, particularly since special arrangements already have been in place for some time. Some of the foreign-owned components firms already view North America as an entity: Robert Bosch, for example, concentrates its electrical technologies in Mexico and its electronics in the USA.[15]

In the USA and Canada the components industry is still dominated by the subsidiaries of the Big Three assemblers. In 1989 the market for original equipment components (value of production) was estimated at US$90 billion.[16] This business was shared as shown in Table 2.13.

In addition to the assemblers' subsidiary firms, there are some large,

Table 2.13 Analysis of US/Canadian original equipment automotive components production

		Value of production (1989)	
		US$ billion	%
In-house[a] subsidiaries of:	Ford	12.0	13.3
	Chrysler	3.8	4.2
	GM	25.0	27.7
Top twenty independents		12.4	13.7
Other independents[b]		36.8	41.1
Totals		90.0	100.0

Notes: [a] includes separately named parts companies and component production within assembly operations. [b] Including component operations of Japanese transplants.
Source: Research interview data from ELM International, Detroit.

51

independent suppliers. All of these are US-owned and most have substantial non-automotive business. They are listed in Table 2.14. ELM International estimates that the top fifty independents account for between US$20 and US$25 billion OE automotive sales in the USA and Canada. The total number of component suppliers in this region is estimated at 1500 companies.

As in Europe, the industry in North America has seen significant change in recent years as a result of merger and acquisition (e.g. Scheller Globe Corporation was absorbed by United Technologies in 1989, Champion by Coopers Industries in the same year) and firms from other sectors have become major players (e.g. Motorola from electronics, GE Plastics and DuPont in new materials, etc.). In some cases these firms have not created a separate automotive division (e.g. DuPont, with an estimated US$1.5 billion automotive sales, out of a total US$40 billion in 1990) choosing to remain influential but slightly removed players.[17] This is an interesting strategy to which we shall return in Chapter 8.

Product technology changes have given rise to the need for change in existing players, too, as exemplified by Holley Carburettor's development of electronic fuel injection expertise (see Chapter 5), while the arrival of Japanese transplant component suppliers, in addition to their assembler customers, has provided major challenges for the industry.

Table 2.14   The major independent component suppliers in the North American industry[a]

Company	Automotive OEM sales (US$ million 1989)	Notes[b]	Corporate sales (US$ million 1989)	% automotive
Allied Signal	3849	1,2	11 942	32.2
TRW	3440	1,2	7340	46.9
ITT	2645	1,2	20 005	13.2
United Technologies	1931	4	19 532	9.9
Eaton	1886	1	3671	51.4
Budd	1400	3,7	1400	100.0
Johnson Controls	1285	2	3684	34.9
Varity Corp	1200	1,2	2285	52.5
Borg Warner	1200	1,2	1200	100.0
Dana	1124	5	4865	23.1
Cooper	886	1,2	5129	17.3
Rockwell	777	2	2518	30.9
Masco	660		1687	39.1
A.O. Smith	600	1,2	976	61.5
Arvin	600	1	1540	39.0
Motorola	500	6	9620	5.2

Notes: [a] figures are generally for total (i.e. global) OE passenger car business. As the following notes show, some cases include commercial vehicles and after market. [b] (1) includes heavy truck and bus sales; (2) includes after-market sales; (3) includes small amount of non-automotive sales; (4) sales of industrial division, primarily automotive; (5) light truck only; (6) includes OE semiconductor and cellular phones; (7) division of Thyssen (Germany).

Source: Research interview data from ELM International Detroit.

Estimates of the number of Japanese component suppliers who have set up in North America vary. In terms of manufacturing plants, Dodwell (1990a) quotes a survey carried out in 1988 by the Japanese Auto Parts Industry Association (JAPIA) in which 128 of its members report such activity: 58 of these operations were recorded as wholly owned subsidiaries of their Japanese parents, 53 as joint ventures with North American partners and 17 as joint ventures with Japanese trading companies and 'complementary material/parts suppliers'. A leading industry consultancy report (Elm International, 1989b) on the same subjects records 146 establishments, of which 81 were wholly owned Japanese subsidiaries, 49 joint ventures with North American partners, 8 joint ventures with other Japanese suppliers, 5 joint ventures with Japanese assemblers and 3 joint ventures with European firms.

When non-manufacturing operations are included, it is estimated that a total of 400 Japanese suppliers has appeared in the North American region in the past decade (see Chatterjee (1991)). Japanese suppliers were building a presence before this, however, and as in Europe, the early settlers appear to have invested before the location of assembly plants was considered. For example:

- Koyo Seiko set up in 1958 to manufacture ball bearings.
- NGK Spark Plug began manufacturing coil springs in 1966.
- NOK has made rubber parts in the USA since 1968.

Since the arrival of the Japanese assembly plants in North America, the attraction for Japanese component suppliers has increased. Some examples are given in Table 2.15.

In addition to the sole ventures, the Japanese have entered into partnerships with American and European component suppliers, some of which are shown in Tables 2.16 and 2.17.

A list of the Japanese component manufacturing investment in North America in the form of Japanese–Japanese joint ventures is contained in Appendix 5. Further examples of Japanese–American joint ventures in North America are listed in Appendix 6, and Japanese wholly owned greenfield sites are listed in Appendix 7.

The Japanese component suppliers have not found their investments in North America trouble free, however:

> In many cases, it started to become obvious to some parts producers that business with the transplants of their traditional Japanese OEM customers alone would not justify the investment they were making in the U.S. To exceed the critical throughput, many other transplant parts manufacturers had expected to have a chance to supply the U.S. Big Three automakers. In reality, such attempts have been successful only for an exceptionally small number of Japanese parts manufacturers . . . a downturn in the U.S. car production in the last few years is working as yet another negative factor.
>
> It is anticipated that sooner or later some of the Japanese transplant parts manufacturer will face serious difficulties in sustaining a viable volume of business in North America. (Dodwell, 1990a, p. 5)

Table 2.15 Japanese component firms: some examples of greenfield sites in North America

Date	Company	Transplant affiliate	Products
1975/86/87	Nippondenso	Various (Toyota Group)	Starters and other electric parts; display meters; radiators; heaters
1976/83/86	Calsonic	Nissan	Radiators; air conditioners; exhausts
1982/86/88	Yazaki	Toyota/Nissan Isuzu/Hino	Wiring; pressed terminals; meters
1985	Kanto Seiki	Nissan	Plastics
1986	Toyoshimna	Various	Leaf springs
1986/87	Jidosha Denki Kogyo	Isuzu/Hino/Nissan/ Honda/Toyota/Mazda/ Mitsubishi	Wipers and aerials
1986/88	Asmo	Nippondenso/Mazda/ Toyota/Daihatsu/ Mitsubishi	Electric motors; windscreen washers
1986/89	Topy	Toyota/Nissan/Isuzu/ Hino/Mitsubishi/ Mazda	Steel wheels; aluminium wheels; fasteners
1987	Nippon Seiki	Honda/Yamaha/Suzuki/ Mitsubishi	Speedometers
1988	Aisin Seiki	Toyota/Suzuki/Daihatsu	Pressings
1988/89	Delta Kogyo	not known	Seats

Source: Chatterjee: The Technology Partnership (1991)/ELM International (1989b)/Dodwell (1990a).

The Technomic Consultants International report (1990) goes further than this, reporting that many of the North American components transplants are still making substantial losses.

The activities of Japanese components transplants in North America have loosened the strict ties between Japanese assemblers and their suppliers (see below). Dodwell reports that:

> In December 1989, Nissan decided to start purchasing electric fuel pumps from Nippondenso [a Toyota group affiliate] for use at Nissan Motor Manufacturing Corp., USA (NMMC), Nissan's U.S. production subsidiary. Nippondenso will start supplying the parts from its plant in Japan in the middle of 1990 and eventually from its U.S. joint venture with Robert Bosch in July 1991. One of the reasons for such movement is that Nissan's current suppliers of the parts, Mitsuba Electric, Jidosha Kiki and Jidosha Denki Kogyo, lacked manufacturing capability in the U.S., while Nippondenso needed orders from non-traditional customers to support the growth of its U.S. production base. (Dodwell, 1990a, p. 19).

Table 2.16 Automotive components manufacturing: some Japanese–American joint ventures in North America: 1982–88

Date	Company	Partner	Japanese ownership (%)	Products
1983	Hayashi–Telempu	Masland	50	Carpets; trim
1984	Diesel Kiki	Wynn's	50	Air-conditioners Heat exchangers
1985	Daikyo	Magna	50	Interior trim
	Kunigawa	Chardon	51	Weather strip
	Ryobi	Sheller Globe	45	Die castings
1986	Asahi Glass	PPG	20	Safety glass
	Usui Kukusai	Bundy	49	Brake pipes
	Sumitomo Metal	LTV Steel	60	Galzanized sheet
1987	NHK	Barnes	45	Suspensions
	Calsonic	Globe	n/a	Soundproofing
	Nishikawa	Standard	40	Weather strip
	Sanoh	Itigbie	50	Brake pipes
1988	Akebono	GM	50	Brake drums/discs
	Namba	Dunglas	50	Seating
	Nippon Glass	Libby Owens	n/a	Safety glass
	Riken Corp.	Sealed Power	50	Piston rings

Source: Chatterjee: The Technology Partnership (1991).

The Japanese transplants are a natural target for political crossfire, in view of the USA's US$41 billion trade deficit with Japan in 1991. One result of this is pressure upon them to source from indigenous component suppliers: in January 1992 MITI required the Japanese vehicle assemblers to double their local (North American) spending to an annual US$19 billion, from April 1994. In September 1992 it was reported that this level would probably be required, in the light of the NAFTA agreement between Mexico, USA and Canada. Under the agreement, Japanese cars made in the region must have 62.5 per cent local content to qualify for free movement between the three countries. The Daiwa Institute of Research in Tokyo estimated that only US$4 billion of the total US$19 billion would be for parts imported into Japan; the remaining US$15 billion would be for use in the NAFTA region (*The Financial Times*, 3 September 1992).

In summary, the North American OE components industry is still dominated by the in-house operations and subsidiaries of the Big Three American assemblers and the top fifty independents, who between them provide over 70 per cent of the value. Several other large independents operate primarily in the after market, whilst almost 1500 smaller firms compete for the remainder of the OE business. Suppliers who have gained contracts with Honda, Toyota, Nissan and the rest of the Japanese assemblers (all of whom have operations in the USA or Canada) have learned how to provide new levels of service and there is anecdotal evidence that

Table 2.17 Automotive components manufacturing: some Japanese–European joint ventures in North America

Japanese partner	European partner	Country	Japanese ownership (%)	Products
Murakami–Kamiedo	FKI	UK	n/a	Mirrors
Japan Brake	T&N	UK	n/a	Brake components
Ishikawa Tekko	Lemforder	Germany	50	Ball joints
Nippon Piston Ring	Goetze	Germany	25	
Nippon Seiko	Electrolux	Sweden	50	Seat belts
Nippondenso	Bosch	Germany	50	Fuel pumps
Sumitomo Electric	Lucas	UK	50	Disc brakes
Yazaki	VDO	Germany	50	Meters
Yokohama Rubber and Yokohama Aeroquip	Aeroquip	France	35	Hoses, air conditioners

Source: Chatterjee: The Technology Partnership (1991).

the benefit of this is being passed on to their American customers.[18] The growing strength of Japanese component suppliers currently searching for new ways of achieving competitiveness with or without non-Japanese partners, appears to threaten the traditional position of the American firms in the long run.

The Japanese automotive components industry

As in North America and Europe, the present structure of the automotive components industry in Japan today reflects its origins and development. The supply groupings around the major assemblers, themselves parts of the larger *keiretsu* groups, have remained largely unchanged. This is principally the result of the continuous growth which the Japanese automotive industry has enjoyed for three decades, and the Japanese dislike of ownership changes brought about by capital market dealings.

The ideas of Kiichiro Toyoda in 1939 (see Chapter 1) on the role of suppliers, and the relationships between them and their customers, have produced an industry in which there are strong ties and some clearly defined responsibilities.

Dodwell (1990a) reports that there are 'about 1,400 parts suppliers and more than 10,000 suppliers of materials and subcontractors for machining, casting and other processes' in Japan. Dodwell quotes the total production of automotive parts in Japan in 1989 as valued at ¥9 625 022 million, or just over US$74 billion (at ¥130:US$1). This includes after-market and original equipment for cars and commercial vehicles. When allowance is made for exports (US$19 057 million in 1989) and imports (US$932 million) the domestic OE and after market may be seen to be almost US$56 billion.

The top twenty suppliers (see Table 2.18) have a combined automotive turnover of US$32 660 million. Allowing for exports it is estimated that the top twenty suppliers account for approximately 40 per cent of the domestic production.

The sourcing patterns (by value of component supplies) of the assemblers are as shown in Figure 2.5. All the assemblers except Honda have their own supplier groupings, or *kyoryokukai*. In Toyota's case, 176 of its 340 suppliers are in this grouping: 56 affiliated companies (i.e. those firms in which Toyota has a significant shareholding and holds effective control) and 120 independents. For Nissan, the numbers are 58 and 106 respectively. Honda has 32 affiliated suppliers and 276 independents – the lack of a *kyoryokukai* meaning that all non-affiliated firms are treated equally (whereas Toyota and Nissan give their non-*kyoryokukai* companies (160 for Toyota, 150 for Nissan) less favoured status.[19]

The suppliers linked to Toyota and Nissan tend to be highly dependent upon the automotive industry, whereas most independents have substantial non-automotive business. The largest Japanese components suppliers are shown in Table 2.18. There is an increasing tendency for suppliers within the *kyoryokukai* to supply parts to other assemblers. This is partly a function of the general search for sources of competitive advantage, and partly a result of the geographical spreading of assembly. There has always been some cross-trading: Dodwell (1990a) reports that forty-nine companies are members of both the Toyota and Nissan *kyoryokukai*.

The new Toyota plant in the South island of Japan – Kyushu, near the town of Fukuoka – is the first domestic assembly plant outside Aichi prefecture for the company. There are no Toyota affiliates on the island and it is likely that many parts will come from Honda and Nissan suppliers already located there.

Nippondenso, one of the world's largest and most sophisticated automotive components companies, still has very strong links to Toyota but has shown through its strategic moves that it increasingly makes its own decisions.[20] It also has a variegated ownership, including a 7 per cent stake held by a competitor – Robert Bosch GmbH of Germany – and its own supplier grouping: Denso Kyoryokukai, founded in 1959.

The moves offshore by the Japanese assemblers inevitably provide challenges for the component suppliers. This is not limited to the transplants in North America and Europe. For example, Toyota has announced plans to cease domestic manufacture of one of its car engines (1.5 litre) setting up a joint venture manufacturing plant in Indonesia, to supply all assembly plants in Asia, including those in Japan. The Japanese suppliers are already well configured to take advantage by supporting such moves. In addition to the investments noted earlier, many other activities are under way, as shown in Table 2.19.

Table 2.18 The largest Japanese component suppliers[a]

Company	Group	Auto sales (US$ million)	Corporate sales (US$ million)	% auto	Parent holdings (%)
Nippondenso	T	8497	8583	99	35.2
Aisin Seiki	T	2937	3124	94	26.9
Hitachi Seisakusho[b]	I	2238	24 862	9	—
Yazaki	I	1997	2736	73	—
Sumitomo Electric	I	1396	4654	30	—
Aisin A.W.	T	1346	1346	100	—
NTN Toyo Bearings	I	1303	1903	68.5	—
Calsonic	N	1303	1303	100	33.2
Toyoda Gosei	T	1289	1302	99	40.5
Nippon Seiko	I	1134	2315	49	—
Atsugi Unisia	N	1029	1029	100	31.1
Tokai Rika	T	1020	1040	98.1	30.1
Yachiyo	H	994	1046	95	41.4
Sumitomo Denso[c]	I	991	1066	93	—
Koyo Seiko	T	978	1577	62	17.7
Asmo[d]	T	934	946	98.7	—
Tokyo Seat	H	906	906	100	20.5
NHK Springs	I	793	955	83	—
Clarion	N	790	964	82	12.8
Koito	T	785	857	91.6	19.0
Araco[e]	T	763	1525	50	81.6
Stanley Electric	H	685	1114	61.5	3.9
Toyoda Machine Works	T	605	1025	59	30.1
Akebono	I	575	618	93.1	—
Kayaba	I	483	1124	43	—
NGK Spark Plugs	I	350	716	49	—
Mitsuboshi Belting	I	237	515	46	—

Notes: [a] Ranked by automotive sales (Total: OE and after market); T = Toyota; N = Nissan; H = Honda; I = Independent. Sales figures for 1989: converted at ¥ 130: US$1. Excludes tyres and glass manufacturers. Several large firms have substantial auto sales, not quoted separately (e.g. Toshiba, which probably has US$1 billion; Matsushita probably has almost US$1.5 billion, mostly in the after market. Other large firms are indirect (materials) suppliers (e.g. Mitsubishi, Hitachi Chemicals, etc.).
[b] Automotive includes 'transportation equipment'.
[c] Also Sumitomo Metals, etc. (large materials suppliers).
[d] 73.4 per cent owned by Nippondenso.
[e] The other 50 per cent is vehicle assembly for Toyota.
Source: Derived from Dodwell (1990a).

■ American vertical integration versus Japanese vertical integration

The Japanese *keiretsu* consist of horizontally connected and vertically integrated groups of companies. The automotive companies are all classifiable as vertically

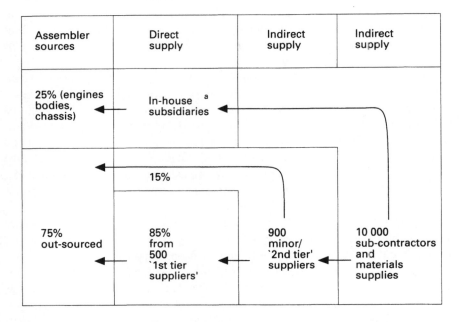

Note: [a] Toyota, for example, has six in-house plants for the production of parts, as opposed to five for assembly of vehicles. Nissan has four parts plants and five for vehicle assembly. Honda's non-car plants produce some parts and other products such as motorcycles, lawn mowers and portable generators. Honda's policy of sourcing as 'openly' as possible is reflected in its lack of a *kyoryokukai* and small amount of in-house component manufacture.

Source: Author's construction, derived from Dodwell (1990a), p. 7 and research interviews.

Figure 2.5 Sourcing of automotive components in Japan[a]

Table 2.19 Overseas activities of Japanese auto parts suppliers

	Manufacturing affiliates	Sales affiliates	Licensing arrangements
USA	115	46	21
Taiwan	51	3	46
Korea	29	—	50
Thailand	28	5	30
Indonesia	20	1	22
Malaysia	15	1	17
India	11	—	24
Brazil	11	—	5
Canada	10	8	1
Singapore	10	6	—
Others	47	62	133
Total	347	132	349

Source: Dodwell (1990a, p. 20).

integrated although with minority holdings by the parent company in most cases.[21] Clearly the level of influence, or even control, by parent companies over subsidiaries (e.g. assembler over supplier) is high, and yet the Japanese version of vertical integration appears to work where the American version has failed. It is important to understand why this is so.

We saw in Chapter 1 how the American version of vertical integration started with frustration (justified or otherwise) on the part of Henry Ford with the attitude of his suppliers to the change from craft to mass production, and with the strategies of Alfred Sloan in giving the giant conglomerate GM a workable structure. The huge companies were pioneering a new form of manufacturing and there was a sense of 'all hands to the pump'. Gradually, however, the initiative was lost and the cosiness of protected positions as a subsidiary within either organization blunted the competitiveness of component suppliers. Total control, it seems, leads to a lack of supplier response and customer service.

Buyers within the assembler, meanwhile, were obliged to buy from subsidiary divisions: threats to the contrary (i.e. re-sourcing to outside suppliers) would be countered with political arguments on the part of the supplier division (job losses, wasted capacity, etc.), and by senior executives in suppliers pulling rank on junior purchasing managers in the assembler). Independent suppliers, while they never gave up on gaining new business from the Big Three at the expense of in-house divisions, would not apply themselves in the manner associated with a free market.

The exchange of information across divisional boundaries within integrated groups in the West was apparently not good and interdivisional politics appear to have played a greater role than customer service. This cannot have been helped by the general atmosphere of complacency present in the American industry (as explained in Abernathy, 1978).

The result of these developments is a relative inefficiency in component supply within vertically integrated groups, exacerbated by the need to embrace and master new technologies. The supplier companies which must perform this latter duty cannot do so without meaningful contracts outside their parent groups but they are prevented from gaining such work by a wariness on the part of other customers in dealing with competitors' in-house divisions. (This may not be the case if the subsidiary is perceived as less strictly integrated – see Chapter 7.) At the same time the independent suppliers would not strive to gain new business in competition with in-house divisions, on technological or other grounds.

In Japan, the vertical integration of the groups occurred initially for similar reasons to those in the USA, although ownership did not develop in the same way. Relationships between customers and suppliers, however, were determined by the economic climate, especially after World War II, when survival was paramount. The extreme pressure under which Japanese industry was placed was converted into a working discipline which ensured that customer service remained a strategic objective, even though the supplier might apparently be assured of the assembler's business (as with its vertically integrated counterpart in the USA). In the Japanese version of vertical integration, therefore, the dynamic tension between customer and supplier remains, to the long-term benefit of both parties.

In 'going global', it is possible that neither model will suffice, however, as suppliers need to be able to deal with new customers on the full strategic level, and with a degree of self-determination. This might not be possible if the supplier were fully controlled (i.e. through 100 per cent ownership) or as heavily influenced as the traditional Japanese relationships require. This will be discussed later.

Vehicle assemblers and component suppliers are facing a time of turmoil. Now, more than ever, they need to innovate and collaborate to compete. In the next two chapters we shall explore the theories and concepts which underpin these two challenges of technical change, beginning with innovation.

■ Notes

1. This was achieved in order to compare like with like. For details see Krafcik (1986).
2. The joint venture, to be 51 per cent owned by Peugeot, represented a very modest investment (FFr10 million) because an existing Jeep assembly plant could be used. Local content was planned to rise from 20 to 30 per cent by 1994. Peugeot encouraged its Parisian neighbour, Valeo, to set up a component plants or make collaborative deals with local suppliers in Egypt to accompany the new assembly venture (*The Financial Times*, 21 July 1992).
3. Ford and Mazda each hold 10 per cent of Kia stock. Ford owns 25 per cent of Mazda.
4. The report was prepared with the help of the US Office of the Study of Automotive Transport at the University of Michigan: *The Financial Times*, 19 June 1992, p. 25.
5. The 'minicar' from VW and Suzuki, whose joint development was announced in July 1992, will be built by VW's subsidiary, SEAT, in Spain, replacing the Fiat-based Marbella (*The Financial Times*, 24 July 1992). GM, Ford, Volvo, VW and Renault all have plants in Belgium.
6. Personal interview with a German automotive industry manager 1988.
7. Author's estimate of the total value of the European components market (i.e. requirements of assemblers for components to be used in Europe – excluding tyres – in 1988 was ECU50 billion original equipment plus ECU20 billion after market (Lamming, 1989a, p. 14). The BCG estimate for the same 1988 statistic (total) was ECU78.5 billion (BCG, 1991, p. 3). An exchange rate of ECU0.8216 1988 US$1 is used, from *International Journal of Financial Statistics*.
8. From Lamming (1989a). The top twenty-five suppliers are not necessarily the same now as they were in 1987–88 but the estimate of concentration remains the same.
9. BCG do not discuss the possible dilution of Germany's high value-added, however. It could be argued that component plants set up in Eastern Germany would be suitable, at least initially, for lower value-added work.
10. These examples were provided by J Chatterjee of The Technology Partnership Ltd (UK): Research discussion, November 1991.
11. See DTI (1992). This report explains in detail the implications of different types of collaboration.
12. In 1991 VW assembled 197 078 cars in Mexico, Ford 167 004, Chrysler 132 488, GM 125 663 and Nissan 98 151.

13. Figures from author's interviews in Mexico (1989) and the Mexican autoparts manufacturers' association, INA. See also ELM International (1992b).
14. Daimler–Benz completed its takeover of the Mexican truck maker, FAMSA in February 1990, raising its stake from 49 per cent to 80 per cent. Plans were immediately put in place to assemble Mercedes Benz saloons (at first from kits of parts made in Germany) from 1993. Daimler Benz Mexico already buys components for its truck assembly operation from local suppliers.
15. From author's interviews in Mexico in 1992.
16. Figures from ELM International, Detroit.
17. DuPont has, of course, been involved with the automobile industry since the early days of GM, and is a major supplier in terms of coatings and paints. The new role referred to here is in connection with new materials, e.g. the role of plastics and composites.
18. Author's interviews in USA and Canada 1988–89.
19. Figures from Dodwell (1990a) and author's interviews in Japan, 1989.
20. Justification for Nippondenso's moves into North America and Europe has been based on business from the local assemblers in addition to that with the transplants. The firm has also undertaken joint ventures in Europe with local components firms (e.g. Valeo, Magneti Marelli) based upon a mix of Japanese (transplant) and non-Japanese business. Nippondenso remains in direct competition with Valeo, however, beating the latter's Delanair division to an important air-conditioning contract for Jaguar in April 1991.
21. In the Toyota group, for example, within the manufacturing sectors (Transportation Machinery (excluding Toyota Motor itself), Fibres and Textiles, Rubber Products, Iron and Steel, Metal Products and General Machinery) there are nine subsidiaries classified as 'strongly inclined' (over 50 per cent influential power from Group), thirty-three are 'inclined, connected, with links' (30–49 per cent influenced) and three 'weakly inclined' (less than 30 per cent). Dodwell calculates this 'inclination' as the ratio of the Group's shareholding in the supplier to that of the top ten shareholders, and other factors, e.g. sources of bank loans, exchange of directors and the company's relationships with non-Group firms. Note that it is the Group's shareholding, not that of the one parent company (e.g. Toyota Motor) which is used in calculation. Toyota Group thus has only minority influence over most of its suppliers, while Toyota Motor has proportionately even less. See Dodwell (1990b, pp. 137 and 252–3). In the Nissan Group, meanwhile, thirty of the thirty-nine companies are 'heavily inclined' although of the thirty-eight subsidiaries to Nissan Motor whose Nissan equity share Dodwell 1986 quotes, only seven are more than 50 per cent owned by Nissan.

3 | Shared Technical Change: The Nature of Innovation

During the 1980s, the focus of attention in the global automotive industry turned to the need for strategic repositioning for competitive advantage. No feature of this search for new strengths was more clearly evident than the recognition of the need for strategies which might enable firms to link together effectively in joint ventures or collaborations for mutual advantage.[1] This trend has continued into the early 1990s and shows no sign of abating.

There were many reasons for this: the technology of the automobile itself and the process of its manufacture were changing quickly; developing countries wished to have their own automobile industries, thus representing complex new sales markets, manufacturing locations and international competitors;[2] and the rise of Japan as a new dominant force in the industry.

In vehicle assembly and in component manufacture and integration (i.e. into functional systems), firms were faced with the need to embrace new technologies in manufacturing and product design (process and product innovation) and to adopt a more dynamic approach to international competition (see Hayes and Abernathy, 1980).[3] This new approach was often based upon collaborative ventures. The nature of such collaboration varied from specific product joint ventures, sometimes requiring new factories to house the new business entities so formed, to long-term strategic collaboration on new product technologies which in some cases might significantly affect the organization of the partner firms.

For some firms, the origins of collaboration lay in earlier decades. The strategic equity link between Ford (US) and Mazda (Japan), for example, which was to prove of such fundamental value to Ford in moving towards lean manufacturing, had started in 1979, whilst Nissan, in Japan, had been revitalized in the 1950s partly on the basis of product technology supplied by Austin of England in 1952.[4] Another form of collaboration, technology licensing, had long been popular, with many Japanese component firms gaining product technology from European and American companies (e.g. almost all clutches fitted to cars built in Japan have been made under licence from Automotive Products – a UK component supplier).[5]

These might be termed 'horizontal' collaborations, since they apply to interfirm links at the same 'level' or stage in the manufacturing process (i.e. vehicle assembly or component manufacture), although the partners were often of very different size and the arrangements involved very different styles (e.g. Ford took and retained a 24 per cent equity stake in Mazda; Austin sold the design and manufacturing knowhow of a proven model – the Austin A50, which became the Datsun 310 – to Nissan, but took no long-term interest; the component licences were essentially 'one-way' transfers of technology). In their comprehensive account of cooperative strategies, Contractor and Lorange (1988) describe such collaborative ventures as representing '*similar* inputs' by both parties. This refers not to the extent of commitment, but to the type or nature of contribution, and thus the type of business each partner is configured to conduct.

Aside from the main spotlight of attention on strategic joint ventures between assemblers (and to a lesser extent, between suppliers), another key form of collaboration for competitive advantage was becoming recognized within the industry during the 1980s: the need for very close links between vehicle assemblers and their suppliers – manufacturers of components and component systems (vehicle sub-systems). Contractor and Lorange describe these 'vertical' collaborations as those in which the partners make *complementary* contributions; they use the term 'vertical quasi integration'.[6]

It might be supposed that such vertical collaborations would depend upon good relations between the partners. In the 1980s the range of relationships between assemblers and component suppliers included arm's length – adversarial dealings in which firms did not trust one another and attempted at every opportunity to gain 'competitive advantage' over their customers and suppliers (see Chapter 6), traditional vertical integration (in which the situation was often similar to the first example in its adversarial nature), and the *keiretsu* and *kyoryokukai* in Japan, in which, it appeared, developments took place as the result of collaboration and consensus: see Nishiguchi (1987, and 1989, Chapter 2).

The 1980s saw a series of realizations in European and North American automotive firms which led gradually to a generally perceived need[7] for better relationships between assemblers and component suppliers, for the simple purpose of gaining mutual competitive advantage – a new concept for many.

But why should closer technological links between companies be thought to lead to competitive advantage? What evidence is there to suggest that collaboration, encompassing shared technical change and collective industrial research, leads to more effective ways of operating commercially? Indeed, collaborating with another business organization, which might be seen as a competitor, or at best a party with non-congruent business ends, is surely the opposite of conventional commercial sense. And for vertical links, is the concept of collaboration not contrary to the ideal of perfectly competitive supply markets, which are supposed to lead to 'efficient' prices through minimized transaction costs?

Traditional collaboration on technical matters starts with the need (shared between competitors) for established design and performance standards. This is the concern of entire sectors, through industrial associations and national or international bodies. An example would be drag coefficients for vehicle bodies: it is useful for the automotive firms to have an agreed method of measuring this (the *Cd* figure) and thus to be able to compare designs. An example of developed or extended use of this type of link would be the research findings published at industry conferences (e.g. the US-based Society of Automotive Engineers). Such findings would naturally not expose 'leading edge' research done by any one firm. Instead, it is the conclusions of consolidation work which are shared, without giving away any secrets to 'collaborators' (i.e. competitors).

This is 'safe' collaboration in which little intellectual property need be exposed. Since it is the basic mode of expressing technical details which is being agreed, there is no threat to competitive position for an individual firm. Indeed, it is the basic technical 'rules' for competition which are thus established.

In some cases, such sector-wide collaboration can lead to shared strengths and competitive advantage for a group (e.g. national) of firms which would otherwise be less well positioned. An example of this is given by the work of Bessant and Grunt (1985, Chapter 4) in the West German foundry industry, where it was found that small firms (95 per cent of foundries employ fewer than fifty people) gained technological strengths and skills through their industry association and their 'willingness ... to license and share their own technology'. When asked how they managed to conduct R&D (in order to compete as small firms in a technology-based industry – mainly process innovations and some product development for manufacturability) – foundry directors would point to the telephone – indicating their link to a very wide network.[8]

Von Hippel found that 'informal know-how trading' was an important function in engineering industries:

> Informal know-how trading is essentially a pattern of informal co-operative R&D. It involves routine and informal trading of proprietary information between engineers working at different firms – sometimes direct rivals. (Know-how is the accumulated practical skill or expertise that allows one to do something smoothly and efficiently, in this instance the know-how of engineers who develop a firm's products and operate its processes. Firms often consider a significant portion of such know-how proprietary and protect it as a trade secret.) Know-how trading exists in a number of industries and seems ... to be an important phenomenon.' (Von Hippel, 1988, p. 6)

If a few firms constitute a significant sub-set of an industry, bound by common technical agreements, they will represent a threat to any firms not included. A recent example of this is provided by the European 'intelligent highways' programme, PROMETHEUS.[9] The European firms included in the programme hope to gain competitive advantage from a technical standard which other, non-European firms will have to follow (at a disadvantage through entering after technical details have been fixed) in order to sell compatible vehicles in Europe.

Another form of knowhow trading is embodied in the role of the independent design house. In the automotive industry these firms have always played a significant part in technical change, often originating in the field of motor racing. Graves gives examples of this, concluding that: 'design sub-contractors can act as catalysts in order to demonstrate to the manufacturers the feasibility of a project, reinforcing the importance of learning by innovating' (Graves, 1991, p. 192).

Knowhow trading and open agreements on specifications can be observed at the industry level in a purely practical sense. In order to discuss the more intimate technical collaboration between firms in search of mutual or joint competitive advantage we must consider the evidence of experience with collaborative technical change and the nature of relationships between assemblers and components suppliers ('customers' and 'vendors').

There are many paths along which this consideration might lead. The pattern of geographical location of firms, for example, is affected by it (the need to establish a 'local' presence throughout the sales market; the logistical requirements of a de-integrated component manufacture and assembly process, etc.),[10] as shown by the case of concentration in the North American industry, discussed in Chapter 1. The technical nature of the automobile is also very relevant, especially the manner in which it is conceived (e.g. modular design – 'corner engineering').[11] The manner of working and human resource policies within the manufacturing plants of the vehicle assembler and components supplier also become relevant when the demands placed upon such firms are considered. All these things must be taken into account in arriving at a comprehensive understanding of the development of interfirm technological linkages in the automobile (or any other) industry.

First, however, it is necessary to understand some observed features of the nature of technical change itself and the merits and demerits of collaboration. This chapter will deal with the first of these subjects; strategic collaboration will be addressed in Chapter 4.

■ The nature of technical change: development of theories

The observation that the fundamental technical characteristics of products and manufacturing processes change continuously – incrementally and radically – is now commonly accepted. Throughout the twentieth century economists have debated the origins of technical change and the importance which this has for economic theory and hence policy making and strategic planning.

The fundamental implication for firms – that continuous and discontinuous technical change must be sought and generated, not simply accommodated – has apparently been less readily accepted, at least in the automotive industry in the West. There have been, until very recently, clear signs of inertia in a conservative industry. These include the preponderance of long product lifecycles (e.g. the Austin, now Rover, Maestro was designed in the late 1970s and was still in production, roughly in its original form, in the early 1990s), the tendency to describe firms in terms of the products they currently produce (Toyota was seen by Western assemblers as a producer of high-volume, mid-priced passenger cars, and was thus able to enter competition in the luxury car sector – with its Lexus marque – against Daimler-Benz, BMW, Jaguar, and Cadillac, etc., almost to the surprise of the industry), and the poor introduction of new manufacturing technologies and working practices (e.g. the troublesome adoption of measured day work, as a replacement for piecework in the UK in the 1970s: see, for example, Willmann (1986)).

In discussing the move from the situation described above to the adoption of a range of strategies which, it is argued, may currently be necessary to compete in the automotive and automotive components industries, it is necessary to consider the nature of technical change, as writers have described it, and the likely manner in which it will manifest itself.

The search for the origins of technical change and its development has centred upon a basic argument on causality which may be reduced to a simple representation, as shown in Figure 3.1. The argument ('Does technical change lead to new markets or vice versa?') is actually crucially important for firms wishing to instigate developments (to innovate) and to recognize when others do so. It is now widely acknowledged that neither of these simple concepts is sufficient to explain the nature of technical change. The path which the debate has taken in reaching this recognition, and the nature of innovation as it is currently understood, are worthy of consideration here. This consideration starts with the origins of the 'push–pull' arguments and leads to their resolution in the interactive model proposed by Rothwell (1983) and shown as Figure 3.5.

The 'cornerstone' theories in the origins and nature of technical change stem from the work of the Austrian economist, Joseph Schumpeter. In his book *Theorie der Wirtshaftsichen Entwicklung* (Theory of Economic Development) (1910: 1934 in English translation), he proposed what amounts to a linear model of technical change (Schumpeter I),[12] although he referred to the process as 'more like a series of explosions than a gentle though incessant transformation'.

This early Schumpeter model stresses the important roles of the

(a) Science discovers, technology produces, firm markets

(b) Need pulls, technology makes, firm markets

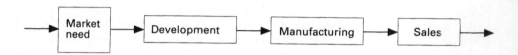

Source: From Rothwell and Zegveld (1985).

Figure 3.1 Basic causality models for technical change

entrepreneur and the inventor in the process, characterizing innovation as exogenous to the firm – something which cannot be 'managed'. The process, as illustrated by Philips (1971), is as shown in Figure 3.2. The division between the first and second stages is interesting: Schumpeter clearly feels that most entrepreneurs are not inventors, and thus the innovation process itself is immediately characterized as a synthesis or partnership of exploratory activity on the one hand and commercial risk taking on the other.

The first Schumpeterian model of technical change may be summarized as the interaction between many, small, innovative, technology-based firms which possess the ingenuity and (just) sufficient resources to pursue the development of original or semi-original product ideas from scientific concept to working prototype, subsequently selling the output of this effort to large, entrepreneurial, mature firms whose research and development departments take the ideas from prototype to commercial reality. Central to this model are the gaps – between basic concept and the commercial firm (filled by the inventor) and between prototype and commercial exploitation (filled by the entrepreneur).

It is almost inevitable that these two roles should come together: that the commercial risk taker should invest in exploration, drawn by the appeal of 'technology rents' available to the 'first to market' and the wish to 'manage' the whole process. Whilst he still stressed the importance of the

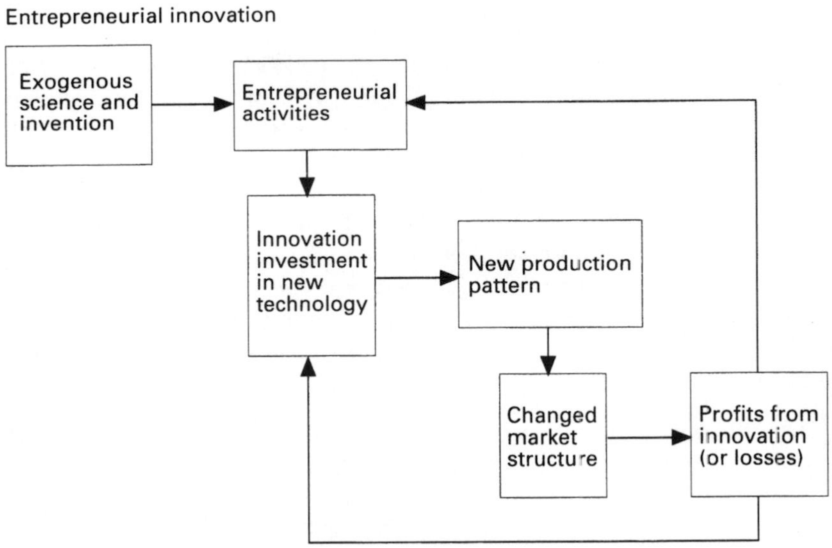

Entrepreneurial innovation

Source: Walsh *et al.* (1979, after Philips (1971).

Figure 3.2 Schumpeter's first model of technical change

independent inventor in the process, by 1928 Schumpeter had recognized that 'bureaucratic management of innovation' was replacing individualistic flair and that the large corporation was becoming the main vehicle for technical innovation in the economy.[13]

Schumpeter developed a very broad definition of innovation, which is particularly useful in delineating strategic developments. In his 1935 paper, *The Analysis of Economic Change*, he identified the following categories of innovation:

- A new product.
- A new process.
- The opening up of a new market.
- The acquisition of a new source of raw materials.
- A structural reorganization of an industry.

In addition to this challenging set of definitions, which extended the scope of the debate from the narrow 'new product/new process' constraint, Schumpeter observed that innovations tended to 'cluster' together, rather than be evenly spread over an economic system or a timeframe. This reinforced his analogy of 'explosions' and led him to describe long cycles (i.e. periods of clustered innovations followed by periods without such clusters) in economic development. At the same time he was recognizing the validity of the so-called Kondratiev cycles[13] and suggesting a new causality for such phenomena: the periodic emergence of clustered innovations (in addition to exogenous factors such as war, etc.), each cluster being characterized by a few key technologies, e.g. steam, railways, electricity and, latterly, electronics. Embedded in this was the conviction that innovation represented irreversible changes, which could not be 'decomposed into infinitesimal steps' (Schumpeter (1935), quoted in Rosenberg (1982)).

An additional feature of the impact of this clustering is the follow on innovation and pseudo-innovation (semi-original ideas from copying) contained in the 'swarming' – the tendency for competitors to develop or copy an innovation in order to share the 'innovative profits' which may be gained. This bandwagoning effect constitutes the adoption of an innovation which, as Freeman points out, is very significant:

> The diffusion process cannot be viewed as one of simple replication and carbon-copy imitation ... but frequently involves a string of further innovations – small and large – as an increasing number of firms get involved and begin to learn new technology and strive to gain an edge over their competitors ... The 'band-wagon effect' is extraordinarily important – it is the main explanation of the upswings in the long waves. It is the steep part of the 'S-curves' characteristics of many diffusion processes. (Freeman, 1982, pp. 214–15)

The result of this realization was a reappraisal of the process by Schumpeter and a new model: Schumpeter II, proposed in 1942 in his book *Capitalism, Socialism and Democracy*, in which he referred to the 'clusters of explosions' as 'perennial gales of creative destruction'. This process is shown in Figure 3.3. At the firm level, this 'destruction' might be described as the effect of innovators focusing their creative attacks (new products to replace existing ones, more efficient process technologies to reduce costs, improve quality, etc.) upon the capital investments of their competitors.

Schumpeter's message is that innovation is not an easy, incremental process, in which new ideas can build on old, but a painful expensive, irresistible task of throwing out the old and re-investing for the new. This challenge, for manufacturers, is as real now as it was when Schumpeter first described it sixty years ago. The company which is able to destroy the old way and embrace radical new ideas is the company which can be truly called an innovator.

This is an enormous task for the manufacturer which invests in major tooling only to find that a competitor has developed a better way of doing the job, or that the market is demanding something beyond the capability of the new plant. An example of this was the investment by Ford in the USA in drum brakes manufacturing in the 1950s, just before the widespread adoption of disk brakes (which for a while lost the company competitive advantage). An example of overcoming the problem through innovation was

Large firm-managed innovation

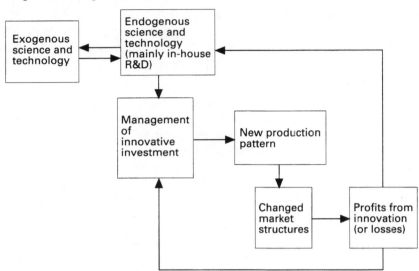

Source: From Walsh *et al.* (1979) after Philips (1971).

Figure 3.3 Schumpeter II: managed innovation

the case of the Japanese assemblers' investment in small, four-cylinder engines in the 1970s when it was thought that Americans would turn away from their traditional, large power units. Both cases are discussed in Chapter 5.

Hayes and Abernathy referred to the destructive nature of innovation, accusing American firms of inertia:

> Innovative design is initially destructive of capital – whether in the form of labour skills, management systems, technological processes or capital equipment. It tends to make obsolete existing investments in both marketing and manufacturing organisations. (Hayes and Abernathy, 1980)

Maintaining their provocative, challenging style, Hayes and Abernathy provide a thought-provoking comment on innovation: 'It is the choice of the gambler.'

The second Schumpeter model acknowledges the profound role of internal R&D (i.e. in the large, bureaucratic organization) in the innovation process and recognizes that technology may thus be seen as endogenous (or internal) to the firm. The role of exogenous innovation (independent inventors) is still noted, however, and it is held by other writers that 'small firms may have some comparative advantage in the earlier stages of inventive work and the less expensive but more radical innovations, while large firms have an advantage in the later stages and in improvement and scaling up of early breakthroughs': see Jewkes *et al.* (1958), p. 232 in Freeman (1982, p. 137). (The role of small firms is borne out further when considering the interactive nature of the innovation process, as characterized by Rothwell. This is discussed later in this chapter.)

Freeman comments:

> (In Schumpeter model II) there is a strong positive feedback loop from successful innovation to increased R&D activities, setting up a *virtuous self-reinforcing circle* leading to renewed impulses to increased market concentration. Schumpeter now sees inventive activities as increasingly under the control of large firms and reinforcing their competitive position. The coupling between science, technology innovative investment and the market, once loose and subject to long time delays, is now much more intimate and continuous. (Freeman, 1982, p. 214)

The nature of the clustering or 'bunching' of innovations was investigated by Mensch (1979) who noted that during the depression periods of the Kondratiev cycles, innovation clustering seemed to increase – there were more innovations in a shorter time period. This, he reasoned, reflected an urgency (or desperation) for discoveries to be exploited, shortening the discovery–innovation time lag. In a nice use of words, he termed this effect 'the depression accelerator'.

If Schumpeter's view of innovation, based upon competitive tension between firms in the same industry ('disharmonious and disruptive'), may be termed 'technology-push', then the opposite view – that necessity is the mother of invention – must be recognized as the 'demand-pull' concept. It has, of course, been argued that all innovation may be seen as a response to market pulls. The best-known work propounding this view originates in the ideas of Jacob Schmookler (1966) who argued that innovation was essentially market led – an assertion that struck at the very heart of the 'autonomous' nature of innovation as seen by Schumpeter.

Schmookler's work in the 1950s and 1960s was based primarily upon the American railway, petroleum refining, agriculture machinery and paper-making industry, and to a lesser extent upon consumer goods. Using suppliers of capital equipment to the chosen industries as the basis for consideration, his research appeared to indicate a close correlation between the level of sales of capital goods to an industry (market demand) and invention of capital goods for that industry (which he used as a proxy for product innovation in the suppliers of such goods). His conclusion – shown in Figure 3.4 – was that innovation followed market demand, not vice versa.

Walsh *et al.* (1979), however, cast doubt upon the value of Schmookler's findings, in some cases directly contradicting him and in others taking issue with the methodology and use of data. Having critically tested Schmookler's model and those of Schumpeter, as well as a fourth, by Hessen (1931), Walsh *et al.* found themselves largely in agreement with Schumpeter, but as Rothwell and Zegveld report, they concluded that there was:

> evidence of 'two-way linkages with strong reciprocal influences.' In some cases demand might lead to technological activity (and production) followed by basic research, to understand the fundamental mechanisms involved (a sort of 'Rosenberg model'); in other cases the results of prior scientific research might be a necessary prerequisite for inventive and then innovative activity, which might then be followed by further basic research better to understand the mechanisms involved. Walsh *et al.* term this derivative scientific activity 'gap-filling' science. (Rothwell and Zegveld, 1985, p. 64)[14]

Rothwell and Zegveld go on to conclude from the work of Walsh *et al.* that:

> the relationship between science, technology and the marketplace is rarely unequivocally unidirectional, nor is it a simple one, and within particular branches of industry causality can switch from being mainly in one direction to being mainly in the other. The linkages between science, technology and the marketplace are complex, interactive, and multidirectional, the dominant driving force varying over time and

Demand-led invention

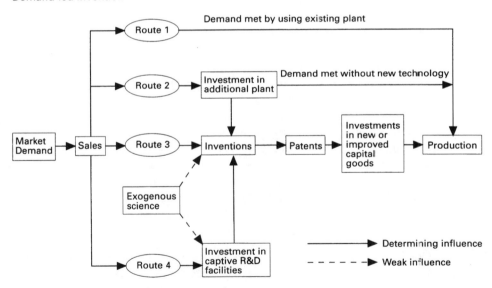

Source: From Walsh *et al.* (1979).

Figure 3.4 Schmookler's model of technical change

between one branch of industry and the next. Innovation is . . . a process of coupling. (Rothwell and Zegveld, 1985, p. 65)

Meanwhile, Mowery and Rosenberg point out that it is inappropriate to compare Schumpeter and Schmookler:

Schmookler's work deals with invention, not commercially successful innovations: thus his use of patent statistics as a measure of inventive output. Rather than explaining the factors underlying commercially successful innovations, Schmookler analyzed market demand forces as they influenced shifts in the allocation of resources to inventive activity – an entirely different matter. (Mowery and Rosenberg, 1979)

Judging that

the demand-pull approach simply ignores, or denies, the operation of a complex and diverse set of supply-side mechanisms that are continually altering the structure of production costs – as well as introducing entirely new products – and that are therefore fundamental to the explanation of the timing of the innovative process

and that 'there is no good *a priori* reason in theory why "market demand" factors should be dominant in motivating innovative activity', Mowery and Rosenberg conclude that 'the . . . widely accepted bit of conventional wisdom concerning the primacy of "demand-pull" forces in the innovation process is lacking in any persuasive empirical support'.

The work of Langrish *et al.* (1972) was based upon innovations produced by the 1966 and 1967 winners of the UK Queen's award to Industry: 111 cases in all. Using four models, entitled the 'technology discovery' (push), 'science discovers, technology applies', 'customer need' (pull), and 'management by objective' (assuming that innovations spring from ideas which occur within the management of the firm), the study found that no one model appeared to be favoured above the rest.

Soichiro Honda was plainly a 'technology push' man. Speaking about the success of his first motorcycle – the Dream – he said, in his later years: 'We do not make something because the demand, the market, is there. With our technology we can create demand, we can create markets. Supply creates its own demand' (Davis, 1987). Another great Japanese innovator, Akio Morita, of Sony, is similarly inclined. Writing in 1986, he said:

Our plan is to lead the public with new products rather than ask them what kind of products they want. The public does not know what is possible, but we do. So, instead of doing a lot of market research, we refine our thinking on a product and its use and try to create a market for it by educating and communicating with the public. Sometimes a product strikes me as a natural. (Morita *et al.*, 1986)

Clearly there is a range of opinion regarding the roles of the market and technology in technical change. Notwithstanding the great success of innovators such as Honda and Morita (after all, Sony and Honda do have large market research efforts and have had their failures as well as successes), there is a need for a less polarized view.

Following work on a research project called SAPPHO, using a comparison of matched pairs to identify factors for successful innovation, Rothwell and Zegveld, (1985) propose an 'interactive' model for the innovation process. This is shown in Figure 3.5. Rothwell and Zegveld use this model to describe innovation as

> a complex net of communication paths, both intra-organisational and extra-organisational, linking together the various in-house functions and linking the firm to the broader scientific and technological community and to the marketplace. In other words, the process of innovation represents the confluence of technological capabilities and market needs within the framework of the innovating firm. (Rothwell and Zegveld, 1985, p. 50)

In other work, Rothwell describes the practical features of this networking. In a 1991 paper describing the activities of innovative small and medium-sized firms (SMFs) in the UK, he characterizes innovation as 'a process of "know-how" accumulation based normally on a complementary

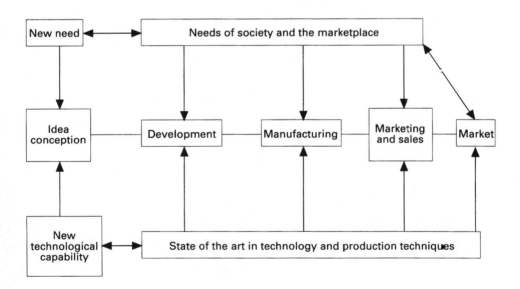

Source: Rothwell (1983).

Figure 3.5 Rothwell and Zegveld interactive model of technical change

mix of in-house R&D coupled to the results of R&D performed elsewhere' and goes on to report that '34.6% of the firms [in a 1986 postal survey] engaged in formal R&D joint ventures ... [and] ... 65% ... took part in collaborative R&D which involved active technical participation, not necessarily on a formal basis.' This is despite the listing in the same paper, amongst the disadvantages for all small firms, of the observation that they 'often lack the time or resources to identify and use important external sources of scientific and technological expertise'.[16]

Summarizing, Rothwell finds that the R&D networking of the innovative SMFs was 'strategic rather than undertaken simply in response to short-term problems' and that

> there are innovation-related links made through activities which, on the face of it, do not have any overt technological content. Perhaps the most interesting area of activity in this respect is marketing links, which some firms use to gain access not only to market know-how, but also to technological know-how. (Rothwell, 1991)

Emphasizing the significance of the innovative nature of firms in the sample, Rothwell notes that, in the Netherlands,

> SMFs operating at the leading edge of the innovation diffusion cycle (i.e. those firms producing newer and more novel products) generally enjoy significantly higher levels of communication with the external environment (technical, business, market) than do their less innovative counterparts

and that SMFs' share of innovation in the UK had grown rapidly from 22.6 per cent in 1965–69 to 38.3 per cent in 1980–83,[17] Rothwell echoes the much earlier ideas of Schumpeter with regard to the importance of the small inventor in the innovation process. Specifically, it is the sharing of roles at different stages of the innovation process which is referred to, using the computer industry in the UK between 1950 and 1983 as a case in point:

> During the 1950s and 1960s, U.K. production was composed almost entirely of mainframe computers, the introduction of which involved very high R&D, capital and mainframe costs. During this period ... U.K. SMFs produced very few innovations in the U.K. computer industry. Following the advent of the integrated circuit, but more especially the microprocessor, entry cost declined dramatically and many new market niches opened up for computers and peripherals: SMFs' innovation share in the U.K. grew rapidly: it was 36 per cent by 1970–1974 and reached 64 per cent during 1980–1983. (Rothwell, 1991)

The innovative role of small automotive components firms and the networking between them are especially important in the current developments in the industry. We shall meet this later, in discussions on strategy in Chapter 8. Rothwell's conclusion is a confirmation both of the ideas of

Jewkes (1958) quoted previously, and also an example of the follow on innovation characteristic of the 'swarming' effect noted above.

Swarming may also be seen as the copycat activity of competitor firms which have been waiting to see if the initial innovation was to be successful. As Rosenberg notes, the uncertainty or discontinuity created by an innovation is not limited to the post-launch period:

> There is a further dimension of uncertainty in the innovation decision of a sort not emphasised by Schumpeter in his stress of the *discontinuous* nature of technological innovation. This is, quite simply, the uncertainty generated not only by technological innovations elsewhere in the economy but *by further improvement in the technology whose introduction is now being considered.* Schumpeter's argument creates a presumption that the first innovator reaps the large rewards. Nevertheless, the decision to undertake innovation X today may be decisively affected by the expectation that significant improvements will be introduced into X tomorrow (or by the firmly held expectation that a new substitute technology, Y, will be introduced the day after) ... The optimal timing of an innovation becomes heavily influenced by expectations concerning the timing and the significance of *future* improvements. (Rosenberg, 1982, p. 106)

The effect of this caution reinforces the clustering of innovations, as firms wait until they are (all) convinced that a new technology will 'take off'. Since this confidence (i.e. in the new technology) is likely to arise in many firms at the same time, their own new products, and technological innovations, will be launched at the same time – a cluster, albeit made up of imitations. The caution stage of this cycle is referred to by Fellner (1957) as 'anticipatory retardation' (quoted in Rosenberg (1982, p. 107)).

Georghiou *et al.* take this point much further. Arguing that 'innovations are rarely fully developed when they are first introduced, and ... their full economic significance depends upon the continued development of the original innovations during a period following their introduction to the market-place', they conclude:

> Once it is grasped that the interaction of technological opportunity and market-need constitute a time-dependent evolving process, it is easier to see that success and failure in innovation is less about the conditions for innovation than about an on-going performance of the firm. From the point of view of the firm, successful innovation is about choosing technologies which embody the potential for a sequence of developments that meet market possibilities as the product or process diffuses into the commercial environment. As successful innovation is linked, therefore, to the ability of firms to provide a stream of post-innovation improvements, so too the diffusion process must be enlarged to include, in addition to demand factors, those supply factors which will

make it worthwhile for firms to embark on a particular path of innovation and technological development in the first place. (Georghiou *et al.*, 1986)

This proposal, and the interactive nature of technical change as modelled by Rothwell and Zegveld (technology-push *and* demand-pull) are reinforced and consolidated by the concepts of 'natural trajectories' (technological trajectories) and 'selection environments', introduced by Nelson and Winter (1977) as tools for building, in their words, a *useful* theory of innovation (to link the economists' ideas to practical reality).

Trajectories, corridors, selection environments and paradigms

Natural trajectory is the term used by Nelson and Winter (1977, 1983) to describe the direction in which a technology may be seen to advance, driven by both technology-pushes (as innovations arise from research and development) and demand-pulls (as the market gets a taste for the technology and demands further variations and developments, offering further profits to exploiters of the technology). Firms which might benefit from adopting the technology must be aware of the trajectory – the direction in which things are moving – and decide whether to follow it (the alternative being to depart from it – employing a different technology in the hope of gaining some advantage thereby – possibly creating a new trajectory, if others were to follow). This is illustrated in Figure 3.6. The technology-push which is seen as irresistible in this context is characterized by Rosenberg as a 'technological imperative'.

In this way, successful technologies can be seen to gather momentum with bandwagoning. No one innovation (necessarily) lasts throughout the trajectory: instead, the original idea is developed and modified by adopters. Georghiou *et al.* (1986) refer to a 'technological corridor' of development, within which many individual, but not independent, innovations follow their trajectories.

Clearly an important issue for firms, therefore, is how they can remain aware of developments in the trajectory, predict its next stage, etc. Coupled to this is the manner in which firms select which technologies to adopt: which factors lead to their choices, and thus, possibly, to the direction the trajectory takes? Nelson and Winter refer to 'selection environments', both market and non-market related. Other writers have called them 'search environments'. The market-related search or selection environment consists of factors which lead firms to choose specific technologies for competitive reasons (cost advantages, product differentiation possibilities, etc.). A non-market-related selection environment is characterized by factors such as government regulations, environmental considerations, professional respon-sibility and prerogative, etc. In either case, it is clear that both technology-push and demand-pull play a part.

Innovation: trajectories and search/selection environments

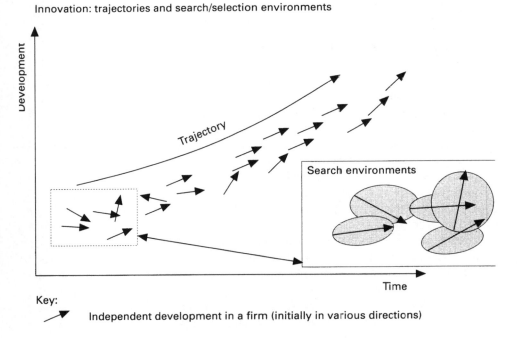

Key:

Independent development in a firm (initially in various directions)

Figure 3.6 The natural trajectory concept

It is likely that some natural trajectories will be more 'successful' (longer lasting, more universal in their acceptance, etc.) than others. Nelson and Winter point to 'the progressive exploitation of economies of scale' and 'the increasing mechanisation of operations that have been done by hand' as 'two natural trajectories that are common to a wide range of technologies'. Other trajectories may apply specifically to one sector, or even to one firm. For example, Gardiner (1984) identified 'design trajectories' applying in the aerospace and automotive industries.

Linking the momentum-gathering characteristic of a trajectory with the intuitive or tacit nature of technology itself (i.e. many factors in technology are normally communicated without the need for explanation), Georghiou *et al.* propose the idea of technological 'regimes':

Technology, then, is a framework of knowledge which guides engineers and innovators in the design of a range of products and their related processes of production. Within such a framework the resultant family of products and processes may then be said to constitute a technological regime ... a set of basic design parameters which embody the principles which will generate both the physical configuration of the product and the process and raw materials from which it is to be

> constructed. The basic design parameters are the heart of the technological regime and they constitute a framework of knowledge that is *shared* by the firms in the industry. (Georghiou *et al.*, 1986)

When a trajectory becomes established to such an extent that it is accepted as a common view or best practice, it may be referred to as a 'paradigm'. Dosi (1982) defines 'technological paradigm' as 'an outlook, a set of procedures, a definition of the relevant problems and of the specific knowledge related to their solution.' He continues to argue that 'each technological paradigm defines its own concept of progress based on its specific technological and economic trade-offs.' Dosi sees technological trajectories as the patterns of normal problem-solving activity 'on the ground of a technological paradigm'. Thus a paradigm might be seen as a cross-sectoral set of new trajectories.

The concept of a paradigm is also addressed by Freeman and Perez (1989) who describe 'techno-economic paradigms' linking developments in technologies with economic events, in relation to 'long waves'. These waves are described by Bessant (1991) as: early mechanization; steam power and railways; electrical and heavy engineering; mass production. Freeman and Perez, and Bessant each point to the likely emergence of a new paradigm: the sub-title of Bessant's book is 'The Challenge of the Fifth Wave'. Interestingly, in both cases there is a clear suggestion of interfirm relations as a vital part of the new paradigm.

In their 1971 book, *Agricultural Development*, Ruttan and Hayami argue that technological innovation and adaptation take place in response to shifting patterns of relative resource scarcities. It is possible to argue that the process might also work in reverse: the innovation borne of a scarcity of resources in one region provides a more efficient way of manufacturing, which requires competitors to act as if there were a scarcity of resources in another region (when there is not), not simply because this is more cost effective, but because the 'carefulness' required (e.g. to run a 'fragile' system)[18] has many spin-off benefits, such as improved attention to quality, motivating of workforce, etc.

Diffusion of technology

In examining the development of technologies within the automotive industry it is also important to consider the manner in which innovations are diffused and taken up (or not taken up) by other firms.

Rogers (1983) characterizes diffusion as a sub-field of communication, identifying the main elements as innovation, channels (of communication), time taken, and the social system (or, presumably, industry) into which the innovation is to diffuse. Taking as a major argument the influence of lead users (whom others copy in adopting the innovation) he categorizes adopters into five classes: innovators, early adopters, early majority, late majority and laggards. Suggesting that adopter behaviour can be modelled using a normal distribution, Rogers shows the expected proportions of adopters for any one innovation (Figure 3.7).

The term 'adopter' is applied by Rogers to individuals (hence the use of the expression 'social system'), but this may be generally extended to firms, in order to allow some identification of strategies formed in the face of new technologies. Starting from the point of view that technical innovation may be likened to an epidemic disease – first a small number of cases is seen, then a rapid increase in the number over a short period, followed by a levelling off (an S curve) – Rogers suggests that it is important to understand why firms catch on and are thus able to identify potentially beneficial strategies for innovators. He provides some useful starting points for identification of the five classes of adopters. Innovators are 'venturesome' (daring, risky, etc.); early adopters are 'respectable' ('the early adopter knows that to maintain a central position in the communication structure of the system, he or she must make judicious innovation decisions'); early majority adopters are 'deliberate' ('follow with deliberate willingness in adopting innovations, but seldom lead'); later majority adopters are 'sceptical' ('their relatively scarce resources mean that almost all of the uncertainty about a new idea must be removed before [they] feel that it is safe to adopt'); and the laggards are 'traditional' ('the point of reference for the laggards is the past'). The behaviour of firms may be examined by employing Rogers's typology to predict how they will respond to innovations (a potentially useful technique in forming competitive strategies).

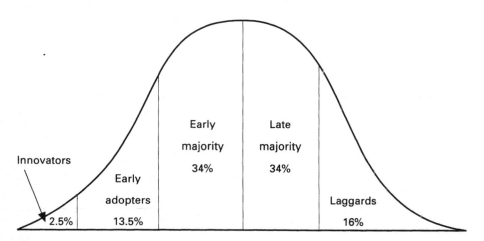

Figure 3.7 Adopter characterization on the basis of innovativeness

It is clear from the various views expressed above that innovation is inextricably linked with uncertainty. The early adopters appear to be more prepared to deal with risk – to accept uncertainty in order to reap potential rewards from socially marginal innovations. To have this attitude they clearly need the appropriate equipment and skills. They need not be alone in this venture, however – the suppliers of innovations have a role to play in encouraging its acceptance and diffusion. It is apparent from the work of several writers (Davis, 1979; Stoneman, 1976; Mansfield *et al.*, 1977; Metcalfe, 1981) that when an innovation originates in one company (a 'supplier') but is intended for use by another (a 'customer'), the perspective of the latter (i.e. with respect to acceptance of risk) may be fundamentally altered by the behaviour of the former.

It may be expected that this theme will be very important in relationships between component suppliers and vehicle assemblers: this will be revisited in Chapters 7 and 8. In preparation for this, the next chapter looks at strategic collaboration.

Distilling the risk and uncertainty embodied in innovation, Hayes and Abernathy called it the choice of the gambler. Kenichi Ohmae (1989) concludes that: 'In a complex, uncertain world, it is best not to go it alone.'

■ Notes

1. As Womack reports (in Mowery, 1988, p. 307): 'Since the full emergence of the Japanese industry in the late 1970s the rate of joint venture formation in the motor sector has accelerated dramatically. More than 100 transnational joint ventures have been initiated worldwide since 1980, the majority since 1984.' Contractor and Lorange (1988, p. xxvi) report that this was a general feature of international business: they refer to a 'surge of interest' in collaborative ventures in the early and mid-1980s. Bessant (1988) finds that most firms wishing to exploit computer integrated manufacturing technologies are unable to do so without collaboration – particularly with suppliers.
2. In Korea, for example, automobile assembly rose from nil in 1960 to 100 000 units per annum in the early 1980s; in Malaysia the rise was from nil to 85 000 per annum in the same period. Some of this was kit assembly, with parts supplied from European and Japanese producers.
3. In their outspoken declaration of the need for more dynamism, Hayes and Abernathy (1980) portrayed 'Europe' as a more effective and successful world player (in addition, naturally, to the Japanese) than North America, using mainly West German examples to argue their case. In fact, the need for more dynamism was just as great in Europe, as subsequent events have shown, and the authors' focus on America can be forgiven as urgency on the home front.
4. For a full discussion of this see Cusumano (1985, pp. 24–5).
5. Quote from author's interview, 1984.
6. The term 'quasi-vertical integration' was first used by Blois (1972), who argued that control of the supplier could be effected without vertical integration. See also Farmer and Macmillan (1976).
7. Perceived at least at the strategic level. Attitude changing at the operational level (buyer–sales rep) did not change, for a variety of factors discussed in Chapter 6.

8. Information from the referenced text and research interview with J.R. Bessant.
9. For a good discussion of the PROMETHEUS (Programme for European Traffic with Highest Efficiency and Unprecedented Safety) and DRIVE programmes, see Graves (1991, pp. 193–227).
10. For a discussion of locational factors (for assembly plants and components manufacturers) see Miller (1989).
11. The term 'corner engineering' refers to the practice of conceiving the vehicle as a cluster of major sections, each of which might be engineered separately, being brought together with other corners for efficient final assembly as a complete vehicle. Note that a major section need not literally be a 'corner' of the car. An example is the radiator/fan/sensors/front sub-frame assembly, which might be termed the cooling system corner. Once specified in this manner, such a corner could be altered significantly in its design, to reduce cost or improve performance, etc., benefiting from controlled pre-assembly, off line. This concept is discussed further in Chapter 5.
12. Schumpeter did not, of course, call his models I and, subsequently II: these terms were used by later observers.
13. These are not discussed further here: for a good explanation see Freeman (1982) or Bessant (1991).
14. The well-researched role of science in innovation, as distinct from technology, is not included here since it is considered to be only of indirect relevance to the main theme of the work (although it is clearly of fundamental importance to the deeper debate on the nature of technical change). Rosenberg's argument may be summarized as assuming that technology leads science, rather than vice versa (as might perhaps be thought intuitively). Rosenberg (1982) provides a full discussion, and Rothwell and Zegveld (1985) add a critique of the proposal.
15. The full name was Scientific Activity Predictor from Patterns with Heuristic Origins. For a full account of this important project see Rothwell (1974).
16. This is noted as a *potential* disadvantage: from Rothwell and Zegveld (1985).
17. Research findings based upon the Innovation Databank of the Science Policy Research Unit at the University of Sussex, UK, which contains details on over 4500 significant UK innovations.
18. In the development of the lean production concept, the IMVP research employed the term 'fragile' to refer to a system (e.g. a manufacturing process) which was intentionally designed without safety 'buffers'. Such a system must be managed carefully – as if it were fragile and thus likely to 'break' if abused. The results of such careful management might be expected to provide higher quality, better use of resources, etc., cf just-in-time principles.

4 Shared Technical Change: Strategic Collaboration

■ Collaboration and shared technology: why collaborate?

The terms 'collaboration', 'joint venture' and 'coalition' are all taken, for the purposes of this discussion, to mean the same thing, at least initially. In a general sense, in an adaptation of the format used by Mowery, the following definition is employed here:

> A collaborative venture is an instance of inter-firm collaboration for significant mutual medium or long term benefit, involving product development, manufacture or marketing that is not based upon arms-length market transactions, and includes substantial contributions by partners of capital, technology, know-how, or other assets. (Mowery, 1988)

Since it is collaborative ventures between customers and suppliers which will form the key focus of this book, the term 'arm's-length market transaction' will be considered especially carefully in the review of relationships in Chapter 6.

In considering the question: 'Why do firms collaborate?' Dodgson comments that:

> It can enable firms to reach the 'critical mass' of financial and human resources that may be necessary to conduct research, develop standards, or enter new markets. Some firms pursue collaboration as a way to improve the flexibility and responsiveness of the organisation to emerging opportunities. (Dodgson, 1991a)

The international nature of the many collaborations in the automotive industry since 1980 is an indication of another major reason for such strategies. As Kogut (1988) says: 'In order to compete in global markets, it is necessary to have a presence in all major markets' – something which is impracticable for most firms without partners abroad. Kogut also says that 'in order to compete in many industries, coalitions between firms have become *obligatory*'. Ohmae (1989) agrees: 'Globalisation *mandates* alliances, makes them absolutely essential to strategy' and the feeling is echoed by Porter and Fuller (1986). These conclusions indicate that companies often cannot face the challenges of working globally without support from strong collaborators. A current example of this is seen in the US and European automotive industry as the Japanese set up transplant assembly operations which are heavily reliant on collaborative support from component suppliers.

Hamel *et al.* (1989) agree with this conclusion but add the caveat that: 'A strategic alliance can strengthen both companies against outsiders even as it weakens one partner *vis à vis* the other.' Claiming that 'collaboration is competition in a different form', Hamel *et al.* go on to point out that successful collaborators are those which see joint ventures as learning exercises.

It is clear that collaboration may imply fundamental alterations to corporate structure, particularly if subcontracting some functions leads a firm to jettison existing resources. The negative view deriving from this point has been expressed as collaborations leading to '*hollow corporations* not engaged in producing goods, employing a small number of highly paid financial and marketing executives and few if any production workers' (*Business Week*, 1986, quoted in Mowery, 1988). This is a firm-specific view, however, (or possibly nationalistic), and for the purposes of this discussion it has to be assumed that employment displaced by lost resources in one firm will be replaced by a similar requirement elsewhere, although the collaboration may lead to a more effective use of resources in general, and removal of duplicative effort, and thus a reduced aggregate resource requirement (including labour) overall.

Macdonald (1991) sees collaboration as an interference in the 'invisible college' (the term coined by Crane (1972) to describe the free flow of technical information and knowledge between firms in an industry)[1] concluding that it may be *anti-innovation*. Cynical views are evident elsewhere: Contractor and Lorange (1988) themselves point out that:

> The most common example (of collaboration) is the joint venture forced on a company because of government mandate, nationalism or protectionism in that country. This is the traditional rationale for joint ventures in Japan, socialist countries and several developing nations. (Contractor and Lorange, 1988, p. xxvi)

In fact, Contractor and Lorange initially characterize collaboration as a feature of centrally planned or strictly controlled economies and remark that the surprising thing about the growth in the number of ventures during the 1980s is that it happened between firms 'in industrial, free-market economies where there were few external regulatory pressures mandating a linkup'.

Other writers argue that the evidence of extensive cooperative networks between small craft firms in Europe before the advent of mass production suggests that collaboration is a 'natural' form of working, only suppressed by mass production and perhaps re-emerging as a feature of post-mass production – what Piore and Sabel call 'flexible specialisation'[2]. This would appear to reflect the evolution of the automotive industry as we discussed it in Chapter 1. Contractor and Lorange balance their own argument with the assertion 'Even if operating alone is an attainable strategy it may be inferior to a strategy of cooperating or linking up with another firm' (Contractor and Lorange, 1988, p. xxvi).

A positive expression of the need for corporate reconfiguration required by collaboration is also provided by the 'competences' approach of Prahalad and Hamel (1990). This speaks of firms 'reconceiving' themselves along the lines of competence rather than function. Alliances are used by such firms (Prahalad and Hamel quote the Japanese giant, NEC – the only firm in the world to be simultaneously in the top five revenue earners in telecommunications, semiconductors and mainframe computers – which had entered into over 100 strategic alliances by 1987) to develop their core competences, by learning from partners. In requiring this 'reconceiving', collaboration may be seen to add a further dimension to the management process, bringing problems as well as potential benefits.

Teece (1986) provides a profound analysis of collaboration, based upon the idea of the assets required for the desired operation being shared by the collaborators. Since they combine to provide the total capability for the operation, Teece calls these 'complementary assets' and focuses on the crucially important identification of what is required in each firm in order for the coalition to succeed. This is discussed later.

Contractor and Lorange (1988) compiled a list of reasons for collaboration, derived from their research:

- Risk reduction.
- Economies of scale and/or rationalization.
- Technology exchanges.
- Coopting or blocking competition.
- Overcoming government-mandated trade or investment barriers.
- Facilitating initial international expansion of inexperienced firms.
- Vertical quasi-integration advantages of linking the complementary contributions of the partners in a value chain (see below).

These are shown in Table 4.1 and discussed further below.

The risk of a new product venture is clearly reduced for each partner in a collaboration; quite simply, the fixed costs may be halved for each firm. In addition to the obvious reduction in capital outlay, sharing the fixed cost may also enable existing facilities to be used, removing the need to build anew. For Toyota, the highly risky business of setting up manufacturing facilities in North America was eased by the joint venture with General Motors – the New United Motor Manufacturing Inc. (NUMMI) project in Fremont, California. By using an existing GM plant and workforce, one type of risk was reduced – that of setting up physical plant. It was more than shared – the land and plant were made available by GM. The risk which Toyota encountered was thus not the financial outlay

Table 4.1   Strategic contributions of joint ventures

Risk reduction
Product portfolio diversification
Dispersion and/or reduction of fixed costs
Lower total capital investment
Faster entry and payback

Economies of scale and/or rationalization
Lower average cost from larger volume
Lower cost by using comparative advantage of each partner

Complementary technologies and patents
Technological synergy
Exchange of patents and territories

Coopting or blocking competition
Defensive joint ventures to reduce competition
Offensive joint ventures to increase costs and/or lower market share for a third company

Overcoming government-mandated investment or trade barriers
Receiving permit to operate as a 'local' entity because of a local partner
Satisfying local content requirements

Initial international expansion
Benefit from local partner's knowhow

Vertical quasi-integration
Access to materials, technology, labour, and capital
Regulatory permits
Access to distribution channels
Benefits from brand recognition
Establishing links with major buyers
Drawing on existing fixed marketing establishment

Source: Reprinted with permission, from Contractor, F.J. 'An Alternative View of International Business' in *International Marketing Review*, Spring 1986, MCB University Press: Bradford, UK.

(probably not a major worry to the very successful assembler at that time) but that of transferring the Toyota production system to the USA. One thing that Toyota was not prepared to risk was its good name for quality: the initial cars from the plant were all shipped to GM for sale as Chevrolet Novas, with the explicit understanding that Toyota would not badge any of the cars as Toyota Corollas until they were good enough.[3]

There are examples of risk reduction through collaboration in R&D. Some technologies are now so expensive that individual firms do not feel able to develop them alone. This is true for major systems (e.g. Moog Inc. of the USA and British Lotus (owned by GM) joined forces in 1986 to work on active suspension systems) and for whole vehicles which represent non-mainstream work for at least one of the partners, or new departures (e.g. GM Cadillac and Pininfarina (Italy) joint design and production of the Allante prestige sports model in 1984 (niche for GM); Ford and Volkswagen multi-purpose vehicle manufacture in Portugal, announced in 1991 (new departure/niche); and the very small cars introduced by the North American assemblers in the 1980s which were all badged versions of

Far East partners' products (Ford–Kia, GM–Daewoo, GM–Suzuki, Chrysler–Mitsubishi)).

In some cases, however, the intended risk reduction is outweighed by management and coordination problems, e.g. Renault of France and Volkswagen of Germany collaborated in 1983 to develop a new automatic transmission but the project was a financial failure because of poor communications and cooperation.

Some of these examples also indicate the economies of scale which may be achieved through collaboration, particularly in models which represent new departures for assemblers. Interestingly, this may be less important for aggressive moves into new regions. For example, Nissan Motor Manufacturing UK, the Japanese No. 2's bridgehead in Europe, was established without a local partner and was run at a loss, well below economic scale, from its opening in 1985 until 1991. This is in contrast to Honda's move into Europe, characterized by very thorough collaboration (several new models and, eventually, equity exchange) with Rover. Honda's approach is another example of Ohmae's 'insiderization' – becoming a part of the local scene.[4]

The international networking of the automotive industry has led to extensive opportunities for assemblers and component firms to amalgamate production in partnerships and subsidiaries in order to gain economies of scale. For example, the joint venture Saab Automobile (50:50 GM and Saab) will receive Vauxhall V6 engines from the new plant in Ellesmere Port, England in 1993; GM plants in Canada, Australia and South Africa receive transaxles from Isuzu and Suzuki plants in Japan (GM's partners).

The union of technological synergies is clearly appropriate for the systems designs concept in automobile manufacture: a system or corner may bring together previously unlinked technologies (unlinked, that is, except in their functions in the vehicle) requiring firms to seek partners with which they would not traditionally have dealt. One example is the concept of modular doors, pioneered by Ford in the USA in 1989. Wishing to receive complete door packages (window, window lift, wiring, loudspeakers, trim, etc., ready for fitting on to the car) Ford asked major suppliers to suggest collaborative consortia which might supply them. The result was a collaboration between Budd, Johnson Controls and Standard Products, three separate suppliers which combined their individuals strengths to meet the new requirements of the customer.[5]

A good example of blocking competition is provided by Contractor and Lorange, from a specialist sector of the automotive industry:

> Caterpillar Tractor is said to have linked up with Mitsubishi in Japan in order to put pressure on the profits and market share that their common competitor Komatsu enjoyed in its important home market, Japan. Japan is said to generate 80% of Komatsu's global cash flow (Hout Porter and Rudden, 1982). Thus, even though the joint venture might not have great importance itself for Caterpillar, it may act as a thorn in Komatsu's side, and thus reduce its competitiveness outside Japan. (Contractor and Lorange, 1988, p. 14)

The automobile is so visible and potentially emotive a subject that direct foreign investment by an assembler is almost always met with arguments over intrinsic value to the host country's economy (and, by implication, damage to indigenous assemblers), centring on local content. Thus collaboration with a local firm can help an inward investor to gain acceptance, both governmental and popular. Nissan in the UK, whilst lacking a partner itself, encouraged component suppliers to form links with Nissan suppliers from Japan, resulting in ventures such as Ikeda Hoover for seating (US Hoover – part of Johnson Controls – with Ikeda Bussan, Nissan's seating supplier in Japan). This 'knock-on' collaboration can have other benefits; for example, Ikeda Hoover is now deemed to be as good at synchronous manufacture (production of sub-assemblies in perfect coordination with the vehicle assembly process to ensure no work in process build up) and just-in-time delivery as suppliers in Japan. Thus the joint venture company has learnt from the Japanese partner. This has further consequences for the American partner's parent as the acquired techniques have been fed back into other areas of the business.

It is apparent that the fundamental motives of each partner may be the same (joining forces to solve a common problem) or very different. NUMMI represented a foothold in the USA for Toyota, at the expense of letting GM 'in on a secret' (the Toyota method), whilst for GM the venture was a learning exercise (GM managers from many US plants were sent to learn in NUMMI) at the expense of letting a competitor into its home market. Toyota also underwent a learning exercise about operating in the USA, benefiting from its local partner's knowhow in a social and cultural sense. The venture itself had its own purposes: to build a successful small car (Chevrolet Nova/Toyota Corolla) and to show that Japanese manufacturing techniques could work with American labour, infrastructure and plant.

Contractor and Lorange analyze in detail the costs and benefits of each of these factors and potential advantages and conclude that 'the strategic rationales prevailing when a cooperative venture was formed may shift over time'. Drawing a distinction between 'ventures in which the partners make similar inputs ("horizontal" ventures)' and 'ventures in which the contributions of the partners are complementary, with quasi-vertical integration providing synergy',[6] they propose 'to view the international firm as a member of various open and shifting coalitions, each with a specific strategic purpose'.

In an extensive consideration of specific reasons for collaboration, Dodgson (1991b) adds the following factors to Contractor and Lorange's list:

- **Technological complexity**: new technologies demand both breadth and depth of expertise (often in technologies not previously directly related e.g. electronics and mechanical engineering combined in mechatronics).

- **Technological uncertainty**: a special case, perhaps, of risk reduction but a highly important one. As Dodgson notes, there may be 'considerable uncertainty as to the most appropriate configurations of the technology and the markets in which it is to be used.' Dodgson quotes Freeman (1991) in concluding that collaboration may overcome this uncertainty, including the problems of the intuitive or tacit nature of technology (discussed later in this chapter).

Collaboration as a strategic option in multi-stage manufacturing

It is appropriate to begin an approach to understanding the workings of collaboration with a review of the 'value chain' concept. This idea, which has many parallels with the supply chain concept, was introduced by Porter (1985).[7] This is shown in Figure 4.1. A value chain is a linear map of the way in which value is added throughout a process, from raw materials to finished, delivered product (including continuing service after delivery). Porter sees this as a series of defined steps, or stages, rather than a continuous process. Since some of these stages may be simultaneous or parallel, and interdependent, the linear map may be developed as a 'value network'.

Initially, this concept may be limited to the process within one firm but it is

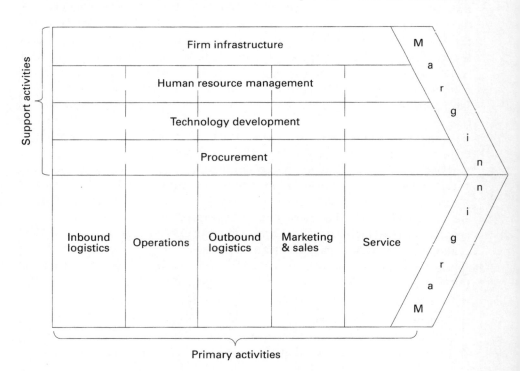

Figure 4.1 The generic value chain for a firm

easily extended to encompass all upstream and downstream stages. Porter does this by identifying firms as role players: the overall value chain consists, he says, of a combination of the value chains of the supplier, the firm (manufacturer/assembler), the distribution channel, and the eventual buyer or owner/user. Having identified these logically separate stages, it is possible to assess how much value is added in each, and what it costs to add that value. From this it is a short step to identifying the objective of optimization of the chain by selection of assets (as proxies for costs) which should be employed at each stage. This is illustrated in Figure 4.2.

Having separated the value-adding process into discrete stages, there is a tendency to focus on those stages themselves: how are they organized, resourced, owned, etc.? Indeed, if each stage in the process were a separate, independent firm, there would be a natural concern within each to define strategies, etc. When the entire chain is viewed, however, it soon becomes clear that it is the way in which the stages interact, and in which their interdependence is recognized, which determines how well the chain functions as an efficient value-adding process (i.e. it is possible to envisage excellent functions, poorly coordinated, which therefore constitute an inefficient chain). The links between stages are traditionally seen as adding no value – an assumption which may be changing. Porter recognizes this in his explanation of the value chain, discussing 'linkages' (in both a general sense, and specifically in a 'vertical' sense) and their relationship to cost drivers.

In addition to requiring an understanding of how the links between the stages

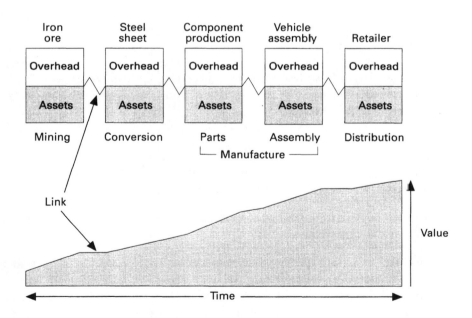

Figure 4.2 The supply chain as a value chain: example using the value chain for metal parts

are designed and managed, comprehensive description of the value chain, and thus appropriate collaboration of companies within it, demands a critical assessment of the various assets (as listed in the definition of collaboration earlier, but not necessarily limited to these) needed for optimal operation at each stage.

Teece's model (discussed above) relates to the value chain, characterizing the asset-based relationships between the stages in the value chain as the 'complementarities' originally identified. Well-matched or balanced complementary assets in adjacent stages, it is suggested, may provide efficient links and thus an efficient value chain. Teece discusses the management of complementarity using two dimensions: the location decision and the governance decision. The first of these is the physical/geographical location of facilities (e.g. in which country or part of a country a manufacturing plant should be placed); the latter (governance) is the practical implementation of a value chain management strategy (i.e. the manner in which the stages in the chain are coordinated).

A firm wishing to perform an entire value-adding process, must divide that process up into stages (each stage having specified necessary assets) and then consider the relationships between the stages (for possible complementarity), and also its ability to carry out each stage. A firm which decides to carry out all of the functions itself (total vertical integration) does so on the basis of its assumed superiority in performance at each stage, or else for some special reason such as secrecy, etc. The decisions are specific to each stage (e.g. 'can we do this in house at best practice/lowest cost, or would it be less expensive to subcontract it?') and to each interstage link (e.g. 'if we are to assemble the circuits ourselves, could we also print our own circuit boards, or is it easier to coordinate their printing elsewhere and have them delivered to our requirements?').

If the decision is against carrying out the stage in house, the firm must opt to subcontract, sharing its value chain management with a partner. This is, in effect, collaboration, or coalition. The view that subcontracting can somehow be done without close cooperation misses the importance of the concepts of the value chain and complementarity of assets.

Porter and Fuller appear to reduce the decision to a simple cost comparison:

> Coalitions arise when performing an activity with a partner is less costly than performing it internally on the one hand, and [than] reliance on arms-length contracts or merger with another firm on the other. (Porter and Fuller, 1986)

Pisano *et al.*, in discussing this work, summarize Porter and Fuller's framework for decisions on collaboration:

> Coalitions are seen as creating four classes of benefit:- economies of scale and learning, access to an incumbents' superior capacities, risk reduction, and 'shaping' competition. Costs include coordination, competitive position, and rent extraction. Ultimately, however, Porter recognises that coalitions must be compared to other organisational forms, such as integration or arms-length contracts. Interestingly, integration is viewed as permitting better information

disclosures and coalitions are viewed [as] providing better incentives than contracts. Coalitions permit faster repositioning than mergers, and the cash requirements are less than for integration. (Pisano *et al.*, 1988)

Porter's ideas as summarized here must be viewed in the light of his well-known strategic planning model (1980), which includes suppliers (presumably including those which would see themselves in the broadest sense as partners in a coalition) as *competitors*. In order to ensure and develop competitive advantage, Porter recommends 'tapered backward integration' (gradually cherry picking the operations of suppliers, to increase control of added value at their expense – potentially leaving them with the most difficult/least rewarding parts of the process) and creating 'the threat of backward integration' to keep suppliers on their toes. This approach to managing links in the supply chain will be discussed further in Chapter 6.[8]

The preferred method of coordination in the automotive industry might have tended towards vertical integration under a traditional logic (e.g. Ford c.1930), as companies followed steps very similar to those described by Porter. Williamson's (1975) model of transaction cost economics[9] would refine this view as the minimizing of the sum of production and transaction costs by simplifying the interfaces between the stages – either by removing them completely (vertical integration) or by effectively cancelling them, by creating perfectly competitive supply markets.

Williamson identifies three factors which may be expected to lead to high transaction costs: asset specificity (i.e. how dedicated the assets need to be to the specific task); uncertainty (i.e. in the supply and sales markets); and frequency (presumed to be proportional to volume requirements for the good). This view does not allow for many non-price factors, however (e.g. quality of production and design), which stem from market imperfections. This is a fault in the assumption that any asset may be acquired if it is desired.

Foxall also lists these three factors, pointing out that an increase in each or any of them may be expected to lead a firm to move from subcontracting to in-house operation. He continues:

> transaction cost analysis ... rests upon two behavioural assumptions: (i) the bounded rationality of decision makers' cognitive process and consequent actions, and (ii) the opportunism to which market arrangements may be subjected by one of the transacting parties. (Foxall, 1987)

Teece points out that it is wrong to assume that the complementarities are easily obtainable. They are, he claims, related to assets (possibly very specific, uniquely developed assets) owned by firms, and dependent upon such factors as market structure and the technology characteristics (to which we might add geographical location and innovative flair). Thus identification of complementary assets within the supply chain which are not necessarily owned by one firm may lead to a more competitive configuration than an attempt to acquire them all under direct ownership and control. Mowery (1988) says that 'The ability of firms to purchase these complementary assets is often limited by high transaction costs', leaving the firm with 'a choice between developing these capabilities internally and trying to gain access to them through licensing, contractual agreements covering marketing or production, or collaboration with a domestic or foreign firm'.

Doz noted that the concept of complementary assets applies not only to present competences but also to the ability to develop those competences in the light of changing requirements:

> The relative values of the respective contributions of the partners vary over time and may be very asymmetrical at almost any given point in time. There is a need, then, to keep in perspective the contributions over the life (potential) of the partnership and not to be swayed by what currently looks like a serious imbalance. (Doz, 1988, p. 324)

This is an extremely important concept for collaboration as represented by customer–supplier relationships and it will be revisited in Chapter 7.

The decision thus becomes how best to organize the complementary assets identified as necessary to support an optimal value chain. Between the two extremes (total integration, and subcontracting everything) there lie many combinations of options from which to choose. As Pisano *et al.* (1988) point out, the decision depends upon three factors:

■ The appropriability regime: the extent to which the practicalities of the environment will allow a firm to retain competitive advantage from control of the process (i.e. whether it is worthwhile trying to do it all in house and keeping it secret). This is a factor which is affected by patenting practice (technology related) and industry structure (concentration, role of small firms, etc.).

■ The nature of the complementary assets: whether or not they are dedicated to the process in question, or usable more generally.

■ The prior market positioning of the innovator with respect to the crucial complementary assets: is the innovator a newcomer to the field, and therefore vulnerable, or, does it have a track record, and thus potential collaborators wishing to do business with it?

The decisions the innovator has to make about subcontracting part of its activity on the basis of assets and 'appropriability regime' are addressed by Teece (1986). The process is summarized in his diagram, reproduced in Figure 4.3.

Von Hippel, Teece, and Foxall have all argued at various times that patenting and other forms of cover for trade secrets rarely provide real protection for the innovator, and that strong or tight appropriability regimes are therefore rare. Foxall (1987) concludes that the innovator will only gain significant advantage from its innovation when it can achieve a 'quasi-monopoly on the basis of sufficient response time' (i.e. stay ahead of the market) and only then when the innovation is represented by 'knowledge that is output-embodied'. In other words, it is essential for the innovator to reach the market with a product based upon the innovation: the

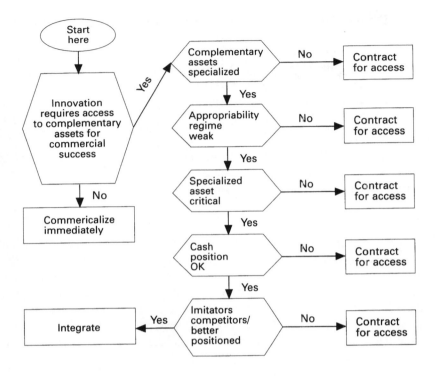

Source: Teece (1986, Figure 10).

Figure 4.3 Teece's model of complementary assets in collaboration

longer a good idea remains unexploited, the less benefit will be enjoyed from exclusive use by the originator.

In discussing the nature of the complementarity, Teece introduces the concept of 'co-specialized assets'. These are between the two extremes of generally usable assets which would cover the requirements of making the new product in addition to other work, and very specialized or 'idiosyncratic' assets which are dedicated (initially at least) to the innovation (i.e. cannot be used for anything else). A special case of this would be when one innovation (e.g. a new product in one company) requires another (e.g. a new process in another) in order to come about. In such a situation, both partners are required to innovate and take risks but both have the opportunity of capitalizing on the innovation entailed and finding further competitive advantages from its extended use possibly with other partners.

It may be seen, therefore. that collaboration as a strategic option is very asset specific and that the asset specificity is itself firm specific. If this is placed in the context of Contractor and Lorange's business environment of 'various and shifting coalitions' it is apparent that a continual review of asset configuration by would-be collaborators is necessary (notwithstanding Doz's warning on the significance of 'asymmetry'). This has two possible alternative implications for management:

- That collaborations have finite lives and that partners should always remain aware of potentially better deals, if they exist.
- That collaborations must be managed on the basis of asset utilization and balance, being periodically adjusted to maintain best fit. Such adjustments may, in the extreme, render a partner's contribution temporarily, or even permanently, redundant to that collaboration.

Kogut describes the 'mortality' of collaborative ventures, remarking that:

> No matter what the initial agreement on control and ownership may have been at the start of the venture, environmental and strategic changes over time may shift the relative bargaining power amongst the partners. (Kogut, 1988, p. 177)

Doz concurs with this:

> While the complementarity of strengths and assets brought to the partnerships is generally obvious at the start of, and even prior to negotiations – since this is usually what brings the partners together in the first place – the convergence of purpose is still difficult to achieve ... Genuine competition over what is contributed over time by each partner translates itself into hidden agendas ... Convergence of purpose may also be hampered by an incomplete or insufficient strategic overlap; current technological complementarity may hide future strategic divergence. (Doz, 1988, p. 318)

It is apparent that not only the business environment, but also factors internal to the collaboration, may be expected to change.

A special form of collaboration, half way between independent partnership and vertical integration, is present in an alliance in which one partner takes an equity stake in the other (or each in each other). The normally recognized advantage of this is reinforced lines of communication between the two parties and a confirmed genuine interest on the part of one (the larger) for the continued well-being of the other (the smaller).

This is often the basis of collaborative relationships between large customers and smaller suppliers and is portrayed as involvement without interference. This portrayal is based upon limitation of the equity holding to a minority stake, although as Doz points out, this is:

> often ... bolstered by various clauses such as preferred stock with higher voting rights, super majority clauses, and other set-ups allowing the larger firm an influence more than commensurate with its equity position. The equity investment itself is usually complemented by various agreements, such as research contracts from the larger firm to the smaller one, exclusive licensing agreements to the larger firm, and loan and other financial arrangements provided by the larger firm to the smaller one. (Doz, 1988, pp. 317–18)

As has been seen from the discussion of captive Western component suppliers and Japanese *keiretsu* and *kyoryokukai* in the automotive industry, there may be many potential benefits from this type of collaboration beyond those traditionally expected.

Focus of collaboration: what is being shared?

In a physical sense, what is being shared in a collaborative venture may be simply described: e.g. employees, capital, equipment, premises, product brands, marketing skills, distribution channels, etc. These complementary assets are, however, the means to the end. It is important to ask what, in a deeper sense, is being shared in terms of the firms' destinies, directions and benefits.

For example, a collaborative venture in new manufacturing technology might be seen as a learning experience: it is this learning that is being shared. A collaboration in a new geographical market (e.g. Japanese and European firms setting up a joint venture manufacturing in the USA) offers a similar learning experience: once again it is benefit of experience in global operations that is being shared. Since the collaborator is also a potential competitor (or a potential collaborator of a competitor – particularly relevant for a supplier–customer collaboration), the implications of this deeper sharing are far more significant than those of setting up shop together (it is relatively easy to retrieve physical assets, thereby depriving a partner of the means of production: the learning gained from the collaboration may not be similarly erasable, despite the intuitive or tacit nature of technology).

In discussing the factors which affect the focus of collaboration, Mowery points out that joint product development is usually involved in situations which may be characterized by high costs of new product development, complicated requirements for systems integration, the difficulty of licensing key technologies, and the need to circumvent political barriers to market access. However, Dodgson (1991b) notes that 'There is a belief that technological collaboration may assist competitiveness by increasing firms' speed to market with new products. There is, however, very little actual evidence of this.' Perhaps this is, as Dodgson concludes, 'Because of the nature of technology, collaboration is a *long-term process*.' Certainly, current developments in collaboration between firms in pursuit of 'simultaneous engineering' are showing that speed to market can be improved through collaboration but only with great care in the preparation. This is discussed in detail in Chapter 5.

What is being shared, then, is an intangible. Many writers have concluded that much technology is 'tacit' or 'specific' to a firm (Polyami, 1962; Pavitt, 1988; Mowery, 1988; Dodgson, 1991b). We have already seen in Chapter 3 how Von Hippel identified 'know-how trading' as an important part of technical innovation. Mowery goes on to say: 'Know-how, in addition to blueprints, is critical to understanding technology and therefore to transferring it.' This immediately raises the issue of risk attached to the deeper meaning of sharing in collaborative ventures – a factor often uppermost in the mind of a 'junior partner' – the smaller firm in a joint venture, or a supplier within a partnership whose prevalent concern is with 'keeping the customer satisfied' in a traditional sense. The problem was precisely identified by Arrow (1962), who pointed out that the necessary revelation of technical details about a product or technology by the supplier potentially enables the customer to do the work itself – but only if it can be easily absorbed and exploited by the latter. The Ford and Excel case, which we saw in Chapter 1, illustrates that this is not as simple as it seems.

It is possible to argue that the intangible assets are, to a degree, interchangeable – almost tradable. In joint ventures, Mowery suggests,

> partner firms make financial commitments to . . . back up their claims for the value of the assets that they are contributing: such financial commitments may substitute for the complete revelation of the value and characteristics of the assets that would be necessary to complete a licensing agreement. Further, the partners may only expose the necessary parts of their overall technological 'portfolio' – just sufficient for the collaboration. (Mowery, 1988)

This 'unbundling' (i.e. of the collaborative contract), as Mowery puts it, ensures for each partner that the necessary complementary assets may be provided, but that neither exposes itself to unwelcome 'knock-on competition' in unintended areas. The partners both play with their cards close to their chests. Such 'selective technology transfer' makes collaboration possible for suppliers which have reason to be wary of partner-customers, especially if the 'bits' of technology they expose are not useful by themselves to anyone else (including the partner-customer). This is one of the most commonly quoted barriers to customer–supplier collaboration in the automotive industry, especially on new product ideas stemming from the supplier.

The true nature of collaboration

It appears that collaborations so far may have be intrinsically *tactical* in nature – perhaps built upon specific projects, rather than general relationships. This conclusion is supported by the results of a survey conducted by McKinsey (1991), which found that most successful collaborators entered (international) alliances expecting them to last less than ten years, and with the firm intention of buying out their partner at the end of that period. This does not necessarily reduce their value as a strategic option, however, but it does perhaps alter the basis of a cost-benefit approach to collaboration.

This is doubly important in the light of another conclusion of the McKinsey report – that successful alliances were likely to be those which involved the *core businesses* of the partners (and were aimed at strengthening them) rather than some peripheral activity. An alternative interpretation is that some long-term framework arrangement is necessary which either removes the doubt, thereby enabling a trusting relationship, or formalizes it into a working method which copes with the lack of trust in a stable manner, perhaps even gaining from it (rather like the role of managing, but not eliminating, conflict in industrial relations). The interfirm relationships necessary to support these two positions (and others between them) have differing implications for strategy: these will be revisited in Chapter 8.

■ Collaboration theories and their relevance to the automotive industries

Dodgson (1991b) concludes that 'no clear theory of collaboration has emerged' from the extensive review of literature which he undertakes. It is possible to identify dominant themes in the theories which have been presented, however, and Dodgson does this. The following analysis of relevance and value of the various theories to the automotive industry uses Dodgson's listing:

- New institutional economics.
- Strategic competitive analysis.
- Technological primacy/innovations networks.
- Lifecycles.
- Industrial districts/restructuring.
- Resource-based perspective.
- Dynamic capabilities.
- Organizational learning.

New institutional economics

New institutional economics refers mainly to Williamson's transaction cost economics.[10] The idea of vertical dis-integration – subcontracting based upon efficiencies in supply markets greater than those in internal transfers – is very relevant to the automotive industry, and a major precursor to collaboration, especially between assemblers and their suppliers. At present, the North American and European industries could be said to have realized the value of subcontracting (reassessing the economics of subcontracting versus vertical integration), but they are hampered by two historical factors: a reluctance to give up ownership of the entire process, and a reputation for poor supplier relationships. These practical factors reveal the limitations of the transaction cost approach: a hierarchy (of subcontracting) ought to be more efficient but it is held back by imperfections in the market. This may be an example of what Argyris and Schon (1978) call inhibitory loops – self-reinforcing error behaviour – which account for the difficulties organizations have in unlearning outmoded practices.

The approach is also limited by the assumption that traditional switching costs must be minimized for most efficient dealing. In developed collaboration, traditional switching costs are apparently raised through the reliance placed upon one partner by the other (i.e. it would be difficult and/or 'expensive' for the customer to re-source the business to an alternative or new supplier). The limits to collaboration (finite life, limited 'cosiness', etc.) may, however, be usefully addressed by reference to transaction cost economics: the high switching costs resulting from investment in longer-term relationships should actually be offset by savings obtained from mutual expectations of high performance between the partners.

Strategic competitive analysis

Strategic competitive analysis is the subject of Porter's work on positioning, barriers to entry and blocking competition, and that of Hamel *et al.* (1989) on collaboration as a form of competition, etc. Since the automobile industry is essentially conservative and technical change is characterized by incremental innovation, firms at both the assembly level and that of component sub-assemblies must seek to establish competitive advantage in ways which employ appropriate combinations of technical skills. Since some of the technologies are very advanced, at least in terms of applications, acquiring the necessary skills through collaboration may be a crucial part of the positioning process. Thus choosing partners becomes a key competence for automotive companies. It is also important to note that the appropriate combinations may change with time – another reminder of the importance of seeing collaborations as tactical. The extension of this principle would lead to a situation in which firms adopt positions in networks, rather than 'monogamous' collaborations: this is envisaged by Miles and Snow (1986) in their theory of 'dynamic networks' and we shall see it later in Allen's (1977) 'gatekeeper' concept.

Technological primacy/innovations networks

There is a need to keep abreast of events in the face of rapidly changing technologies. Granstrand and Sjolander (1990) suggest that firms are increasingly looking outside themselves to satisfy technological needs, and to achieve or retain technological primacy. In doing so, such firms may be said to form innovation networks (DeBresson and Amesse, 1991, Freeman, 1990) – characterized by Crane (1972) as the 'invisible college' .

To the extent that such networks lead to standards and standard practices (e.g. dominant technologies in electronic data interchange) it would seem reasonable to expect them to occur in the automotive industries. They would also appear to be the practical manifestation of 'healthy' search environments – firms listening in to whatever is happening in the industry. As strategic moves within the field of collaboration, however, it would seem that for automotive firms, specific links with partners offer more than do the looser ties of general networks.

Lifecycles

As already discussed, Kogut (1988) and others have shown how the basis for partnerships may be expected to change over the life of the collaboration. The lifecycle approach to collaboration analysis emphasizes this point and attempts to identify the reasons behind ventures at the early, middle and late stages. This is useful as it serves to remind partners of the need for reassessment of the collaboration on a regular basis (against targets, etc.).

The resource-based perspective

The resource-based perspective (Teece's complementary assets, etc.) has a natural affinity with the automotive industry: it matches the ways in which both the product and the process of manufacture are constructed. It fits particularly well with the notion of systems, aiding the process of revising the vehicle: it has been fashionable to speak of a 'system of systems'. Whilst this might be going too far in simplifying the complicated design of the car, it is useful in looking for new supply strategies. A developed case of this approach is represented by Teece *et al.* (1990) in which they introduce the idea of 'dynamic capabilities' – an extension of firm-specific competences.

Organizational learning

The main thrust of Dodgson (1991b) is the need for organizational learning within technical development and the role which collaboration can play within it. Quoting Doz and Shuen (1988), Dodgson notes that there are three learning processes in continuing partnerships: learning about the partner, learning about the task, and learning about outcomes. This, when combined with the concepts of 'single loop', 'double loop' and 'duetero' learning by Argyris and Schon (1978),[11] provides for a very lean organization indeed.

As Imai *et al.* have shown, Japanese firms tend to place a great deal of importance on learning:

[Japanese firms exhibit] an almost fanatical devotion towards learning – both within organizational membership and with outside members of the interorganizational network. To them, learning is something that takes place continuously in a highly adaptive and interactive manner. (Imai *et al.*, 1985)

and, with specific reference to learning growing from product development:

Everyone participating in the development process is engaged in learning, even outside suppliers. Learning also takes place across all phases of management and across functional boundaries. It is this kind of 'learning in breadth' that supports the dynamic process of product development among Japanese companies. This learning emanating from the development process, in turn serves as the trigger to set total organisational learning in motion. In this sense, new product development is the particular device that fosters corporate-wide learning. (Imai *et al.*, 1985, p. 372)

This is certainly reflected in the policies of the Japanese firms abroad. To become a supplier to Honda in Marysville, Ohio, for example, the US component firms have to go through eighteen months of intensive grooming – fundamental learning – about how to perform and what to expect of Honda. Once through this process, however, they have learned how to learn and carry on doing so. They have also won a permanent place in the Honda supply base, provided they maintain performance (i.e. they do not live in fear of the business being placed elsewhere at any time, as they have traditionally with American assemblers). One supplier described this as 'the agony and the ecstasy!'[12]

Summary of collaboration theories

In examining tendencies towards collaboration, or potential benefits to be gained from collaborative ventures in the auto industry, it appears that the following should be borne in mind:

- There is a need to understand transaction cost economics, but to develop the ideas to allow for imperfections in the market possibly caused by the historical relationships and attitudes, and to redevelop the notion of switching costs. Identification of assets and dynamic competences (in a very broad sense, i.e. to include intangibles such as knowhow) may be critically important.
- Choosing partners for positioning (as a result of joint competences) is a central function for strategic planning. Combinations of competences achieved by collaborations may be only temporarily appropriate. Techniques should be in place to assess the collaboration for validity and against target objectives.
- It may be necessary for firms to join 'invisible colleges', or innovation networks, in order to maintain efficient search and selection environments. It is not clear, however, that such a position will directly benefit a firm unless it

is combined with more specific partnerships, based upon actual business dealing.

■ The collaboration process will require companies to formulate policies on organizational learning and should be seen as a learning exercise itself.

Sources of innovation in customer–vendor relationships and supply chains

When the link between two (or more) firms, however tenuous it may be, results in some innovation, it is important to identify from whence the idea sprang (the 'locus' of the innovation) and how each partner contributed to its development and exploitation. If such identification can be clearly made, then it should be possible to say what contribution can be expected of firms in similar positions, and thus what strategies might be followed to achieve those expectations.

This identification process has been formalized by the work of Von Hippel (since 1978), which has given rise to the concepts of the manufacturer-active and customer-active product idea generation paradigms (MAP and CAP) (1978, 1982). Significant development of this work has been carried out by Foxall (1987) and Shaw (1987). In much of this work, the research has concentrated especially on the interface (supply chain link) between the manufacturer of process equipment and the user of that equipment. Von Hippel's ideas are shown in Figure 4.4.

For the automotive industry this link only exists in a tenuous definition – the 'user' is the eventual driver of the vehicle. The components supplier and systems integrator are 'manufacturers' in Von Hippel's sense, but their customer – the assembler – is not the user in the same way. Indeed, it is immediately apparent that the components supplier/integrator may be seen as an *intrinsic* part of the vehicle-manufacturing process and that functional demarcations between supplier and assembler are almost arbitrary, relating to ownership more than technical development or manufacturing logic. In value chain terms, the stages of production (and associated product technology competences) may be interchangeable across the assembler/supplier interface).

Von Hippel sees the CAP developing out of a situation in which a customer is frustrated at being unable to obtain what is needed from manufacturers (which, it is assumed, ought to be able to satisfy the customer's need for new products) and resorts to in-house innovation – typically developing the specification for an instrument or piece of process equipment and then asking a manufacturer to make it. In some of the cases quoted by Von Hippel (especially Von Hippel, 1988), which look at materials for use by another manufacturer in products for an eventual customer further along the supply chain, Von Hippel's own observations support the MAP – the customer is reliant upon the manufacturer for the innovation as well as the physical/commercial realization of the product.[13] Some of these cases are analogous to the situation of automotive components suppliers – the output from their process is not a complete product, to be retained by the immediate customer, but an intermediate, to be transformed by the customer as

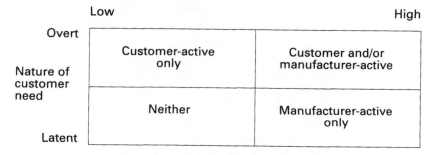

(a) Characteristics of new industrial product opportunity, appropriate to customer-active and/ or manufacturer-active idea generation paradigm

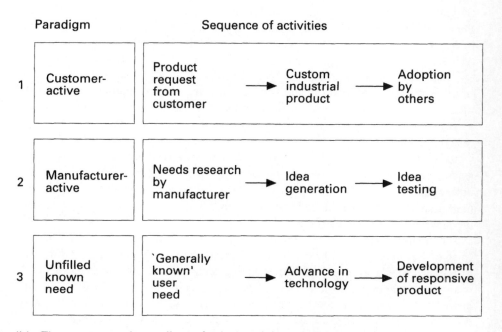

(b) Three proposed paradigms for industrial product idea generation

Source: Von Hippel (1978, Figures 3 and 5).

Figure 4.4 Manufacturer-active and customer-active idea generation paradigms

part of a product for the further customer. In his later work (1988) the variety of loci for innovation is recognized by Von Hippel and he proposes that 'analysis of the temporary profits (economic rents) can ... predict the source of innovation'.

In his discussion of CAP/MAP, Von Hippel concludes that a manufacturer-active product idea generation paradigm may be economically executed (and thus expected) when:

(i) The proportion of all consumers using an existing product in the functional category being studied is sufficiently large and/or known to allow economical identification of a sample of users via a survey or other manufacturer initiative. Therefore identification of users with a new product need/dissatisfaction with existing products ... appears economical – the cost of such identification is low.

(ii) A sample of current users of ... goods is effectively a sample of future buyers ... because the products are frequently repurchased;

(iii) User/buyers can switch relatively easily to a new brand if they see it as preferable to their present brand because the switch involves little adjustment effort/cost on their part. (Von Hippel, 1978)

Von Hippel says that when the duration of 'new product selling opportunities' (defined as starting when a customer first develops a need for a new product, and ending when that customer is no longer willing to consider purchase of a responsive product offered by a would-be supplier) is long, then either MAP or CAP may apply. When a long duration is accompanied by a relatively simple marketing research task (such as in the automotive components industry where there are few customers, all making roughly similar products), then the MAP may be expected.

For a components manufacturer/supplier, the marketing research task – in terms of planning sales to the automotive assemblers – should be relatively straightforward: the number of vehicles to be built is usually reasonably well forecast in the medium term; their technical constitution is predictable; and the customers are all well known. A manufacturer of alternators, for example, knows that virtually all vehicles require alternators, and that a proportion of alternators require replacing after a number of years of use. Thus original equipment and replacement equipment markets (which are fundamentally different in many respects) are relatively simple to describe in quantitative terms. Similarly, the technology required (particularly along Von Hippel's 'dimensions of merit')[14] is predictable: in alternators, the developing requirements for size and weight reductions, power generation, and energy consumption, are all 'targetable' technical paths.

Foxall (1987) extends the idea of the CAP to several closely defined variants:

- MII (manufacturer-initiated innovation): the idea and the exploitation of the idea lie solely with the manufacturer.
- UII–1 (user-initiated process innovation): the user develops the process but does not market it.

- UII–2 (passive user-initiated product innovation): basically Von Hippel's CAP – the user has the idea but the manufacturer (whom the user asks to make the product) does the exploitation.
- UII–3 (active user-initiated product innovation): the user joins the manufacturer in developing the idea commercially.
- UII–4 (vertically-integrated user-initiated innovation): the user has the idea and carries out all the exploitation himself.

Foxall concludes that all these models are possible and discusses them in the light of appropriability regimes and transaction approaches. In common with other writers he feels that there is little chance of the user benefiting from non-embodied knowledge, even with the protection supposedly offered by patenting. Shaw follows up this theme, identifying several strategies used in the interface between medical equipment manufacturers and their health service customers. Following Teece's (1986) suggestion that firms wishing to capture the initiative in innovation need to establish a 'prior position' in terms of appropriate complementary assets, Shaw concludes that:

> the locus of innovation benefit is determined also by the nature and levels of co-operation existing among the parties to the innovation process, the relative closeness of user requirements to the 'state of the art', and the perceived non-embodied and output-embodied benefits arising from this co-operation. (Shaw, 1987)

Technology flow within a group of linked firms

If it is accepted that innovation can take place jointly within a group of separate firms, on the basis of mutual benefit from harnessing complementary or co-specialized assets, then it might be useful to consider such a group as analogous to a single firm. In this way, the lessons learned about innovation and the flow of technology within a firm can be tested on the group of firms, in order to identify possible sources of improvement in shared technical change.

Of particular interest here is the notion that the various assets, or individuals, within an organization do not contribute equally to innovative processes – there are often crucially important individuals, known as 'technological gatekeepers'. This concept was proposed by Allen (1977), who observed that within the scientific laboratories he studied, there were people to whom others frequently turned for advice, information or ideas on technological matters. 'They differed from their colleagues in the degree to which they exposed themselves to sources of technological information outside their organisation. They read more – the refereed journal, significantly more.' Thus, the technological gatekeeper, as a function of personal choice (rather than contractual agreement with the employer) becomes an especially useful and potentially powerful person and a key link in the path by which technology enters the firm. A further stage of this concept is exhibited by a networking of gatekeepers – the key individuals set up and maintain

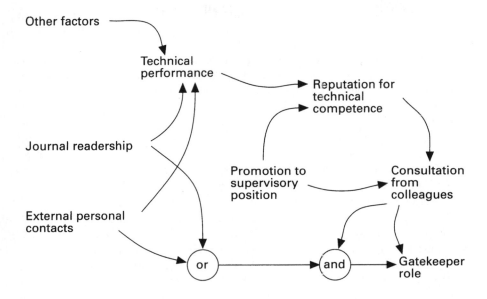

Other factors

Technical performance

Reputation for technical competence

Journal readership

Promotion to supervisory position

Consultation from colleagues

External personal contacts

or

and

Gatekeeper role

Source: Reprinted with permission from *Managing the Flow of Technology* by T.J. Allen, © The MIT Press, 1977.

Figure 4.5 The logic of the technological gatekeeper concept

communication links with each other, to reinforce their technical knowledge development. Figure 4.5 explains the logic of this process, as recorded by Allen.

If the group of firms can be likened to an organization consisting of individuals, then perhaps the flow of technology into such a group could be facilitated by some firms acting as technological gatekeepers – conducting intelligence activities comparable to those of Allen's original model. This theme will be revisited in Chapter 7.

■ Expected attitudes to shared technical change between customers and vendors in the automotive industry for optimum positioning

The successful innovation process involves considerably more than technical problem solving. Good market knowledge and linkages, effective overall management, effective inventory and cost control, and effective quality control are all essential to the creation of products that have an appropriate combination of price and non-price attributes to satisfy market requirements. (Rothwell, 1991)

This very practical comment on innovation suggests that firms which need to deal together on a daily basis, in the mundane areas of materials management, quality control and manufacturing, should have the basis for good collaboration in product technology development: shared technical change.

There is sufficient evidence to conclude that the automotive industry has recognized the role of collaboration within strategic positioning. It is also apparent that collaboration between firms at different 'levels' (or stages) in the supply chain is similar in many ways to 'horizontal' coalition. It might be expected, therefore, that firms in the automotive industry would have set up strong customer–supplier links as practical attempts to gain competitive advantage from collaboration. Before discussing the nature of technical change within the automotive industry, it is perhaps useful to conclude this chapter with a scenario-building exercise. What would the foregoing evidence and theory lead us to expect to find?

Automotive vehicle manufacturers are large firms. In very recent years, the last few small firms have been absorbed by the larger ones: Jaguar by Ford, Lotus by General Motors, Aston Martin by Ford, etc.[15] This has been a trend which we have already seen (Chapter 1) throughout the life of the automobile.

Automotive component suppliers vary in size, but most are small in comparison with their customers. We might therefore expect to see collaborations typical of those between small and large firms. This would imply 'special' minority equity stakes in suppliers taken by assemblers, as noted by Doz (1988).

As we have seen in the discussion of Von Hippel's work (see the alternators example above), the industry characteristics might lead us to expect a manufacturer-active paradigm for idea generation – where the manufacturer is the components supplier and the customer the vehicle assembler. The component suppliers and vehicle assemblers are united in the role of 'manufacturer' and there is little 'natural' gap between them to generate the dissatisfaction which Von Hippel would expect to give rise to frustration and thus in-house innovation by the customer (assembler) – a sort of 'intra-manufacturer customer-active paradigm'.

Thus with the need to develop new products at an increasing rate, in an industry in which the component supplier and vehicle assembler act as one in the effort to satisfy the eventual customer, and in which the possibility of achieving optimum transfer costs through efficient long-term subcontract of manufacture and design should be high, the recognition of the potential value and strength offered by collaboration – vertically as well as horizontally – might be expected to lead to a close-knit bond of shared technical change between assemblers and component suppliers. The vehicle assemblers might be expected to develop innovative specifications for their complex products, in their highly competitive global markets, but the suppliers will surely be required to use such specifications in a creative innovative manner. The next chapter will investigate this idea.

■ Notes

1. The term 'college' is employed by Crane in this expression to denote a learning network to which the firms belong. It is 'invisible' because it is only apparent to those sharing in it.

2. Piore and Sabel (1984) summarize their concept as 'a strategy of permanent innovation ... based on flexible – multi-use – equipment; skilled workers; and the creation, through politics, of an industrial community that restricts the forms of competition to those favouring innovation. For these reasons, the spread of flexible specialisation amounts to a revival of craft forms of production that were emarginated at the first industrial divide' (p. 17). See also Zeitlin and Hirst (1988).

3. See Krafcik (1986) for a full account. The NUMMI project also provides a comment on the pragmatism necessary for collaboration – particularly in choosing partners. Toyota had originally (June 1980) wished to collaborate with Ford, not GM. However, Ford's position on the Arab 'blacklist' (they had a plant in Israel) frightened Toyota off – the danger of turning Arab countries away from Japanese products was too great (see Sakiya, 1987, p. 16).

4. Ohmae (1990). Sony's word for this is 'glocalization'.

5. Information from author's industry interviews in USA, 1989.

6. Hegert and Morris (1988), report that of 839 cases of collaboration in a mainly European survey, 15 per cent were between buyers and sellers; 71 per cent were horizontal, between rivals; and 14 per cent were devised for new market entry. Fransman (1990) reports, however, that many large Japanese firms undertake horizontal and vertical collaborations. See also Levy and Samuels (1991).

7. Porter credits the business system concept, developed by the consulting firm, McKinsey and Co., as the origin of his value chain idea.

8. This view comes from the first of Porter's two important books in the 1980s. In the second he does refer in a more enlightened sense to developing relationships with suppliers, but still shows signs of a mechanistic approach, e.g. 100 per cent inspection of incoming deliveries is suggested as the best method of ensuring improved quality of supplied components (1985, pp. 49–50).

9. Transaction costs are nicely defined by Kogut as 'the costs of monitoring efforts, of investing in ways to bond performance, and of cheating' (Kogut, in Contractor and Lorange, 1988, p. 174).

10. The concept was first discussed by Ronald Coase (1937). Other writers on transaction cost economics include Klein, Crawford and Alchian (1978), Masten (1984), Monteverde and Teece (1982a and 1982b), Walker and Weber (1984a and 1984b), Flaherty (1981), Langlois (1989) and Globerman (1980). See also Helper (1987).

11. Briefly put, *single loop learning* is the process of gaining competence in specific tasks. *Double loop learning* is the process of understanding what is required to continue the learning process – learning how to learn (as an organization). *Duetero learning* is the term used to describe what occurs in an organization in which learning becomes the norm for everyone – so that double loop learning occurs all the time. This notion is akin to the concept of *kaizen*, in that each learning process changes the status quo.

12. From author's industry interviews, USA 1988.

13. The cases (from his own research and that of others) which Von Hippel cites in support of the customer-active paradigm were scientific instruments, process equipment and plant, chemical products, semiconductor and printed circuit board processing, and the 'pultrusion' process (see 1988). Those which supported the manufacturer-active paradigm were plastic additives, engineering plastics (1978) and the mechanized tractor shovel (1988). It is not intended to contest Von Hippel's conclusions in any way here – as already stated, the customer–supplier interface in the automotive components supply situation is not directly analogous to Von Hippel's customer–manufacturer model.

14. Von Hippel (1978) characterizes the development process (within manufacturers) which springs from 'not resting on their laurels' as 'dimensions of merit.' This, he claims, occurs because the customers' needs are 'generally known' by the manufacturer (in the absence of specific instructions, which would constitute a customer-active paradigm).

15. Those that are left are effectively not in the automotive industry: products such as Morgan and TVR sports cars, and the myriad 'special' versions of cars such as Porsche 911 coupés (which proliferate on the stands of small 'customizer' firms at the Geneva motor show) are subject to a very different set of market characteristics – arguably closer to jewellery or toys than automobiles.

5 | Development of New Automobiles

A new car is almost never a totally new product. Instead, some new parts and new styling are combined with a considerable number of pre-existing, 'carryover' parts. Traditionally, the construction of a car has involved three major areas of engineering:

- The chassis: the frame, upon which everything else is supported or suspended.
- The power train: the engine, the clutch, the transmission (gearbox) and the final drive to the wheels – the propeller shaft, differential gears and rear axle.
- The body assembly: including trim, seating, glazing, etc.

The three fields of engineering require three different fields of production technology. A chassis consists of a frame, welded (or riveted) together from steel members, some 3 mm thick.[1] Attached to it are various components such as suspension springs and dampers, axles, steering equipment, braking systems, and the wheels and tyres.

The engine is an assembly of machined castings (iron, steel or aluminium), forged or cast shafts, precision-machined metal parts, gaskets and seals, fasteners of many different types and sizes, fuel/air supply, filtration and mixing equipment (carburettors/fuel injection, valves, etc.), chains, belts, manifolds and several separate electrical systems (low tension, high tension, sensors, signals and control, etc.).

The body consists of a series of panels (originally wooden, later steel, sometimes plastic, aluminium or composite materials), attached to one another and to the frame. The interior of the body is 'trimmed' (with plastic, leather, wood, etc.) and fitted with seating, instrumentation and electrical and mechanical controls. The body also has several electrical systems, glazing and lighting systems. Finally, the body is decorated in various fashions, starting with protective paint coatings and finishing with decals, bright metal and special coverings (e.g. vinyl).

Two widespread fundamental changes to this configuration have occurred during the recent history of the automobile. The first of these was the demise of the chassis, which was replaced by monocoque construction ('unit construction' in American) in which the body itself becomes the major frame (a structural, stressed member) while sub-frames are attached, fore and aft, to support and suspend the engine, drive train and running gear, wheels, springing, etc.).[2] The second was the gradual move towards front wheel drive, obviating the need for the propeller shaft and rear axle. This was intended to reduce weight, cost and fuel consumption, while improving handling.

■ Applying new technologies to the automobile

It is clear from the above analysis of the product that to renew every item in a new model would be commercially impracticable, and almost certainly unnecessary. As with many other products, the looks, touch and feel of the car can be altered without changing it 'under the skin'. Indeed, this was the basis of Henry Ford's product differentiation for the Model T (nine body styles on one chassis) and to a much greater extent the success of General Motors's 'full-line' policy.

Thus the complexity of the car enables the manufacturer to launch apparently new models whilst retaining a large proportion of the technology unchanged. This is referred to as 'carryover'. Much of the North American market demand, during the years in which that region's industry was losing its competitive advantage, was satisfied by the 'this year's model' practice: the addition of visually interesting features (e.g. tail fins, new colour schemes, different chrome-plated external fittings and trim, etc.) to an otherwise unaltered vehicle. This policy of annual model change started in General Motors in the early 1930s and was soon copied by Ford (who had previously held on to each model for as long as possible).

All this was very good news for the mass producer of components. Retaining the same engine for a new car extended the production runs of the components used in the engine, etc., whilst changing just the colour of a seat cover simply meant using different shades of material. The components producers in this system were thus even more apt to rely upon mass production than their customers.

The complexity of the car also provides a potentially low-risk option for the assembler to try out new technical ideas by fitting one new system at a time.[3] It is quite possible, for example, to fit fuel injection to a carburettor engine, modify the engine accordingly, and then to use it into a production car. Thus a new model (with appropriate minor visual alterations) may be launched on this basis, marketed on technological benefits. Altshuler *et al.* note that this process may be extended:

> vehicle designers tend to add new systems one at a time or to apply new technologies to one area at a time. For example, microprocessor controls were added to engines beginning in the mid 1970s, to transmissions in the early

1980s and suspensions in the mid 1980s. This is the preferred course of the assembler because it builds step by step on experience, minimising the chance of wasted development funds and the risk of a disastrous error. (Altshuler *et al.*, 1984, p. 79)[4]

It is clear, therefore, that technical change in the automotive industry is linked with new product development in a multi-faceted way. An apparently new vehicle may be launched which is in fact almost unaltered in technical terms from its predecessor, and a visually unchanged model may be introduced which has, under its skin, an entirely new technology, working for the benefit of the customer.

As Altshuler *et al.* (1984) note, innovation in the automobile must be directed towards at least four different markets at once: the utilitarian consumer, who wants the vehicle to be a workhorse (from the company sales rep's car to the farmer's four-wheel drive cross-country vehicle); the performance-minded consumer, seeking ever greater acceleration, sleeker styling (and traditionally, but seldom nowadays, higher top speed); the economy-minded consumer, conscious of fuel and maintenance costs and resale value, in addition to initial price; and the luxury consumer, whose motives are a mix of comfort, delight, ego satisfaction and public image.[5]

To these must now be added a further class: the ecological or environmentally conscious consumer. This set of market factors appears to cut across the entire spread of the previous four.[6] For example, in Europe, lead-free petrol is priced significantly lower than leaded (via national excise duty policies) and thus engines which can use it were immediately required by economy-minded consumers. At the same time (1970s–1980s), performance engines were redesigned to run on lead-free fuel. Interestingly in North America, unleaded fuel was priced higher than leaded: even so, all new cars in the last decade have been designed to use unleaded.

The other major anti-pollution measure of the 1970s, the catalytic converter (fitted to the exhaust system and designed to reduce the harmful carbon monoxide and dioxide in emission gases)[7] was fitted first to high-specification cars in Europe – principally because of the significant increase in the price of the vehicle (the construction of a catalytic converter includes the use of platinum). Once again North America took the opposite path, requiring all new cars to be fitted with catalytic converters.[8] Meanwhile, the first advances in two other environmentally orientated moves – recyclable cars (materials, components, etc.) and the vehicle dismantling processes (a new role for distribution networks in the future)[9] were made by BMW, a firm clearly targeting the performance and luxury markets.

The differentiation of vehicles across a full line helps the assembler in meeting these multi-dimensional markets. In Europe, each volume assembler (those producing over 1.5 million units per year) has a range of models which incorporates four or five separate sizes (for example the Ford Fiesta, Escort/Orion, Sierra and Granada). In the USA the classes are known as sub-compact, compact, full size and luxury. Within each range, there is a spread of model specifications, which also helps the innovation process, e.g. the Ford Escort range encompasses models from the economical Popular through to the sporty XR3i and the luxury Ghia. Thus one model can be made to appeal to several types of consumer.

New systems which offer major advances (such as fuel injection, or anti-lock braking systems) are usually introduced on high-specification vehicles, subsequently being fitted to models lower in the range as an option, and finally becoming standard equipment. Abernathy (1978) refers to this process as 'packing down' the technology on each vehicle; the implication being that it is necessary to introduce new ideas 'on top' of everything else. Once all cars have servo-assisted brakes (an option in the 1970s, standard equipment in the 1990s) the differentiated product must have anti-lock braking systems (microprocessor controlled) and so on.

In some cases, this pattern is broken. The diesel engine, for example, was developed principally for economy reasons and was not therefore a selling point for performance and luxury cars. It was introduced in Europe in the 1960s (North Americans would not have been interested in saving on fuel consumption at that time) on mid-range models, subsequently spreading up and down the range as enabling technologies were developed (e.g. to overcome weight problems in small cars – the diesel engine is intrinsically heavier than the petrol engine).

The problem for the innovator in the automobile assembler is to launch a new, high-technology, system which will perform perfectly at once. This is because the cars in which the system will be fitted are high price, high visibility. Modern consumers cannot be expected to tolerate failures or drawbacks (as they were, for example, with the diesel, which was noisy, smelly and sluggish, for a car engine, in its early days). This has fundamental implications for automotive innovation: it means that it is essentially incremental. As Altshuler *et al.* (1984) point out, the radical alternatives are very high risk. Henry Ford took the risks with the Model T (several product innovations at once) and thought through the implications (principally connected with manufacturing technologies and pricing ability). British Leyland took the risk with the Mini in the 1950s and did not succeed in commercial terms.[10]

This may be compounded by the success of previous innovations in the vehicle which make it increasingly difficult to convince the essentially conservative consumer that it is necessary and desirable to accept the new ideas. This problem applies not only to radical departures which affect the car as a whole (the Mini, for example, had a transverse engine, was very small, but incorporated four adult seats, rubber suspension, front-wheel drive, minimal front and rear overhang, etc.), but also to the introduction of new major systems. Citroën attempted to introduce front-wheel drive in 1934, almost bankrupting the company in the process because of technical problems, despite the model's eventual success (Altshuler *et al.*, 1984). It was only two decades later that the idea became a commercial technical reality – initially in the BMC Mini but more so in its followers – thanks to the innovation carried out in a components supplier: the constant velocity joint by GKN.

The UK company Pilkington, world leader in automotive glass technology, achieved major success in the 1960s with its Hotline heated rear screen; almost all new cars made today are fitted with such a device. Its following innovation, the 20–20 laminated safety windscreen, was not a success, however: the consumer was not convinced of the need for it (a special form of lamination to prevent injury and loss of forward visibility in a crash) and for the related increase in the vehicle price. (Safety features have rarely proved to be long-term success factors in selling cars, other than image-related safety – arguably more the product of clever advertising than engineering and design).

■ The need for innovation in automobiles

Altshuler *et al.* (1984) note three reasons for innovation in automobiles, and situations in which it may be expected to occur:

■ **A dramatic change in the automobile's operating environment**: The obvious example here is the environmental issue, which requires a move to zero emissions in the medium term. This may necessitate a replacement for the internal combustion engine. This would naturally be a radical or 'epochal' innovation although possibly not a new idea at the time of its introduction, perhaps being the realization of an old theory. Altshuler *et al.* (1984) note that adaptation to such a change would normally be met by 'coping innovations', which would probably be invisible to the consumer. This would apply even to the radical innovation required to replace the internal combustion engine – the best selling proposition might be *'nothing has changed, except that there are no harmful exhaust emissions!'*

■ **Intense competition in the auto market**: This comes about when there are a large number of firms in the industry, especially during a recession or in other stringent market conditions such as adverse exchange rate movements. Product technology as the basis for competition would fit all the market categories mentioned above.

■ **Exogenous development of new technologies with applications in the automotive industry**: The automotive industry has always borrowed technologies from other industries. The best recent example of this is the microprocessor, which was developed for defence systems and computers but is used in the automobile for many different control functions. The turbocharger, aluminium engines, and anti-lock braking systems are all technologies transferred from the aerospace industry to vehicles. In each case, however, the application of the idea to automobiles required ingenuity, e.g. to enable the turbocharger to function reliably in the stop/start, accelerate/decelerate operation of the motor car, instead of the relatively constant load in an aircraft engine.[11]

Lastly, product innovation leads to the need for process innovation. This can threaten entire businesses, e.g. small metalworkers whose product is redesigned by the customer in plastic. This would mean the potential obsolescence of the workforce skills and capital equipment, such as presses and lathes, requiring massive investment in new machinery and retraining (a good example of Schumpeter's 'destruction of capital').

An example of success in the face of this threat is provided by the parts supplier Holley Carburettors Inc., for a long time the largest independent manufacturer of carburettors in the USA. Faced with the advent of fuel-injection systems, Holley shifted its core technology from mechanical engineering/fluidics to electronics. As a result, the company is now the leading independent US manufacturer of fuel-injection systems and is patenting innovations which may remove some of the controlling edge held over this technology by the world leaders, Robert Bosch GmbH. Holley's successful development from mechanical to mechatronic technologies is remarkable in that it was completed without resorting to merger and acquisition. The necessary engineering resources were recruited and developed internally – a singular achievement in the modern industry.

■ Technical change in craft, mass and lean automotive production

Innovation in craft production

As we saw earlier, the technology for the early motor vehicles came largely from the joint efforts of assemblers and component suppliers. Even for the relatively simple vehicles of the day, collaboration was necessary between such firms in order to develop the entire product. Differentiation between assembler and component firms was somewhat arbitrary since they were all so deeply involved in producing the vehicle. Some firms were established as pure components producers, however (e.g. Bosch in Europe, Budd in the USA), whilst the major assemblers (Olds, Ford, Mercedes, Renault, Fiat, etc.) remained assemblers throughout. The rest either left the industry or became subsumed (e.g. the component firms which were absorbed by GM – see Chapter 1).

Abernathy implies that the initial innovation (i.e. the birth of the motor car) was actually a need-pull, at least in the USA:

> Emerging consumer needs, not new technological capabilities, triggered
> the rapid development of the U.S. automobile industry at the turn of the
> century. A practical steam-powered car could have been produced twenty
> years earlier. Allan Nevins observes that the industry was born from the

consumer's desire for a light personal transportation vehicle – a desire stimulated by the bicycle boom of the 1890s. (Abernathy, 1978, p. 11)

Since each car was slightly different from the last, technical development could be said to be a continuous process in craft production. This was partly because the manufacturing method was not designed to produce similar products, and partly because the customer was able to specify the technical details of the car he or she wanted. Since parts were not required to be interchangeable, a new idea could be tried out on one model without the worry of after-sales service, which would today inhibit experimentation on production models. Many of the product innovations noted in later years actually originated in the craft production era. As Abernathy (1978) notes, commenting on the industry up to the mid-1970s, 'Changes in market preferences ... may call earlier design approaches back into use.'

Just as the emergence of the automobile in the USA had been a response, based on readily available technologies, to the market need which grew out of dissatisfaction with the limitations of the bicycle, so periodically some new market requirement was identified by the assemblers and satisfied by the development of existing ideas. A summary of some of the innovations chronicled by Abernathy (Table 5.1) reveals the strength of this argument. Each of these innovations was hailed as a major advance decades after its original introduction – usually in a more developed form.

Another interesting addition to the list is that of continuously variable transmission (CVT). This system – involving the substitution of steel belts and variable pulleys as an alternative to the use of gears in the drive train – was developed in the craft era in vehicles such as the Cartercar, B.M. and Certus (Altshuler *et al.*, 1984, p. 86). It did not succeed, but reappeared in 1955 in the Dutch Daf Variamatic car, developed as a system by the engineering designer, Van Doorne. It met with more success this time but was never really accepted, despite its use in later Volvo saloons. In the 1980s it was redeveloped, with the use of microprocessor control to optimize the ratio variation. Once again, it was more

Table 5.1 Origins of product innovations in the automobile

Innovation	Date	Remarks
Four-stroke petrol engine	1876	Dr Otto, Germany
Independent front suspension	1878	Amédée Bollée, France (in a steam car)
Aluminium engine body (not cylinder)	1895	Haynes-Apperson Co., Indiana
Aluminium pistons	1900	Clerget, France
Monocoque/unit construction[b]	1903	Vauxhall, UK[a]
Automatic transmission	1904	Sturtevant, USA
Disc brakes	1904	Lanchester, UK
Closed steel bodies	1912	Budd, USA[a]
Windscreen wipers	1916	Trico, USA[a]

Notes: [a] Companies still in existence in 1991. [b] The first monocoque car was an open two seater, before the development of the closed steel body.

Source: Adapted from Abernathy (1978, Appendix 1, pp. 183–218). Last item added by author (*The Financial Times*, 3 August 1991).

successful but not completely acceptable. Development continues, in pursuit of fuel economy and possibly safety (by removing the need to change gears, etc.).[12]

Abernathy sums up this delay in the exploitation of product innovations with a nice use of symbolism:

> The important performance-improving innovations – like automatic transmission and power steering – that have advanced over the years, were all envisioned from the beginning of the industry. They were, in fact, the targets of innovative effort from the beginning. Once these improvements were realised, it was as if the mainspring of a giant clock had unwound.
> (Abernathy, 1978, pp. 66–7)

With so much raw ingenuity being poured into the industry, it is perhaps not surprising that the technologies which would satisfy almost a century of consumers were spawned in the few early decades of the automobile's life. What is surprising is the realization that the very unruly nature of craft production itself may have been a crucial part of this fertile innovative process.

Abernathy's observation was written just at the time when the microprocessor was being developed. Innovation since that time has been almost entirely based upon microelectronics.

Innovation in mass production

The American version of mass production, as practised by Ford, suppressed technical change within the company in the 1920s to such an extent that the company lost its market leadership and much of its momentum. During the building of that leadership, however, the concentration on one design provided Ford with the simplicity to consolidate performance. Having employed some major product innovations, therefore, Ford failed to continue to develop in an incremental fashion and was overtaken by General Motors.

Realizing, in 1921, that there was no hope of beating Ford on process innovation – his strongest suit – Sloan decided to 'take a bite from the top of his [Ford's] position' – to 'go up market' by producing high-margin, high-specification vehicles, thereby providing funds to underwrite the development of the Chevrolet models, which would compete directly with the Model T. (This policy would also lead to a useful boost to the GM corporate image.) The GM version of technical innovation was still fairly conventional. This was intentional, and came from the top. Alfred Sloan was later to comment: 'It was not necessary to lead in technical design or run the risk of untried experiments' (Sloan, 1963, p. 72).[13]

GM's differentiation policy worked and was emulated by Chrysler and eventually Ford. The market shares in the USA were to remain the same for the next fifty years or so, while the Big Three ran a race of equals, in which competition was a matter of keeping up with one another. When radical innovation threatened to upset this balance, it was a common enemy for them to fight together. Examples such as Cord, Tucker and Kaiser automobiles, with radical ideas such as rear engines, aluminium bodies, electric transmissions and front-wheel drive, were dismissed, apparently by market forces, which were in fact driven by what amounted to collusion on the part of GM, Ford and Chrysler (see Halberstam, 1985, pp. 328–33).

Halberstam comments on this situation thus:

> What had happened, of course, without anyone realising it, was that the industry had become monopolistic – what Patrick Wright [a Detroit journalist] called a shared monopoly – and monopolies, free of fresh challenges and new ideas, inevitably become cautious and staid. At the time, George Romney of American Motors, which was struggling along, warned of what was happening. While the Big Three, he pointed out, were muscle-bound and mindless in the domestic market – increasingly locked into practices that their best people knew were destructive but were unable to break out of so profitable a syndrome – their European subsidiaries were often innovative, because on the Continent they encountered genuine competition . . . in his [Romney's] words: 'there is nothing more vulnerable than entrenched success'. (Halberstam, 1986, pp. 327–8)

In the mid-1950s, a senior Ford executive, Ted Yntema, reporting to the US Senate Monopoly Subcommittee, likened the competitive situation to 'a boxing game where you try to guess what your opponent is going to do'.

Summarizing, Womack *et al.* (1990) remark:

> the world auto industry has lived during its first century in a benign environment – demand for its products has increased continually, even in the .most developed countries; space has been available in most areas to expand road networks greatly; and the earth's atmosphere has been able to tolerate ever-growing use of motor vehicles.[14]

Nowhere was this more evident than in North American mass production in the mid-twentieth century.

In analyzing and criticizing the nature of innovation under mass production, Abernathy (1978) concludes that the search for productivity gains in the manufacturing process leads to standardization of the product, actually inhibiting product innovation. This is more than a simple case of sunk costs – investments in one technology which, through the need to achieve a payback preclude a switch to a new technology. As Abernathy notes:

> Since the Model T, [up until 1976] no one firm has achieved a major production-process advantage over others, for they have all evolved in a very similar way. In practice, this means that no firm sustains a competitive advantage through product innovation. When all firms have the same process capabilities, then any one firm can replicate the product innovations of any

other. Under these circumstances, the incentive for significant product innovation is weakened. (Abernathy, 1978, p. 62)

A remark by Donald Frey, a vice president of the Ford Motor Company, in 1964, sums up the mass production attitude to innovation. The last significant innovation in the auto industry, he said, was the automatic transmission, which went into production in the late 1930s.[15]

As radical innovation was suppressed in the USA by standardization of mass production and the lack of dynamic competition, the importance of incremental innovation increased. This might have emphasized the significance of the component suppliers' role, had not the industry been so heavily integrated.[16] As it was, the situation degenerated until, as Abernathy puts it, as of 1976: 'The car itself is now a styling concept, rather than a technological concept ... The technology is embedded in the components' (Abernathy,1978, Chapter 6).

The industrial sclerosis observed by Abernathy certainly applied fully to the USA but was less observable in Europe – and it was directly opposed by the lean production system, developing in Japan.

Innovation in European mass production

For reasons discussed in Chapter 1, the European industry never standardized in the same way as the North American mass producers. The different requirements for the various countries and the plethora of assemblers, coupled with the lack of real scale economies, led the Europeans to experiment more radically, giving rise to such concepts as rear engines, mid-engines, transverse engines, front-wheel drive and fuel injection. The three drivers for innovation – environmental change (provided by intra-regional trade such as the need for Italian cars to compete in the UK), intense competition from many firms (Europe had many assemblers), and exogenous innovation (never in short supply, as we have seen) – were all present.

In addition, the strength of the components industry meant that the systems made available to the assemblers were often well developed, while the component needs of the vehicle designers resulting from their radical innovations (e.g. rear engine, or front-wheel drive) were competently met by the supplier firms. Thus, the European component suppliers played a significant part – sometimes *the* significant part – and developed technical strengths.

In recent decades, however, the limitations of the European version of mass production and the striving for economies of scale in fragmented markets have led to a concentration of assemblers and a gradual convergence of designs. In France, Peugeot absorbed Citroën, Matra became a subcontractor to Renault (building the Espace multi-purpose vehicle), Simca disappeared, etc. Germany saw the demise of NSU – an innovative company until the end, responsible for early use of the Wankel rotary engine (later used successfully by Mazda, achieving first place in the 1991 Le Mans 24 hour endurance race). The UK lost many firms which were absorbed by British Leyland (Riley, MG, Wolsely, Vanden Plas, Standard, and later, Triumph, Morris, Austin and, temporarily, Jaguar), following the merger of British Motor Holdings and Leyland in the 1960s, and those which had been absorbed first by Rootes Group, then by Chrysler, and finally by Peugeot (Humber, Hillman, Singer and Sunbeam). In Italy, all the major assemblers except the niche specialists, Lamborghini and Maserati, were gradually absorbed by Fiat.[17]

In parallel with this development has been the apparent demise of innovation and genuine fundamental product differentiation. Front-wheel drive has been adopted by all the volume builders, as have transverse engines and servo-assisted brakes. The specialist assemblers have all stayed with rear-wheel drive. Rear-mounted engines are to be found only in exotic cars, most designed decades ago (e.g. Porsche 911) and volume assemblers have reached the point where products are differentiated only by minor technological factors and minimal styling differences. This was reinforced by the predominance of national champions in the domestic markets (see Table 5.2).[18] By the 1970s a situation almost akin to that in North America had arisen – mass production acted against sustained innovative activity within the assemblers and the low level of competition from outside Europe meant that little pressure existed for change.

The top half of the table shows how the domination of national markets in Italy, France and, to a lesser extent, the UK has been reduced (despite limitations on Japanese imports in these countries). Germany (which has no such limitations) appears to remain more balanced. In the UK, the reduction in home market share has not been balanced by a strong export drive by the British-owned firms – reflecting the significant reduction in size of BL (Rover).

Rothwell and Gardiner note:

In the automobile sector the basis of design robustness [the scope of a design for continued refinement] appears to be not so much technological, but

Table 5.2 National champions in Europe

		Share of home market (automobile sales) (%)		
		1970	1980	1990
Fiat, Alfa Romeo	Italy	73.6	58.5	52.4
VW, Audi, Mercedes, BMW	Germany	41.5	46.7	40.4
Peugeot, Citroën, Renault	France	79.8	76.9	60.8
BL (etc.), Jaguar	UK	32.0[a]	18.2	14.5

		Exports expressed as % of total production			
		1960	1970	1980	1990
Fiat, Alfa Romeo[15]	Italy	33.3	36.8	35.4	39.6
VW, Audi, Mercedes, BMW, Ford, Opel	Germany	46.3	54.8	59.9	57.3
Peugeot, Citroën, Renault	France	41.9	43.2	46.2	43.4
BL (etc.), Jaguar	UK	42.1	42.0	38.9	31.9

Note: [a] 1973 data.

Source: D.T. Jones, University of Wales, Cardiff Business School, MVMA *Yearbooks* (various years).

rather to reflect the product/market strategy of the firm. This can be illustrated by comparing the evolution of the BL1100 [British Leyland: Austin Morris] and the Ford Cortina during the 1960s and 1970s. While the BL1100 essentially changed little over this period, with only one model available during the first generation, three rather similar models during the second generation and three during the third, the Cortina evolved as a sophisticated design family offering a much wider choice of models over the first three generations of development (4, 7 and 3 respectively), which between them covered a much greater spectrum of price and performance characteristics. The evolving Cortina family enjoyed considerably greater commercial success than did the much more limited BL1100 series, being much better adapted to meeting an ever-increasing range of user requirements. (Rothwell and Gardiner, 1989)

The BL1100 was more radical in its technology (front-wheel drive, transverse engine, gas suspension, etc.) than the very traditional Cortina, but it was the apparent developments rather than the truly technological features which underpinned the Cortina's success. The extreme variant of the Cortina was the Capri – an entirely different body with Cortina mechanical parts. Ford used the American principle (first used by Henry Ford on the Model T) of quasi-product differentiation. The Cortina's simplicity also appealed to UK company car fleet managers, who saw potential for lower maintenance costs than those suggested by the radical designs of the BL1100. This was a further factor in its great success. Ford did try front-wheel drive in the German version of the Cortina – the Taunus – in the 1950s, but decided it was too complex for available components and manufacturing techniques.[19]

Thus, the intraregional competition which, for example, led Ford to enter the small car market for the first time with the Fiesta in the 1970s (designed to compete with the very small Italian and French cars) left the volume assemblers with the semi-rigid product structure described above (large, medium, small, very small) which was in turn used as the basis of a reduction in the number of different models offered.

This situation was measured by the work of Sheriff (1988) developed in Womack *et al.* (1990) which showed that the European volume assemblers reduced the number of models[20] offered to the market by 12 per cent between 1982 and 1990 (from forty-nine to forty-three). This reduction involved the removal of old models from the range, which reduced the average age of the overall European offering from 4.6 years to 3.4 years between 1982 and 1985. However, the tardiness in new product introduction shown by the European assemblers meant that this increased again to 4.6 years by 1987 (i.e. models had to remain in production and on the market longer, awaiting their replacements, and thus the average model age increased).

In the USA, Sheriff's research shows that the assemblers did increase the number of models available over the period from 1982 to 1985 but did not replace old models. Thus model ranges increased (often as a result of collaboration with Japanese firms, sometimes including 'badge engineering'),[21] but incremental innovation for existing models was not carried out efficiently. Sheriff's work indicates shortcomings in the mass producers' product strategies in both Europe and the USA. In sectors such as sports cars the initiative was taken over by lean producers. In other sectors, the mass producers still managed to lead, e.g. multi-purpose vehicles (Renault Espace/Chrysler Minivan) and sports hatch (Golf GTi/Peugeot 205), but lean producers were quick to learn.

The work of Clark and Fujimoto (1985–89, and 1987–91) has attributed the weakness in product development within mass producers partly to policies in organization and supplier integration. The traditional practice of appointing new-model development teams, formed by the secondment of functional specialists on a short-term basis, is seen by Clark as 'lightweight' commitment by companies to the process. The individuals thus seconded see their activity in the new-product team at best as an interesting experience and at worst as a waste of time. The need for advancement up the functional ladder (promotion within the home department) is not necessarily satisfied by time spent on special projects. As Womack *et al.* remark:

> The members of the [new product development] team know that their career success depends on moving up through their functional speciality – getting promoted from chief piston engineer to deputy chief engine engineer to chief engineer for example – and they work very hard in the team to advance the interest of their department. (Womack *et al.*, 1990, p. 114)

As will be seen in the comparisons (by Clark) shown below (see Table 5.3), mass producers in the USA and Europe still appear to require component suppliers to 'make to drawing'. Clark shows that the parts supplied to mass producers were mostly 'detail-controlled' (developed entirely by the assemblers from functional specification to detailed engineering).

Despite this, innovation appears to have continued in mass production component suppliers. As Table 5.4 indicates, a review of the international patents,

Table 5.3 Comparison of component supplier technical inputs to product development in the auto industry: Japan, Europe and USA

	Nature of supplier involvement in parts engineering (%)		
	Japan	USA	Europe
Supplier proprietary parts[a]	8	3	7
Black box parts[b]	62	16	39
Detail-controlled parts[c]	30	81	54
	100	100	100

Notes: [a] Those parts which are developed entirely by parts suppliers as standard parts. [b] Those parts whose functional specification is performed by assemblers, whilst detailed engineering is carried out by parts suppliers – see Endnote 25. [c] Those parts which are developed entirely by assemblers from functional specification to detailed engineering.

Source: Adapted by the author from Clark, K.B. *Project Scope and Project Performance: The Effect of Parts Strategy and Supplier Involvement on Product Development* Management Science, Vol. 35, No. 10, October 1989, pp. 1247–63 Table 1.

Table 5.4 International patenting by automobile companies, 1981–86[a]

European firms	Patents	US firms	Patents	Japanese firms	Patents
Component suppliers					
Bosch	1625	Allied S	2033	Hitachi	3399
Lucas	624	Rockwell	947	Mitsubishi Electric	1364
SKF	227	UTC	872	Nippondenso	620
Valeo	180	ITT	862	Aisin Seiki	600
ZF	156	GTE	688	Sumitomo Electric	278
Fichtel Sachs	132	TRW	385	Diesel Kiki	204
VDO	115	Dana	140	Toyoda Gosei	73
GKN	112			Nippon Seiko	67
BBA	97			NHK	41
T&N	64				
Vehicle assemblers					
D Benz	419	GM	2203	Nissan	1910
Fiat	275	Ford	974	Toyota	1585
VW	210	Navistar	196	Honda	1043
Renault	210	Chrysler	119	Mazda	287
MAN	164			Fuji (Subaru)	186
BMW	109			Mitsubishi	62
Porsche	109			Suzuki	35
Volvo	103			Isuzu	20
PSA	76			Daihatsu	11
Saab	58				
Rover	25				

Note: [a] Figures for Fiat include Magneti Marelli (36). BBA includes Automotive Products, Valeo includes Nieman, etc. Rover includes Jaguar. PSA is Peugeot/Citroën. International patents are those taken out in the USA. Patents are for automotive and non-automotive applications.
Source: D.T. Jones, University of Wales Cardiff Business School, 1989.

taken out in North America, shows that the suppliers were often more innovative than the assemblers.[22]

In a comparison of Germany and Japan between 1982 and 1986, Jones (1988) shows that over two-thirds of their international patents were taken out by component firms. Of the German total, one-third were by Bosch. These data are shown in Table 5.5.[23] Jones finds also that the German firms exhibit technical strengths in mechanical engineering – engines, brakes, clutches, hydraulics, etc. – while the Japanese lead in electrical equipment including computers, semiconductors and data storage devices.

There is an apparent contradiction here: mass production has hampered innovation in automobiles and yet the companies in the industry – particularly the component suppliers – appear to be patenting at a healthy rate. Part of this is explained by the diversity of the supplier groups, particularly in the USA, as discussed in Chapter 2 (i.e. the component firms are very advanced and active in other, non-automotive technologies). It is apparent in addition, however, that imperfections in the relationships between assemblers and component suppliers in

Table 5.5 Share of US patents, 1982–86, by German and Japanese automotive firms – assemblers and component suppliers

| | US Patents 1982–86 | |
	German firms	Japanese firms
Assemblers	1098 (28%)	4369 (32%)
Component suppliers	2825 (72%)	9385 (68%)
Total	3923 (100%)	13 754 (100%)

Source: Jones (1988).

the mass production regions might be responsible for this waste of innovative resources.

Thus innovation in automobiles under the mass production paradigm may be seen to suffer from three main limitations:

■ The need for economies of scale in production and product development, leading directly to standardization and indirectly to limited competition through industry concentration.

■ Functional demarcation, a characteristic of mass production, is extended to the new product development process.

■ The tendency in the assemblers towards retaining control over all design and technology decisions – a result of high levels of vertical integration.

Innovation in lean production

Lean production directly counters the three limitations listed above. The concept of economies of scale is based upon some assumptions of fixed costs (such as setting times for machine tools) which are not allowable in lean production. These assumptions have traditionally led to many incalculable manufacturing costs being brought together into overhead allowances, tied to direct labour costs by some notional ratio. In lean production, however, the system is under control (systematically problem solved, fully choreographed, and capacity fully utilized, with all waste eliminated) and activity-based costing may be used to identify all costs precisely. Labour is also treated as a fixed cost ('non-productive' time, so-called in mass production, becomes continuous improvement, etc.), so the traditional differentiation between direct and indirect labour costs becomes redundant. The practice of *kaizen* has led to a situation in which lean producers can effect die changes which require hours in mass production, in a few minutes (see Schonberger, 1982, p. 20).

The functional demarcation inherent in mass production is not accepted in lean production. This is clearly shown in the area of new product development. Womack *et al.* (1990, pp. 104–10), in tracing the development of one mass production product – the GM10 series – and one lean product – the Honda Accord

– illustrate succinctly how lean product development relies upon 'heavyweight' commitment (Clark's term) to development teams.

In terms of investment in R&D, lean producers in Japan have shown a remarkable emphasis on its importance. As Graves reports:

> Major changes have taken place in the ranking of the leading countries in the automobile industry. [From 1970 to 1985] R&D expenditure in real terms remained relatively constant in the UK, while rising by 25 per cent in West Germany, 28 per cent in Italy, 55 per cent in the USA, 88 per cent in France and by more than 428 per cent in Japan ... The Japanese share of R&D total expenditure by the big six auto-producing countries rose from 11 per cent in 1969 to 28 per cent in 1984, while that of Western Europe fell from 31 per cent to 27 per cent and that of the USA fell from 58 per cent to 45 per cent. (Graves, 1991, p. 60)

The work of Clark (1989a and 1989b) also shows that the different integration policy in lean production leads to a greater involvement of component suppliers in the new vehicle development process.

The contrast between product development in mass production (North American and European versions) and lean production is summed up by Womack *et al.* in a table based upon the work of Clark *et al.* (1987) and Fujimoto (1989), which is reproduced as Table 5.6.[24] The full version of the data from the work of Clark, Fujimoto and Chew shows major benefits accruing to the lean developer: products are brought to market more quickly, and with less effort and interruption. The role of the supplier is clearly one of the key factors – the lean producer needs fewer people in the development team and fewer engineering hours to develop the new car.

In another paper, Clark comments on the data on which Table 5.6 is based:

> The contrast between the Japanese and the Americans is intriguing. The American projects make only modest use of suppliers in design and engineering but they rely relatively heavily on common parts [common with other vehicles and thus not new for the new car]. The engineers in the American projects thus spend more time making a larger set of common parts fit into a new design. To the extent that common and carryover parts pose constraints for product design and engineering, the greater use of unique parts in the Japanese projects suggests a possible advantage in product performance. Most of the Japanese firms use suppliers to sustain development of more uniquely designed products without substantially increasing their internal engineering workforce. (Clark, 1989a)

In addition to qualifying his own data, in this conclusion Clark summarizes mass production's problem with new product introduction and innovation itself: the practice of retaining parts and controlling all the technology is less efficient than changing a greater proportion of the vehicle but trusting suppliers to do the development work. As Clark points out, however, this is only the case if the coordination work between customer and supplier goes well and does not become more time consuming than the internal effort it obviates.

Table 5.6 Automotive product development: lean production versus mass production (volume assemblers only, mid-1980s)

	Japanese (lean) producers	American (mass) producers	European (mass) producers
Average engineering hours per new car (millions)[a]	1.7	3.1	2.9
Average development time per new car (months)	46.2	60.4	57.3
Number of employees in project team[b]	485	903	904
Number of body types per new car	2.3	1.7	2.7
Average ratio of shared carryover parts (%)	18	38	28
Supplier share of parts engineering (%)	51	14	37
Supplier share of total engineering effort (%)[c]	30	7	16

Note: [a] Corrected for differences in supplier involvement, use of off the shelf parts, and product content: see Clark (1989b, p. 10 and Exhibit 10). [b] See Endnote 24. [c] From Clark and Fujimoto (1991, p. 37, Figure 6.3). Share of total engineering effort is calculated as the product of the fraction of supplier engineering in total parts engineering and the ratio of parts engineering to total engineering effort.
Source: Womack *et al.* (1990, p. 118). Based on Clark, K.B., Fujimoto, T., and Chew, W.B. (1987) 'Product development in the world auto industry' *Brookings Papers on Economic Activity, No. 3 1987*, and Fujimoto, T., *Organisations For Effective Product Development: The Case of the Global Motor Industry* Ph.D Thesis, Harvard Business School, 1989 Tables 7.1, 7.4, 7.8).

Further analysis of Clark's data shows the manner in which suppliers contribute in each case: see Table 5.3.[25] This shows that the lean producers (the Japanese in this example) rely to a much greater extent than mass producers upon developed relationships with their component suppliers. In lean production, the parts suppliers are mainly providing their own technology (which is, nevertheless, developed in close communication with their customers), while the mass production suppliers, especially those in the USA, are still required to comply with instructions from the customer.

Clark is quite convinced of the value of the suppliers' contribution:

> The ability of the Japanese firms to operate efficiently while using a larger fraction of unique parts is due in significant part to the capability of the supplier network. The implication is that it is not only the extent of supplier involvement that is important but the quality of the relationship and the way that it is managed that matters ... It is important to note that such benefits are based in a relationship of reciprocity. Not only do suppliers have valuable capability, but the auto firm manages the process so that capability plays an important role. Moreover, the auto firms cultivate capability in their suppliers. (Clark, 1989a, p. 1256)

In an interesting extension to this principle, Clark's work confirms the limitations of mass production's obsession with vertical integration:

> There is some evidence from the interviews that project managers and engineers [in mass producers] found external suppliers easier to work with

than their internal parts divisions. In several cases, managers suggested that working with the internal parts divisions gave the project less control over the engineering work and involved them in a more bureaucratic process than working with outside suppliers. (Clark, 1989a, p. 1260)

And finally:

There is evidence in this data that integration of capability between upstream and downstream firms without financial ownership (i.e. an integrated supplier network) may be more effective in developing new technology and new products than an enterprise where the upstream firm is a wholly owned subsidiary of the downstream firm. At least in the development process, the implication is that the vertically-integrated firm actually is less integrated than the network of independent suppliers. (Clark, 1989a)

As noted in Table 5.6, lean producers have fewer people involved in the project team for a new model. There is a further dimension to this, observed by Clark and described by Womack *et al.* New product development in lean production begins with a very large team of people who see their position in the team as equally important to their position in their functional department. A great deal of effort is spent in defining specifications and sorting out problems at this stage. This investment of time at the early stage of the project helps to save time later. Indeed, fewer people are required on the team as the date of launch for the new model approaches (the individuals thus released turning to new projects, or returning to their functional departments). The reverse occurs in mass production. The lightweight commitment shown by senior management to a new model in its early stages, and the transient nature of the project leader's position (contrasted to the 'superstar' status of the Japanese *shusa*[26] in lean production) lead to a failure to resolve basic problems early on. This leads to a heavy problem-solving load later in the project – involving many more people.

The traditional involvement of suppliers in new model development in mass production is similar to this. Component firms in mass production are not involved until most of the design work has been done. At that stage, specifications are prepared and tenders are invited for the business. It is too late to alter designs fundamentally, even though the component supplier might see many ways of improving the product. In lean product development, the suppliers of major components are identified early on and involved in the design process, ensuring that potential faults are identified and rectified and that the value which the supplier is able to provide is built into the product early, to the mutual advantage of assembler and supplier. Finally, lean product development takes the concept of market orientation to a new level, or perhaps back to the bespoke nature of craft production. In the latter, the customer was able to specify the design features of the car to a degree which is unheard of in mass production.

The closest mass producers come to this is 'clinicking' the new car – soliciting the views of customers during the design or (even prototype) stage. Potential customers – expert and inexpert in automotive design – are invited to view the almost completed vehicle prior to launch to say what features they do or do not like. This process can lead to removal of extreme features and often to bland designs.[27] When it is carried out at prototype stage, clinicking can mean the early death of radical ideas before they have even been tried out.

A good example of lean product development is the Toyota Sera – a two-door sports car produced and sold only in Japan in 1989–90. Toyota produced only 10 000 of this model and all were sold. This was achieved in part by radical production techniques (the steel body panels were formed in dies which had only a female half, the male role being taken by pressurized water). Toyota's new fourteen-storey Amlux Centre, opened in Tokyo in September 1990, is the consolidation of this concept. The Amlux Centre contains:

> a vehicle design studio. Powerful computer systems, normally used only
> by research and development engineers, have been adapted to offer a 'menu'
> of styling and other parts, thus allowing members of the public to spend
> as much time as they want designing their own vehicles on screen – and in
> the process providing Toyota with insights into potential customers' 'ideal'
> vehicles ... finally there is a two-way information centre. Here, visitors
> wishing to ... expound at length on what they think Toyota should be doing
> or making, have an attentive audience of note-taking Toyota staff. There is
> no attempt by the latter to sell cars. (*The Financial Times*, 9 April 1991)

Mazda have taken this idea even further in their M2 Centre, built in Tokyo during 1991. Here, a similar design studio for the public is envisaged, but with a radical follow-on strategy: 'Mazda ... plans to take an unprecedented step in the world motor industry: to produce and test-market two or three new model lines a year, each in volumes as low as 100 [cars].'[28] Perhaps this is not unprecedented: in seeking to define niche products, Mazda is returning to craft production – or rather moving up to lean production.

This situation was predicted by Womack *et al.* (1990) and is illustrated in Figure 5.1. This traces the development of the automobile supply market from craft production, where there were many different products on offer and only a very small number of each built (high degree of customer specificity but at a high price), through mass production, when there were few different products for sale and a large number of each type made (low customer specificity, low price), to lean production, where there are many different products made and a low to medium number of each made (high customer specificity and medium to low price).

The integration of efforts on the new product development process is a natural part of lean production. This is shown in a 1987 paper by Graves in which he reports an observed difference between lean and mass production practice in product development, focusing on the relationship between functional departments. He finds significant differences in the two approaches, as shown in Figure 5.2.[29] In mass production, the demarcation between functions is prevalent in communications between production and R&D departments. The new product is

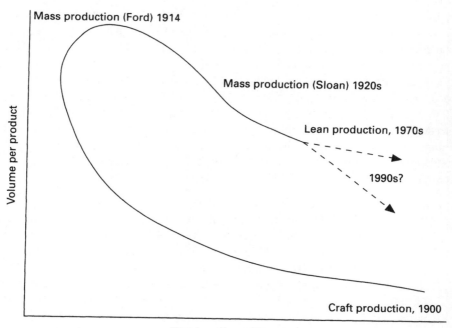

Source: Womack *et al.* (1990, Figure 5.7, p. 126).

Figure 5.1 The progression of product variety and production volume in the auto industry

'finished' by one department and responsibility is transferred to the next. Subsequent problem solving is a complex affair requiring backtracking and apportioning of blame. In lean production all departments are involved throughout the process of development. As Graves comments:

> In effect, the US system of R&D is uni-directional, whilst the Japanese process, with its inbuilt feedback mechanisms, tends to be cyclical and dynamic. [In the Japanese system] the relationships are more organic with key engineers and managers maintaining a flow of information throughout the system. (Graves, 1987)

This process has become recognized in recent years in the West and has become known as simultaneous engineering, or the 'rugby team' approach (because all the departments run together with the project from start to finish, passing the problems and solutions between one another all the way – the mass production model is known as 'relay race' using the same metaphor). Awareness of the principle is one thing: practising the concept is quite another. Recent evidence from the industry indicates that the mass producers are moving from the first model to the second, becoming lean in the process – at least in their intentions.

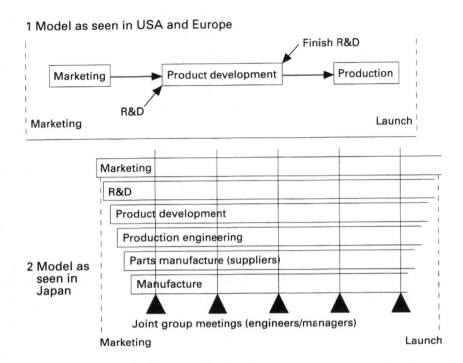

1 Model as seen in USA and Europe

2 Model as seen in Japan

Source: Graves (1987). (The Japanese diagram is based upon Nissan.)

Figure 5.2 Relationships between R&D, product development and production

A final contrast between mass production and lean production in innovation provides an example of the way in which each faces the destructive nature of the process. In the 1960s Ford in the USA invested heavily in drum brake manufacture, just before the commercial application, in mass production, of disc brakes. As the new technology took a hold, Ford retained its capacity in drum brakes and was subsequently late to market with discs – by that time an important selling factor.

In the 1970s the oil shocks convinced many people – including the Japanese – that smaller, less 'thirsty' engines would be required for the 1980s. The Japanese invested heavily in four-cylinder engine production technology, intended to penetrate the North American market where the producers were still wedded to the V6/V8 pattern. In fact, the worry caused by the oil shock did not last and the Americans returned to their preference for large engines. The Japanese lean producers, faced with a market poorly matched to their technology, had to innovate radically. This they did by applying immense concentration to the four-cylinder engine, adding every technology they could to achieve the maximum performance from the basic design. This meant developing expertise and refinement in several technologies at once: four valves per cylinder, turbo charging, balance shafts for smooth running, fuel injection, etc., as well as basic engine design. To this were added true innovations such as Honda's VTEC – variable valve timing. The result, as Womack *et al.* record, was more than just a success:

> As these features were added during the decade of the 1980s, they had an interesting effect on public perceptions – one that was perhaps unanticipated. Even as they raised the power of the same basic engine, in some cases by a factor of two, these innovations convinced buyers, particularly in North America, that Japanese cars were now 'high-tech', that they now had the most advanced features. They had grown from 'low-tech' weaklings in 1980 to 'high-tech' wonders by 1990 while preserving their manufacturers' basic investment in production facilities for small engines. (Womack *et al.*, 1990, p. 132)

It is interesting to note that Toyota's first entry to the large-engine, prestige car market – the very successful Lexus – was built on a 32 valve V8 engine: the lean producer had moved into the new area with a complicated product which was immediately successful.

■ Comparison: the automotive industries and innovation

Pull, push and the destruction of capital

As noted earlier, Abernathy (1978) concludes that the original innovation of the automobile may be seen as a need-pull phenomenon: consumers in the USA wanted a better form of personal transport than the bicycle. This is a limited view, however: the motor vehicle had existed in Europe and America for some time (Abernathy notes that it was seen mainly as a carrier of freight in the USA). It is not clear, therefore, that the motor vehicle itself can be called the result of need-pull innovation: it is more likely that the various technologies developed in other industries (e.g. steam power) gave rise to the concept of a mobile, lightweight, individually powered carriage or wagon. It may also be argued that this is a case of technical substitution rather than innovation *per se* (i.e. the need for personalized transport was already being answered by horses and horse-powered vehicles; the automobile was simply a substitute for the horse, and was only exploited fully – the innovation process – once the horse was no longer seen as a competitor).

As it has developed, the automobile has been the subject of both technology-push and need-pull innovations – often in the form of an interesting but unsuccessful idea being subsequently improved and commercially accepted (e.g. front-wheel drive, CVT, etc.). This is an example of what Rothwell and Gardiner

(1985) call 'reinnovation' – the constant redevelopment of a technology leading to new versions. In many cases in the automotive industry, however, there have been long periods between innovations, as noted earlier. It is thus possible to identify some technologies which appear on each generation of a vehicle, updated and improved in some way, (e.g. cabin ventilation systems, alternators), others which appear once and then disappear until much later, returning in a very developed form (e.g. disc brakes)[30] and still others which come and go (e.g. CVT).

The large number of inventions which arose in the early years provides an example of the 'clustering' expected of innovation, and the number of automobile builders which sprang up shows how 'bandwagoning' occurred in the industry on both sides of the Atlantic. The demise of craft production in the face of mass production was certainly a case of Schumpeter's 'destruction of capital', as was Ford's crisis in 1927. A similar example is now provided by the demise of mass production in the face of lean production – the destruction being represented by the need to renew capital equipment (for flexibility), to retrain workforces (for 'up-skilling') and reduce labour levels.

The internal combustion engine, using petrol, has been continuously refined through incremental innovation, but remains fundamentally the same today as those in use a century ago. Need-pulls within this long natural trajectory include economy in fuel consumption, cleanliness of exhaust gases, noise and vibration reduction, power and torque generation (for long running at high speeds and for acceleration), mechanical and electrical reliability, ease of maintenance and weight reduction. To these must be added the needs of the manufacturers themselves, such as ease of assembly and a reduction in engine size (to fit in low profile designs for cars). Current development of lightweight two-stroke engines may be seen as the next step in this trajectory.

On the broader front, technology pushes have come from outside the industry, the microchip being the clearest recent example. As noted previously, the industry has benefited constantly from developments occurring elsewhere, particularly in aerospace. Currently, many ideas for safety (anti-lock braking systems), comfort ('memories' in seats, steering wheels and mirrors, to fit personal driving positions), and convenience (computer/satellite navigation systems) are being developed – all examples of technologies originating elsewhere. The concept of 'head-up displays' is well established in aircraft design and provides a good example. At the basic level, the dials of the control panel in the cockpit are lit so that they reflect off the windscreen in the pilot's line of sight, placing an image in focus a few feet in front of the glass. In this way, the pilot need not divert the eyes from the direction of flight to see the information on the dials. In aircraft this concept has been taken a lot further – much more complicated data are represented, including computer simulations. A simple version of this (e.g. the speedometer, turn indicators and some warning lights) has now been installed commercially in some cars in Japan and the USA, with the same 'safety' reasoning. It is probably safer if drivers do not need to lower their eyes to see the speedometer (although the reverse case could be made – that having the information constantly in view is distracting), but it is hardly arguable that the development of head-up displays for cars was necessary: this is a clear case of technology push.

Graves summarizes the situation:

> Continuous incremental organisational and technical change is more significant than radical or 'revolutionary' innovation. Technological change in the industry is more the result of innumerable adaptations, cumulative improvements, technological fusion between firms and the adaptations of long-built-up technical skills, rather than technological breakthroughs. In the automobile sector, demand pull (particularly regulatory pressures, e.g. environmental control, fuel efficiency and traffic safety) is important in the early stages of technology development, while technology push becomes more important as the technology matures. (Graves, 1991, Abstract)

Sources of innovation in automobiles

It seems that the focus of innovation within the automobile industry may be about to change. In the craft production era, innovation clearly came jointly and simultaneously from the assembler of the vehicle and the companies that contributed to its construction. This reflected the nature of the companies – rich in engineering skills and with long experience in inventiveness – and that of the product – immature and in demand. The assemblers and the components companies worked very closely together because each knew that they needed each other; the relationship was based upon mutual respect and interdependence as well as (presumably) tough commercial dealing.

This situation changed with the onset of mass production, as standardization and vertical integration, coupled with the deskilling inherent in mass production itself, gave rise to a customer-dominated innovation environment. Assemblers limited their own search and selection environments, by largely failing to recognize the value available from independent component manufacturers and, in the USA, by choosing to dictate to the market (in Ford's case, mainly on the basis of accounting decisions taken by the new breed of management recruited in the 1950s: see Halberstam (1986, pp. 204–23).

The capacity for innovation evident in the component suppliers, coupled with the success gained by lean producers in using the efforts of their suppliers in new product development, suggest that the source of innovation should not be restricted, as it appears to be in mass production: some new model of development is required which exploits the innovation resident in component suppliers and allows it to grow.

The lean producers have also begun to show the importance of customer-led innovation, even to the extent of putting the customer in control of the CAD terminal. The visitors to Mazda's M2 centre in Tokyo will inevitably include hundreds of Japanese school children, possibly spending much of their time 'playing' at design. By the time they are ready to buy them, the cars they have styled for themselves will have been developed and built by Mazda and prepared for delivery.

■ Implications for component suppliers

If the above is true, then all parties in the industry have to re-assess strategies on product design. For component suppliers the recognition of technical abilities, including the ability to innovate, should presage a new era of development. There are, however, many factors involved in moving to a situation in which the supplier and assembler share new product development in a lean manner.

Not the least of these is the cost of investment required to achieve critical mass in R&D. As we saw in Chapter 2, some suppliers are already investing heavily in this, and doubtless these will be the firms best positioned to take advantage of the new order (sharing the opportunity with large, technology-rich firms from other industries which find applications for products and processes in the automotive sector).

Above all, the relationship between a vehicle assembler and its component suppliers appears to be crucial in the move towards lean product development. In pursuit of shorter introduction times for new vehicles, lower engineering efforts for increased technical output, and simultaneous multi-technology development, more efficient collaboration between customers and suppliers ranks alongside organizational policy (Clark's 'heavyweight' teams) as a priority concern for emerging lean producers.

For component suppliers, the challenge is to develop new strategies which position the company correctly for such collaboration. This is a major task, following decades of dealing with mass producers which wished not only to design and build the vehicle, but also to retain – in some cases jealously – control over all the technology contained in it.

■ An opportunity to collaborate

The reasons for collaboration and the potential benefits available to the collaborators find a resonance in the above. The innovation required is a mix of the radical and incremental (as identified by Graves), and clearly involves risk. The sharing of risk for an assembler may be effected via collaboration with a supplier; but only if there is sufficient potential benefit for the supplier in taking on the challenge. The success of the lean producers appears to be due in part to their ability to learn – another of the factors in collaboration, as identified by Dodgson, and discussed in Chapter 4. Once again these arguments lead to the need for an evaluation of relationships between customer and supplier. This we shall discuss in Chapters 6 and 7.

■ Notes

1. Early chassis members were thicker than this – up to 6 mm (0.25"). Assemblers gradually learned how to use fabrication better to gain strength from thinner metal. Early welding techniques sometimes distorted the metal and had to be given up in favour of brazing or riveting. Subsequent developments have made welding possible in virtually all cases. Heavy vehicle chassis are still bolted together, however (JLL).

2. This development took place first in Europe. The chassis/body design remained popular in North America well into the 1970s. The chassis is still a feature of some vehicles, e.g. those with plastic bodies. An interesting problem faced the assemblers whose custom it was to produce pick up versions of saloon cars: the monocoque construction would not provide the necessary strength for such a vehicle. So, for example, in the UK in the 1960s, Morris was making the Morris Minor pick up with a monocoque front attached to a chassis-based rear (JLL).

3. This in itself may be a major investment. Altshuler *et al*. (1984) note (p. 78) that 'to incorporate a new component system – after it is developed in prototype form – into a new model takes four years on average.' This was referring to Western practice and was written before the revelations of lean production.

4. In the mid-1990s it may be expected that microprocessor control will be added to the body of the car – in automatically controlled glass roof technology (changing translucency to control solar gain) and noise reduction/modification systems (in which anti-noise is introduced to produce silence inside the car, or any desired sound, such as the throb of a performance engine which would, however, not be heard outside the car).

5. It is interesting to note that for their introduction of high-specification vehicles in the USA in 1989, the Japanese chose to concentrate on the word 'luxury', playing what appeared to be semantic games. The actual effect of this technique was in fact more profound. For example, the Nissan-built Infiniti cars were advertised as directly redefining luxury as 'whatever you have always promised yourself but never been able to manage' – a specifically non-price-oriented approach. This was coupled with a definition of the Infiniti as a driver's car – not cluttered by superfluous technologies which separated the driver from the road. The Japanese therefore debunked the high-price European cars (sold at extremely high levels to consumers who simply wished others to see that they could afford such 'luxuries' – classic conspicuous consumption) and the Detroit prestige cars, which had interiors which appeared to be designed to 'insulate' the driver from the outside environment and road conditions. This marketing move came at the time when wealthy Americans were turning away from spending money on cars – perhaps bored by the lack of innovation and change in European specialists – in favour of other indulgences (boats, holiday homes, etc.). The move worked: Toyota's Lexus (which admittedly had many high-technology features) immediately began to compete aggressively with Mercedes Benz in the USA and was outselling the equivalent products of the German manufacturer by mid-1991 (over the first six months of the year, Lexus outsold BMW and Mercedes Benz). In the same year Infiniti and Lexus were first and second in the prestigious quality survey issued by the US consultants, J.D. Power, Inc.

6. In July 1992 Honda President Nobuhiko Kawamoto said that making cars more environmentally friendly was the most important challenge for manufacturers. One

month later, Honda withdrew totally from motor racing, apparently to concentrate more on environmental aspects of development. Mazda began a major advertising campaign in the same month, stressing the company's concentration on environmental issues and almost thirty years of achievements in the area (*The Financial Times*, 16 July 1992, and 21 July 1992).

7. Catalysts convert carbon monoxide and nitrogen oxides into safer gases and convert unburnt hydrocarbons into less harmful water vapour and carbon dioxide. In 1993 the EC joined the USA and Japan in requiring catalytic converters to be fitted on all new cars.

8. A car fitted with a catalytic converter must use lead-free fuel. The combination of mandatory catalytic converters and higher-priced lead-free fuel gave rise, in the USA, to many cases of 'catalyst poisoning' as motorists opted for the lower-priced, leaded fuel in cars fitted with catalyst converters.

9. The Euromotor (1991b) report predicts that recycling technology will be required to process 220 000 vehicles per day by 2010.

10. As Altshuler *et al.* (1984) record (pp. 81–2), it was BL's competitors, Fiat, Volkswagen, etc., who benefited in the long term. Despite its popularity, the Mini was not a commercial success until much later in its long life.

11. Examples exist of technology transfered in the other direction, with aircraft benefiting from the production volumes (and thus economies of scale) in the car industry. For example, alternators, starters, voltage regulators, fuel and hydraulic pumps, fuel quantity senders and some instruments originally designed for cars have found their ways into aircraft. *Flying* magazine (USA) of September 1992, pp. 66–8, reports that 'the linear activators that drive the flaps in some airplanes were originally made to adjust the seats of luxury automobiles'.

12. In July 1992 Rover relaunched the Metro automatic with a CVT drive replacing the previous conventional automatic transmission. The CVT was the same unit used by the Fiat Uno and Tipo, and the Ford Fiesta and Escort. *Car* magazine reported that although the CVT was lighter and more efficient than the torque converter automatic transmission, the manual Metro was still 12 per cent better on fuel consumption, and the CVT had a tendency to 'creep' when stationary in gear. CVT has never been exploited in North America.

13. This is still a popular strategy with large firms in high-technology industries. For example, the computer giant IBM have massive R&D resources but have preferred to let smaller, more dynamic firms (e.g. Apple) test market acceptance of radical ideas for new product features (e.g. graphic user interfaces, mouse control, etc.).

14. As Womack *et al.* point out (1990, p. 129), when a 'crisis' did occur GM was able to respond quickly: the need for emissions control led GM to develop – at short notice – the catalytic converter.

15. Quoted by Abernathy (1978, p. 3) from US Senate Hearings, 70th Congress, 2nd Session, 10–23 July 1968.

16. Abernathy attributes some of the success at Chrysler to its lower level of integration: 'Because Chrysler produced fewer of its own components, it was less constrained in adopting advanced innovative components. Thus Chrysler could seek competitive advantages though flexibility in product engineering and in styling. Chrysler pioneered high-compression engines in 1925, frame designs permitting low centre of gravity in the 1930s and the experimental introduction of disc brakes in 1949, power steering in 1951 and the alternator in 1960.' (1978, p. 37).

17. Maserati is now 49 per cent owned by Fiat and effectively dependent upon it for its survival.

18. By the end of 1991 Fiat's share of its home market had dropped to 47 per cent (the first time that the majority of cars sold in Italy were of non-Italian origin) with exports at 35 per cent of sales. It still accounts for all but 1300 cars (0.08%) made in Italy (*The Financial Times*, 26 November 1991 and 30 June 1992).

19. From research interview with A. Graves, 1992.
20. Sheriff defines a model as 'neither as narrow as a nameplate nor as broad as a platform ... a Volkswagen Golf and Jetta (Golf with a boot/trunk) would be viewed as one model just as a Mazda 323 hatchback and sedan [saloon] are viewed as one model.'
21. Badge engineering is the practice of buying a vehicle from another company and selling it under a different name (e.g. the Mazda 323 exists in some countries (including the USA) as the Ford Laser) or of launching several models using one platform (e.g. GM engineered five models off the 'J' platform and four off the 'W' platform. The term is used in a pejorative sense.
22. As Jones points out, the use of patenting statistics to measure technical activity has limitations: patents are only one route to appropriation of technology – an alternative being secrecy. The Science Policy Research Unit (University of Sussex) data are as quoted by the US Office of Technology Assessment (OTA) on all patents registered in the USA. Jones cross-references his findings with data on R&D spend (see Jones, 1988).
23. Data based upon all car and component firms taking out more than five patents a year between 1982 and 1986: twenty-seven German firms and forty-three Japanese. Bosch's counterpart in Japan, Nippondenso, had just 4 per cent of the Japanese total.
24. The Project Team refers to the personnel within the assembler who are directly involved in the new product development process. Not all of these would work on the project full-time or for the full duration of the process. Supplier personnel are not included in this number. Clark and Fujimoto also found that the Japanese companies who were using so-called 'heavyweight' teams (where product development is given priority over line responsibility) used only 333 team members. The European assemblers with least emphasis on the role of product development had 'lightweight' teams, in which the members were only weakly committed to the project, with an average of 1421 members: see Clark and Fujimoto (1991) and Womack *et al.* (1990, pp. 114–15).
25. The concept of black box engineering has been a traditional feature of automobile engineering for some time but is currently discussed frequently as a sign of increased closeness between assemblers and component suppliers. The idea is that the customer specifies the interface details and performance requirements for the component and leaves the supplier to develop the technology. These data show the practical results of black box operation. The idea of a grey box has also been mooted: this is similar to black box but with the customer having more of an idea (and, possibly, an influence) on its internal workings.
26. For a full explanation, see Womack *et al.* (1990, pp. 104–10).
27. The 1990 Ford Escort/Orion was severely criticized by the motoring press for being characterless – apparently the result of excessive use of clinics. In an interview with *Car* magazine (September 1991), John Oldfield, Head of Product Development, with responsibility for the CE14 (1990 Escort/Orion), said ' We took too much notice of market research with the CE14 and we made fundamental mistakes in the early stages – being too conservative ... We screwed up and we're going to have to do a damn sight better next time ... The problem with market research ... is that you put your finger on the pulse of today. In two or three years time when the new car is launched, the findings aren't valid.' This is reminiscent of Akio Morita's remarks – see Chapter 4.
28. *The Financial Times*, 9 April 1991. Mazda's radical approach to new products is not limited to the market niche strategy: in 1992 it took a lead in hydrogen-powered vehicles (in the pursuit of 'zero-emission engines') with a non-polluting prototype (the HR-X) travelling 200 km between refuelling, at speeds of up to 150 kph. BMW claims similar achievements using hydrogen.
29. Graves notes that the Japanese assemblers vary in their techniques for product development but that there are organizational similarities.

30. Disc brakes appeared on Lanchester Cars in 1904 and AC Cycle Cars in 1914 (both British companies). It was thirty-five years before they appeared again on cars (Chrysler in the USA) only to be phased out after five years. In 1956 Citroën is credited by Abernathy (1978, Appendix 1) with the first successful long-term application of disc brakes in volume production, although Jaguar had fitted them to all its cars for some time before this having had a connection with the original Lanchester company.

6 Customer–Supplier Relationships

We saw at the beginning of this book that the vehicle assemblers and component manufacturers have always had important relationships – starting with technical collaboration in craft production. Mass production reduced the importance of these relationships: lean production requires them to be renovated and revised. This demands a new study of customer–supplier relationships, to provide a framework for analyzing them and for making strategies accordingly.

■ Development of concepts

The classification of the repeated transactions between a selling company and a buying company as 'a relationship' is relatively new. Traditional marketing-oriented management literature tends to extend the themes of consumer marketing to industrial situations. One of the results of this is the tacit assumption that industrial customers (like consumers) are passive and that the activity in the transaction comes from the supplier. Such literature does go as far as discussing 'buyer behaviour' but, again, this is grounded in consumer, not industrial, markets (Kotler, 1976; McCarthy, 1978; Corey, 1976). More recently, marketing writers have begun to amend this situation. Roy Shapiro (1986) and Benson Shapiro (1988), describe new approaches to relationships, caricatured by the latter as 'close encounters of the four kinds'.

For its part, traditional purchasing literature is similarly presumptuous. Negotiation, for example, has been treated as the means whereby the 'active' buyer gains control over the 'passive' sales representative (England, 1970; Lee and Dobler, 1971; Westing, Fine and Zenz, 1976; Webster and Wind, 1972; Sheth, 1973). New editions of old texts have, during the 1980s, made passing reference to relationships (Baily and Farmer, 1990; Baily, 1987; Dobler et al., 1990) but it is only recently that new books have appeared which pay more serious attention to the subject (Carlisle and Parker, 1989; Farmer and Ploos von Amstel, 1991; Slack, 1991; Bessant, 1991; Sako, 1992; Syson, 1992).

In the 1960s, Macaulay hinted at the role of relationships when pointing out that formal contracts are rarely the most important part of interfirm deals: '[The] contract ... often plays an important role in business, but other factors are significant. To understand the functions of contract[s], the whole system of conducting exchanges must be explored fully' (Macaulay, 1963). The 'whole system' which Macaulay suggests we should explore is what we now call the 'relationship'. The work of the international group of university-based researchers known as Industrial Marketing and Purchasing (IMP) Group (Hakansson, 1982, pp. 10–27) has begun this exploration and produced an 'interaction approach', based upon the observation that both buyers and sellers are active in the transactions connected with industrial groups. This concept, grounded in interorganizational theory (Van de Ven *et al.*, 1975) and those of the new institutionalists (characterized by Williamson's transaction cost economics) is summarized in Figure 6.1.

The IMP model begins by identifying four types of variable which describe and influence the interaction between buying and selling companies:

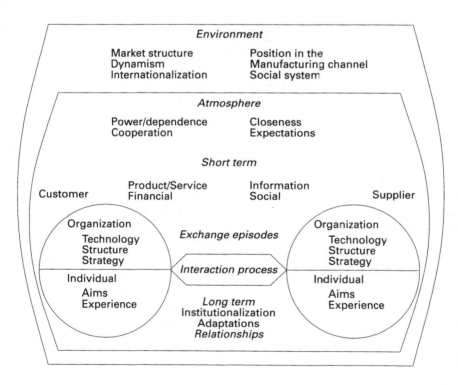

Source: Hakansson (1982). Reprinted with the permission of John Wiley & Sons Ltd, from *International Marketing and Purchasing of Industrial Goods*, by H. Hakansson © 1982 John Wiley & Sons.

Figure 6.1 IMP interactive model for buyer–seller relationships

- The **elements** and **process** of interaction.
- The **participants** involved in the interaction (individually and organization- ally).
- The **environment** in which the interaction takes place.
- The **atmosphere** affecting and affected by the interaction.

The IMP findings, and those of some of the individual writers within it (e.g. Ford, 1980) stress the importance of considering both the short-term interaction process – 'episodes': a selection of exchanges (product/service, information, financial, social)' – and the long-term: the 'relationship'. The latter is characterized by Ford (1978) as 'routinized', implying that the episodic relationship becomes a matter of expectation and behaviour patterns which are taken for granted. The product/ service and financial exchanges appear to be straightforward (but none the less important in their detail: e.g. delivery on time, payment by due date, etc.). The social exchange is characterized by IMP as the means for reducing uncertainty in the relationship (a subject comprehensively covered by Hakansson *et al.*, 1976) and credited, in the long term, with an 'interlocking' effect on the two firms, developing trust between them.

The information exchange is understood to cover several types of communication of data although there is no direct reference in this part of the IMP interaction model to technology: perhaps a 'technology (design) exchange episode' should be added to the existing four to complete the picture.[1]

Within the routinization of the relationship, IMP specify the institutionaliza- tion of expectations and contact patterns (taken-for-granted assumptions), and adaptations which each partner must make to propagate the relationship. Ford (1980) notes that the level of adaptations grows with the life of the relationship, with changes to practice becoming institutionalized and resulting in cost savings (mutual benefit for both partners).

Among the interacting parties, IMP identify three organizational and two personal factors. At the level of the firm, there is the matter of technology – different levels of ability will, it is argued, affect the nature of the relationship, and the structure and size of each partner. For the individuals concerned with the interaction, personal aims and experience will affect behaviour and performance, and thus the relationship. This is true both in the direct sense (e.g. inexperienced buyers may not manage effective relationships with experienced sales representa- tives) and in the indirect, or policy-making, mode (e.g. inexperienced buyers are always put in charge of machined parts, because they are simple to buy and there is no tooling, with the result that machined parts suppliers deal with a series of inexperienced buyers, each of whom stays only a short time before being moved on to more complicated buying responsibilities).

The IMP model places the interaction within an 'atmosphere' – defined as the combination of specific variables. The economic dimension of the interaction is captured by assessing the 'closeness' of the relationship – the transaction costs may be reduced by improved closeness of the partners – while the control dimension is addressed by analysis of the power/dependence position of the partners. In developing this point, Hardwick and Ford (1986) conclude that the dependence of the buyer upon the supplier may be involuntary, but that the commitment shown is necessarily a positive factor.

Finally, the IMP model defines relevant 'environmental' factors: the structure, internationalization and dynamism in the marketplace, the prevalent social system, and the stage in the manufacturing channel (one could say value chain) at which the interaction takes place.

The IMP model is a very useful bridge between the two fields of theory on which it draws and the operational arena it addresses. It does not refer to collaboration *per se*, but much of the related IMP literature, particularly that on 'networking', bears a close relationship to the theories described in Chapter 4.[2] Much of the casework subsequently related to the model has been carried out in manufacturing industry, suggesting a relevance of the interaction concept to the automotive industry. This does indeed appear to be the case, and further reference will be made to the interactive approach in discussing the models for relationships which are introduced below.

Oliver Williamson's (1975) transaction cost economics approach, with its contrast between hierarchical organization (in which transaction costs are supposedly minimized through reduction in opportunism on the part of the subcontractor) and subcontracting, later (1986) developed into a model of 'obligational contracting' – somewhere between the two extremes. In this case, Williamson suggests that the asset specificity (discussed in Chapter 4) becomes the crucial factor in deciding upon how developed a relationship should become. In other words, the decision on which firm should carry out the operations in question depends on more than short-term considerations: investments in skills and equipment on the part of the supplier, for example, cannot be ignored by the customer in deciding between vertical integration and subcontracting.

This concept, in conjunction with Dore's (1987) 'relational contracting' – based upon the concept of perceived and actual high levels of trust and moral trading in Japan – are brought together conveniently by Sako (1992) in her spectrum of relationships from arm's-length contract relation to obligational contract relation (ACR–OCR). Sako echoes the ideas of Hirschman (1970), who characterized relationships as ranging from 'voice' at one extreme (i.e. the supplier and customer engage in a discussion on matters regarding the relationship), to 'exit' at the other (i.e. if the supplier does not comply exactly with the customer's demands, the latter looks elsewhere for a supplier) (see also Helper, 1987 and 1991). Developing this idea, Sako discerns a remoteness at one extreme and a closeness at the other (cf IMP model), arguing, on the basis of British and Japanese case studies in the electronics industry, for the potential efficiency offered by the latter.

The key dimensions differentiating the arm's-length relation from the obligational are seen by Sako as the degree of interdependence between the two parties and the timespan for reciprocity. The first of these, analyzed by Sako in terms of 'goodwill trust' and 'competence trust' is similar to the interaction concept discussed above. The second is particularly interesting in that it captures a practical factor of subcontracting ('looking after No. 1') in the social networking concept which runs through much of the literature on relationships (particularly that of the IMP). As Sako says:

The greater specificity and underlying calculation involved in reciprocal activities in ACR [arm's-length contract relation] are a reflection of the reluctance of ACR traders to accept a favour which they feel they cannot return in the near future. In contrast, OCR [obligational contract relation] traders feel that mutual indebtedness or obligatedness at any time is a normal state of affairs which sustains a relationship. (Sako 1992, p. 10)

Carlisle and Parker (1989) also centre their argument on the commitment (cf Sako's indebtedness) required on the part of customer and supplier in order to establish effective relationships, with a 'win–win' objective. This is seen as realizable or operable through a 'mandate team' approach, which the authors have developed as a practical method, basing their analysis of organizations on the work of Lievegoed (1973). This approach and the conclusions of Axelrod (1984) regarding the benefits of a tit-for-tat strategy in the classic prisoner's dilemma game (implying that treating a supplier well will result in being well treated as a customer) find resonance in the concept of firms 'serving' their suppliers. This has been suggested by Kanter (1985), characterizing suppliers as the 'fifth constituency' for which companies must seek to provide in addition to themselves (the others being customers, employees, communities and society at large). Kanter herself redevelops this concept (1989) towards the general concept of partnerships (i.e. characterizing customer–supplier interdependence as an example of the strategy of collaboration).

Extension of the relationship concept invokes the subject of 'supply chain management' (Macbeth *et al.*, 1989a, 1989b; Macbeth and Ferguson, 1990) and 'pipeline management' (Farmer and Ploos van Amstel, 1991). These are basically sub-sets of logistics, concerned with optimizing the whole value chain through balancing, resource auditing and relationship monitoring. Macbeth *et al.* have developed this concept to the stage of using a 'tool' to measure, or position, relationships by assessing the extent to which selected factors have been optimized.

The basis of the positioning tool is that these factors can be applied to any pair of firms (customer and supplier) and the relationship may be compared with the 'ideal' defined through research of a wide sample of firms. Inevitably, weightings are necessary for some or all of the factors to make the method relevant to any given context. Macbeth *et al.* explain this as follows:

Ideally, the positioning tool will be able to easily accommodate these context-specific aspects and it will then be able to be used stand alone, in a repeating cycle of applications to inform and monitor the improvement paths. The real utility of the tool ... is that it provides an agenda for discussion between the companies. (Macbeth *et al.*, 1989b)

Cousins (1992) has developed a more sophisticated technique, which he calls the Vendor Management Model – a supplier selection and development approach employing multi-criteria decision-making methodologies. It is clear from such developments that there is much scope for use of such computer-based models to aid purchasing managers in their practical approaches to supply relationships.

Viewed broadly, the supply chain management concept can be seen as a part of networking as discussed by IMP (see Ford, 1990). Slack (1991) pursues this idea, concluding that a network can be described a series of supply relationships and that supply chain management is, by derivation, a networking approach to value chain optimization. A diagrammatic summary of writers on relationships, and connections between them, is given in Figure 6.2.

■ Discussion of theoretical approaches

The grounding for relationship theories identified by several writers – Williamson's transaction cost economics – provides a rich and useful mix of personal attributes (e.g. opportunism, guile) and systemic factors (e.g. asset specificity). This is very helpful in expanding the theory to apply to the sorts of relationship studied in this book.

The preoccupation with networks, apparent not only in IMP literature but also in other recent writing, is relevant to this research and must be addressed in the factors into which relationships are segmented for analysis. The nature of

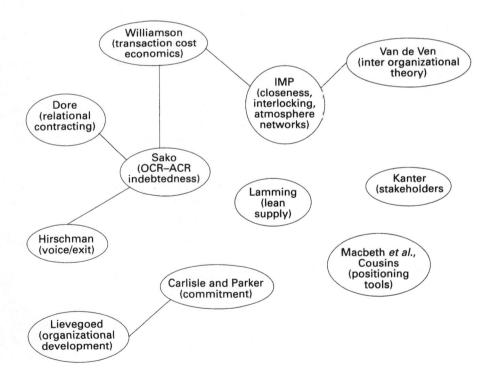

Figure 6.2 Summary of writers on relationships

competition (and within it, collaboration) is the factor which provides this address in the models which are described below.

Supply chain management must also be considered, although perhaps not as a factor of the individual relationship. The manner in which the customer becomes involved in 'suppliers' suppliers' is connected to the relationship between buyer and supplier, but is addressed more specifically later in discussion of strategies for suppliers, since it is deemed to lie outside the individual link.

The practical problem of make or buy is also concerned here, and examination of its traditional use suggests a basic reason for development of relationships. It has been used traditionally as a tactical tool, principally for achieving utilization of capacity. This represents a stark choice between Williamson's subcontracting (buy) and organizational hierarchy (make). Nowadays it is seen as a more strategic matter – defining a company's core business (what to include within the organizational hierarchy – vertical integration). All non-core business may be strategically subcontracted.

The basic problem with the make or buy decision was traditionally that the customer rarely knew, as a result of the choice, how much value was being added and at what cost. Cost accountancy within the organization was generally not good enough to show these two factors accurately, so the make option would be more influenced by political factors (e.g. using existing capacity – including labour – because it was there) than by genuine cost/value calculations. The extreme of this is, of course, the stagnation of vertical integration in mass production, in which the supreme factor was ownership of the process: a mixture of myopic greed and insecurity.

The buy option would also not provide the necessary value/cost data, since all the buyer was provided with was the price – a complex factor hiding many different costs.

A developed relationship, however, should be able to provide better cost/value data through the process of the two parties working closely together, sharing information, etc. This, after all, was the basis of success in Japan after World War II. In searching for a model of relationships, therefore, the need for strategic make or buy techniques should be borne in mind.

The need to develop a useful model was the foremost consideration throughout this research and the remainder of the chapter is devoted to a discussion of this, taking account of the points above.

■ Selection of factors in a relationship

The author's early interviews revealed that the relationship between an automotive assembler and its components supplier should be considered in the light of practices (similar to IMP's 'episodes'), attitudes and immediate environmental factors – specifically the nature of competition in the supply market. These factors could be used as a framework for analyzing relationships and thus for developing a better understanding of them.

The initial list was compiled during these interviews. The list consisted of the factors shown in Table 6.1. Employing a series of face-to-face interviews for this purpose meant that the factors could be extensively discussed and developed gradually. The interview method was thus seen as a more appropriate approach than a postal survey, which might have reached more firms but left more of the interpretation to the researcher.

Each of these factors is discussed in detail below. First, however, it is important to consider the rationale for this selection.

The nature of competition in the components supply market is the practical manifestation of many other environmental factors – economic activity and dynamism, technology trajectories, international developments, etc. As such, it might be argued that it is a context within which the relationship exists, rather than a feature of it. It is possible to trace an influence in the reverse direction, however: the manner in which the relationship is built and developed will itself determine, to an extent, the nature of competition for the supplier. For example, if customers are encouraging suppliers to vie with competitors for the lowest piece price, then competition will become cutthroat. If customers require suppliers (via closer relationships) to develop new technologies – beyond those suppliers' existing

Table 6.1 Factors selected for analyzing customer–vendor relationships[a]

Relationship factor	Examples
The nature of competition in the components supply market	Price-based, cutthroat, driven by negotiation, technology-based, collaborative, etc.
The basis upon which sourcing decisions are made	Competitive bids (price-based), supplier accreditation, long-term track record, etc.
The role played by data and information transfer, and the approach towrds managing it jointly	One-way, closed or open book, transparency of costs, electronic data interchange, etc.
The attitude to capacity planning and the approach towards managing it jointly	Independent, shared problem, tactical make or buy, strategic planning, etc.
Delivery practices	Buyer's whim, eratic, JIT, etc.
The manner in which price changes are dealt with, and the attitude towards them	Traditional price negotiation/game playing, price hikes, suicidal pricing, collaboration on progressive cost reductions, etc.
The attitude towards product quality and the approach towards managing it	Inspection – retrospection, goods inward inspection, aggressive campaigns, joint efforts, parts per million quality, etc.
The role of research and development (products and processes) in the relationship, and the approach towards managing it	Assembler designs and dictates – supplier follows instructions, shared development, supplier leads in specific technologies

Notes: [a] This is the original list: see text for a ninth factor added later.

capabilities – competition in the supply industry might be characterized by collaboration, and so on.

The basis upon which sourcing decisions are made is one of the clearest indicators of development in relationships provided by the interviews throughout the research period. The use of bids, coupled with the choice of lowest price, is perhaps one of the most defined characteristics of primitive purchasing, evoking similarly basic responses from suppliers. The adopted research method of testing purchasers' assertions by cross-checking with suppliers was especially enlightening with regard to this factor.

The role played by data and information transfer, and the approach towards managing it jointly have both personal and technical aspects. On the first level, the relationship is affected by the integrity of communication and information transfer between the individuals involved in it, e.g. is the buyer honest in intimating the level of business which might be forthcoming for a particular component (i.e. projected vehicle build rates)? At the second level, data transfer between companies has taken on a new meaning in the 1980s with the advent of electronic data interchange (EDI) and the general growth in use of microcomputers in business. Thus a measure of a relationship might be the extent to which the parties have invested in compatible technology for transmission and reception of data (an example of asset specificity), and coped with the concomitant problems, e.g. intellectual property ownership/protection.

The attitude to capacity planning and the approach towards managing it jointly is another major area raised by interviewees throughout the research. At one level a special case of information transfer, capacity planning also has about it the air of strategy: investment in appropriate new plant for a new contract – complementary assets – is more an act of faith on the part of the supplier than simply a provision for guaranteed business from a particular customer. The 'faith' is a reflection of the closeness of the relationship.

Delivery practices are once again related to both the business and technical environment within which the relationship exists and to the closeness of the relationship itself. The recognition of just-in-time and the development and application of some associated concepts in the West during the 1980s[3] provided targets for suppliers which could be easily set by customers. The closeness of relationships could thus be assessed by analyzing the degree to which customer and supplier co-operated in developing true just-in-time delivery, rather than simply the imposition upon the supplier of the buyer's demands.

The manner in which price changes are dealt with is a central theme of purchasing, theory and practice. The traditional approach has long been one of confrontation and negotiation. It was clear from early interviews, and reinforced by subsequent research in Japan (where the situation is very different, as will be discussed later), that such practices were wasteful in the long term: the customer's short-term gain from forcing down prices would eventually lead to poor supply, and consequently higher real costs. The approach to price agreements and changes and the fundamental attitude towards them were thus chosen as a focus for attention in modelling relationships.

The attitude towards product quality and the approach towards managing it have changed significantly in many industries over the 1980s. The development of this factor from traditional 'inspection' techniques (and related disputes) to a more strategic approach was an obvious factor for inclusion.

As seen earlier, the technological capabilities of suppliers appeared to have been largely neglected by assemblers in the West, but have been more integrated with the efforts of the automotive firms in Japan, to good effect. **The role of research and development** in the relationship, and the approach towards managing it were thus selected as a factor for monitoring, in order to identify where best practice might lie.

Having selected these factors as the basis for analysis of the relationship, subsequent interviews were focused partly upon testing the validity and completeness of the list. Only one further factor was added – by an interviewee in North America (who had extensive experience in dealing with Japanese customers): **the level of pressure in the relationship**.

The IMP interactive model was initially criticized for concentrating too much on cooperation within relationships and omitting discussion of competition. This reflects, in part, a danger in assuming that developed relationships, with high degrees of commitment and dependence, become steady and comfortable positions with goodwill between the parties compensating for operational problems. In fact, it seems that low pressure, or the absence of stress, in a relationship may be a sign of decadence and potential disaster: the concept of *kaizen* (continuous improvement) has within it the notion of never reducing the operating pressure. In other words, the better the relationship, the harder each partner must try to improve it. Level of pressure was thus added to the list of factors.[4]

■ Identification of timescale and phases

The initial interviews were conducted in the UK. From these it was apparent that three distinct phases had occurred in the previous decade. The reference years were only approximately identified. They are indicated in Table 6.2. Between each phase there had been a transformation. In the first phase, business had been good

Table 6.2 Timescale for first four models of customer–vendor relationships

First phase	Until about 1975, before the impact of the oil shocks and the consequent recession, and before the increase in international competition in the automotive industry. This was a period of relative calm with domestic demand and supply well balanced for mass producers
Second phase	Between 1975 and 1980: a period of great difficulty for assemblers and suppliers as demand fell and became unstable
Third phase	Since 1980: noticeably better attitudes towards relationships, but still difficult and unstable

for the mass producers in the UK. This had changed drastically during the mid 1970s. This is illustrated in Figure 6.3. The shock to the automotive assembly industry was severe: the impact upon suppliers was immense. Relationships between the two suffered as a result. By the turn of the decade, the supply industry was in dire straits, a situation exacerbated by the destructive relationships dominated by assemblers. Some resolution of this situation had to occur and it took the form of better relationships – or at least the public affirmation of this intention by the assemblers.

In constructing the models to describe and plot this development, customer–supplier relationships in the three phases were characterized as the traditional model, the stress model and the resolved model. In order to complete the trajectory (to best practice), a fourth model was posited. This was initially called the Japanese model – a title which was subsequently changed to the partnership model, to avoid excessive emphasis on national culture (considered inappropriate) and in order to generalize the approach for application in countries other than Japan.

■ Testing the model structure

Early interviews provided both the structure of the model and details for tracking the nine factors over the three phases and into the (proposed) fourth phase. The initial four-phase model was based upon the UK, which was clearly too limited a field for useful broadening of the results (the UK is a small player in the automotive industry, and was beset by peculiar national problems during the 1970s in addition to the economic events referred to above). Accordingly, the model was tested in Europe and North America, by many further personal interviews. It was discovered that, with some minor variations, discussed below, the phases and models were recognized by assemblers and suppliers in all cases.

It appeared that the stress model could be attributed as much to the crisis faced by mass production in the 1970s as to specific economic events. This was a significant revelation, since it pointed to a feature of the decline of mass production (cf the demise of innovation, productivity and product quality) rather than to some 'blip' in the fortunes of an otherwise healthy paradigm. It suggested furthermore that some post-mass-production component-supply best practice should be sought.

After extensive testing and refinement, therefore, the first, four-phase, model resulting from this research could be said to serve the functions of recording part of the transition from mass production to its successor (i.e. the decline of the old paradigm) and of indicating some characteristics of that successor (a new 'best practice' for customer–supplier relationships in the automotive components industry).

The model was published in an early form in 1986 based upon the UK survey, and in a developed form in 1987 (see Lamming 1986 and 1987b). A more

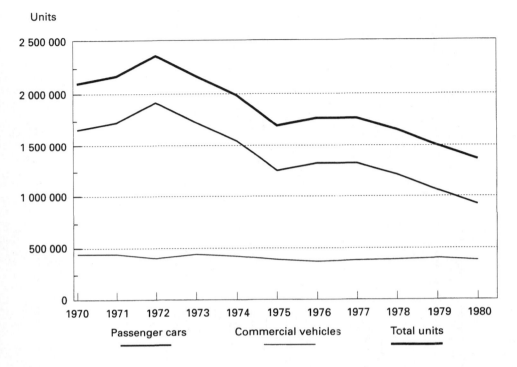

Units

Note: [a] This period is chosen in order to highlight the market conditions which were in place during the fundamental change in relationships referred to in the text.
Source: MVMA Yearbook (various years).

Figure 6.3 Vehicle production in the UK, 1970–80[a]

developed form, benefiting from continued research (1987–91) is shown in Table 6.3.

■ The four-phase model explained

The four-phase model grew from work in the UK but was substantially developed during interviews with 129 companies[5] in twelve countries in four continents.

Throughout the research in the West, interviewees in suppliers and assemblers have added to the model and analyzed and developed specific features, but never refuted its basic appropriateness to their national situation. As might be expected, national variations appeared, reinforcing some of the observations made regarding the industry in Chapter 2 (e.g. the closeness of national ties in some European countries: the stress model was not as severe in West Germany).

The data in Figure 6.4 show that the severe market collapse experienced by UK component suppliers during the 1970s also happened in a general sense

Table 6.3 The four-phase model of customer–supplier relations

Model	Nature of competition	Basis of sourcing decisions	Role of data/information exchange	Management of capacity	Delivery practice	Dealing with price changes	Attitude to quality	Role of R&D	Level of pressure
Traditional before 1975	Closed but friendly; plenty of business	Wide; enquiries; lowest bid; price-based	Very restricted – minimum necessary	Few problems: some poor scheduling	Large quantities; buyer's choice: steady	General negotiation (annual); a game win/lose	Inspection: arguments/ *laissez-faire*	One-sided: either assembler or supplier	Low/medium: steady: predictable
Stress 1972–85	Closed and deadly; chaotic	'Dutch Auctions'; price-based	A weapon; one-way; supplier must open books	Spasmodic; no system to deal with chaos	Unstable; no control; variable; no notice of changes	Conflict in negotiation; a battle lose/lose	Aggressive campaigns; SQA, etc.	Shared, but only for cost reductions	High/unbearable: volatile
Resolved 1982 onwards	Closed; some collaboration; strategic	Price, quality and delivery	Two-way: short-term e.g. forward build	Gradually improving; linkages appearing	Smaller quantities; buyer's demands stabilizing	Annual economics plus; negotiation; win/lose	Joint effort towards improvements	Shared for developments	Medium: some sense of relief
Partnership/ Japanese 1990 onwards	Collaboration; tiering; still dynamic	Performance history; long-term source; costs	Two-way: long-term e.g. knowledge of costs	Coordinated and jointly planned	Small quantity; agreed basis; dynamic (JIT)	Annual economics + planned reductions win/win?	Joint planning for developments	Shared: some black or grey box	Very high: predictable

Auto production (000s)

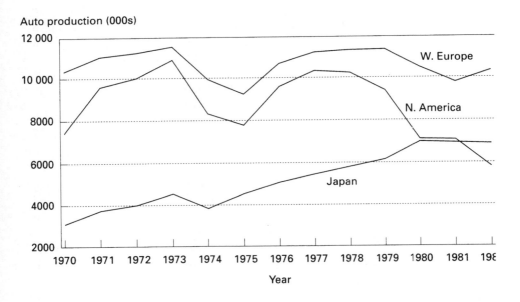

Source: MVMA *World Motor Vehicle Data Book*; SMMT *The Motor Industry of Great Britain* quoted in Altshuler *et al.* (1984, p. 19).

Figure 6.4 Automotive production in North America, Europe and Japan, 1970–82

elsewhere. Before long the severe world recession brought about major problems throughout the West. Altshuler *et al.* provide useful comment on this:

> At just this point [the late 1970s] the extraordinary period of post-war economic growth came to a close. Worldwide auto use and the demand for new cars suddenly levelled off in response to broader economic phenomena, many of them related to energy. The environmental and resource issues of the 1970s were temporarily deferred because the more ominous forecasts of resource shortages and environmental crises had all assumed a continuation of world economic growth at 1960s rates. However, the new situation of prolonged worldwide recession quickly raised even more pressing problems for the world auto industry and for persons who earned their livelihoods from auto manufacturing. (Altshuler *et al.*, 1984, p. 6)

This period had a severe effect upon employment. Altshuler *et al.* estimated that in 1979 between five and six million people were employed in auto-related business in France, Italy, Japan, Sweden, the United Kingdom, the United States, and West Germany. Two years later, they found, up to a million jobs had been lost.

The conditions which led to the stress model and its subsequent resolution occurred, to varying extents, in all the mass production countries. These were features of the demise of mass production, indicating a failure of the system to sustain a competitive position in the international automotive industry of the 1970s and 1980s. In fact, the stress model could happen at any time in a cyclical industry, simply as a result of recession. With hindsight it can be seen that a new form of competition – on the basis of partnerships in supply (in Japan) – was already beginning to influence the industry in the 1970s, bringing with it a shift in relationships more long term than those associated with business cycles.

The traditional model

As we have seen from Figure 6.3 and Figure 6.4, production of automobiles had increased steadily, in all areas, between 1969 and 1973. The long-term trend had been upward since the 1950s. During this time, assemblers had tended to buy almost all their components from their home markets.

This situation existed in Europe and in North America. The European assemblers bought between 85 per cent and 97 per cent of their components from their home country, while in the USA a similar proportion would come from within a 300 mile radius around the assembly plant. As an example, local sourcing trends in the UK are shown in Table 6.4. The data in this table illustrate the high degree to which assemblers in the UK bought from UK suppliers, and the growth of 'captive imports' (cars which appeared to the British but were actually built elsewhere) between 1973 and 1983.

The buoyant market of the early 1970s, coupled with the inherent lack of dynamism in mass production, had led to a situation in which component suppliers and their assembler customers usually had a fairly stable relationship with a moderate pace of change. Since there was plenty of business, competition was fairly friendly, but perceived to be closed – a gain of business for one supplier was a loss of business for another. This suggests that the observed growth in production was the result of an increase in existing business rather than the addition of new products.

In the context of a specific contract, competition for suppliers was defined by the buyer. This meant that the terms upon which suppliers would bid were fixed by the enquiry process. This tended to discourage innovation in the supplier: few competitive points could be gained by suggesting alterations to the customer specification. Wherever possible, the buyer would ask many suppliers[6] to bid for business and use the enquiry and post-bid negotiation process to reduce the piece price.

The basis of sourcing decisions in the traditional model was thus relatively simple: the supplier with the lowest bid would be awarded the contract, unless there were severe technical restrictions on choice. Having placed the business, however, the buyer would continue to seek cheaper sources. When this was achieved, the business could often be re-sourced easily, usually giving the

Table 6.4 Dependence of UK assemblers on local parts supply, and growth of captive imports as a proportion of vehicle sales, 1973–83

	Local content (%)[a]	Share of UK car market (%)		
		1973	1978	1983
Austin Rover production	> 90	31.9	23.5	15.8
+ UK-assembled	70–90	—	—	2.1
Total Rover sales		31.9	23.5	17.9
Ford UK production	90	22.6	16.1	15.5
+ captive imports[b]	—	—	8.6	13.4
Total Ford sales		22.6	24.7	28.9
Vauxhall and Talbot				
UK production	85	18.7	8.3	1.0
+ UK-assembled[c]	< 60	—	3.7	7.9
+ captive imports[b]	—	0.3	4.4	10.2
Total Vauxhall/Talbot sales		19.0	16.4	19.1
Other imports:				
Japanese	—	5.6	10.9	10.8
European	—	20.9	24.5	23.2
Totals:				
UK-produced	85–90	72.3	47.8	32.4
UK-assembled[c]	60–90	—	3.8	10.0
Captive imports[b]	—	0.3	13.0	23.6
Other imports	—	26.5	35.4	34.0

Notes: [a] Local content relates to factory gate price in the UK including local assembly, labour, and plant operating costs. Stamping, welding, painting, trim and final assembly account for just under 50 per cent, engine for up to 15 per cent and bulky components another 10–15 per cent. Assemblers interviewed confirmed that they were buying between 80 and 95 per cent of components in their home country at this time. [b] Captive imports refers to cars which were built outside the UK but appeared to the buying public to be British cars. [c] UK-assembled refers to cars whose engines, transmissions and major stampings were imported for kit assembly in the UK.

Source: Society of Motor Manufacturers and Traders, London, UK. Prof. D.T. Jones, Cardiff Business School, UK. Science Policy Research Unit, University of Sussex, UK.

incumbent source a chance to reduce its price to beat (or match) the new quote. Piece price is only one aspect of a bid, however, and in many cases the need for customer-funded tooling would restrain the free hand of the buyer in re-sourcing.

Underlying this practice is the assumption that the supplier and customer exist in two separate but related industries which come together only to trade. The preoccupation of the buyer with short-term advantage from finding a cheaper piece price creates this assumption. The natural response of the supplier – to gain as much from the business as possible while it has the chance – reinforces it. This is close to commodity buying, where the assumption is that the supplier either cannot or will not differentiate the product offering: price is the only criterion for choice of source. In extreme cases, this preoccupation with price made the automotive business unattractive. In the USA, as we saw earlier, the integration policies of the mass producers led the major suppliers to base their corporate business largely on non-automotive industries (see Table 2.14).

In this atmosphere, it is not surprising that exchange of data was very limited.

The two main types of operational data required for an effective relationship are product related (technical and financial) and capacity related (projected volume of required production and delivery stipulations). As we saw above, this meant that analysis for make or buy decisions rarely provided genuinely strategic choices.

Since the buying tactics were clearly aggressive (despite the relatively affable relationship) the supplier would be unwilling to provide details of cost structure, etc., since these would simply be used by the buyer in beating down the price. Similarly, if the supplier could see technical paths to reducing the piece price, it would keep them to itself, knowing that they might be needed to reduce prices quickly when the buyer found an alternative, cheaper source.

The buyer, meanwhile, was aware of the importance of volume predictions to the supplier: they were the basis of scale economies, tooling costs (including amortization), commitment of capacity, etc. In order to encourage the supplier to reduce piece prices, therefore, it would be in the interest of the buyer to inflate expectation of volume. The supplier, knowing that the buyer would do this, would allow for the exaggeration and work on a lower volume prediction in calculating the costs and price. The result of this bluffing process was complicated. If the supplier was new, it would not know that the buyer was inflating the requirements and might submit a low quote, based on the high expectation. The supplier which did know the game would thus be undercut and the price reduction process would begin. In this case, either the new supplier would get the business but subsequently find that the actual level of requirement was insufficient to make a profit, or the existing supplier would reduce its price to the required level and then fail to perform properly (cutting corners – on quality, etc. – in order to regain profitability from the business) or, having gained the dependence of the buyer, demand a price increase after an initial period of supply, on the basis of the reduced demand.

This process of bluff and manoeuvre, whilst it sounds grotesque, was the generally accepted basis of the traditional relationship. Moreover, it was conducted in a cavalier manner on the part of the supplier's sales representative and jovial grandeur shown by the buyer. Both sides knew that it was a waste of time but both had their motives: the buyer could show 'savings' on piece price while the supplier generally knew what he was doing and managed to win the trick.[7]

Once business was placed, therefore, the conditions set up by the traditional model meant that uncertainty remained. For the supplier this was represented by the constant risk of losing the business to a cheaper source; for the buyer, there was the perpetual risk of the supplier failing to supply, because of the corner cutting and lack of trust. Capacity planning, delivery performance and product quality were the natural casualties.

The normal method of indicating delivery requirements within the mass-production supply process in the automotive industry was the material control schedule. The purchase order, issued by the buyer, would stipulate price details and reference to technical specifications (the customer's drawing, etc.), and an indicative volume requirement. It would not contain delivery dates, etc., this being the responsibility of the material control (or similarly named) department. This technique is called blanket ordering and is widely used in manufacturing industries where variable quantities of standard or specified components or materials are required regularly over a long period.[8]

The material control schedule would be issued under the auspices of the blanket order, in relation to forward-build projections for vehicles. Details of this projection varied from one assembler to another but always included some 'firm' commitment (e.g. quantities of the component which should be delivered in the next month) and usually some indication of the second and third months into the future, specified in weekly amounts. Sometimes, the medium-term requirement (i.e. the second month) would be 'firm for materials', meaning that the customer would cover the supplier's purchase of raw materials for this period (recognizing the lead time of material deliveries to the supplier). Attached to each class of commitment on the schedule would be a legal arrangement regarding responsibility, recompense for cancellation, etc.

Despite the steady nature of mass production mentioned above and the apparent logic and well-planned nature of the scheduling systems, assemblers found difficulty in forecasting a model mix to match their own market. Thus the material control schedule was traditionally regarded with deep suspicion. Short-notice changes were commonplace and deliveries covered by schedules would be 'turned round at the receiving dock' (i.e. delivery would be denied by the customer) when, for example, mistakes had been made in requesting them, or a strike at the assembler meant that no parts were required. The suspicion became institutionalized to such an extent that suppliers would regard schedules as an indication at best, and an irrelevance at worst. Thus capacity planning at the operational level was as hit and miss an affair as the original planning of investment for a new contract, under the traditional model of the relationship.

Mass-production delivery requirements were based upon batch quantities, sometimes calculated by economic batch quantity theory but more often a matter of storekeepers' judgement/guesswork. The relatively high volume of automobile manufacture and large size of some of the sub-assemblies and major components meant that weekly and sometimes daily deliveries were commonplace in the industry. Nevertheless, the large amount of indirect labour employed to sort out problems of non-delivery (material control departments, progress chasers, roving troubleshooters, etc.) revealed that delivery practices were not under control.

The blanket ordering system had provision for technical and price amendments to be added without the need for a new order. The latter formed a large part of the traditional purchasing role, entailing significant amounts of negotiation. The need to increase prices would be argued by the supplier, in connection with rising costs (labour, materials and 'economics').[9] The buyer would employ all the tactics seen above (i.e. at the sourcing stage) in trying to reduce the amount of the increase. In common with bargaining practised worldwide for centuries this would consist of the supplier asking for more than was needed and the buyer beating the price down (thereby earning a 'saving' to his or her credit) to a level probably not far from what the supplier actually needed. A supplier who did not practise this custom (arguably a part of human nature), submitting instead a genuine claim based upon true figures, would end up with less than was needed to remain profitable in that contract.

Thus the traditional model treated negotiation as a 'game' – ostensibly win/lose (i.e. the buyer was supposed to win the argument and achieve a saving, whilst the supplier was supposed to have lost some of the increase originally requested). Considerable managerial effort and thought went into systems which ensured that the price increase demand and, consequently, the saving, were genuine – in order to judge the buyer's performance. The insinuation was that the buyer might get a supplier to submit a high price increase – even in writing – and then agree to reduce it to a predetermined level, to make the buyer look good. Add to this the considerable quantities of expensive lunches and Christmas appreciation gifts, etc., accepted by automotive industry buyers, and it is not difficult to grasp the atmosphere which existed in relationships under the traditional model. The level of pressure was low, with occasional increases during arguments or re-sourcing exercises, or when dealing with crises arising out of mistakes or short-notice changes.

The attitude towards quality in mass production was generally one of inspection of work followed by rectification where necessary. In the IMVP assembly plant world survey, the areas set aside for rework were measured and found to be very large in mass producers (and very small in lean producers) (see Krafic and MacDuffie, 1989). The same *laissez faire* attitude was evident in the relationship between buyer and supplier and in the expectations of the former with regard to the latter. The traditional model phase occurred before the realization of new (or rediscovered) quality techniques (statistical process control, employee involvement groups, etc.) despite the fact that they had been in operation in Japan for over a decade.[10]

Initiatives in R&D, as we saw in Chapter 5, came largely from the assemblers under mass production. The suppliers, whilst they had technical skills, were seldom involved in new vehicle development. Some larger suppliers who had proprietary technology would naturally provide most of the input in specific cases, but the atmosphere even then was often one of providing what the customer had requested, rather than the supplier advising what was needed. In short, R&D were not shared. This was expressed in an interview with a German assembler who referred to the *unterschrift* of the car (literally, the signature). The interviewee explained that whilst the supplier might make an excellent component, only the assembler's engineers could ensure that the car had, for example, its 'Mercedesness'. Whilst there is an obvious intuitive attraction in this view, the traditional model took the principle to extremes: the supplier was rarely required to offer advice or to innovate.

Discussion of the traditional model

It would be wrong to say that customers and suppliers did not have long-term relationships in the traditional model phase: many had dealt together for half a century. The nature of each specific transaction, however, was transient and long experience of the other was no guarantee of stability or satisfaction. This was, perhaps, the natural result of the lack of pressure leading to a lack of effort to improve: mass production had led to the demise of 'drive' in the relationship. This was a situation akin to the problems of vertical integration: the long-term suppliers were exhibiting some of the indolence of the in-house divisions in competitive terms. In vertical integration, where there was no turnover of suppliers at all, the pressure to perform was very low and had to be artificially created periodically by edicts and 'initiatives' from group headquarters.

The constant search for price reductions by re-sourcing (or the threat of it), which was a feature of the traditional model, seems at first to be a reasonable activity for purchasing. The nature of full costs was not revealed by piece price, however, as explained above. Furthermore, it was generally recognized that a new source might be lower in piece price than the existing source for many reasons (a low price – even a loss leader price – offered in order to gain access to a new customer; no sunk costs to write off since no technical involvement in early trials for new component/vehicle; a misinterpretation of the specification of component requirements, etc.), but the traditional model ignored this.

In summary, then, the traditional model provides a picture of haphazard purchasing, dealing in an inefficient manner with poor information, in a buoyant market, with little real competition requiring it to improve. The threat of re-sourcing (which might have led to increased competition, in theory) was outweighed by the stability of the old-boy network and lack of real alternatives for buyers.

It might have remained that way, until competition overtook it. However, the demise of mass production was accelerated by the macroeconomic shocks caused by the oil crises in the mid-1970s and, to an extent, by labour management problems. The result was that the level of automotive production dived in 1974, exacerbating all the factors which had been causing difficulties in component supply, exposing the weaknesses of the traditional model relationship and resulting in a great deal of stress.

The stress model

It is possible to envisage the stress model evolving from purely technological pressures, with the buyer urging favoured suppliers to invest and gain benefits from the competitive advantages available in new practices and plant. There are some ideas here which might be incorporated in best practice and it is not unlike the situation in Japan in the 1950s which we saw earlier. In the Western car industry in the mid-1970s, however, the stress was generated by fear for survival. (It has reappeared since in various guises, as we shall see later.)

The first step in the move towards the stress model was a desperate attempt to reduce unit costs. The problems followed because a fundamentally long-term objective (cost reduction) had to be met quickly – by a squeeze on suppliers' prices. The balance of the traditional model was upset since one side – the buyer – had not only to 'win' in price negotiations but having won, to squeeze a little more out of the supplier to achieve a further saving. The rational approach towards improvement in competitive position broke down: the resultant marginal costing led to suicidal pricing and, inevitably, to insolvencies.

During the stress model phase, all the inefficiencies of the traditional model were exposed and performance worsened. The pressure on buyers to achieve price reductions increased to a level where the understanding between individuals, built up in many cases over a long period, despite the traditionally transient nature of contracts, was often destroyed. Mass production, under which firms had become accustomed to growth and relative stability, was unable to deal with major change and instability.

Competition between suppliers inevitably became fiercer as components markets were reduced in size. The pressure passed on by buyers to suppliers, however, was itself a cause of increased competition in the supply market, as suppliers stretched themselves to find ways of cutting their prices and costs. The bidding process described above degenerated into what is sometimes known as the Dutch auction. This is the set of tactics employed by a buyer which persuades a supplier to reduce a bid price by indicating that a competitor for the business has quoted a lower price. Having achieved the reduction in bid price, the buyer then goes to the other supplier and does likewise, gradually forcing the bid price down, possibly to a level below that needed by the supplier for basic profitability. So desperate were component firms to retain business during this phase that sound business sense was not always in evidence. Competition in the components industry became chaotic.

As might be expected, concern for planning capacity, both at the strategic level and operationally, became obscured by the more basic worry over survival. Delivery practice also became spasmodic as assemblers tried to balance material requirements with unstable sales forecasts. Some of the basic instruments of communication were set aside: one component supplier in the UK said in an interview that he had been supplying one assembler on the basis of a daily telephone call, without material control schedules, for eighteen months. At the time, of course, it was not realized that this system might actually be better: with hindsight, the comparison with *kanban* in a just-in-time delivery system is obvious.[11]

The exchange of data between customer and supplier also changed during the stress model phase. As noted above, a feature of traditional negotiation had been the relative weakness of the buyer in technical and product-specific details. This weakness meant that suppliers, whilst rarely pulling the wool over buyers' eyes, were usually able to rely on better knowledge of real costs and thus to control the negotiation. The response of the customers to this was the creation of purchasing intelligence teams – specialists in product and process design – who could advise the buyers on target prices and also help in negotiations with such matters as tooling costs, overhead rates, labour rates, and production process costs. This development had taken place during the traditional model phase,[12] but became a major strength under the stress model, giving buyers an advantage to which the suppliers' sales representative was unaccustomed. At the same time, the desperation of suppliers to obtain and keep business meant that buyers, backed up by their new advisers and under stress themselves to find cost reductions for the vehicle, were able to insist that suppliers relinquish their traditional weapon – retention of cost details.

The costs that the customers were trying to identify in their suppliers' processes were, however, just the current costs. The assemblers had little idea of how to reduce them, so most of the negotiations employing the cost data were directed at squeezing the supplier's margins rather than actually lowering the costs in the long term.

The suppliers were forced to open their books to buyers, but at the same time they had to cope without any real volume forecasting or the quasi-legal coverage of material control schedules. The mass production paradigm relied upon scale economies, which had disappeared and would probably never return in some cases. The price increases which were required, under mass production, to offset the instability and lower volumes were not forthcoming. Indeed, piece prices were being forced down by buyers who held all the cards.

Not surprisingly, many firms left the components industry at this time. For those that managed to stay, however, there were two further fundamental challenges: the need to improve product quality and the need to become involved in cost reductions through product redesign – including research and development.

By the mid-1970s it was becoming clear that the basis of international competition was moving towards product quality. It is not clear where this started but it is probable that the North American assemblers felt that superior quality would be the way to combat the Japanese cars imported to the USA in the 1960s which were inexpensive, and the European cars which were prestigious and, in the case of Volkswagen, reputed to be reliable. It was the American assemblers who brought systematized quality control for suppliers (supplier quality assurance: SQA) into Europe, in the late 1960s and early 1970s. Thus when the stress model phase arrived, suppliers were not only faced with the challenges outlined above but also the need to invest in systems to ensure quality control, in line with assemblers' requests. Nor were those requests uniform – each customer had a different set of criteria. It was possible to pool the ideas, however, and please all parties, but this represented extra indirect costs for the suppliers (not immediately recoverable in piece price) at a time when pressure on prices was already threatening to remove any margins. Once again, the mass production paradigm could not help: increased product quality meant increased quality control and extra cost. The traditional trade off in mass production terms is shown in Figure 6.5.

It is not clear whether or not the aggressive SQA campaigns of assemblers in the 1970s did actually improve product quality. Suppliers reported improvements in approaches to quality (use of manuals, formal systems, adoption of techniques, etc.),[13] and those who subsequently gained formal approval, almost always (perhaps inevitably) gave credit to the schemes for improvements in their level of control over quality and production. It is clear that adoption of SQA formalities,

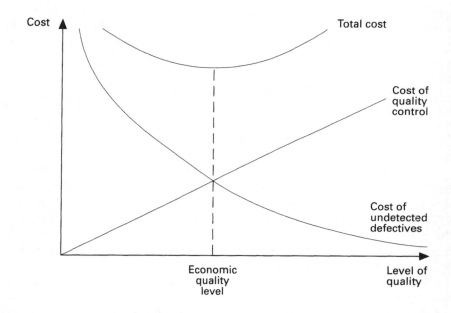

Note: [a] This is a traditional concept. The straight line marked 'cost of quality' implies that the level of quality (measured by reject rates, etc.) improves, as the number of inspectors, amount of equipment, etc. increases. The notion of economic quality level – often expressed operationally as acceptable quality level (AQL) – is based upon a trade off between this cost and the cost (lost sales, rework, etc.) of defective work which is not detected by inspection. It is traditionally assumed for the diagram that only these two costs exist; thus the total cost of quality is the sum of the two.

Figure 6.5 Mass production approach to cost of quality[a]

which became a precondition for being considered as a supplier for new business, represented extra cost for the suppliers. In other words, the mass production ethic caused people to think in terms of strengthening traditional quality efforts (extra inspectors, measuring machines, better rectification processes, etc.) rather than using lateral approaches such as employee involvement and 'quality is free'.[14]

The idea of suppliers becoming involved with product development appears at first to have been an enlightened move for the assemblers. In fact, it was another sign of the desperation which was abroad in the stress model phase. The supplier involvement which was solicited was directed towards cost reduction – perhaps recognizing that this potential had been present all along, and that now the customer wanted the benefit. Thus another of the supplier's traditional tactical strengths was to be stripped away. Ford, often the innovator in such practices, instituted a programme in which suppliers which came forward with ideas for reduction in a piece price through redesign could retain half of the saving. This showed a relatively mature approach to the problem. The programme was successful and has been used again subsequently.

Suppliers which had previously eschewed R&D did not begin to invest in it during the stress model phase. Some larger suppliers had significant R&D resources already, of course, and these remained. It does appear, however, that suppliers which managed to remain in the industry realized that product technology was now perceived to be partly their domain and began to think accordingly.

Clearly the level of pressure in relationships during this phase was very high. Indeed it was not simply pressure but stress itself. It was a volatile period and some firms found it unbearable.

Discussion of the stress model

When the stress model was first developed during this research, it appeared to be a phase in which control was lost. Subsequent research and the process of ideas generation have changed this picture to one of an inevitable development in which some tough lessons were learned. The curious thing about the model is the number of features which come close to lean production principles: the opening of information channels; the acceptance of working to short-notice requirements; the involvement of suppliers in product development; the adoption of disciplines in quality control (notwithstanding the omission of employee involvement) and working under pressure. In each case, however, the application was incomplete or misguided and appears to have been involuntary.

Clearly the stress model phase was a crisis for the components industry, but perhaps it was one which had to occur for a more fundamental change to take place. The damaging effects of the stress model led to a situation in which assemblers in some countries began to find difficulty in identifying competent sources of supply, as suppliers either left the industry voluntarily or went into liquidation. By the end of the decade, it appears that the assemblers realized this and a new form of relationship began to emerge, bringing with it a resolution of the stress.

The resolved model

There was not, of course, any sudden change, nor was every assembler affected to the same extent.[16] The realization of the importance of relationships, as opposed to individual deals, occurred to assemblers towards the end of the stress model phase and gradually resulted in a redefinition of roles.

Since the components industry had been through a shake out there were naturally fewer competitors for most suppliers. Thus, competition in the resolved model phase was less chaotic than during the stress model phase, although whilst vehicle production stabilized and began to increase there was still the notion of 'closed' competition. Some collaboration between European component suppliers began to be evident, although mostly as a result of Nissan's plans to set up in the UK (e.g. Nihon Radiator/TI Silencers, 1982; Ikeda Bussan/Hoover, 1985). At the same time there was talk of 'systems' in automobile design, giving rise to the concept of suppliers collaborating to supply extended technologies. Thus, several factors related to competition brought together component supplier companies who would not normally have dealt with one another. Collaboration appeared as a potentially necessary part of competition during this phase, beyond the licensing arrangements with which some of the firms were familiar.

The investments made in improving supplier quality assurance during the late 1970s,[17] plus the recognition of the value of quality methods employed in Japan (many of them American), meant that by the early 1980s some assemblers were beginning to include quality performance as well as price in sourcing decisions. To be considered as a potential supplier for most of the assemblers by this time, a firm had to satisfy the customer's SQA requirements. Once approved in this way, suppliers had another hurdle to jump: in addition to price the delivery requirements were now more stringent. The Western assemblers had begun to learn about just-in-time (JIT) methods.

With hindsight and the benefit of research it is possible to conclude that a great deal of misconception arose about JIT methods during the resolved model phase. First, JIT was seen as a way of reducing inventory. This was helpful for assemblers who were still trying to face volatile markets (in terms of product differentiation) with mass production methods. The prospect of removing raw material stores and being able to demand whatever materials were required from the supplier, as and when they were required, was naturally appealing to buyers. Moreover, some assemblers were accustomed to receiving frequent supplies and appeared to miss the deeper significance of the JIT approach. A senior supplies manager of Ford of Europe was quoted thus: 'I think we have always had just-in-time deliveries . . . We always run the A class parts, which have the highest daily value usage, between one and two days in the plant, so we've always had just-in-time from that point of view'.[18] Quite apart from the question of degree (Ford's competitors in Japan at the time were working with hours of inventory, not one or two days) this statement indicates the view that just-in-time is a matter of stock levels and delivery frequency, rather than involving the much more fundamental principle of quality improvement, elimination of waste and motivation.

Delivery practices did change during the resolved model period, and with them capacity planning. Three variations on just-in-time developed:

- **Apparent just-in-time** see (Figure 6.6): the tactical transfer of the inventory from the assembler to the supplier. The levels of raw materials previously held by the assembler were reduced to a minimum and the supplier was required to provide JIT deliveries. Interviews, especially those with small firms, revealed that this led to an increase in finished goods inventories for the suppliers who felt unable to move to true JIT operation internally. The assemblers were either oblivious to this problem or chose not to 'interfere in the internal affairs' of their suppliers. It is clear, however, that no one actually benefited

The customer demands
and receives supplies
just-in-time for use
on the assembly
line...

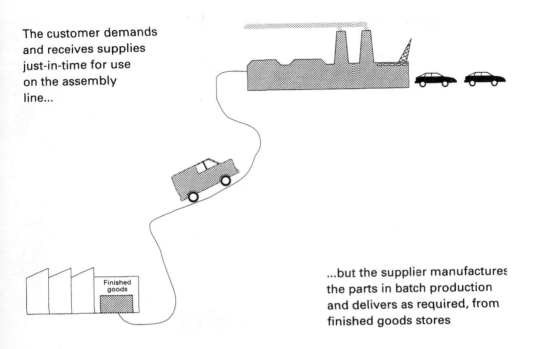

Finished
goods

...but the supplier manufactures
the parts in batch production
and delivers as required, from
finished goods stores

Figure 6.6 Apparent just-in-time

from this practice – despite the apparently JIT operation achieved by the
assembler – since the cost of holding the inventory remained in the supply
chain, simply transferred from one stage back to another.[19]

- **In-line warehouses**: suppliers were required to maintain stocks of their
  components in a warehouse close to the assembler's plant – at their expense
  (even, in some cases, charging the supplier rent for the space used). Once
  again, this gave the impression of JIT operation at the assembler with no real
  benefit to the supply chain, since the cost of the inventory remained. Instead
  of moving the assembler's raw materials to the supplier's finished goods
  stores, this system took them a little way down the road and required the
  supplier to invest in what was effectively further finished goods (separately
  for each customer). This system has some similarity with the 'consignment
  stocks' employed in some chemical industries: the customer has a large tank
  of the supplier's product on site and only pays for it as it is used.[20]

- **The milkround, or ex-works delivery system** (see Figure 6.7): the assembler
  has parts collected from the supplier's site (usually by a third party logistics
  firm) and delivered to consolidation points. From there the parts, together with
  appropriate selections of other components, are delivered to the assembly
  plants. This system was popular with suppliers for several reasons. Firstly, it
  meant that the worries of delivery were removed:[21] the supplier was required

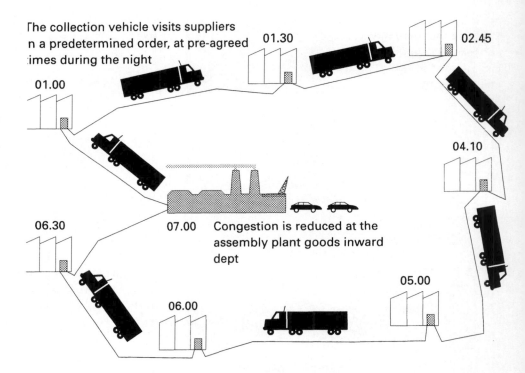

The collection vehicle visits suppliers
in a predetermined order, at pre-agreed
times during the night

01.00

01.30

02.45

04.10

06.30

07.00 Congestion is reduced at the
assembly plant goods inward
dept

05.00

06.00

Figure 6.7 The milkround delivery system

to ensure that the parts were placed ready for collection at a certain time (usually during the night – convenient for daytime delivery to the assembly plants and also for less congestion in transportation). Secondly, the assembler gave commitment to take the parts, in return for the supplier's working to daily phone calls (approaching true just-in-time). Thirdly, once the driver had signed for receipt of the parts, the documentation for payment was in the supplier's hands. Lastly, the parts made by, for example, a Ford supplier in the UK might end up on an assembly line in Spain or Germany. The pan-European logistics of Ford, and later GM, meant that suppliers who would normally serve only domestic customers were given the chance of supplying markets greater than that in their home country.

Use of all three approaches was evident in resolved model relationships. The first approach was understandably unpopular with suppliers and served to exacerbate the bad feeling built up during the stress model phase. It was later to be developed by the addition of assembler involvement, as discussed below.

The second approach was similarly unwelcome although it was soon modified to include a sort of *kaizen*: the space allocated to a supplier in the warehouse could be used as a *kanban* square – the supplier had to keep each part's space allocation full. If the space became empty, that was the signal for another delivery of that part. Coupled to this was the notion of reducing the size of the allocated space for each part, dealing with consequent problems of supply as they arose – a genuine JIT concept.

The milkround was especially appropriate to established assemblers whose old factories simply could not cope with the volume of heavy goods vehicle traffic involved in traditional supply. Assembly plants which had grown in a piecemeal fashion were just not appropriate for planned JIT deliveries.

Thus, delivery practices began to improve during the early 1980s. In conjunction with this, capacity planning improved and some suppliers were offered long-term projected involvement for the first time. Information was exchanged – volume forecasts from the assembler and cost structures (very cautiously) from the supplier.

Pressure on costs was still very high and little comfort was available for suppliers in terms of price increases. Some lessons had been learned by the assemblers in the stress model phase, however, and more concern was shown for actual needs. The mass production paradigm was still dominant and the lateral leap to cost reduction as the norm had yet to be made by the hard pressed suppliers. There was an air of relief at this time. The notion was that the suppliers who had survived the stress period could now relax. The level of pressure in performance was reduced – a dangerous development, as noted above.

Part of the relief for the supplier was mixed with concern and challenge, caused by the assembler's attitude towards research and development. On the one hand there was an opportunity to control more of the added value, in a part of the chain which had always seemed the natural role for the supplier but which had been jealously denied by the assembler. On the other, immense investment was required for such activity. Assemblers exhibited an expectation that suppliers would start to provide product solutions, but did not see a collaborative role for themselves in the process (reminiscent of the single-sided traditional nature of R&D in the industry). For firms who had only minor presence in the technology fields up to this point, the possibility of gaining competitive advantage from R&D investment was remote. The European suppliers which were already there were spending amounts on R&D which were in some cases larger than the total sales turnover of the medium-sized firms, as shown in Table 6.5.

The developments in quality control which had been under way for some ten years began to bear fruit in the resolved model period, with suppliers which had gained control over their processes being accorded respect by their customers and in some cases, taking the lead in quality initiatives. Quality was still not good enough, however, and further quality campaigns were to come. Data captured by Nishiguchi between 1987 and 1989 relating to this are shown in Table 6.6.[22]

Discussion of the resolved model

It is clear that many genuine improvements occurred during the resolved model phase. Suppliers interviewed in the mid-1980s spoke frequently about better

Table 6.5 Research and development expenditure of European component suppliers[a]

Suppliers	1986–87 annual spend (million ECU)	% of automotive sales spent on R&D
Bosch[b]	389	5.9
Epeda Bertrand Faure	6	1.6
Gilardini	26	7.4
GKN	80	2.6
Lucas	96	5.6
Magneti Marelli	81	4.6
Valeo	107	5.0
VDO	65	10.0
ZF	130	5.0

Note: [a] Levels of spend vary year by year. For example, Valeo was reputely spending up to 10 per cent of sales turnover on R&D in later years than those shown. [b] Figures for 1987.

Source: Published data/and author's estimates.

Table 6.6 A comparison of Japanese, North American and European components firms

Average of samples	Japanese in Japan	Japanese in America	American in America	All Europe
Inventory level (in days)[a]	1.5	4.0	8.1	16.3
Number of daily JIT deliveries	7.9	1.6	1.6	0.7
Resultant defect parts per car[b]	0.24	n/a	0.33	0.62

Notes: [a] For discussion on inventory, see Endnote 22. [b] Quality figures relate only to cars sold in the USA: from initial quality survey of new owners by the US consultancy J.D. Power. Resultant refers to a link suggested by Nishiguchi between component quality and reported defects in new cars. Discussions with assemblers indicated that these data compare well with their own surveys on non-USA build.

Source: Nishiguchi (1989, pp. 313–47). From a matched sample of 54 supplier plants in Japan (18), America (10 US and 8 Japanese owned), and Europe (18).

relationships. It is also apparent, however, that the relaxation in working pressure was a sign that lessons had not been learned well enough. The true nature of just-in-time and *kaizen* calls for continuous improvement – never being satisfied with achieved performance. In view of the decade of shock which they had been through, the component suppliers and assemblers can perhaps be forgiven for missing the point – discussed here with the benefit of hindsight. However, the competition was only just beginning, as the Japanese assemblers began to move into international locations, raising the game once again.

The partnership model

The resolved model was not sufficiently progressive for best practice relationships. Some of the features were grudgingly developed (on the part of both assemblers and suppliers) and were clearly expedient. For example, the exchange of information was not liked by either side, since the customer's tendency to use cost data against the supplier in negotiation was still apparent, whilst the supplier found that forward build figures could still not be trusted. Working to daily phone calls was more patiently accepted in many cases but there were still frequent cases of requests being cancelled at even shorter notice and deliveries not accepted – traditional problems for relationships.

As noted above, it was initially decided to call the proposed best practice the Japanese model. This was for two key reasons. Firstly, it was recognized that the manner of dealing with suppliers was a major strength for Japanese assemblers in Japan. Secondly, it was becoming clear that Japanese assemblers would have to set up plants overseas in due course and that suppliers would have to deal on the new customers' terms if they wished to deal with them.

Thus, the Japanese model elicited interest from both suppliers and assemblers interviewed in the mid–1980s. No one in the West claimed to be practising it; most admitted that some of its features were beyond their current capabilities.

In order to set the scene for the Japanese or partnership model, it is useful to revisit, briefly, the tenets of subcontracting policies in Japan, which we saw in Chapter 1. Toyota's policy (as defined by Kiichiro Toyoda in 1940) rests upon three major assumptions:

- The assembler controls the relationship – is the senior partner (or, in Japanese terms, the parent).
- The specialist abilities of the supplier, which are not present in the assembler, are recognized as crucially important.
- It is necessary to have some sort of shared capital or financial tie in order to effect a secure relationship. Without these, suppliers may be switched at will.

Any model of customer–supplier relationships which purports to re-create and learn from the Japanese way must naturally reflect the above factors. They are present in the policies of the other Japanese assemblers clearly providing them with a sound technical and commercial basis upon which to build competitive advantages.[23]

For Western assemblers and suppliers there were some apparent limitations to adoption of the Japanese way of working. Shared capital and financial ties had been created progressively in Japan in a protected industry rising from the ashes of war – with the benefit of a strong national determination to resurrect itself. In the stressful Western automotive industry of the 1980s, it would evidently not be easy to create a common concern for mutual benefit, or even survival. The resolved model phase had brought some improvements in relationships but the Japanese model would need some step changes in attitudes in order to provide a competitive basis for Western suppliers and assemblers.

It was realized that the chosen name for this phase of the model was counterproductive, both in the research and in the objective of providing a useful framework for policy making. Referring to debate in the industry at large, some interviewees complained that there was too much fascination with the Japanese culture and perceived tendency towards consensus and harmony. Others said that the Japanese way was really only vertical integration by another name. Another complaint was that the Japanese model might work in Japan, but not elsewhere. (This last comment, whilst reminiscent of the 'not invented here' syndrome, was to lead eventually to a posited post-Japanese model, discussed in Chapter 7.)

Thus, a better title for the final part of the four-phase model was needed. The essence of the best practice appeared to be partnership between the two firms engaged in the relationship – indicating the need for each to value and respect the other. This was the title chosen, therefore, and the features of the partnership model are discussed below.

Competition under the partnership model is dynamic and fierce in the sense that every company knows it must work with customers and outperform other companies seeking to provide similar services. The methods of achieving this are, however, very different from those employed in earlier phases of the model. The structure of the supply chain is created to provide optimum combination of complementary assets in subcontracting firms – tiers of companies taking responsibility for specific parts of the manufacturing process. A supplier towards the top of this tiered structure (a child, in MCI's terms, rather than a grandchild) has a solid, long-term relationship with its customers and knows that it must constantly provide better service: the security of remaining a supplier to any particular customer is provided not by right but by fulfilling expectation.

In order to fulfil this highly demanding role, it is necessary for the supplier to use all available resources – including the abilities of other suppliers. Thus cooperation is essential for the partnership model supplier – both with other suppliers (including competitors) and with customers. This naturally poses challenges for customers: cooperating with suppliers is the reverse of many features of the traditional relationships.

The use of enquiries and bids for sourcing decisions is clearly inappropriate in partnership. Unless the item has not been bought before and bears no similarity to items currently purchased (e.g. in its principal production process requirements) an existing source which has a well-developed history of excellent performance is the obvious choice for supply. The customer still needs to know that the price paid is the lowest possible, but better mechanisms are employed for this, avoiding the inefficiencies of competitive tendering.[24] Open discussion of costs is practised and the genuine position on vehicle build is made clear. This does not, however, mean that regular, stable deliveries may be planned but rather that the supplier has a good comprehensive picture of volume requirements and is flexible enough to work within this, responding to specific short-notice requests.

Efficient information exchange is of fundamental importance to the success of the partnership model. In Japan, as we saw in Figure 2.2, the assemblers and suppliers are able to monitor, predict, and influence levels of return of assets, by the use of constant exchange of operating and financial data. This is underpinned by the positions in *keiretsu*, as noted earlier. When a Japanese assembler squeezes a supplier, it is with knowledge of the implications of such action. Meanwhile, information exchange is a major challenge for firms in the West, where such openness is not traditionally practised, and strategic information rarely flows across the company's internal or external interfaces.

Partnership sourcing does not necessitate single sourcing. Several factors will determine the number of sources for any parts, including the traditional factor of price competition for some items (e.g. commodities, or Kiichiro Toyoda's (a) class items). The following types of sourcing, all revealed in interviews in Japan, are contained within the model:

- Single sourcing: where the supplier is able to provide the entire volume/variety/delivery requirements of the customer.
- Dual sourcing: strategic parts, where any of the volume/variety/delivery factors makes it difficult for one supplier to provide the whole supply – shared sourcing.
- Dual sourcing: non-strategic parts, where classical competition is used to drive prices down.

For the most part, partnership sourcing in Japan results in small supply bases (number of direct suppliers to the assemblers). This reflects predominantly single sourced, or shared-sourcing supply. This is shown in Table 6.7.

The partnership model thus includes provision for dual sourcing where a supplier is unable to provide all the volume required (a capacity management decision which, whilst it may not be made jointly, would certainly be clear to both parties), the variety required (i.e. where different variants of a component represent significantly different products, and thus may be sourced separately) or delivery needs (e.g. supply of the same part in different areas or different countries).

There is another aspect to dual sourcing in the first case, for volume reasons. If two suppliers share the sourcing, fluctuations in requirement levels should represent half the problem for each of them. Provided the supplier has a good aggregate level of business from the customer, it is less important to have 100 per cent of any one item in partnership sourcing than in traditional mass production.

Capacity in the partnership model is therefore coordinated, with deliveries being controlled and made on a just-in-time basis. The development from the resolved model in this respect hinges upon the attitude of the customer in becoming involved in the supplier's move to true just-in-time and that of the supplier in letting the customer 'interfere'. This is a complex matter because it attempts to recreate the situation which gave rise to competitive advantage (from relationships) in Japan in the 1950s – a very different industrial climate, as seen in Chapter 1. The initial premise is that the assembler agrees to help the supplier by becoming involved in the production process for the components. There is a precedent for this in the SQA programmes of the 1970s. There are, however, two further conditions. Firstly, the manner of intercompany involvement must be appropriate – it is clear from the Japanese case that improvement comes from cooperation (possibly including financial links, as foreseen by Toyoda) and this requires the assembler to learn, not dictate terms. Secondly, it is assumed that the assembler is able and competent to help the supplier – this is by no means always the case.

Table 6.7 Number of direct suppliers to assemblers[a]

Assembler	No. of direct suppliers (domestic supply)	Vehicles built (domestic production: includes commercial vehicles)
Japan		
Toyota	340	3 968 697
Nissan	310	2 213 506
Honda	310	1 293 416
USA/Canada		
GM	2500	5 876 013
Ford	1800	3 982 209
Chrysler	2000	2 207 104
Europe		
Fiat	900	1 880 856
Renault	1050	1 680 636
PSA	900	2 017 508
VW/Audi	1580	1 879 748
D Benz	1650	698 600
BMW	1420	442 776
Porsche	600	25 969
Rover	850	520 299
Jaguar	540	51 939
Volvo	590	331 218
Saab	485	152 406

Note: [a] All figures apply to 1988 except for BMW, which is 1987. (See also Figure 7.1.)
Source: Author's interviews, 1988–89, and *MVMA* (1988).

The involvement of the assembler in the processes within the supplier also provides the basis for the partnership approach to price changes. As noted by Cusumano:

> Productivity at [the] larger [components] firms ... rose throughout the 1950s and 1960s [in Japan] as they received direct assistance from Nissan, Toyota, and other Japanese automakers, in addition to foreign companies such as Robert Bosch and the Bendix Group. Higher productivity then made it possible for the Japanese automakers to demand price reductions from all their suppliers of around 10 per cent a year during the late 1950s and early 1960s. (Cusumano, 1985, p. 245)

The challenge of partnership is thus significant for supplier and customer: the idea of reducing costs, and therefore prices, each year turns established thinking on its head.[25] Clearly some elements of component prices are beyond a supplier's control. In more recent years, cost reduction through *kaizen* of those elements which are controllable has been used by Japanese suppliers to remain competitive through such macroeconomic events as the hardening of the yen against the dollar in 1988.

Once the concept of the assembler's involvement in improvements to the supplier's processes is established, the joint approach to total quality and product development become natural. Suppliers whose quality control procedures had been developed by successive campaigns in supplier quality assurance, etc., found new challenges more acceptable. The introduction of statistical process control (SPC) in the mid–1980s meant that suppliers had to invest in employee training and began to operationalize the concept of cost reduction through quality (cf mass production, as shown in Figure 6.5).

In the partnership model, suppliers become involved in the new product development process very much earlier than before. As shown by the results of Kim Clark's work (see Chapter 5) the involvement of suppliers in the development of a new vehicle gives the Japanese a major advantage. Earlier involvement and black/grey box development, both key aspects of the participation in new product development, are features of the partnership relationship.

The complexity of the partnership relationship and its dependence upon commitment from both assembler and supplier clearly lead to a high level of pressure to perform. The relaxation noted above as a feature of the resolved model is thus shown to have been inappropriate. The notion that Japanese supplier relationships lead to 'cosy' and stable consensus-based cooperation could not be further from the truth.

Discussion of the partnership model

When the partnership model was proposed it was only partly accepted by the assemblers and some of the suppliers interviewed. It was said by some interviewees that some of the features went too far in their extrapolation. In order to develop the model and to test it further, more interviews were undertaken. These, in addition to repeat interviews and discussions, indicated that the developed model did indeed provide a valid framework for best practice relationships. Few relationships in the West exhibited many of the partnership features, however, and nowhere was there an example with all of them. This was not surprising – it was a model, proposed as a target.

Gradually features of the model appeared in the industry: public affirmation of the importance of supplier relationships (by assemblers) became commonplace. Suppliers reported that they were becoming involved in new models earlier, etc. It seemed as though the Western automotive industry was preparing itself for competition by planning to establish Japanese-style relationships with its suppliers.

The idea of assemblers holding shares in suppliers, which was limited to vertical integration and 100 per cent ownership under mass production, spread slowly to the West. In 1985, for example, Ford in the USA followed such a strategy after its difficulties in mastering the technique of glass encapsulation for side and rear windows. (The process entails fitting a plastic edging to the glass panel, to reduce drag, wind noise, etc.) Its supplier, Excel Industries, was dismayed when the assembler decided to do this work in house, after some years of working together to develop the process in the supplier's plant. Ford subsequently admitted that the encapsulation would be better done by the supplier and sold its factory to Excel to carry out the work on a long-term contract (seven years). Following Ford's initial decision, however, Excel was in no financial position to support the process, so Ford agreed to buy a 40 per cent stake in the supplier. The case has been hailed, somewhat prematurely and simplistically, as a sign of an emerging American *keiretsu*. It does appear to illustrate commonsense and the principles of asset specificity and complementarity in operation. The contract has been a major success for both customer and supplier.[26]

■ Reflection on causes of the evolution of relationships

It appears that the traditional model was a feature of mass production. The stress model was caused by mass production's failure to provide solutions to the problems caused by the major downturn in the market coupled with the increased threats of international competition. The resolved model was the necessary, expedient, antidote to the problems caused by the stress model and laid the foundations for the full transition to the partnership model – a 'me too' strategic emulation of the successful Japanese companies.

The four-phase model was deliberately constructed as a matrix in order to reinforce its use as a framework in identifying positions (for companies, individual relationships or national industries) and for planning strategies. Inevitably, companies characterized their own situation in terms of a selection: some traditional features, some stress, some resolved, etc. This was a very productive response for the research since it enhanced the understanding of evolution and provided foci for developmental work. For example, if several interviewees reported progress in data exchange practices in a certain country, the likely causes for that specific progress could be discussed further in isolation. In the case of Australia, for example, the peculiar geographical factors coupled with the history of the automotive industry lead to a situation in which capacity planning is very difficult. Use of the model in this case led to clarification of issues, at a time when national policies were being decided (see Lamming, 1990, and Automotive Industry Authority, 1991, pp. 58–60).

The four-phase model illustrated the lumpy, piece-meal and involuntary nature of evolution on relationships – an important factor in relationship management approaches. We shall return to this concept in Chapter 9.

It may be seen that the relationship between customer and supplier in this industry has, in the West, evolved to a stage where a best practice model is discernible. There was a recurrent view provided by interviewees, however, that the partnership model was desirable but possibly not achievable: it was too reliant upon the unique situation in Japan for some of its strengths. It was also apparent that the Japanese assemblers which were venturing abroad, whilst they were demanding and creating great changes in their suppliers' attitudes (and indirectly influencing the attitudes of Western assemblers towards suppliers), would need to take into account the limitations of their system when extended to international operation in autonomous regions (see Womack *et al.*, 1990, pp. 192–222). This was confirmed in interviews with Japanese suppliers in Japan in 1989.

Other factors of change were apparent. For example, the shake out in suppliers during the 1980s (which occurred throughout the West), coupled with the development of long-term customer–vendor relationships, led to the need for a better defined responsibility in major component suppliers – to avoid the reduction in working pressure which might result from monopoly positions.

It became clear that a new best practice model would be required – based largely upon the partnership model but developed for global operation. This was initially called the post-Japanese model, and latterly, the lean supply model. This is discussed in the next chapter.

■ Notes

1. This shortcoming (in the early modelling work) has been recognized by IMP (Ford, 1990, p. 541). The research of IMP members did turn to technology later in the 1980s – see, for example, Hakansson (1987).
2. For a good summary of IMP work in the 1980s see Ford (1990).
3. Just-in-time was an observed feature of the Japanese system: see Schonberger (1982); Monden (1982); Voss (1987); Voss *et al.* (1987).
4. The term 'stress' was initially chosen for this factor (and was actually the word suggested by the interviewee who contributed it). This word has negative connotations (destruction, lack of control, etc.) however, and was replaced by 'pressure' later in the research. The substitution has resulted in better identification with the model by interviewees.
5. The model has been presented at many seminars, etc., at which the input from suppliers and assemblers, who were not otherwise interviewed, was gained. The actual exposure of the ideas has thus been rather greater than the 129 companies interviewed. Some firms were interviewed more than once.
6. The number naturally depended upon the commodity or type of component being bought. Examples have been given of enquiries sent to fifteen companies for some components. New potential suppliers would constantly be sought for parts which were available from one or only a small number of suppliers.
7. The buyer was usually motivated by a personal assessment process which included the value of savings achieved during the month. The expression save your salary was commonplace – indicating that the buyer could provide a profit for the company by saving more than he or she cost. The short-term logic of this is obvious; the long-term fallacy is only apparent with hindsight. The supplier's knowledge of the product and detailed cost factors was inevitably better than the buyer's, who had to deal with several different types of commodity and probably had no actual experience of the production processes, etc., connected with the product. In the case of small suppliers, the buyer would usually be dealing with the company owner, or another director. If the supplier was large, the full strength of a technical department would back up the sales representative, as opposed to the buyer's reliance upon his or her limited experience.

8. While the individual styles of customers varied, the basic system was the same for material control throughout the industry. This uniformity of approach reinforces the concept of a 'model' of customer–supplier relationships within the industry.

9. This term was commonly used in the industry with little formal explanation. Factors subsumed within it included: inflation, interest rates, exchange rates, prices for services, exogenous shocks, etc.

10. For a good historical account see Bessant (1991, Chapter 9).

11. For a good explanation of *kanban* see Schonberger (1982, Appendix I).

12. Naturally, some assemblers had these in place earlier than others. In Europe, Ford was an early adopter – apparently as a result of success with the concept in the USA.

13. The early SQA schemes did not include explicit use of statistical process control – this was to follow. Statistical quality control was included, however, in addition to requirements for bonded stores for some materials, systems for routine responsibilities for quality control engineers, etc.

14. The proponents of this concept (Feigenbaum, Crosby, Deming, Juran, etc.) had by this time turned their attention to North America following success in Japan, but had yet to influence thinking in Europe. Even when they did, the implementation lag between theory and practice would mean that true applications of the concepts would only be apparent some years later: see Bessant (1991, Chapter 9); Halberstam (1986, Chapter 17).

15. The term resolved may be seen to suggest a removal of the problems caused by the stress model. This was, of course, not the case. The title is chosen, however, to reflect not simply the resolution of the stress but also the apparent belief on the part of the assemblers at the time, that this was all that was necessary.

16. In many cases, suppliers were keen to talk (in confidence) about specific assemblers and even to rank them in order of performance. This is, of course, just as pertinent as assemblers vetting suppliers (and may have relevance to future partnership structures). Since the discussion here is about generic models, however, no formal attempt has been made to identify particular companies, although specific pointers to best practice may be seen in the models of strategy in Chapter 8.

17. The SQA schemes represented major investments for assemblers as well as suppliers. For example, training programmes for SQA engineers were necessary, with associated expenditure on equipment, facilities and documentation (manuals).

18. Vice President of Supply for Ford of Europe, quoted in *Ward's Automotive Reports*, Detroit, October 1988.

19. It could be argued that this form of pressure had been effective in Japan, as the inventory in the system was broken down and reduced by passing it back down the supply chain. In each level of supply, the inventory would present a problem to be tackled and in this way the overall amount could be reduced. Two important differences existed, however: the less vertically integrated, 'tiered' subcontracting system in Japan (more firms involved in the supply chain) (see Nishiguchi, 1987 and Ikeda, 1987) and the collaboration evident between companies with their suppliers (and their suppliers' suppliers) in the problem-solving process. Research in the USA in 1989 by Helper indicated clearly that component suppliers had reduced their delivery cycles significantly since 1985 but were still manufacturing in the same batch size as before (see Helper 1991).

20. A surprise answer (carefully double-checked) to an interview question with a supplier in Japan revealed that this is not purely a Western concept. A very lean supplier of brake parts, north of Tokyo, which supplies Toyota, some six hours' drive to the south (through the congestion of peripheral Tokyo), on a four-hourly basis (i.e. Toyota holds only four hours' inventory of the supplier's parts) admitted that Toyota requires the firm to hold one day's worth of parts in a warehouse near the assembly plant. This is not an in-line warehouse, however: the parts are never used for normal supply (apart from turning the stock over periodically) and deliveries go directly from the supplier to

Toyota. The warehouse is there as an 'insurance policy' demanded by Toyota. The supplier is not a member of the Toyota group.

21. Small price reductions were negotiated for this: generally between 1 and 2 per cent.
22. The figures in the table referring to inventory cover in-process and finished goods. Nishiguchi carefully omits stock at JIT depots and customer-stipulated holdings, to ensure accuracy of measurement (see Nishiguchi, 1989, p. 337).
23. Conclusion drawn from repeated interviews with Honda and Nissan purchasing directors and with suppliers to other Japanese assemblers, in Japan, North America, the UK and Australia.
24. Competitive tendering is, of course, still widely considered to be the best way of awarding contracts for major one-off, or infrequent projects (e.g. building construction work) and has largely replaced the older concept of fixed-cost contracts in areas such as military procurement. It implies, however, that there is a learning curve with every new contract and that all competent suppliers will have similar abilities to learn the client's requirements. A similar situation exists in commodity buying, where the supplier is asked simply to provide the goods, i.e. no learning is involved. The difference between these and partnership sourcing is that the supplier deals continuously with the customer and builds up a better knowledge of its requirements than the customer has itself. In construction works, for example, the lean producers tend to use the same contractors each time, while commodity purchasing is also being reviewed in the light of partnership sourcing techniques.
25. Such was the dismay of North American suppliers at this conclusion when it was first proposed by the author at the MEMA seminar, Boston, 1987, that few of those attending agreed that it was plausible, despite the evidence from Japan thirty years earlier. After four such annual seminars, when the lean supply model was presented to the same group in 1990 this factor was automatically accepted by participants as a necessary part of the proposed new best practice.
26. Transfers such as this may also be seen cynically as exploitation of cheaper, non-union labour (Excel is a non-union plant). Whilst this is clearly a factor in the case, there is enough documented evidence to show that the technology, coupled with the drive for better supply chain relationships, was the dominant reason for this exercise. The Excel case also provides an example of an assembler investing in the supplier for mutual benefit but not overall control (Excel has major contracts with other assemblers). See Marler (1989) and *Business Week* magazine, 27 January 1992, pp. 38–40.

7 | Lean
Supply

The Japanese automotive industry clearly owes a great deal of its success to its operation in Japan. The influential factors include: the determination born of the nationalism of a country rebuilding itself after a devastating war; the formation of the self-supporting groups to fend off foreign intervention, giving rise to a rare source of concern for mutual benefit; the early practice of reverse-engineering American and European products (learning and criticizing designs, etc.); the role of national initiatives – especially those of MITI;[1] a protected domestic market; inspiration from American process innovators (Deming, Juran, etc.) frustrated by the lethargy of their own country; and some genuine brilliance of leaders such as Kiichiro Toyoda, Taiichi Ohno and Shoichiro Honda.

There is a limitation to the Japanese/partnership model, however, and it stems paradoxically from its strength: the assemblers and their component firms have developed, in almost all cases, as senior and junior partners. Collaboration between customer and supplier in these circumstances misses the richness of an equal's contribution: for lean supply, something beyond partnership is required.

The development of industrial dynamics in Japan, including the demise of the *zaibatsu* and the rise of the business groupings (*keiretsu*) has led to what Imai (1989) terms 'the network industrial organisation' in which there are 'fuzzy' organizational forms. The companies in these new industrial organizations are interdependent in a fundamental way, relying upon close information and supply relationships for constant development, and yet employing looser formal ties (e.g. equity) than those of the *keiretsu* or their forebears. This network industrial organization only exists to this extent in Japan and the relationships which underpin it appear to rely upon the Japanese national economic situation for their continuity. For the supply systems to work globally, therefore, something else is needed.

In reviewing partnership-type relationships, therefore, it becomes apparent that a further development is necessary in order to arrive at a true best practice for the immediate and possibly medium-term future, outside Japan. It is clear that the automotive industry is developing globally, rather than internationally, with firms operating in and between several countries or regions at once. Examination and development of the partnership model was necessary, therefore, to see how it would fare in this context. The result of this development was a further model – a proposed fifth phase which was not already evident in practice. The proposal was that the partnership model, as described above, would be insufficient in a global industry. The title initially given to this fifth phase was the post-Japanese model. The model was constructed in 1988, and presented to many assemblers and suppliers in several countries (including, of course, Japan) for further development.

Use of this title in this development work always required immediate qualification. It was not being suggested, it had to be explained, that Japanese firms would cease to be the influential force in the industry and in relationships, nor that they would necessarily lose any of their competitive advantage. It was proposed instead that the best practice firms under the partnership model would need to modify and extend their practices, developed in the special context of Japan between 1940 and 1980, to take account of a new operating environment. Close working relationships between, say, German assemblers and German suppliers in Germany would need to be developed similarly for global operation.

With the emergence of the lean production concept in 1990 (Womack *et al.*, 1990) it became apparent that the need for a forward-looking model applied to the entire automotive industry, not simply the component supply process: hence the adoption of the title – lean supply – in place of post-Japanese model (which was always seen only as a working title).

We saw in Chapter 3 that research suggests that when an innovation originates in a supplier but is intended for use by a customer, the customer's perspective on accepting risk may be fundamentally altered by the behaviour of the supplier. This is the principle upon which lean supply rests, and this is why it is beyond partnership. (This is discussed further at the end of this chapter.) The post-Japanese model is an industry scenario whereas lean supply is a strategic model for assembler–supplier relationships. Before discussing the latter, therefore, we shall review the former.

Throughout the research, the term supply system had been used to indicate the comprehensive consideration of the combined strategies and practices of the assemblers and the suppliers. The four-phase model had reflected this in its selected factors. The initial expression of the lean supply model developed this approach, and discussion of the model begins below with this framework.

■ The characteristics of the automotive components industry in lean supply: the post-Japanese model

This model describes best practice in supply systems and the development of the automotive components industry thus:[2]

- The global automotive components industry will consist of significantly fewer companies. They will be larger than the present companies and will offer a broader range of services to their customers – the assemblers: they will be more 'talented'. They will also take more responsibility in the development of the industry. Other types of company may be expected to play only minor roles in the industry.

- The supplier industry will be structured in 'tiers' or separate levels, differentiated by the nature of the suppliers' connections to the customer, the level of product technology for which they are responsible, and the complexity of production and supply functions which they coordinate or control.

- There will be stronger vertical strategic relationships between customers and suppliers throughout this tier structure, including those between the assembler and the direct suppliers.

- There will be stronger and more common horizontal strategic relationships at the higher levels, linking suppliers through joint ventures, technology partnerships, supply agreements, etc.

- A first-tier supplier will have very close ties to one assembler whilst maintaining more distant but still important links to others.

- Suppliers will need to have multi-market presence. This means that original equipment automotive business alone will probably not be sufficient. Either the supplier will need substantial after-market business (depending upon the product type) or activity in other industries (e.g. electronics, aerospace, etc.) or both.

- As the assemblers set up global operations, assembling in several countries (in the three major regions)[3] and designing in two or three, so they will need to obtain supplies locally around the world. Suppliers will need to match this strategy by setting up production facilities or links in these countries.

- Sourcing of components in low-labour-cost countries, where it makes economic sense (to achieve reductions in production costs) will be the responsibility of first-tier suppliers (including the component-manufacturing subsidiaries of assemblers).

- Competitive advantage for suppliers will continue to be based upon achievement of best practice, world-class manufacturing, incorporating the implementation of new technologies and working practices and continuous improvement. This will give the supplier leverage to reduce unit costs, improve quality, and develop new products and tooling in a fraction of the time taken traditionally.

Fewer, more talented and larger suppliers

As we saw earlier, the heterogeneity of the European industry meant that its vehicle assemblers had developed significant technical relationships with their suppliers. The work of Clark and Fujimoto (see Chapter 5) indicated that while the

American assemblers were doing 81 per cent of the detailed design work on components, and the Japanese 30 per cent, the figure in Europe was 54 per cent.

However, the European assemblers, like the Americans, have amassed very large supply bases, as shown in Table 6.7. Supply bases in both regions are being reduced by assemblers, in order to have better relationships with fewer companies. The analogy sometimes used is the formation of a small circle of close friends – reminiscent of Toyota's ideas in 1940. This is shown in Figure 7.1.[4] Reduction in supply bases is more than a 'weeding out' process: a strategic reasoning is necessary to select the small number of suppliers with which an assembler intends to maintain supply relationships.

This reduction may be achieved in several ways:

■ Removal of any supplier which does not achieve the required levels of performance in supplier quality assurance (SQA) and similar supplier-assessment processes (the business being re-sourced to an approved supplier, resulting in a reduction in the total number of suppliers). The first screening-out process of this type in Europe began in the 1970s with the introduction of SQA. For the first time there was a restriction placed upon purchasing departments in their choice of supplier – even for purely comparative quotations. This idea was developed in the USA and brought to Europe by the

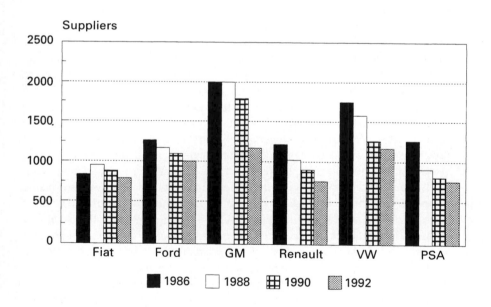

Note: [a] See Endnote 4 for comments.

Source: Actual/forecast data from author's interviews/estimates.

Figure 7.1 An example of strategic reductions in supply bases: European volume assemblers[a]

American assemblers. Fifteen years later, however, the supply bases were still large, in both regions. Use of the techniques to rationalize supply bases has taken a long time to develop and it is only now that Ford (the earliest adopter in Europe) is prepared to demand that 100 per cent of suppliers have Q101 approval (by autumn 1992).[5] Assemblers sometimes employ a grading system, encouraging suppliers to work towards approval as A class (or similar status). B class suppliers are those on this path; C class may be those who are being phased out (at least in theory – see below).

- Removal of multi-sourcing: suppliers used as second or third sources (or those currently not performing well in dual-sourced situations) can be removed. As we saw earlier, however, Japanese firms do practise dual sourcing and at the same time maintain very small supply bases. This practice may thus be seen as a 'cleaning-up' exercise: it would not, on its own be sufficient to bring about the consolidation sought.

- Integration of several separate components into a system or corner, requiring some redesign by the assembler (or by the supplier): suppliers of smaller components are then asked to switch supply to the systems integrators, thereby quitting the direct supply base of the assembler. Full use of this approach is most demanding for the assembler since it requires real commitment to the principle of lean supply. The engineering required to enable it may represent significant investment of time. The transfer of control, or 'sovereignty', over sourcing of components – from assembler to first-tier supplier – requires some nerve and a great deal of confidence on the part of the assembler. There is also the need to retain some in-house expertise in the transferred technology in order to maintain a dialogue with the supplier. In July 1992, the new President of Nissan, Yoshifumi Tsuji, said 'We intend to thoroughly reduce the number of components [used in a car] and also vigorously promote common use of parts among different models. We intend to focus even greater emphasis on design for manufacturability'. Tsuji's words were interpreted to mean a general reduction in complexity of the car – a process which would inevitably have implications for component supply in systems. Shoichiro Toyoda, however, has said that the use of common parts, whilst an attractive concept, is very difficult in practice without compromising the quality of different models, with differing engineering requirements.[6]

- Use of first-tier suppliers to coordinate supply from minor firms; this is similar to the above, but does not necessarily involve redesign of the components sub-system. This is basically a case of out-sourcing assembly work – often in order to exploit lower labour rates in suppliers' companies.[7] It also recognizes the value of specialism in manufacture. The prime example is seats (consequently called 'seating systems') where the type of labour required bears little direct relation, in terms of skills, to that more generally associated with automobile assembly (i.e. the cutting and sewing of fabrics and leather, and the assembly of foam rubber on tubular steel frames). In this way, a system such as a seat, which would traditionally have been supplied in, say, fifty pieces, by thirty suppliers (for assembly in the vehicle plant), can be supplied whole by one supplier. An example of this is supply of seats for Nissan's luxury model, the Infiniti, by one supplier: for a similar model, GM (in the USA) still has separate parts delivered by twenty-five suppliers (Womack *et al.*, 1990, p. 146).

Seating suppliers now usually deliver 'car sets' of seats just-in-time, thus avoiding the need for storage space at the point of assembly (seats are bulky items) and quality problems (they are vulnerable to damage in storage). Overall inventory is also reduced (i.e. in the supply chain) as seats are made in the required colour and specification only hours before their use – synchronous manufacture. When this approach works well, it can develop into the more technically committed practice described immediately above: for example, Renault eventually transfered design responsibility for all its seating to its expert supplier, Epeda Bertrand Faure.[8]

The nature of mass production supply bases is such that a small number of suppliers account (in all observed cases) for a large proportion of the value of component supply. This is illustrated in Figure 7.2, which is an actual example from North America. The 'tail'[9] identified in the diagram is a feature of every Western supply base which has been plotted in this manner. Clearly, it represents

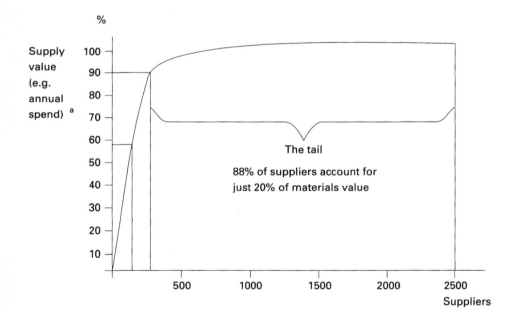

Note: [a] Annual spend refers solely to production components and materials.
Source: Author's interview: Ford, USA January 1989.

Figure 7.2 Typical mass production supply base profile: actual example

waste: the purchasing department of the assembler has to maintain records and contacts with firms who provide only a very small amount of the value bought in. The firms themselves are not necessarily small, of course, but the amount of business transacted clearly is. It is feasible that such supplies could be conducted in a partnership mode, but unlikely. Very small tails exist even in the supply bases of lean producers, as shown by the example in Figure 7.3.

There are two major reasons commonly given in interviews for the existence of a tail:

■ The companies in the tail are the only sources available for the parts or materials purchased from them. The assembler would like to obtain the item from one of its major suppliers, but cannot.

■ The small-account suppliers are retained in order to provide a price comparison for major suppliers (a weapon, in traditional negotiating terms).

The apparent pragmatism of these arguments has until now meant that tails have survived. In the near future, however, lean purchasing in the assemblers may be expected to change this situation. Lean assemblers also have tails to their supply bases, but they are very small (there will always be some entry and exit activity).

The challenge for the supplier is to influence the manner of its customer's

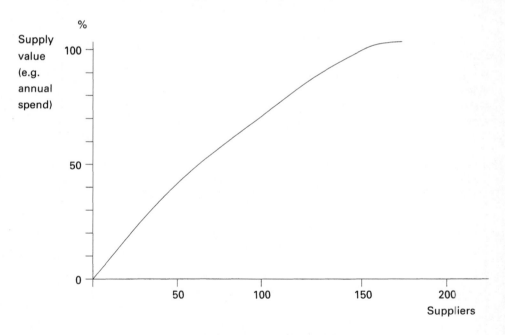

Note: [a] The example given is that of Toyota in Australia. This assembler's supplier base provides an interesting example of emerging lean supply. See Lamming (1990) for a full account. In 1991 Toyota announced plans to build a new assembly plant near Melbourne to assemble 100 000 cars a year.
Source: Author's interviews, Australia 1990.

Figure 7.3 Example of a lean supply base profile[a]

supply base reduction. There is nothing new in this principle – it is the traditional practice of trying to get a larger slice of a fixed-size cake. As relationships between customers and suppliers strengthen, however, traditional sales techniques may be expected to count for less in this endeavour – the alternative being a technology/service-oriented strategy.

In partnership relationships it is clear that the second reason for the tail would only apply in a very small number of cases – ideally none. If a lean approach is being taken to cost analysis, etc., there is no need for such primitive tactics, except perhaps in the purchasing of the most basic parts (see Toyoda's categories: Chapter 1). As we have seen, however, basic parts are being 'designed out' – integrated into systems.

The first reason is often a fact of life for purchasing, although there are some observed approaches for tackling the problem. These include having the supply directed through a 'first-tier' supplier (see below) who has more business with the source (which might therefore support a more comprehensive relationship), and designing out the item, so that the supply is no longer required, e.g. use of a substitute material. In either case, the trade off decision will be between the benefit gained from taking the action and the cost of keeping the supplier in the supply base.

Assemblers are restructuring the way in which components are classified for engineering and purchasing purposes. This means grouping items into 'families', determined by function, physical characteristics, etc. For example, in the mid-1980s, Peugeot identified 257 families, Fiat 250 and Renault 150. In each case, for each family, the company intends to identify two or three suppliers. This would result in a supply base of between 300 and 750 firms. To this would be added some further suppliers – perhaps between 50 and 100 – for specific requirements, etc., although in a truly lean supply base these would be very few.

The responsibilities of the suppliers which remain in direct contact with the assemblers (as partners) will clearly be great. It would appear that the only suppliers capable of maintaining such a service will be large firms. The amounts of expenditure on R&D alone, as seen earlier, are large. Investments needed to support the activities and responsibilities listed above are always described by suppliers as a cause for concern. Firms unable to accept this challenge will join the second tier of suppliers, where the necessary competitive strengths may be less onerous.

During the interviews designed to test the post-Japanese model, it became apparent that Western firms did not intend to become tied to any one or two assemblers.[11] In almost all cases, interviewees said that the Western industry was accustomed to suppliers dealing on an intimate basis with several competitors which were themselves direct competitors. This even extended to competitors' subsidiaries. For example, Renault buys instrumentation equipment from Jaeger (a French company), relying upon them for significant development advice in an area of the vehicle which is directly related to customer satisfaction. In 1987, Jaeger was acquired by Magneti Marelli – a subsidiary of Renault's competitor, Fiat. Renault, however, continued to deal as before with Jaeger. Similarly, the subsidiaries of GM, e.g. AC Delco, can point to component development work carried out for other assemblers.[12]

This feature looks likely to remain and is a challenge for Japanese firms in their moves abroad. It appears to be in contrast to the close, sometimes exclusive, technology relationships (as distinct from supply relationships) built up by Japanese assemblers and suppliers – an example of the developments needed to the Japanese/partnership model in the move towards lean supply.

Tier structures

As assemblers reduce their supply bases, the number of direct or first-tier suppliers may be expected to fall. Many firms who were previously direct suppliers to assemblers will become second-tier suppliers. It is also apparent that the actions of the suppliers themselves will bring about a reduction in numbers. For example, the sale of several businesses by Lucas to Magneti Marelli in 1988 reduced the number of major lighting suppliers in Europe. Similar effects are generated by merger and acquisition, and by joint ventures.

The terms first tier and second tier have been widely but loosely used for some time in a general description of the situation in Japan (the *keiretsu*) and the assumption that the roles in the supply chain can be clearly defined. This is not the case, as we shall see. In transferring the terminology to the West several misconceptions arise. To clarify this we shall use a hypothetical example, shown in Figure 7.4. In this case, there is a Western assembler which has rationalized its supply base, so that it is receiving integrated systems from its major suppliers. The many smaller items that it used to receive from a host of companies are now routed through its direct suppliers. In Figure 7.4, the assembler is dealing directly with supplier A, which integrates several components into a system. The system is delivered to the assembly line, ready for fitting into a vehicle, with a minimum of interfacing effort (it is 'plug compatible').

Suppliers B, C, D and E are supplying components into supplier A, for integration into the system. It might be claimed that this makes them 'second-tier suppliers' in this supply system, with A as a 'first-tier' supplier. Strictly speaking, however, they are not actually a tier at all: they have no formal relationship to A, other than a commercial contract to supply parts, or to one another, or to the assembler. In fact, they should be called indirect suppliers to the assembler, and direct suppliers to A. To call B, C, D and E (collectively) a tier, implies that there is some industry organization similar to that in Japan. The post-Japanese model indicates that the industry will be structured in tiers, but not in the Japanese sense of layers of an integrated ownership structure such as the *keiretsu*.

Supplier B is a special case. It supplies parts to A for integration into a system, but it also supplies directly into the assembler, on another contract, possibly coordinating supplies from other suppliers. It is thus a direct and indirect supplier. This is quite natural and it is easy to see how this situation might change, either way. B could be phased out of the direct supply base for the assembler, or it

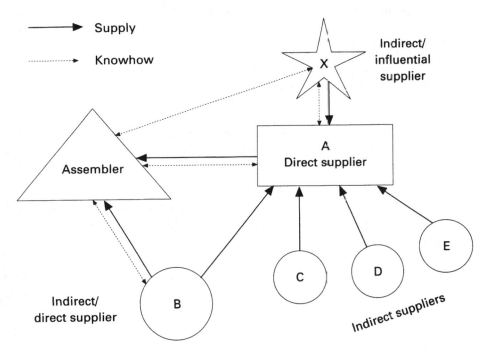

Figure 7.4 Hypothetical case of direct and indirect supply

might increase its direct supply, taking on more technological responsibility and raising its importance in the assembler's supplier list. There is no reason, however, why B should not maintain its dual role.

To make a transition to a wholly direct supplier (which would clearly involve investment and extensive strategic management effort on the part of B) the firm would need to align itself more with the automotive industry. The strictly indirect suppliers (C,D and E) are not so aligned; they are probably making components for several different industries, either through efforts to hedge their bets or because of their technical capabilities.

So suppliers may be described as direct or indirect, and aligned or unaligned, to varying degrees. There remains the special case of supplier X. X is a very influential supplier that probably makes a high-technology product or material which must be incorporated (e.g. microprocessors) or transformed (e.g. composite materials) by another supplier to be of use to the assembler. Thus the supply route is indirect from X to the assembler (in this case, through A) but the communication is direct. X is also clearly an important influence, but may be unaligned. It is hardly appropriate to call X second tier.

The automotive industry-aligned supplier may thus be direct or indirect. The non-aligned supplier will almost certainly be indirect. Suppliers that are (for historical reasons) unaligned but direct suppliers (except the very large firms) will be the first targets for removal from supply bases.

We shall return to this subject in Chapter 8, when discussing strategies. For now, the terms first and second tier, as applied to suppliers, are used to indicate the degree of influence the supplier exerts in the supply chain, rather than some fixed position in a hierarchy:

■ First-tier suppliers are those that integrate systems for direct supply to the assembler, or have a significant technical influence on the assembler while supplying indirectly.

■ Second-tier suppliers are those that supply components to first-tier firms for integration into systems, or provide some support service, such as metal finishing, etc.

In Figure 7.4, A and X are first-tier suppliers; C, D and E are second tier suppliers. B has some characteristics of each: its classification depends on how influential it is (on product technology) for the assembler, and whether or not it will remain a direct supplier. This situation is represented in Figure 7.5.

As the need for collaboration between suppliers increases (in order to supply increasingly complex technologies to the assembler), so it will be commonplace

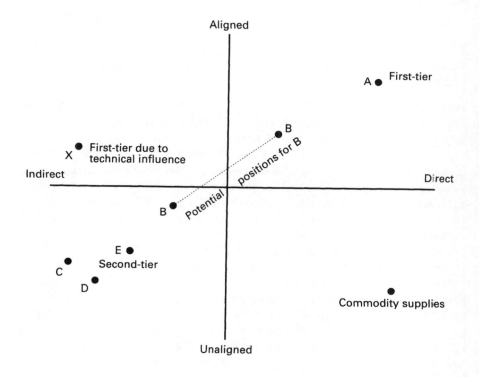

Note: [a] For a true representation it would be necessary to draw a three-dimensional model, the three axes being alignment, direct supply and technological influence. Identification of suppliers refers to Figure 7.4.

Figure 7.5 Definition of first-tier and second-tier suppliers[a]

for first-tier suppliers to share responsibility for jointly developed systems. In cases where one collaborator has responsibility for delivery, the others are technically indirect suppliers. This situation will not affect such suppliers' standing as first tier (at least not in the short term). Those firms who remain as first-tier suppliers will need to provide a greater range of services to the assemblers. These are listed in Table 7.1.

As we saw earlier, the structure of the Japanese components industry is as much the result of a set of historical factors as a strategic industrial configuration. A replication of this structure is not likely in the West. Two themes do emerge, however. Firstly, much of the competitive advantage required for lean production comes from the ability to deal as collaborators with subcontractors – at all stages in the supply chain. This indicates that the 'meshing' of first-tier suppliers with their own suppliers (second-tier) must be efficient to enable the removal of waste from the whole system or chain. Secondly, the development of systems in the vehicle can provide a good basis for tiering by identifying suitable areas of responsibility for the first-tier supplier – the systems integrator – which then subcontracts to the second tier the components and possibly assembly work, etc.

In this streamlined system, the assembler becomes the chief systems integrator of the vehicle. The detailed work is the responsibility of the first-tier supplier.[13]

The question may therefore be asked: why should tiers form? The first reason is that the systems which the assembler will ask the first-tier supplier to integrate, contain diverse technologies in which one company does not have all the necessary skills.

Secondly, some of the components required for systems will be very specialized and thus made by a small number of (large) firms, in large quantities. It makes sense for the first-tier supplier to buy them rather than integrate their

---

Table 7.1 Responsibilities of first-tier suppliers

- Research and development, especially in technologies which are being applied to the automobile for the first time

- Management of subcontractors: coordination previously undertaken by the assembler, including responsibility for sourcing decisions, logistics, total quality, and payment

- True just-in-time supply, possibly with 'paperless accounting' (a dynamic system necessary to support JIT supplies without the traditional formal invoice/advice note process (this might be achieved by electronic data interchange)

- Customer-dedicated staff – especially product engineers, possibly working full time in the engineering departments of the assembler

- Responsibility for warranty: a difficult problem and one traditionally avoided by suppliers since their item will probably be dependent upon other items for correct function, etc. As first-tier suppliers take responsibility for larger sections of the vehicle, it will be necessary for them to become involved in warranty (i.e. end-customer claims) procedures

---

production. Small electronic parts are a good example of this. The supplier may well have only a minority of business in the automotive sector, e.g. Motorola has at least one microchip on every car built in the USA (and most cars in other regions) and yet has only 7 per cent of its sales turnover in automotive business.

The third traditional category of subcontracted work – simple, low added value items (small presswork, etc.) will probably remain a tiering factor for the short to medium term, i.e. they will be bought by suppliers from subcontractors, rather than integrated. As component design develops, however, such parts will be obviated: an example of this is the development of specialized fasteners which do several jobs at once but can only be used in the situation for which they were designed. The demise of general purpose fasteners may be expected to follow, as well as the development of more physically integrated systems.

When the tiering is carried out for the first or second reason, the relationship between the two suppliers becomes more akin to a strategic joint venture than to a purchasing link. The product technology resides in both firms: the first-tier supplier would find it just as difficult to replace the specialist second tier supplier as *vice versa*. In this situation, the suppliers talk about collaboration and may even set up special companies to conduct the business as joint ventures.

The policy implication here is that second-tier suppliers would probably not be able to remain a significant part of the industry (i.e. they would become general engineering subcontractors) if they were to rely on traditional skills-based manufacturing services to their customers. The critical competence for a second-tier supplier is thus technology based: it is the ability to collaborate with a first-tier supplier in complementing the latter's efforts to provide solutions for the assembler.

The tiers in the industry indicated by the post-Japanese model are thus not quasi-ownership tiers (as in Japan), nor are they fixed company classifications. They are groupings formed by collaboration for specific supply purposes. Companies may be first and second tier at the same time, even with the same customer. While *keiretsu* are unlikely outside Japan, supplier associations or *kyoryokukai* are already being formed, in an experimental manner, in the UK – as we saw in Chapter 2. Such groupings might reinforce ties between second-tier companies – possibly leading to a more appropriate use of the term in this context.

In Chapter 8 we shall examine the strategic models for lean suppliers, including a revision of terminology to clarify the positioning choices.

Multi-market presence

There are two aspects to this factor: the combination of original equipment and after-market automotive business, and the combination of automotive and non-automotive business. The technical demands which the post-Japanese model suggests assemblers will place upon components suppliers will require research and development investment which will often not be justified on the basis of original equipment automotive work alone. Many components suppliers already derive significant proportions of revenue from the after-market (varying from 10 to 40 per cent),[14] whilst others have significant non-automotive business to underwrite development costs: see Tables 2.7, 2.14 and 2.18.

The recession experienced in the industry during 1991 served to illustrate this point further. Components suppliers found profits falling faster than sales in many cases, and multi-market groups had to rely upon non-automotive business for survival. For example in Europe in the first half of 1991, Lucas Industries saw automotive sales fall 2 per cent but profits were down by 35 per cent. The group's aerospace business, meanwhile, remained steady in both sales and profit. The argument that after-market and OE business are countercyclical was contradicted by a major drop in sales and profit in this sector also for Lucas. A similar picture was evident at TI (sales down by 7 per cent, automotive sales down by 14.4 per cent, automotive profits down by 29 per cent) and at BBA, where automotive business (about half of total sales) was blamed for 'most of the downturn': 6 per cent in sales, 45 per cent in profits). At Bosch, sales were up by 3.4 per cent, but automotive sales by only 0.8 per cent. Marcus Bierich, chief executive officer at Bosch, said that automotive profits had fallen 'drastically' and that 'higher profits from communications technology, consumer goods, and capital goods were not enough to make up for ... the fall on the automotive equipment side.'[15] Nevertheless, non-automotive business was clearly supporting the firm at this time.

The search for stability from multi-market presence may thus come from such strategies as:

- Being situated in several regions, serving a range of assemblers.
- Being active in non-automotive sectors to spread risk and cyclical effects.
- Providing original equipment and after-market parts.

As skill levels increase for the lean supplier, so it will become more important to retain skilled labour during downturns. Thus the need for stability will increase.

Global operation

The availability of low labour costs in the newly industrializing countries presents the vehicle assembler with an opportunity and a dilemma. Whilst great progress has been made in improving quality and technical ability in some countries (e.g. Mexico), the more strategic services required from a components supplier (e.g. R&D, systems integration, etc.) are generally not available from such sources yet. In addition to this, true global operation is a reality for only a handful of assemblers, and global sourcing even less so.

As lean production develops globally, there will be diminishing returns for assemblers in sourcing parts in low-labour-cost countries for assembly in traditional locations, as suppliers everywhere improve their leanness. It is possible, however, that assemblers will produce vehicles in these countries, e.g. Mexico for North America, Eastern Europe for Europe, Thailand for Japan, etc., and it will make sense to source a great deal of the parts for such vehicles close to the point of assembly. The commercial benefit to be obtained from component production in low cost countries will thus come mainly from the achievements of the major global component suppliers.

The assembler will expect the first-tier supplier to provide benefits in cost reduction, etc., and the latter must compete on the basis of using global sourcing. This may entail manufacturing in several countries, or forming collaborations with companies overseas or both. The supplier, in this way, is able to combine the strengths and cost benefits of various economies, providing at the same time the local services needed for the assembler. The Japanese assemblers' transplants in the USA, for example, have relied to a great extent upon supply from the Japanese suppliers' transplants – for reasons of competence (technology, prices and quality) as well as proximity.

Global sourcing is still a policy of some assemblers, however, and may yet be expected to alter some established domestic relationships fundamentally. For example, in July 1992, the then Chairman of General Motors, Robert Stempel, warned his US and German suppliers that his company's plans for global sourcing could mean loss of business for them (*The Financial Times*, 3 July 1992). Such a policy does not have much in common with lean supply.

Global operation for suppliers also leads to a productive internal competition between national companies within corporate groups. Thus, for example, the Australian and North American divisions of a supplier compete for the supply business to Japanese assemblers – especially where both divisions have experience in dealing with Japanese customers on their home territory. This situation presents a real challenge to the supplier: to ensure that the internal competition is not biased by the location of the group headquarters (see Lamming, 1990).

A slightly different example of this competition is provided by the suppliers' efforts to gain qualification under the assemblers' quality schemes. The Mexican division of Champion, a manufacturer of spark plugs, provided a productive stimulus to its parent group by beating its larger US sister to Ford's Q1 full approval in 1988. Such achievements lead to dynamism within supplier groups which may be a key to the essential pressure under which a lean supplier has to operate.[16]

■ From the post-Japanese model to lean supply

The post-Japanese model provided a basis for discussing the future shape of the automotive components industry and the challenges facing the companies within it. In test presentations and interviews around the world it received substantial input from assemblers and suppliers. During this time, the work of the International Motor Vehicle Program at MIT was reaching its conclusion with the formulation of the concept of lean production.

Whereas the post-Japanese model broadens the scope of discussion to encompass industry structure, etc., it is now appropriate to refocus on customer–supplier relationships, and subsequent proposals for lean supply strategies. Thus, from the post-Japanese model is drawn the concept of lean supply, with a lean supply model for the customer–supplier relationships.

To be a useful stimulus for strategic planning, lean supply has to be seen as a practicable and realistic model – a target for continuous improvement programmes. Since none of the assembler–supplier supply systems is currently exhibiting all the features of the lean supply model, it is not possible to use an example as a guide. Some firms are very close to lean supply, however, and are completing the strategy through the addition of a few last 'pieces'.

Japanese assemblers abroad, for example, may set up lean supplier bases but it will take some time for the R&D relationships to become developed. Working with established suppliers in North America or Europe is very different, as we have seen, from the historical circumstances in which the Japanese model originated.

Lean supply is practicable – the developments in the industry all point to it. In most fields, however, there is some way to go before it becomes a reality.

In discussing the lean supply model, the nine-factor framework is employed: this encourages the focus on development from the previous models – a journey of continuous improvement. This is shown in Table 7.2.

■ The lean supply model

The nature of competition

During the 1980s the lean assemblers began a programme of setting up global manufacturing and design capability. This should be largely completed by the end of the 1990s. Meanwhile, the Western assemblers who already had international operations are learning about lean production (see Womack *et al.*, 1990, pp. 244–5). Component suppliers may thus expect to find lean production, in various stages of development, in all regions, and must thus be able to respond accordingly.

Some of the European assemblers have reduced or reconfigured their international activity. Peugeot and Rover both withdrew from the North American market in August 1991 but both subsequently developed plans for assembly plants abroad: Peugeot in Egypt and Rover in Bulgaria. Volkswagen closed its Westmoreland, Pennsylvania assembly plant in 1988, having invested US$650 million since 1974: 3000 jobs were lost. Others are beginning to expand globally: in July 1992 BMW announced its plans to assemble cars in Greenville, South Carolina, USA, from 1995,[17] while Mazda announced its entry into the North American luxury market with a new marque called Amati, planned for introduction in the latter half of the 1990s (*The Financial Times*, 26 July 1991 and 2 August 1991 and 27 October 1992).

Whereas the US-built BMW cars (a small sports model (the E36–7) derived

Table 7.2 The lean supply model of customer–supplier relationships

Factor	Lean supply characteristics
Nature of competition	Global operation; local presence Based upon contribution to product technology Organic growth and merger and acquisition Dependent upon alliances/collaboration
Basis of sourcing decisions	Early involvement of established supplier in new vehicle Joint efforts in target costing/value analysis Single and dual sourcing Supplier provides global benefits Re-sourcing as a last resort after attempts to improve
Role/mode of data/ information exchange	True transparency: costs, etc. Two-way: discussion of costs and volumes Technical and commercial information Electronic data interchange *Kanban* system for production deliveries
Management of capacity	Regionally strategic investments discussed Synchronized capacity Flexibility to operate with fluctuations
Delivery practice	True just-in-time with *kanban* Local, long-distance and international JIT
Dealing with price changes	Price reductions based upon cost reductions from order onwards: from joint efforts
Attitude to quality	Supplier vetting schemes become redundant Mutual agreement on quality targets Continual interaction and *kaizen* Perfect quality as goal
Role of R&D	Integrated: assembler and supplier Long-term development of component systems Supplier expertise/assembler systems integration
Level of pressure	Very high for both customer and supplier Self-imposed Not culturally specific

from the 3 Series saloon – produced at a rate of about 70 000 a year, for sale in both North America and Europe) will probably be assembled from kits at first, and the Amati vehicle will be imported from Mazda's Japanese plants, in both cases these developments represent challenges to the assembler's supply strategy. BMW will need to purchase locally, if only to appease US legislators, keen to see local content grow (including, of course, R&D),[18] and Mazda's top-line vehicles will affect designs lower down the range, requiring suppliers to lift their game accordingly.

The conclusion is that competition in lean production will be global and that part of the lean supply relationship must be a readiness on the part of the supplier to provide a local service to the assembler wherever it is required in the world. A first-tier supplier that provides excellent service in its home country but is unable to offer similar support to the assembler elsewhere in the world will not be a comprehensive competitor in lean supply. This comprehensive support may either be in the form of setting up a transplant close to the assembler's plant or through joint ventures – the observed approach in Europe (see Chapter 2).[19] In this way a supplier can provide technical input to a vehicle or engine which is to be developed in one region and assembled in another. This is a feature of lean supply which goes beyond partnership and the Japanese model. The supplier must form strategies for global cover separately from the requests of its customers. Rather than simply following a senior partner, the lean supplier has to decide for itself how to balance a portfolio of customers and relationships, in order to exploit its resources and assets in a complementary manner in several directions at once.

The principle of a supplier contributing to product technology, via the medium of collaborative effort with the assembler, is now well accepted. There remains much to accomplish in the West, however, in developing the partnership model to a state where this acceptance is converted into a norm. Lean supply goes beyond this – requiring the supplier to develop technologies independently of the assembler's requests. In lean supply, the supplier may become the technology leader, the innovator, the 'pushy' partner.

For the assembler, there remains the organizational superstructure designed to carry out the majority of detailed engineering: the engineers, the facilities, the technical centres. These are by no means redundant, of course – but a transformation is required, to convert the product development process to lean practice (see Womack *et al.*, 1990, Chapter 5). The labour implications alone will provide major headaches for assemblers, as shown by the experiences of Ford in Europe in July 1992, when trade unions, after a long period of complying with company proposals, joined together to demand that 'no core processes [would] be sub-contracted within the next five years.' Seat assembly (see above) in the UK was singled out for special concern, with unions claiming that sub-contracting the business could lead to a loss of 800 jobs in Ford. In the same month, Ford engineers at the UK Dunton development site staged a one-day strike over the proposal to move 300 engineering jobs to Germany.

In lean supply, competition will centre on such out-sourcing and reconfiguration within the assembler: other factors such as quality, delivery and price must be mastered as 'entry criteria'.[20] As the economic and technological logic points increasingly towards a realignment of assets and responsibilities in the supply chain, both customer and supplier will face difficult challenges in repositioning (this is discussed in the next chapter).

The need to provide all the services will, as described above, require firms to grow and acquire the appropriate resources. Most large suppliers intend to grow: the two basic strategies of merger and acquisition and organic growth appear to be equally favoured.[21] The 1980s were characterized by such activity: at one point, the chief executive officer of the second largest component supplier in Europe said that his firm, Valeo, intended to acquire 'a company every one or two months from now on'.[22]

Despite this growth, even the largest suppliers will need to enter into alliances with other firms, including competitors, in order to provide the service required by the lean relationship. Competition in lean supply thus includes collaboration with competitors and between customers and suppliers.

The basis of sourcing decisions

Since a basic principle of lean production is the elimination of all forms of waste – including superfluous procedures – it is clear that sourcing through traditional competitive bidding is not compatible with lean supply. As seen earlier in the partnership model, sourcing to long-term suppliers provides a more stable basis for the assembler to plan model development as well as production.

It had long been assumed that the traditional 'advantage' of competitive bids was the knowledge of 'best available price' which it gave the buyer. As we saw earlier, however, this is not the case.[23] The intense competition by bid and counter-bid which was characteristic of the stress model might lead to lower prices but not to lower costs. The allowances built into the price by suppliers and the false low pricing, followed by subsequent demands for price increases, mean that the buyer gets a distorted view of the actual costs of the component. Relieved of the need to build in allowances, but challenged with the need to reduce costs continually, the lean supplier works under a great deal of pressure but with less need to apply the same cunning to negotiations.

In the partnership model, based as it was upon the Japanese system, the presence of appropriate partners was assumed: Toyota would always buy from Nippondenso; Honda from Stanley, Nissan from Ikeda Bussan. Nor was this assumption based strictly upon the *keiretsu*: the independent brake manufacturer, Akebono Brake, is a long-term source of brakes to all Japanese assemblers: whilst Nissan and Toyota each own about 15 per cent of Akebono, it is not in either *keiretsu*. In the Westernized version of this – partnership sourcing – a similar assumption is made. This is discussed in Chapter 9.[24]

In lean supply, this assumption cannot always be made: competition will be more dynamic, since there will be many more component firms in the global industry than there were in Japan during the formation of the Japanese model. Accordingly, sourcing to long-term suppliers will be a more complex affair. The demands of lean product development require early identification of the suppliers for key technologies for a new vehicle, but the assembler will be unable to ignore the wide choice on offer from potential suppliers. A situation in which the assembler is faced with a new supplier offering something different (a new type of product or some new technology) might lead to one of three scenarios:

■ The assembler stays with the established supplier and applies pressure and cooperation to enable that supplier to provide competitive technology for the new vehicle.

■ The assembler decides to award the contract to the new supplier, having first given the established supplier an opportunity to develop competitive technology (again with pressure and cooperation).

■ The assembler encourages the two suppliers to collaborate, thereby gaining the advantage of the technology without sacrificing the benefits of the working relationship built up with the established supplier.

The difference between this situation and the partnership model is the extent to which new suppliers play a part in the process. Like partnership sourcing, lean supply places great importance on the developed working relationship in making sourcing decisions – a factor militating against the entry of a new supplier. Unlike the partnership model, however lean supply must allow for such entry, providing the means for retaining dynamic stability during the entry process.[25]

The role and mode of data/information transfer

In the same way that negotiators in the early models of relationships were seen to recognize the importance of information by using it as a tactical weapon, lean suppliers and customers use the same factor as a means of gaining joint competitive strength, to use as a weapon in the final market (i.e. vehicles).

This has several implications. Firstly, the supplier must relate its own business to the sales market of its customer. This requires initiative in assessing that market and also confidence in the information provided by the assembler. For this to be the case the supplier needs to understand the end market in general as well as the specific factors which relate to its business. For example, a manufacturer of micro-electronics may know most about the potential use of microprocessors in telecommunications in vehicles, but must work with the assembler to understand the opportunities and limitations of applications of such technologies with regard to the eventual customer.

Secondly, the supplier must be able to work with more than one assembler in confidence. The degree of reliance upon the supplier on the part of the assembler suggests a threat – strategic information could leak from the supplier to a competitor. Throughout the interviews this subject was revisited constantly, always with the same response: since cars are always examined in minute details by competitors – sometimes prior to launch – an assembler would know immediately if such a leak had taken place and end the relationship. Thus the nature of the end product provides a form of security for the assembler in this respect: the lean supplier will take care to protect technology developed with one customer from reaching another, at least until it becomes public domain (upon the launch of the vehicle). Thereafter, there may be joint licences/patents or other devices to control the transfer of technology.

The third implication of this factor is the need for suppliers to relate their operation to the final market, without the batch production smoothing which traditionally insulated them from it (albeit causing other instability problems in the process). In Japan the very effective automotive selling activity (for the domestic market) has meant that vehicle assembly could be smoothed through the practice of *heijunka* (smoothing of vehicle production over shorter forecast periods by effective connection of the selling activity and production control: see Womack *et al.*, 1990, p. 151 and Monden, 1983). It is not clear that this market situation can be replicated outside Japan, and whilst some major changes in vehicle retailing are expected (see Womack *et al.*, 1990, Chapter 7) it is probable that the supply link between assembler and components supplier will be characterized by fluctuating demands – linked to similar fluctuation in the sale of different varieties of vehicles.[26]

It has been possible since the late 1980s for technical and operational computerized information to be transmitted electronically between firms. The early electronic data interchange (EDI) initiatives in the automotive industry, whilst technically successful, led to problems of mistrust. Transmission of technical specifications was approached with caution by suppliers (still in the stress, or perhaps resolved phases of relationship models), because once the details had been passed from their computer to that of the assembler, designs could be printed on the latter's paper, losing the supplier's name in process. This simple problem was the tip of an iceberg of relational problems which have remained in the EDI field, causing more difficulty than the technical limitations. Suppliers were also faced with the need to invest in several different systems at once to deal with the spread of hardware and software chosen by the assemblers.

The confidence built up within the partnership model relationships provides the basis for full use of EDI, without the fear of piracy discussed earlier. The need for component firms to deal with many customers remains a problem, however, and it is expected that further technical developments in EDI will be 'pulled' by the spread of lean supply. Here, again, is an example of the limitations to the Japanese/partnership model as a strategy and the need for greater autonomy in the supplier. This is discussed further in Chapter 9.

The management of capacity and delivery practice

Given the nature of information exchange discussed above, the planning of capacity and the operational communication related to it must clearly be jointly undertaken for lean supply to be effective. Whilst the long-term nature of their customer relationships has helped Japanese suppliers in investment decisions, including those requiring transplants in North America or Europe, it is centrally important to the principle of lean supply that such decisions are made solely by the supplier on a normal business basis (albeit within the positive atmosphere of healthy, developed, goodwill).

There is no evidence to suggest that close geographical proximity is a requisite part of lean supply: several companies in Japan, the USA and Europe are achieving just-in-time deliveries over considerable distances. In one documented Japanese case, this is being achieved with quality defects at better that 50 parts per million (ppm) in a complex, safety-critical, assembly,[27] over a distance of 200 miles working with four hours' work in process at the customer. It is clearly not the distance but the travel time between supplier and customer which is important – a factor which presents a particular challenge when the goods must flow across international borders. There are obvious benefits to synchronized manufacture of components and vehicles involving 'door-step plants' (component production plants built very close to the assembly plant). It has become common to find seating plants built close to assemblers to provide JIT delivery and synchronized manufacture.

It is interesting to note that in Europe, Toyota has chosen to buy seats from the American supplier Johnson Controls, who are to invest £8 million in a new door-step plant (Burton-on-Trent: less than ten miles from the Burnaston plant). Johnson's subsidiary, Hoover, already supplies seats to Nissan in the UK, through a joint venture with the Nissan group company Ikeda Bussan. Johnson has experience of supplying to the Japanese in the USA (in addition to Ford, GM and Chrysler) and the group vice president of Johnson was instrumental in establishing supply strategies at the GM Saturn plant in Springhill, Tennessee, as member of the supplier panel. The autonomy of the supplier in lean supply is shown in this example: in the Japanese model such interplay would be limited. Whilst the suppliers to one Japanese assembler are encouraged to supply others outside the group, the degree of closeness required for lean supply (technical/design partnership, not simply supplying the parts) is only provided to the group assemblers.

Seating is a special case, however, due to the physical difficulties presented by the large, vulnerable assemblies involved, and the wide variety of specification. In a more general sense, transplant component manufacturing plants will locate in Europe and North America within appropriate travel distances from several assembly plants, in order to serve more than one customer. There will thus be 'door-step' plants, just-in-time (but at a convenient distance) plants, and out-of-area plants. It is possible that the last category will become uneconomic, once lean supply is established as a basis for competition but managing logistics over long distances, including internationally, in a just-in-time manner, will remain an occasional requirement within lean supply. This has major infrastructural implications for some countries, especially those with developing economies.

Dealing with price changes

Joint efforts towards cost reduction form a key part of information exchange in lean supply: there is a combination of working pressure and cooperation, coupled with transparency in costing (i.e. both partners being aware of the relevant parts of the cost structures of each other's process and the implications for one of changes in the other).

As we saw in Chapter 2 (Figure 2.2) the Japanese assemblers and suppliers appear to have controlled the return on assets (ROA) achieved by each company in a partnership. In the West, however, cost accountants are seldom able to give ROA information on a line item basis, even though it is at this level that such intelligence is often needed (in order to know true costs and value, etc.). Perhaps lean accounting would provide the means for such information, upon which lean production might be based in the search for reducing costs, improving value and gaining a better understanding of the behaviour of both. If, as we saw earlier, lean supply requires knowledge of the cost of value-added at each stage, and joint planning on capacity (complementary assets), perhaps it is necessary to agree to similar rates of return on assets in assembler and supplier, in order to optimize the value chain, and thus provide shared competitive advantage.

Within this area the technique of value analysis plays a vital role. Value analysis and target costing are recognized in the West and have been features of mass producers for some time but usually within the confines of the assembler, i.e. the assembler works backwards from the market price of the vehicle through to the maximum price that must be paid for each component. This is then used in negotiations with the supplier.[28] Value analysis only works, however, with accurate information on costs, which is only obtainable via good teamwork, i.e. between accountants and manufacturing engineers, and between customers and suppliers. The identification of costs, which is central to lean production, makes value analysis and target costing especially powerful techniques. In lean supply, the target costing process is extended into the supplier, in order to identify specific needs for cost reduction which become targets for attention of both parties, working together.

As we saw earlier, the Japanese firms began achieving cost reductions through cooperation in customer–supplier relationships in the 1950s. In lean supply this process is incorporated and blended with the need for mutual benefit. Thus, as material supply or economic pressures force cost increases on the supplier, it is the joint responsibility of the partners to find ways to counteract the problem. The skill required in both partners is to ensure that ways are found constantly to improve the process and thus reduce the costs, whilst allowing for factors outside their control. Thus if the raw material price increases by 5 per cent, ways must be found to reduce use of material by 5 per cent, or to reduce another cost to compensate. This is illustrated in Figure 7.6.

This concept is naturally attractive to customers and threatening (in traditional terms) to suppliers. If it is seen as a joint responsibility, however, rather than the traditional ultimatum issued by customer to supplier, the true nature of lean supply emerges. The cost reductions (and hence lower prices) can only be achieved, in a lasting sense, through collaboration. When the full extent of the customer's responsibility is realized, it may even be the customer, not the supplier, who finds the role more onerous. An agreement on sharing the benefits of *kaizen* is required between the customer and supplier in order to make this technique work. Careful use of the process leads to a situation as seen in Figure 2.2, where Japanese suppliers and assemblers show the practical reality of shared destiny.

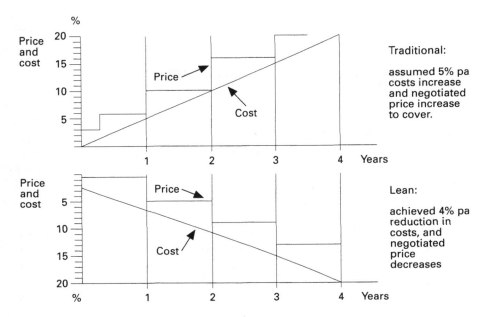

Figure 7.6 The principle of progressive cost reduction through collaboration – an example

Attitude to quality

The approach to quality observed in mass production may be characterized as aggressive and dogmatic. The legacy of twenty years of this approach is a range of supplier quality rating schemes from the Western assemblers which require suppliers to perform in accordance with specific targets, increasingly designed to test strategy in suppliers rather than simply short-term achievements.

The idea of partners constantly vetting one another is contrary to lean supply: such schemes will eventually become redundant for all except new suppliers. It makes no sense for the customer to be constantly checking up on its partners. Nevertheless, performance measurement against agreed criteria is a feature of lean supply when it is used to help the supplier and the assembler to improve achievements within the relationship, and in related areas. Assessment of the relationship itself is the goal, as discussed in Chapter 9.

Thus in lean supply, the ability to provide product quality at defects levels measured in parts per million (so called six sigma quality)[29] is an entrance criterion. Once this has been achieved, the relationship exists on the assumption that quality levels will be constantly improved: the assembler/supplier relationship is only concerned with the subject when there are problems which warrant joint efforts in solution.

As in some of the other factors, a lean supplier is required by the relationship to lead in quality control initiatives, not simply to follow the instructions of the assembler. This changes the relationship into more of a true collaboration and lessens the likelihood of the supplier being seen as the junior partner.

Role of R&D

R&D practice provides the most important link between lean customers and suppliers, since it is one of the clearest manifestations of collaboration on the part of both partners. For the assembler, a move towards the situation noted in Japan by Clark and Fujimoto (see Chapter 5) requires a new approach to becoming interdependent with the supplier. For the supplier, increased activity in R&D must be based upon the belief that the assembler will not exploit the results of that activity unreasonably, to the general disadvantage of the supplier.

In basic terms this might be called trust. In lean supply trust is a vital factor, but it is not naive trust: it is more a matter of mutual agreement on the principles and important points, transparency of information and correct behaviour. It can be likened to arms' control with mutual verification: the need for trust is very small because each party can see what the other is up to and verify that it accords with the shared principles.[30]

As the assembler requires the supplier to develop engineered solutions to vehicle problems and requirements, and as specific technologies such as microelectronics, composite materials, signal multiplexing, etc., increase in their sophistication, complexity and potential, so suppliers may be expected to become the acknowledged specialists. Assemblers in the lean supply model turn their attention to core activities in the vehicle, relying on suppliers to develop sub-assemblies and functional sub-systems. Duplication of effort is removed and the most appropriate assets and resources are applied to the task. At the same time, assemblers reduce the number of suppliers with whom they wish to work (as we saw earlier), thus concentrating the technical responsibilities further into the remaining partners.

In lean supply, the suppliers become involved in the earliest stages of new models – advising on basic technologies. The synchronous engineering practices (see Chapter 5) involve the suppliers as deeply as the assembler.

Level of pressure

From all the above points it is clear that there is a great deal of pressure to perform to the very high levels expected within the lean supply model. The special nature of this pressure appears to stem from its source: self-imposed as well as customer imposed. The lean supplier must drive itself harder than the customer does.

This attitudinal change appears to be the most difficult aspect of lean supply for component manufacturer. In Japan in the 1950s, the pressure was provided by fear for survival. Perhaps this fundamental fear is necessary for lean supply to develop. Success can bring complacency, however, and management ability to retain dynamism in competition is a key requirement of lean supply. An example of this problem is shown in Case-study 7.1. It is a real case, from a Japanese transplant assembler, in 1992.

CASE STUDY 7.1

The need for attitudinal change

One of the greatest complaints of American and European components suppliers in their quest to obtain business from Japanese transplants is the need to have component samples approved and compared to original Japanese sources – a process which normally takes place in Japan. Accusations of unfair treatment abound: clearly the Japanese supplier back home has a strong link into the customer and can apparently influence the appraisal process.

The transplant purchasing offices are therefore at pains to help their local suppliers, and to be seen to be fair. In this case, a local supplier was asked to provide samples for new business on a certain date – a Friday – when a Japanese engineer would be visiting the plant, from Japan, and could see them. Testing procedures were planned to run through the weekend, while the visitor was available.

The Friday came, the visiting Japanese engineer was there, but no samples appeared. The Japanese engineer went home on the Monday without seeing the samples.

On the following Tuesday, the supplier paid his regular monthly visit to the assembler's purchasing office, to discuss general matters, and presented the samples. When asked why they had not been delivered on the specified Friday, the supplier said that, since he was coming on the Tuesday anyway, he thought he might as well bring them with him then.

The working pressure demanded by lean supply must clearly be instilled in the supplier company first as a market-driven requirement but also as a cultural change within the company. This has implications also for the customer: a constant improvement in the pressure on both sides to perform to mutual advantage will only result from genuine collaborative teamwork in the relationship.

■ Lean supply as an example of collaboration

The challenge of lean supply represents a radical innovation for suppliers and assemblers: many traditional values and assumptions are questioned and many established practices are reversed. Perhaps the greatest challenge, however, is that lean supply cannot be achieved by any one company alone – it is intrinsically the combination of the strategies of the supplier and the customer together – true interaction.

Lean supply requires collaboration and might itself lead to further collaboration. We saw earlier how Rothwell noted the importance of developing the day-to-day interactions (market knowledge, inventory control, quality control, etc.) as a sound basis for the technical roles of collaboration and this is clearly reflected in the framework of factors describing lean supply. On almost every count – exchange of information, shared R&D, shared approach to quality, delivery practice, etc. – these factors require collaboration from customer and supplier in order to work. The classic reasons for collaboration, as discussed in Chapter 4, all find resonance in lean supply.

Risk reduction

For the assembler, the risk of moving into an unknown technology (for a new product) is reduced by depending upon the supplier to develop the ideas. In this way, the variety of cars demanded by the 'micro-niche' market may be addressed by the assembler, unencumbered by concern for detailed component development. The supplier, whilst accepting increased technical risk in responding to this, is better assured of the business which will follow successful development and thus can plan accordingly. Since the supplier will invest in assets specific to the collaboration, the assembler's investment risk is reduced. The supplier is likely to acquire assets which are non-specific to the contract, however, and may therefore spread the investment over several customers – including non-automotive industries – naturally ensuring the necessary confidentiality to the assembler.

Economies of scale/rationalization

As already noted, some component technologies are so sophisticated that R&D economies of scale prevent the assembler from vertically integrating their development and production. Lean supply goes beyond this 'no choice' strategy, however, to encompass technologies in which the assembler could invest, but which are assigned to the specialist supplier in order to allow the assembler to concentrate on excellence in other areas whilst reinforcing the supplier's strengths.

Such rationalization clearly requires careful strategy and choice of partner on the part of the assembler, which may have to lose the ability to develop certain technologies (a true transfer of sovereignty) in order to concentrate on core technologies. Partnership may not be sufficiently comprehensive for this to occur, however: lean suppliers may have to make assemblers 'offers they cannot refuse' (i.e. become so good at lean production of their speciality products and technologies that there is little point in the assembler attempting to produce them in house: the Excel Industries example, given in Chapter 6, is a case in point). The assembler retains the ability to switch suppliers if necessary and may thus overcome fears of exploitation (i.e. opportunistic behaviour) from the empowered supplier.

Complementary technologies and patents

This is perhaps the core of technical change in lean production: the union of innovations between customer and supplier, in order to operationalize inventions, is made possible by the concept of shared R&D, the deployment of engineers between firms, etc. In this way Mercedes Benz and Bosch developed anti-lock braking systems technology, whilst Ford and Lucas developed a different technical solution to the same problem.[31]

Co-opting or blocking competition

Joint development of innovations in lean supply inevitably leads to a wish on the part of the partners to obtain technology rents (early profits from being first in the field – before competition begins to reduce the premium which may be charged for a new idea) – shared according to the degree of collaboration. There are many examples of joint licences in which each partner agrees not to use the specific technology with others for a certain period of time. This strengthens individual bonds and may help assemblers to rationalize supply bases.

Overcoming government-mandated investment or trade barriers

This has been seen to encourage the beginnings of lean supply in the transplants of Japanese firms setting up in Europe and North America. The collaborative work between Japanese assemblers and local suppliers (sometimes enhanced by a joint venture between the supplier and a Japanese supplier to the assembler) may be seen cynically as involuntary, but it is a good example of basic lean supply. This is also, of course, an example of *initial international expansion* – another of the classic reasons for entering into collaborations.

Vertical quasi-integration

This is perhaps the most interesting of the factors in this context. The benefits which lean supply offers are those which it was assumed vertical integration should provide. Indeed, it is the redefinition of transaction costs (the basic factors in deciding between vertical integration and subcontracting) which appears to lie at the heart of lean supply.

Competence versus function

There is also a good deal of resonance between lean supply and the concept of collaborators reconceiving themselves in terms of competences instead of functions. A lean first-tier supplier may be more valued by the assembler for its coordination abilities than for being good at, say, machining metal – more important as an expert in microelectronics than as an assembler of printed circuit boards. As the technical challenge facing the assembler accelerates, so it is the higher level competences of the supplier which the assembler seeks. For the supplier, the ability of the assembler to work in a lean supply mode, eschewing the traditional master–servant relationship – or even the senior–junior partner roles – is an important factor in the success of the collaboration (and its absence may even cause the supplier to avoid dealings with that assembler in the long term).

Learning

Throughout the development of the Japanese industry the importance of learning, both individually and organizationally, has been a constant theme. The importance of acquisition of American and European vehicle technology was soon replaced for the pre-war Japanese by the vital ability to learn from what they observed, to recreate, to improve and eventually to innovate. The astonishing success in learning from American influencers in quality control after the war shows the power of this learning ability in the 'studying' sense. The concept of *kaizen* is similarly a manifestation of disciplined personal learning (essentially double loop – see Chapter 4) as an organizational development process. As discussed earlier, a large part of this process in Japan involved the assembler collaborating with the supplier to ensure competent supply was developed.

Networks

Lastly, we saw earlier that specific collaborations (i.e. between one supplier and one assembler) appeared to offer more benefit to automotive component firms than networked relationships. It may now be seen that the need for suppliers to work closely with several assemblers in confidence is an example of both: a network of individual, confidential collaborations, connected by the suppliers and by collaborations between pairs of assemblers. This leads to a controlled leakage of ideas (affected by the 'publication' of technical ideas with every new vehicle) which, as the technical roles of suppliers develop, may be expected to lead to circumstances akin to the 'invisible college' (see Chapter 4), in which some firms play the parts of technological gatekeepers. It is interesting to use a modified version of Allen's diagram (see Figure 4.5) to express this concept, replacing the individuals with, in this case, component suppliers. This is illustrated in Figure 7.7.

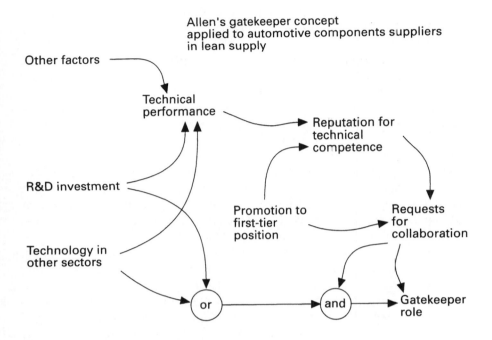

Allen's gatekeeper concept
applied to automotive components suppliers
in lean supply

Note: [a] The following substitutions are made for the factors in Allen's original: 'Requests for collaboration' for 'Consultation from colleagues'; 'Promotion to first-tier position' for 'Promotion to supervisory position'; 'R&D investment' for 'Journal readership'; 'Technology in other sectors' for 'External personal contacts'. The other factors are as defined by Allen for the personal model.

Source: Adapted with permission from *Managing the Flow of Technology* by T.J. Allen, © The MIT Press, 1977.

Figure 7.7 Use of Allen's logic to describe technical flows between 'technological gatekeeper' firms[a]

Allen's diagram, modified in this way, may be taken to represent the supply base for an assembler. Suppliers manoeuvre within the network of relationships by following strategies of 'enrichment'. These may include developing technological expertise in non-automotive sectors, as well as more mainstream R&D for their customers' immediate requirements.

Whatever approach is chosen, each supplier has to build a reputation for technical competence (supported fully by a comprehensive commercial/logistical, lean supply capability). This will lead to promotion to a first-tier position and 'requests' from the customer to collaborate in technical developments (new models). Once the supplier has reached this position, it takes on the role of gatekeeper, i.e. becomes responsible for its chosen technologies, on behalf of the assembler and the other suppliers in the network.

The assembler might view this process as the supplier earning its position in the supply base. The suppliers become part of the assembler's search and selection environment (see Chapter 3) – its eyes and ears for new technologies. The supplier will see it as the strategic repositioning to a point where the assembler has no choice but to operate in a lean supply manner. This concept has clear resonance with the Japanese *kyoryokukai* principle which we discussed earlier.

Whereas in the Japanese *kyoryokukai* systems the technology appears to be led by the customer (the junior–senior nature of Japanese/partnership relationships) in lean supply the technology is the product of the collaboration of the supplier and the assembler as equals. Thus a supplier can work in depth with several assemblers at once and in each case the outcome will be unique. The basic technology and knowhow move forward, however, as a result of the spill over from one project to another (amplified by a network like that shown in Figure 7.7). A collaborative project between a supplier and one customer remains secret until the car is launched, after which, either side is free to exploit the idea (notwithstanding patents, etc.) with other partners. Each assembler can expect the best from the supplier, except for that technology which is the current, unlaunched product of collaboration with another assembler.

In this way, lean supply avoids the problems faced by vertical integration: in-house divisions could not innovate in a fundamental way with competitor assemblers. The Japanese suppliers face the same problem. For example, it is assumed that Toyota will always get the best technology from Nippondenso, so competitor assemblers would not invest their time in trying to develop leading edge competitive technologies with the supplier. In a fully developed lean supply scenario, the supplier acts independently and any assembler is able to collaborate to mutual, temporarily secret, advantage.

■ Why is lean supply beyond partnership?

This question will be discussed fully in Chapter 9, but it might be useful to make some early conclusions at this point.

Partnership, whether it is seen as described here (i.e. deriving from the Japanese model) or in a broader sense (e.g. as implied by the partnership sourcing debate) is clearly a major change of strategy for suppliers and customers. Within partnership, however, the roles of customer and supplier remain senior and junior – the lead comes from the customer, who nevertheless wishes to 'empower' the supplier, for the benefit of both parties. Supplier accreditation schemes and supplier development teams are features of a senior partner helping a junior partner – not a collaboration of equals.

This partnership may have come about as a result of national or regional economic conditions (such as those described in Japan) or as the object of some conscious programme (such as the UK CBI's partnership sourcing initiative). It may be a necessary stage in the development of the relationship but it remains an unequal alliance and consequently misses some of the richness foreseen in lean supply.

For lean supply to go beyond partnership, then, some fundamental shift of position within the partnership is required. The supplier, instead of applying all its efforts to the pursuit of price increases and beguiling the customer, directs it attention towards a new strategy of equality – leading its customers technologically, in areas which it knows best and is best suited to explore.

The difference between partnership and lean supply can thus be seen to a matter of strategy. In the next chapter, strategies for lean supply will be developed.

■ Notes

1. For a good discussion on the role of MITI and the Japanese industrial policy in general, see Johnson (1982) and Morishima (1982).
2. Discussed in full in Lamming (1988) and (1989b). The Post-Japanese model was initially developed in discussion with academic and industrial colleagues on the IMVP – especially Professor Daniel Jones and Ms Maryann Keller of Furman, Selz, Mager, Dietz and Birney, Inc., New York.
3. The three major regions are North America (USA, Canada and Mexico) with inroads into South America (Venezuela, Brazil, Argentina, etc.), Europe, gradually including the old Eastern bloc countries, and the Far East: Japan, Korea, China, Taiwan, Australia, Malaysia, Indonesia, Thailand and India.
4. It should be noted that the number of direct suppliers to an assembler is a very difficult statistic to obtain with practical accuracy. The assemblers do not have any standard way of counting (e.g. if three divisions of a supplier deal directly with a customer, under different trading names, is it counted as one or three? etc.). BCG (1991) report 1990 figures for the European assemblers as follows: Fiat, 900; VW, 1760; Renault, 800; Peugeot, 1100; Ford, 1700; and GM, 2000. The data in Figure 7.1 are from the author's own face-to-face interviews with senior purchasing executives in each of the assemblers, checked in subsequent written confirmation from the interviewees.
5. Only 25 per cent of UK suppliers to Ford have been awarded the more stringent Q1 award (NEDC, 1991).
6. *The Financial Times*, 6 July 1992 and 23 July 1992. See Chapter 5 for a discussion on the use of common or shared parts in new models.
7. Direct labour rates are usually lower than those in assemblers: see Womack *et al.* (1990, p. 139, especially note 2) and Nishiguchi (1989, pp. 155–6).
8. From author's interview with Renault, February 1988.
9. The term 'tail' was first suggested in this context by the author although it has been understood and accepted so readily by interviewees and other discussants that it may be assumed to be common parlance in the industry.
10. Since the plot of a supply base is essentially a snapshot, we must add to these reasons the cases of suppliers who are about to leave the supply base as a result of failing to achieve required performance, and those who are entering it, with small contracts in initial stages.
11. In fact only one interviewee said that his firm (in the UK) had decided to concentrate on one assembler (Ford, Europe). He gave as his reason the good relationship he had with them and the problem he would face in investing in extra capacity to serve other (UK) assemblers with whom he felt relationships would not be good enough to justify the expansion. This view appeared to be based upon a parochial view – seeing the UK as the home market – and a strong emphasis on the value of the relationship. There appeared to be no restriction placed upon him by Ford.

12. The automotive industry is a surprisingly close-knit community. If a supplier were to leak information of a truly strategic nature from one assembler to another, it would soon be known and the supplier's credibility would be destroyed. Leakage in the other direction – from one supplier to another via an assembler – is more difficult to detect accurately but appears to more commonplace.

13. There, it seems, the functional similarity between the Western version of tiering and the Japanese practice ends. It is not the conclusion of the author that this process would give rise to third, fourth and fifth tiers, occupied by many small subcontractors, as found in Japan. The Western version of tiering (for both Western and Japanese assemblers) will have to work without the benefit of the extreme flexibility offered by large numbers of microsuppliers: see Ikeda (1987).

14. Figures from interviews and published data. These compare with the market figures given in Chapter 2, which show for Europe, for example, that the total after market is estimated as ECU20 billion while the OE market is ECU50 billion (1988).

15. Figures from *The Financial Times*: 5 July, 2 August, 6 August 1991. Bosch figures are for five months only.

16. Author's interview, Champion, Mexico, November 1988.

17. *The Financial Times*, 26 July 1991 and 2 August 1991. Whilst this is primarily a reaction to rises in labour rates in Germany (German rate = DM44.47 per hour: US rate = DM35.05), it does suggest that the traditional importance of national identity of the automobile, perhaps stronger in Germany than anywhere else, must now be seen in the light of international competitive factors. BMW will be investing about US\$400 million in the US plant and employing some 2000 people by 1999.

18. A Lucas automotive plant close to the new BMW site in South Carolina makes petrol injectors for BMW engines. Due to BMW's engine build policy, however, Lucas will have to ship the injectors to Germany where they will be fitted to engines bound for re-export to the new plant in South Carolina (*The Engineer*, 2 July 1992).

19. For a comprehensive account on setting up joint ventures in the European industry, see the DTI/SMMT report on supplier innovation (DTI, 1992).

20. This is not to suggest that these three vital factors disappear from the competitive arena; indeed they will increase in importance as technical demands and *kaizen* activities raise the stakes. It is clear, however, that strategies must be based upon the assumption that excellence in quality, price, and delivery is already achieved: any supplier not reaching this basic level of performance will not remain in the industry.

21. Conclusions for author's interviews between 1987 and 1990.

22. M. Noel Goutard, speaking at the Financial Times Motor Conference, London, March 1989. Valeo has not actually maintained this rate, however, due perhaps to the recession in the European industry since then, and the poor fortunes (until very recently) of the two French assemblers.

23. This is confirmed by the extensive and highly detailed research carried out in many supply sectors by the London based consultancy, Purchasing Index Ltd. By confidential, cross-sector benchmarking over ten years, PI have found that what the customer pays for any specific item is a factor of sales behaviour by the supplier and not related to scale of purchase or tendering process. In short, competitive tendering does not even indicate best price, much less the true costs.

24. See the Confederation of British Industry publications on Partnership Sourcing: CBI (1991, 1992).

25. The traditional or stress model would have encouraged the entry of new players – but usually for price reasons, not technology – and failed to retain stability, either in the relationship or in the supply base of the assembler.

26. Most interviewees, both in assemblers and suppliers, referred to the move towards more niches in the vehicle market. This was put succinctly by Wolfgang Reitzle, R&D Director of BMW, in a *Financial Times* article (26 July 1991): 'Even market segments are splitting into fragments. There are niches in niches.'

27. The supplier, Akebono Brake, claimed up to 70 ppm (for a disc brake assembly with about twenty parts in it). The customer, Toyota, said they were receiving as good as 40 ppm. The two figures are generalized: the difference can be attributed to the supplier's modesty.

28. The logic of this process has not always been reflected in practice. Engineers, accountants, and purchasing staff have not always enjoyed good communications and the lack of information exchange between them has resulted in anomalies. In one interview, the buyer said that the design engineering department had, until recently, always withheld the planned vehicle cost data from purchasing, apparently waiting to see how the actual prices compared with their estimates.

29. Six sigma quality is a term derived from statistical process control and statistical quality control which is used to denote products which are manufactured to a defect level of 3.4 ppm, at the process step level (see Harry, 1986).

30. The metaphor is from James Womack's presentation on lean production, 1992.

31. In 1987 Lucas (through its Girling brakes division) also licensed Mazda and Sumitomo Electric Industries to develop an electronic, four channel, anti-skid braking system for the Mazda 626 saloon. The system was not to be offered in Europe, however: Lucas Girling simultaneously developed its own advanced anti-skid system to offer to European assemblers, claiming it could undercut the price of other European systems by half.

8 | Strategies for Going Lean

■ Positioning in the supply chain

As we saw earlier, the concept of the supply chain has become popular parlance in recent years. It is generally discussed in the same terms as the value chain – an association which leads to the assumption that the same strategic goals apply to both, i.e. that the supply chain can be optimized so that value can be added at minimum cost for each stage.

If some comprehensive 'map' of the value chain could be superimposed on the supply chain, this might be practicable. Specialist firms might emerge to carry out each specific step in the process of manufacture. This would be akin to the Japanese situation, where several lower tiers of subcontractors exist, contributing to the efficiency of the total manufacturing sector. The optimized complementarity of assets in the supply/value chain would be an excellent example of lean supply in operation.

The full implications and scope of value chains are rarely seen in practice, however. Few companies can actually identify the stages of their value chain or quantify the value-added at each stage and costs of doing so. The current practical limitations of the principle for European and American firms, (e.g. sunk costs in capital investment, search for economies of scale, growth through merger and acquisition, incumbent labour, etc.) make it unlikely that such an optimized supply chain will emerge in either of these regions in the near future. It is likely, nevertheless, that vehicle assemblers will realize the need to pass on some of the value-adding activity to their immediate suppliers, in order to concentrate on their core business (which need not include designing and assembling vehicles and engines).

The first-tier suppliers will probably want to retain this work and thus grow in their significance. As the proportion of added value for which they are responsible increases, so the first-tier suppliers will need to expand their own technical capabilities. There are three ways for them to do this:

■ Invest in growth (organic or through merger and acquisition) specifically to extend technical skills. The assets thus acquired include people (i.e. skills), equipment, knowhow and organizational strengths (partners, geographical locations, reputations and brands, etc.).

■ Subcontract technical responsibilities – to second-tier suppliers who would develop technical specialisms accordingly.

■ Form alliances with other first-tier suppliers to provide appropriate joint technical abilities as required by the assembler – probably with one company acting as coordinator/integrator.

There will probably be a 'bulging' effect in the companies of the first tier, as suppliers tend to retain all the new business (resulting from the assemblers' passing on the responsibility). It is likely that this will lead subsequently to an overload in first-tier suppliers who will then look to subcontracting technical (as well as production) roles to a lower tier. This process, illustrated in Figure 8.1, is likely to take some time.

• In each of these processes, the customer company will be reluctant to surrender control (and perceived advantage from controlling the added value) to

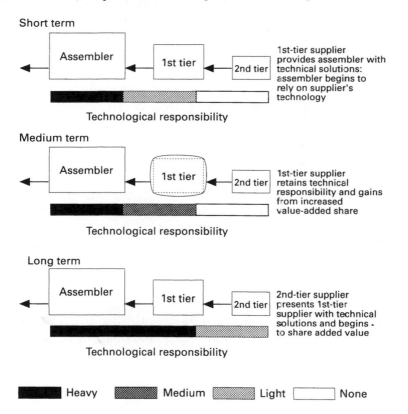

Figure 8.1 Gradual sharing of technical responsibility and added value – short, medium and long term

the supplier. In each case, the supplier will need to present cogent reasoning and attractive commercial packages in order to convince the customer. It is unlikely that customers will exhibit vision in more strategic subcontracting until it becomes an imperative.

The structure of the supply chain will thus become as shown in Figure 8.1. The assembler will identify core business and devote resources to it. The first-tier supplier will absorb the technical work shed by the assembler and enjoy control over more of the value-added. The second-tier subcontractors will continue to be seen as elastic capacity in a production only sense (perhaps with some specialist abilities, e.g. metal finishers (electroplaters) etc.) until they develop technological capabilities which match or exceed the marginal technical responsibilities which will eventually overload their customers – the first-tier suppliers.

There is another aspect to this sharing of responsibility (which can be observed in the Japanese experience) – the lessening of the administrative load at any one level through breaking down and sharing the tasks. As the core technology for each tier is clarified, so the managers and staff in each firm can keep clear targets for achievement and improvement, unencumbered by the complex administrative systems of large, bureaucratic mass production organizations. The simplicity of such systems as *kanban* and *andon* grew from this approach: see Monden (1983).

■ Cost transparency and the value chain

Cost transparency means the sharing of costing information between customer and supplier, including data which would traditionally be kept secret by each party, for use in negotiations. The purpose of this is to make it possible for customer and supplier to work together to reduce costs (and improve other factors).

This transparency of costs across the customer–supplier interface, identified as a feature of lean supply, presents strategic challenges for both customer and supplier in the development of control in value chains. The implications are illustrated in Figure 8.2. The accumulation of value in the supplier's process (including the supplier's own supply chain) is the obvious focus for cost transparency. The customer needs to understand this process and requests information (including overhead recovery rates, etc.) from the supplier. In practice, the customer should only require directly relevant data and should be able to justify any and all requests (i.e. rather than requiring *carte blanche* access to the supplier's costing system). All costs factors are potential targets for improvement, however, including overhead recovery rates, etc.

Revealing this information represents a risk for the supplier: strategies may be exposed, etc. Cost transparency is of no value in reducing total cost of adding value, however, unless it is two way. The customer must share data (including costs and added value calculations) with the supplier about the procedures between the delivery of components and their subsequent use in the assembly process. This

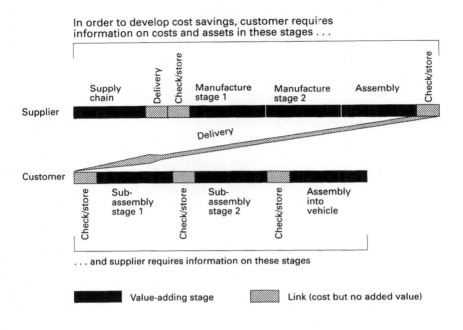

In order to develop cost savings, customer requires
information on costs and assets in these stages . . .

... and supplier requires information on these stages

Figure 8.2 Cost transparency in lean supply: a combination of the
supplier's value chain and part of the customer's

sharing may lead to suggestions by the supplier on potential cost savings which
might accrue from de-integration of the value chain.

Cost transparency is essential in lean supply for the sharing of pain in difficult
times. Customers and suppliers have to find ways of preventing the effects of
recession from causing lasting damage (e.g. to R&D abilities). As the
interdependence of lean supply grows, so the problem of declining markets for
vehicles (and thus components) must be faced together. The collapse of a lean
supplier due to such a recession would be a major blow to its customers. As we
saw earlier, a presence in non-automotive markets helps the supplier to cope in
such situations. The Japanese industry has enjoyed substantial growth for many
years and the Japanese model of relationships does not have a clear answer to the
problems which are faced in recession.

■ Supplier development

The natural companion for cost transparency is supplier development by the
assembler. Once the information is shared, joint efforts can be made to reduce
costs and rationalize the value-adding process. Supplier development is not

215

something traditionally practised by assemblers in the West and indeed examples still abound of their ignoring its importance. General Motors's demand to North American suppliers in 1992 for example – to reduce prices by at least 20 per cent over four years[1] – is perceived in practice to bear only minimal relation to genuine supplier development.

The Japanese assemblers in the USA, meanwhile, realizing the need for massive improvements in their local supply bases during the next phase of their consolidation as manufacturers in the region, are investing heavily in supplier development. The same is true for the Japanese transplants in the EC, where some of the European assemblers are following suit. In 1991, for example, Nissan in the UK began holding purchasing seminars for its first-tier suppliers, to help them in selecting their own suppliers. Nissan also helps to develop its non-first-tier suppliers – over thirty firms from the second tier benefited from Nissan's advice in 1991.

The two-way nature of cost transparency, discussed above, also has a relevance for supplier development. The supplier may well be able to help the assembler to improve processes in the early part of its value chain (Figure 8.2). This is still a distant prospect for most customer–supplier relationships but should be borne in mind as part of strategic collaborations in the future.

The case described in Case-study 8.1 is a true story from the European auto industry, in 1992. Customers A and B are actual assemblers whose identities are disguised for obvious reasons.

CASE-STUDY 8.1

A purchasing manager from Customer A was visiting a components supplier. He knew that one of his supplier development teams was currently working at the supplier's plant and was keen to see what progess they were making. He visited the team members who were working side by side with the operators in one of the supplier's workshops, trying to improve details of the production process. The customer's engineers were wearing their usual company overalls but they fitted in well with the supplier's operators, with whom they had obviously established a team spirit.

The purchasing manager was interested to hear from his host that a supplier development team from another assembler – Customer B – was also working in the plant, on another process. He asked if he might see how this team was operating and was taken to the workshop where they were currently working.

Customer B's team consisted of three people. The first man wore a sports jacket and rollneck sweater: he looked very smart but somehow out of place on the shopfloor. The second man wore jeans and T-shirt. This was perhaps in an attempt to be casual but he had overdone it and looked much less workmanlike than the supplier's operators. The third member of the team was a woman who wore a full length, stylish fur coat. This incongruous team was standing apart from the supplier's operators, holding clipboards and stop-watches, and observing in the traditional work study manner.

The supplier did not have to tell his guest which team was taken seriously by the operators nor which he expected to provide real help to his company.

■ Positioning choice

The customer services required of a first-tier supplier in lean supply, whilst they have some relation to traditional roles, clearly represent new challenges for all firms. There should therefore be a series of strategic 'positioning' choices for component suppliers, perhaps delineated by levels of necessary investment (barriers to entry for new players).

There is little choice for the large, well-established suppliers. They will be expected by their customers to assume a range of first-tier roles: coordination and integration of systems, fundamental research and development, regional invest-ment in manufacturing, global operation capability, etc. A large supplier which does not develop and exhibit such capabilities will miss the opportunities offered by tiering and may be forced to become 'indirect' or even assume a place in the second tier – possibly representing a major involuntary shift of strategy. Developing first-tier capability is not easy, however, even for the largest suppliers in Europe and North America. The prospect is affecting each differently.

Bosch, for example, has formed joint ventures in the USA with two of its licensees in order to supply transplants and the American assemblers. Japan Electronic Control Systems (JECS) is a Nissan supplier and Bosch licensee in Japan (for fuel injection systems). Bosch holds 12.5 per cent of JECS equity, Nissan has 54.2 per cent and Zexel 25 per cent. Bosch also holds 13.1 per cent of Zexel equity (compared to Nissan's 11.2 per cent) showing just how far the German company is involved in the *keiretsu* system (Dodwell, 1986, updated by research data, 1992). Since Nissan could not buy fuel systems from JECS in the USA (because licensees are usually not allowed to compete directly with Bosch in the same region), the two suppliers formed a joint venture company specifically for this contract. Bosch also has a joint venture with Nippondenso in the USA to manufacture fuel pumps: Bosch's production levels and Nippondenso's import quantities (for similar products) were both insufficient, so the two joined forces. Bosch, which has a technology centre in Yokohama with a staff of 130 (over 100 of whom are Japanese), has an ABS licence agreement with Nippondenso (who supply Toyota) and a joint venture (Nippon ABS) with a Nissan supplier – Nabco. In addition there is a link with the Japanese brakes company, Akebono. At the same time, the company has grown by acquisition, buying Airflow Research and Manufacturing in the USA , Voest-Alpine (diesel fuel injection), and a 49 per cent stake in the Brazilian communications technology firm Telmuti in 1990. Lastly,

Bosch has formed joint ventures in Germany with the Japanese firm TDK, to make sintered products, and with Varta Batteries AG, to manufacture starter batteries.

Valeo is to ally itself with Motorola in an interesting partnership which brings the French company access to first-class expertise in microelectronics (a naturally systems-oriented technology), whilst the American partner gains access to mechanical systems business in Europe. Similarly Siemens has gained French R&D resources by the purchase of Bendix Electronics in Paris. Siemens also has a joint venture with GKN – Emitec – to exploit the increase in the catalytic converter market, using patents bought from the German company, Behr. In turn, Emitec has licensed the Japanese substrate manufacturer, Usui Mishima, to supply the assemblers in Japan. The North American company, TRW, is planning to collaborate with Magneti Marelli, of Italy, to produce active rear steering and suspension systems for sale in Europe. TRW (a global organization) will develop similar products on its own, for sale in North America, where Magneti Marelli already has a strong presence. The organizational flexibility shown by these examples illustrates the extent to which a first-tier supplier must develop to provide customer service.

It might also appear that smaller firms have a natural place in the second tier. This view is based largely upon their lack of the financial resources which are necessary to secure a place in the first tier. Some of these firms, however, are rich in technology and have long experience of direct supply: they will be a natural part of the responsibility sharing identified above. Firms which have built an expertise in one or two product types are thus faced with the choice between adding competences (with implications for resources and skills – an investment decision) to become a systems integrator (first tier) or maintaining their narrow expertise and facing the prospect of second-tier status. In the latter case, however, a technology link may still be required (i.e. between the second-tier supplier and the assembler) despite the physical supply link being directed through the first tier. It is clear that second-tier firms will be driven (by their customers and by the final market) just as hard as those in the first tier. A strategic choice to reside in the second tier is not, therefore, the easy option.

An interesting situation exists for large companies who clearly feel that they are the natural members of the first tier (a view not always shared by the assemblers). Such firms may not have an obvious direct link with the assembler and therefore face the challenge of creating one. The obvious path for this is acquisition. An example of this is Mannesman, which has been building a presence in the components sector by acquiring Europe's largest clutch manufacturer, Fichtel and Sachs, in 1987, and Boge (shock absorbers and struts) and VDO (instrumentation) in 1991.[2] Mannesman now has interests in wheels, clutches, suspension, brakes, axles, instrumentation and body mouldings, in addition to its traditional core businesses of steel and electronics. From a small automotive components business four years ago, the company has established a sales level approaching US$4 billion.[3] This is a clear first-tier strategy.

On the other hand, Philips of the Netherlands has an even larger level of components business (US$4.8 billion in 1990)[4] but lacks an automotive division (no official automotive sales figures are ever published by the company). As a result, Philips is often omitted from discussions on core companies in the industry. Its influence, however, defies second-tier classification.

The Valeo–Motorola alliance is another form of first-tier access strategy, reflecting the gap that has existed in Europe for some time for an electronics first-tier supplier, equipped with mechanical technologies, to challenge Bosch. The developments of Siemens during the late 1980s, from a non-automotive position, was another example of this strategy. (Siemens is still on the acquisition trail and was beaten to the VDO acquisition by Mannesman.)

■ Requirements of the assemblers

In addition to the technical relationship discussed above, the assemblers' requirements for partnership sourcing and innovation in logistics are strategic opportunities for suppliers.

Partnership sourcing

Partnership sourcing[5] is the term widely used to refer to a purchasing strategy based upon partnership (broadly as discussed earlier) rather than traditional competitive tendering processes. It is now clear that all the Western automotive assemblers wish to explore partnership sourcing and eventually move to a position approximating to lean supply. There are several different manners of approach to this; however, ranging from a 'get tough' policy (e.g. GM Europe),[6] to a developmental, problem-solving cooperation (e.g. Nissan in the UK, Honda in the USA, etc.). Examples of the former include across the board demands for blanket reductions and bravura in public appearances: the latter is typified by assemblers working with a potential supplier, before awarding a contract, to improve the quality and reduce the cost of its components (which may even be destined for the assembler's competitor) in order to teach the new supplier the principles of lean production.

Many European suppliers have not grasped the full implications of partnership and there are still some significant national differences. For example, in summarizing the situation, the NEDC (1991) report on Nissan in the UK concluded that: 'Quality from other European and Japanese suppliers tends to be better than from the United Kingdom: on a rough and arbitrary scale, Nissan sees Japan as being 100, other European countries 80 and the United Kingdom, on average, 65–70.' This situation may be reflected in the supplier choices of Toyota in the UK, setting up their supplier base some four years after Nissan, who have chosen a higher proportion of non-UK European suppliers.[7]

Further in the same report, a postal questionnaire (*n*=30) of existing suppliers to Nissan in the UK and 'potential' suppliers (those not supplying the Japanese assembler at present), it appeared that '46% of existing suppliers think it reasonable to hide cost savings from the customer, despite the implications for a relationship based upon trust.' Of the total number of suppliers surveyed, 51 per cent thought it unreasonable that a supplier should be expected to pass on reductions in its manufacturing costs to the customer.

This very traditional attitude to engineering improvements and cost savings is perhaps connected to another published feature of the same suppliers: Nissan's UK purchasing director warned in February 1992 that UK suppliers' greatest collective weakness was their lack of research and development capability, whilst delivery and quality were much improved. Interestingly, the purchasing chiefs of Ford and Rover said they were not able to get the same quality from British suppliers as they received from firms in Germany and Spain.[8]

Partnership is based upon commitment, trust and continuous improvement. The fact that Japanese assemblers do not have written long-term contracts, relying instead on short-term stipulations for deliveries but very long-term (next vehicle model) involvement of the supplier, based upon mutual trust, is an indication of the very different business culture that partnership requires.

As discussed above, some misconception surrounded early Western responses to the partnership concept, often focusing upon the perceived 'cosiness' of such relationships. In fact, close working relationships between customer and supplier operate under a far higher level of pressure than traditional mass production arrangements.

As Western assemblers develop their requirements for lean supply, from their American and European suppliers, it is clear that a great deal of attitudinal change has still to occur in the supply base, as well as in the purchasing organizations of the Western assemblers. This change will go beyond that needed for partnership – especially in terms of the assembler's attitude towards the status of the supplier.

Logistics

Since the recognition by the Western industry in the early 1980s of just-in-time delivery practices in Japan, all assemblers have been seeking ways of implementing the ideas in Europe and North America. This has often been expressed publicly by senior management as a 'philosophical' move, but practised at operational levels as another tactical ploy by the customer to reduce internal costs and shift the burden (e.g. of inventory) on to suppliers. Tactics have varied from requiring suppliers to hold stock in local warehouses (most assemblers have done this, including Toyota in Japan and Nissan in the UK) to so-called 'milkround' plans (see Chapter 6).

In Europe and North America there has not been a clear preference for localized manufacturing plants (door-step plants) to be built close to assemblers, although some evidence of this is now clear at Nissan in the UK, where the assembler has leased local land to some key suppliers. There have been, however, new location strategies brought about by the arrival of the Japanese assemblers in the UK (e.g. plants in the north-east, Nippondenso in Telford, etc.) and door-step plants for specific types of components (e.g. seating assemblies are assembled close-by for most assembly plants).

As noted earlier, experience in Japan has shown that just-in-time can be carried out over long distances, even coping with peripheral Tokyo traffic, and it is reasonable to expect similar service from suppliers in Europe and North America without the necessity for door-step plants for all assembly plants.

The need for just-in-time logistics does, however, have a bearing upon choice of supplier for the Western assemblers. Local content pressure (heightened by the Europe–Japan and US–Japan negotiations on import and local build levels) will continue to encourage assemblers to source locally, regardless of ownership nationality. It is clear, however, that if the local suppliers are not able to satisfy the very stringent requirements of assemblers (newcomers and established firms who develop lean strategies) then inward investment from other regions, principally the Far East, must be expected. Reports so far appear to agree that no great influx of Japanese components suppliers is likely in Europe in the wake of Nissan, Honda and Toyota (Technomic, 1990), but the requirements of lean manufacturing, including those of toolmaking and material supply, will not be compromised in the long term. Examples exist in other industries of Japanese inward investment in the UK to replace non-lean operations in raw material manufacture (e.g. white chemicals[9]) and the reliance of lean automotive manufacture upon a lean supply chain has already been amply demonstrated.

Thus Western-based assemblers (transplants and indigenous) will urge Western component suppliers to become lean until the mid- to late-1990s. If specific areas of lean supply are not available to the assemblers by then, inward investment from the Far East in the late 1990s seems inevitable. In some cases, e.g. support functions such as lean production in toolmaking, this timescale may be much shorter. When inward investment is perceived as inevitable, the political debate will shift from trade barriers to investment controls (limitations on foreign ownership). This has already begun in the USA and the 1993 EC–Japan negotiated 'understandings' include 'expectations' (from the Europeans) on the rate of expansion of Japanese inward investment.

■ Strategies available to suppliers

Automotive components suppliers face a choice in positioning themselves for competition within lean supply. There are at least two paths, either of which could be successfully followed. For each path, there is a model strategy.

These models apply not to the relationship between customer and supplier but to the manner in which the supplier presents itself to the customer – its positioning. They refer to structural factors (size, configuration, etc.), strategic planning (approaches to competition, etc.) and to operational approaches (policies of continuous improvement, etc.). Whilst it is the supplier who must formulate the strategy, the challenge of lean supply, as captured in the model, also applies to the assembler. The role of the customer is crucial in enabling and encouraging the development of these strategies – the supplier cannot be expected to make all the running.

There may, of course, be other possible strategies – no discussion can be seen as exhaustive. There are almost certainly many variations of the models derived: the two which are perceived to be of fundamental significance are addressed in connection with each of the strategies: these are referred to as 'modes' for purposes of this discussion. The two model strategies are named key player and loyal collaborator; the two modes are called leader and follower.

■ The key player strategy

Several factors of lean supply suggest the necessity for suppliers to achieve 'equal' status through growth and consequent power. This is not a case of fighting might with might but of assuring the customer of the supplier's competence in critical areas. The required competences vary with the circumstances and may be expected to include critical mass in basic infrastructure (quality systems, delivery ability through location, R&D, EDI, etc.). Taken to their logical conclusion, these suggestions lead to a vision of the lean supplier as a large, technically expert, authoritative, international corporation – strong enough to support the high-risk technologies required for modern automotive development, and flexible enough to respond at the operating level to the demands of the high-variety, microniche market.

Such companies do already exist and may be presently observed in the process of consolidating their strengths (notwithstanding downturns in the market which cause even the strongest firms to adopt consolidation strategies for a while). These suppliers may be seen as adopting the key player strategy. This involves the following:

■ Establishing a technological lead, possibly in several related areas.
■ Having a defined innovation strategy.
■ Having a policy of absorbing or acquiring technologies fully rather than simply 'borrowing' them via collaboration.
■ Growing, through a mix of merger and acquisition and organic development.
■ Establishing a global presence.
■ Taking the initiative on improvements in delivery performance, quality control, and pricing.
■ Competing on traditional strengths and also through collaborative ventures.
■ Being a first-tier supplier, direct or indirect.

Establishing a technological lead

A technological lead, in specific technologies, is required on the part of the supplier to assure the assembler that the long-term relationship will produce appropriately timed product innovations required for the development of competitive vehicles. The stability given to the assembler's component supply system by retention of suppliers, even occasionally in the face of lower price competition, is created by this assurance and must be continually maintained.

The supplier must therefore seek to lead both its competitors and its customers: for traditional competitive reasons in the first case and for lean supply reasons in the second. Collaboration between suppliers also fits into this picture: the supplier with the technological lead will have a better chance of securing the coordinator role in a joint venture (and with it, possibly, the opportunity to control more of the value-adding process).

As the role of the supplier develops (both for the individual company in a specific relationship, and as an industry norm), the technological lead will probably encompass skills in several related areas (e.g. steering, suspension and electronics) leading to a systems integration capability not previously seen. The lead position is necessary for the supplier to ensure that the technical means of satisfying market requirements can be provided through the collaboration.

This lead must be supported by significant patenting activity, derived from substantial R&D investment. To be a key player it is necessary for the firm to be genuinely more expert in its chosen technologies (including related integrative skills) than its customer. An essential part of this strategy is identification by the supplier of the technologies over which the assembler will wish to retain control and those which are likely to be the responsibility of suppliers. The key player can influence this decision and it is apparent that assemblers will vary in their definitions of core technologies. Maintaining a collaborative position in product technology will require the key player to employ design engineers who work constantly between supplier and customer companies.

As technologies tend to become more sophisticated, so the likelihood of necessity for substantial non-automotive technology expertise increases for suppliers. The key player strategy is thus probably linked, in the medium to long term, to spill-over technology – transfer of technological solutions from one part of the firm's R&D to another. In electronics this is clearly already the case (e.g. development of microprocessors for high volume non-automotive applications) and in new materials, transfers are currently becoming apparent (e.g. composites developed for aerospace applications).

A defined innovation strategy

Making the correct technological choices means that the key player must define an explicit policy on innovation, and a resulting strategy. This includes articulation of technological/design trajectories with which the company associates itself and strategic approaches to managing search and selection environments (see Chapter 3). There are clearly human resource policy implications (e.g. how to identify, encourage, develop and reward technological gatekeepers?), investment decisions (e.g. allocation of financial, human and collaborative resources to particular paths), and commercial choices (e.g. which customers to align with).

The technology trends in automobile design will force key players to choose specific trajectories (specific technologies/design approaches, and possibly integration methods). It will not be sufficient to claim a general technical awareness in a broadly defined area.

The Key Player may need to be involved in scientific research (blue sky R&D) as well as applications engineering, including links with other research establishments, including universities, etc. The role of organizations such as the Society of Automotive Engineers (SAE) and supplier industry organizations (on a regional level – requiring better collaboration between national associations) might take on a new importance in such developments.

A policy of absorbing or acquiring technologies

The approach a company takes to collaborations – especially in light of the finite nature of such ventures as discussed earlier – will clearly be important. The key player will plan, perhaps aggressively, to absorb and acquire technologies (process and product) rather than simply to borrow them. The latter path will be an important route for acquisition, however: the key player may be expected to conclude collaborations by buying out its partner. In short, the key player needs to have a strategy for organizational learning contained within its growth strategy.

Growth strategies

Whilst size itself is not a guarantee of success or partnership ability, it is evident that many of the goals of a key player will be attainable only by companies of substantial size. Key players may be expected to grow, therefore, through a mix of merger and acquisition and organic development, to a size of at least US$2 billion automotive sales, probably within a context of corporate sales of US$5–10 billion (depending upon the principal product technology).[10] Corporate spend on R&D would be at least 5 per cent and possibly as high as 10 per cent for short periods (one to two years) with transfer of technologies to automotive from other areas encouraged.

Another way of expressing this is by market share (i.e. in specific component types). Some of the current leading firms in Europe have stated that they would need at least 20 per cent of their market in order to support the responsibilities of the new roles. This seems a reasonable minimum but it must be remembered that component applications technologies are tending to converge (via systems design), whilst geographical markets are tending to coalesce (regionally and globally).

Establishing a global presence

This is partly a matter of reflecting the developments in the assembly industry (as cars are designed worldwide by assemblers, so component suppliers must be able to operate as partners in several locations at once) and partly a feature of critical mass – the necessary ability to draw on international resources for technology and optimum manufacturing. Thus the key player will be able to conduct multi-site product development projects (coping with the very complex communications networking required for this) and also employ assets within a global corporate structure to ensure value is added at minimum cost, etc.

Initial signs are that this would probably be accomplished mainly through wholly owned subsidiaries in the three main regions. In many cases, this will be approached via local joint ventures, either with an indigenous firm or a partner from another region. The Siemens–GKN joint venture – Emitec – discussed above, provides a good example of this. The TRW-Magneti Marelli collaboration (which will not include a separate joint-venture company) shows that even the largest firms will need to be flexible and imaginative in the development of global capacity. As we have seen, however, joint ventures and collaborative arrangements have finite lives: the eventual scenario for a key player is to have wholly owned divisions in each region.

Taking the initiative on improvements

This is perhaps the most enigmatic of the features of a key player strategy – partly because it has always been theoretically possible but rarely attainable. The principle of equal partners is not fully understood by assemblers and, in some cases, not totally accepted. There is therefore an onus placed upon suppliers to convince through persuasion and performance.

Taking the initiative encompasses exceeding expectation and leading by example. Areas in which key players need to accomplish this include delivery performance, quality control and pricing (through cost reductions). The key player must constantly anticipate the moves of the customer and exceed the requirements. This requires a policy of continuous improvement and a close working relationship with the customer. This extraordinary performance by the key player will in time develop the dynamic stability of the long-term relationship, assuring the customer of the benefits contained within it.

Competing on traditional strengths and collaborative ventures

The key player will clearly be a company rich in traditional strengths – products, broad technologies, process and delivery capabilities, etc. These will always be required and will require constant development. Given the need for both merger and acquisition and organic growth, as discussed above, such strengths may have been within the company for a long time or acquired recently. The ability to embrace collaboration as a competitive strategy will be almost as important a characteristic for the key player, however, as the need to gain new skills grows, to satisfy increasingly sophisticated customer demands. Thus the focus of strategic planning moves, in traditional terms, from the strengths of the SWOT analysis, to the opportunities.[11]

The benefits of collaboration to the key player were discussed earlier as part of lean supply. It is likely that the key player will generally take a leading role in collaborative ventures: the need for a clear, finite-term objective on entering such a venture is paramount.

Being a first-tier supplier: direct or indirect

The distinction between direct and first-tier suppliers was also discussed earlier (see Figure 7.4). For the key player, a first-tier position is important because of the influence which will be associated with it, in terms of technological developments. Systems integration takes place at the first tier also and this has been shown as the domain of key players.

The need to maintain daily contact with the customer in operational matters and to conduct the activities outlined in the lean supply model will be central to the role of the key player but the methods of achieving this position are likely to vary. The need for significant presence in non-automotive markets, discussed above, implies that some of the major firms in the industry will rank automotive business as a minor part of their portfolio and accordingly not wish to become direct suppliers, where this would require them to embark upon fresh technological paths (e.g. producers of electronic components which are supplied to sub-assembly manufacturers, which then ship directly to the assembler). Such firms remain influential, because their product technology is pervasive in its influence, and first tier, because assemblers need to involve them in fundamental development work, including potential systems integration, but they are indirect suppliers.

■ Problems faced by key players

Clearly, reaching key player status is a massive challenge for any company. Once this level has been attained, there are inherent problems in managing the customer interface. The principal problems for a key player will be as follows:

■ Maintaining and increasing the pressure to excel. This is a general problem associated with success but applies specifically to the need for continuous improvement and the process of cost reduction within the supplier. In particular it appears to be more difficult for larger suppliers to countenance transparency of information exchange with regard to cost structures, etc. Operational approaches to this problem must be found by the key player.

■ Creating the 'closeness' of the individual buyer–supplier relationship. The attraction for the buyer of the small, loyal supplier is absent when the partners in the relationship are equal. In the light of experiences discussed in earlier chapters, the buyer may even feel real discomfort with a 'powerful' supplier. The key player must maintain the new role of equal partner whilst ensuring that the customer does not become contemptuous.

■ The loyal collaborator strategy

The lean supply base does not exclude firms who choose not to follow the key player strategy – many of the requirements of the assembler may be met by other types of firm. It is useful, therefore to bring together the attributes of such non-key players as an alternative strategic model, starting from the same premise – that lean supply will be an essential part of any supplier strategy.[12] The core strengths of the non-key player will be the ability to form a collaboration with the customer on an unequal basis – as a responsive partner, rather than a true 'equal'. The concern of the customer in this case will be that the supplier exhibits loyalty. Hence the title of the second strategy model: the loyal collaborator.

This model will involve:

■ A sound, proven competence in specific component technologies.
■ An excellent response to customer demands on delivery, quality, and pricing.
■ A direct contact, first-tier or second-tier position.
■ A growth strategy.
■ International links to assist the assembler in global supply.
■ Competing on the basis of closeness in the relationship and flexibility of supply.
■ Maintaining significant presence in other, non-automotive markets.

A sound, proven competence in specific component technologies

The loyal collaborator will require a sound competence and proven track record in specific component technologies, including the ability to provide engineering solutions to complex vehicle problems, possibly in collaboration with other suppliers. This means that the supplier must conduct some R&D activity, though probably not blue sky. While it is likely that the company will not be the integrator, the skills of working in systems integration mode (with competitors and customers) must be developed by the loyal collaborator.

Excellent response to customer demands on delivery, quality and pricing

The loyal collaborator must be as lean as the key player in the ability to use *kaizen* in cost reduction and in flexible use of capacity. Cooperation with the customer's engineers (i.e. in process development to reduce costs, etc.) is a basic requirement and transparency of costs is required. This factor provides an important differentiation between the two strategies: the loyal collaborator is essentially in reactive mode whereas the key player is proactive. The need for self-imposed working pressure – an essential feature of lean supply – is the same in both cases.

A direct contact, first-tier or second-tier position

In a second-tier position, the loyal collaborator may not be a direct supplier to the assembler but must be prepared to conduct technical developments in conjunction with it. Thus, for example, the door locks which are made by the loyal collaborator may be designed and developed in close cooperation with the assembler but delivered to the first-tier, door supplier, for sub-assembly and integration with the electronics system, prior to despatch to the assembly plant. Similarly, the manufacturer of seating fabric sells its material to the seat assembler (second tier to first tier), but must maintain close contact with the vehicle assembler. It is possible that the loyal collaborator might hold a first-tier position, particularly in situations where the assembler has significant in-house investments in the technology and requires a responsive partner for development purposes, as opposed to a proactive systems integrator to take broader responsibility.

Growth strategy

The responsibilities envisaged for the loyal collaborator indicate the need to grow to an annual sales turnover of between US$500 million and US$1.5 billion, with between 3 per cent and 5 per cent spend on R&D.[13]

International links to assist the assembler in global supply

The same rationale on global operation, discussed above, applies for the loyal collaborator but to a lesser extent: the supplier may be asked to operate internationally but need not take the initiative. International links (i.e. interregional but not necessarily global or comprehensive) may involve joint ventures in some cases.

Competing on the basis of closeness in the relationship and flexibility of supply

The advantage of the loyal collaborator strategy is contained in the responsive partner status, which fits well with the traditional purchasing approach (i.e. it does not threaten the established position of the customer). This closeness in the relationship and the flexibility of supply which the supplier must engineer, characterize the loyal collaborator company.

Maintaining significant presence in other, non-automotive markets

The need for maintaining significant presence in other, non-automotive markets (or automotive aftermarket) is present for the loyal collaborator but not necessarily for the technical reasons given above for the key player. Significant business in other markets will help the supplier to present a confident image to capital markets and to survive through recessions in the automotive industry. The transfer of technology from other markets to automotive business is a possibility but not a priority for the loyal collaborator.

■ Problems faced by loyal collaborators

The problem which the loyal collaborator will face is the traditional product-development risk: the supplier must expect to be asked to develop new components despite the low R&D involvement it has chosen to provide. This will increase the need for trust and loyalty in both partners and will tend either to bind the supplier to the assembler or to shift technical responsibilities to the key players, moving the loyal collaborator to the second tier. Loyal collaborators who wish to retain a first-tier position but not to grow to key player status must therefore maintain a dynamic balance in order to avoid having their choices being made for them.

■ Leader or follower?

From the discussion so far, it might appear that a key difference between the lean supplier and the traditional supplier (even under the partnership model) is the need to 'lead' the customer in several operational aspects (e.g. quality). It may be, however, that a supplier can develop lean attributes but remain an excellent follower – ensuring that the customer receives the service required whilst choosing to limit automotive investment.

It might be assumed at first sight that the key player is a natural leadership strategy whilst the loyal collaborator could best be seen as a follower. The nature of the components industry contradicts this assumption, however. Many high-technology firms are involved only to a minor extent in the automotive industry and do not regard it as their most important division. This is often true, for example in fasteners, raw materials, electrics and electronics.

So, key players may choose not to be leaders but to follow the movements of the automotive customers, ensuring that they receive what they want and need as it is required (an approach which still requires the considerable R&D investment identified above for key players). Innovation is still important in such a follower key player and the benefits of technologies developed for applications in other markets may be significant contributions to the automotive industry.

Similarly, the loyal collaborator may take a leading role in specific projects, developing solutions beyond the specifications of the customer. As we saw in Rothwell's research in Chapter 2, small to medium-sized firms may often provide more than their share of innovation to an industry. The two models of strategy and the two modes of approach may thus be combined, as shown in Table 8.1.

■ Discussion of the strategies

It is clear from the discussion above that the two strategies, operating in the two modes, may overlap; that is, companies adopting different strategies may find themselves in direct competition. This will produce a dynamic supply market for the assemblers, offering a range of technological solutions to problems. Since it is expected that, for a given technology, assemblers will specify differing requirements for supplier involvement (e.g. as a result of different identified core technologies), it may be assumed that suppliers will need to operate a mixture of strategies to accommodate several customers.

This situation may be expected to lead to collaboration opportunities for the suppliers, in response to varying demands. For example, a key player which is requested to integrate a system which includes a particular technology or component type for the first time may collaborate with a loyal collaborator firm which has specialism in that area. If the requirement becomes long term, the key player might choose to acquire the technology (or the collaborator company) itself.

Another example of the dynamism would be provided by a loyal collaborator whose level of expertise might be insignificant one year but very important the next, as automobile markets change. In this case the company might become a key player, on the basis of its technology, thereby facing the extra onus of that role as described above. Whilst it is unlikely that a firm which has invested sufficiently to become a key player with one customer will accept a lesser role with another, it is

Table 8.1 Models of strategy and modes of approach: lean suppliers

	Leader	Follower
Key player	Proactive innovation: selects automotive technologies and leads customer Sees automotive business as core activity/image First-tier supplier: direct, systems integrator Configures company to fit own strategy (in automotive field)	Proactive innovation: identifies automotive applications for technologies developed for other original purposes Sees auto business as one (minor) arm of multi-market operation First-tier, indirect supplier; not systems integrator Does not necessarily have an automotive division
Loyal collaborator	Innovator/developer: works in response to customer-identified problems Capable of gaining better expertise in specific technologies than the customer First or second-tier, direct or indirect: not systems integrator Potential for key player status may be limited by customer decisions on core technologies	Developer (e.g. cost reduction through design for manufacture) of customer's ideas Risk averse: unwilling to develop products without customer undertakings Second-tier; potentially non-direct, lower tier supplier

possible to imagine firms moving from one state to the other – by a strategic change.

The Japanese suppliers, accustomed to the senior–junior partnership discussed earlier, are mainly loyal collaborators. The Japanese transplant suppliers (in the USA and in Europe) have begun operating in this mode despite their apparent capacity to take key player roles eventually (based upon their domestic resources, established relationships with lean producers, and positions in Japan). A progression from this position to the other (i.e. to key player status) would seem a logical strategy for such firms, despite the difficulty which they will face in achieving it. Their success would constitute a major threat for Western suppliers.

■ Examples of the strategies

The framework of four strategic positions describes the developments in the industry as they are foreseen. In a sense, therefore, they are future strategies. It is possible, however, to suggest some current examples which bear similarities to the positions discussed. The different histories of the European, Japanese and American components industries (Chapter 2) result in differing implications in the three regions. In Japan, for example, the companies are smaller but traditionally take more responsibility for technology, whilst in North America the reverse is true. The following examples are made in the context of lean supply as we have seen it above, i.e. in a global sense.

Robert Bosch GmbH is a clear example of the key player/leader strategy. The company is large and technology rich, with explicit innovation policies constantly explained in its public documentation. It is configured to reflect the needs of the automotive industry and has extensive global operations and links. Other contenders might include ZF, Magneti Marelli, Valeo, GKN, and several others of the top few suppliers in Europe. The history of the American industry, as discussed earlier, might lead to the expectation of fewer such supplier companies in the region. There are some who appear to fit the bill, however, especially TRW and Allied Signal. In specific sectors a supplier may count as a key player even though it is smaller than others – for example, Johnson Controls (in seating systems).[14] The same is true in Japan, where alongside the obvious inclusion of Nippondenso and Hitachi, the relatively small Akebono would rank as a potential key player, because of its technological ability and influence.

Motorola might be seen as following a key player/follower strategy, having fundamental influence upon the automotive industry but restricting its exposure to a small proportion of its total business. The link up with Valeo is an example of a move from follower to leader via the collaboration route: Motorola will maintain its first-tier operation despite the indirect nature of its product (microprocessors and other electronic equipment). Other examples are given by Siemens and Philips in Europe (the former following a similar strategy to that of Motorola, but employing acquisition rather than alliance), Du Pont in the USA and Toshiba in Japan.

An example of the loyal collaborator/leader combination strategy is provided by the UK firms Britax Wingard and Britax Vega, both wholly owned subsidiaries of the UK group, BSG PLC. These firms are relatively small (£125.9 million sales between them in 1990) but each has a technical lead in its field. Wingard is a leader in electronic mirrors; Vega manufactures rear lights. Both have international links through the BSG group and experience of dealing with lean producers. Thus, though their size probably limits them from key player status, they remain leaders.

Since we may expect to see only a few key players in the industry, it follows that most firms will become loyal collaborators. The challenges in doing so are still considerable.

■ Strategic transformation in lean supply

Moving from one position to another requires clear strategic thinking – particularly if the transformation is from loyal collaborator to key player, or from follower to leader – see Figure 8.3. This will require significant acquisition of resources,

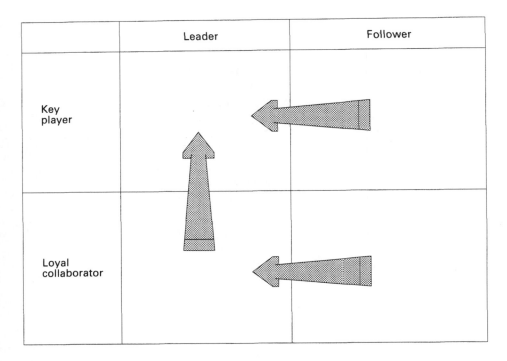

	Leader	Follower
Key player		
Loyal collaborator		

Figure 8.3 Some examples of strategic transformations for lean suppliers

development of skills, and growth. The loyal collaborator which builds a technological strength that gradually convinces customers to rely upon the supplier for product development in that area may shift strategy to the key player level. Such a move is only likely for a loyal collaborator which has already become established in the leader mode: the follower/key players are all firms which were already large before becoming involved with the automotive industry (e.g. plastics, electronics, etc.). The new key player must earn this position with the full complement of skills – especially the management ability to create dynamism within the organization so that it drives itself harder than the customer, etc. The acquisition strategy of Valeo throughout the late 1980s is an example of this shift. From being a nationally based, medium-sized components supplier, the firm grew in stature, and latterly in technology through massive investments in R&D. Valeo is a contender for key player/leader status, having started from a position closer to loyal collaborator/follower.

An example of a firm moving from follower to leader is Mannesman. Following the acquisitions described earlier, the firm now has the potential to mount a key player/leader strategy, provided all the individual firms can operate together. If the shock absorber supplier, Boge, the clutch manufacturer, Fictel Sachs, and the instruments firms, VDO, were to remain separate entities, however well supported, then they would be individually loyal collaborator/leaders (like the

Britax companies within BSG) and Mannesman would be simply the holding company.

The shift from follower to leader at the key player level has profound implications for a supplier – perhaps one reason why Philips chooses not to form a separate automotive division. The investment for competition would be massive: the development of technologies specifically for automotive projects is fundamentally different from the spin-off applications enjoyed by followers, and potentially very expensive. The attractions are clearly sufficient for some raw materials producers to integrate forwards, however. In 1992, for example, the large American aluminium producer Alcoa announced plans to set up an automotive components plant in Germany and joint ventures in Japan. In the same year another aluminium producer, Reynolds Metals, announced plans to invest $26 million on a new components plant at Auburn, Indiana, using technology developed at the firm's site in the Netherlands. Both these moves must be viewed in the light of forecasts of the average aluminium content of cars more than doubling, from 170 lbs in 1991 to 350 lbs in 1996.

The UK company, Lucas, has strategically reduced its reliance on the automotive industry over the past decade, selling its lighting business to Magneti Marelli and its instrumentation to Nippon Seiki. A change of top management at Lucas in 1992 also led to the establishment of an electronics technology division, which is not dedicated to either of its traditional sectors (aerospace and automotive). This almost appears to be shift of strategy from leader to follower for Lucas, perhaps as a precursor to further reductions in investment specific to the automotive business.

■ Which strategy to choose?

The key player and loyal collaborator strategies represent a choice for component suppliers which may be summarized as positioning on a proactive–reactive axis. The decision to follow a key player strategy involves the components supplier in taking the initiative with customers – literally exceeding expectation, in technical and logistical matters. The loyal collaborator strategy requires lean supply from the supplier, but is tenable without the high degree of influence upon the customer's strategy which is characteristic of a key player.

Both strategies are aimed at improving competitive advantage through a customer, or market, orientation. The mode in which the supplier chooses to operate reflects not how well it has succeeded in penetrating the technological market but rather how it sees itself with regard to the automotive industry *per se*. This is illustrated in Figure 8.4. Choosing the leader mode should provide the supplier with a greater opportunity to control the added value – not as a threat to the customer, but as a service, and as part of collaboration. The key player/ follower does not have this control, unless working in concert with another supplier, as an integrator.

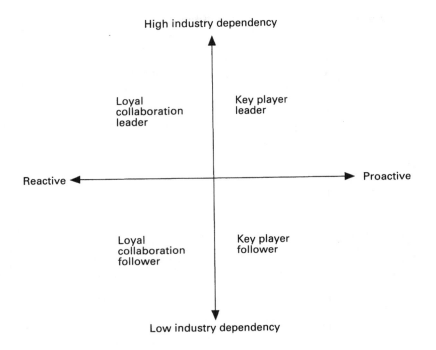

Figure 8.4 Key player/loyal collaborator strategies: an alternative view

To be a lean supplier a company must choose the extent to which it wants to gain control over the added value (key player–loyal collaborator) and the degree to which it wants to be involved in the automotive industry (leader–follower). A clear choice of position on the part of the supplier will be recognized by the lean assembler and should result in a firm basis for collaboration in the supply chain. The supplier will need to be persuasive in this matter but use of traditional sales techniques in such a process would clearly result in loss of credibility.

The stage is set for lean supply, as a necessary complement to lean production, to develop. The final chapter focuses on the future prospects for this development and looks at some of the implications.

■ Notes

1. Some reports put the figure much higher – up to 50 per cent. The scheme – called purchased input concept optimization with suppliers (the acronym is PICOS – the Spanish word for peaks, symbolic of high achievements; the word can also mean pickaxes) is based upon supplier workshops and has achieved reported improvements

of 63 per cent in productivity, 56 per cent in materials costs, and 61 per cent in lead time reduction: see *The Financial Times*, 28 August 1992, p. 19. See note 6 below.

2. In the cases of Boge and VDO, Mannesman bought a controlling stake.
3. *Financial Times* estimate of DM6 billion (22 October 1991).
4. Estimate compiled by the Economist Intelligence Unit; see EIU (1991).
5. See the two CBI documents on Partnership Sourcing (CBI 1991, 1992) for a full explanation of this term. The cases studies include Nissan Motor Manufacturing UK.
6. GM ran supplier seminars in Europe (seven within GM by 1990, with an average of almost fifty suppliers each time, and at over 158 supplier locations by 1992) presenting a strategy for supplier development, and they can point to positive comments from suppliers. By 1990 some DM3.4 billion worth of spend in Europe was covered by lifetime contracts (29 per cent of component spend). The carefully planned and executed cost reduction process was a major success: averaging 51 per cent. In 1989 GM calculated they had achieved almost 5 per cent better cost savings than Ford across Europe – a cost advantage of over DM0.5 billion. In interviews, however, suppliers said they felt that a great deal of coercion was used. For an interesting early account of this situation see the article 'Die Faust im Nacken' ('The iron heel in the neck') in the German *Manager* magazine, August 1988. GM claimed that VW and Ford were openly copying their techniques. A similar approach is now in place in GM in the USA, following the transfer to Detroit of the architect of the European project. The scheme is also to be applied to GM's in-house divisions in the USA, representing a potential threat to the company's agreement on long-term employment contracts with its US employees.
7. Of Nissan Motor Manufacturing UK's 177 suppliers in March 1991, 125 were based in the UK and 52 in mainland Europe. Nissan spends 70 per cent of its European purchasing total within the UK and is expanding its supplier base to 195 with the introduction of Micra in 1992. Its final target for the first tier is 200 suppliers. Of Honda UK's European 138 suppliers, 89 were in the UK. For a summary of Nissan's approach to suppliers in the UK see Syson (1992, pp. 94–106). The account is by Terrence Hogg, Production Control Manager from Nissan Motor Manufacturing UK.
8. All quoted in *The Engineer*, 5 March 1992. A report written for the NEDC, (UK National Economic Development Council) quoted in the same journal in June 1992, noted a general paucity of engineering skills in the UK supply chain, with specific reference to automotive fixings and in-car entertainment equipment, and composite materials. The report was critical of government support for British engineering and manufacturing industry. The NEDC was disbanded by the UK government in the same month.
9. The case refers to Sterling Health, in 1990, which lost its substantial market share for a staple product (DL acid) to Japanese competition. Sterling's version of the 'white' chemical was in fact slightly yellowish – a standard which was assumed to be satisfactory. The Japanese import was pure white, half the price and had a consistency quality measured at 5 ppm, compared to the UK product's 97 per cent purity. The market penetration of the Japanese product took less than one year, from no presence to market leadership. (Author's research interview, Glasgow 1991.)
10. Financial figures estimated by the author at 1990 levels. It should be noted that some important opinions depart from the view on non-automotive business. Two of the most significant European component suppliers, Valeo and Magneti Marelli, are 100 per cent automotive and do not agree with the need for spill over from other sectors. Both firms gain support from their ownership position, however, in some of the factors identified as benefits of a position in a multi-market organization (Magneti Marelli within Fiat; Valeo within the conglomerate organization of Carlo De Benedetti).
11. Strengths, weaknesses, opportunities and threats: traditional strategic analysis framework (see Drucker, 1967).
12. The DTI/SMMT Report (DTI, 1992) discusses (using a modified version of the

original key player/loyal collaborator model described here) the role of a non-lean supplier – a local supplier. In view of the focus on lean supply strategies, the local supplier is not discussed here.

13. Financial figures estimated by the author at 1990 levels.
14. The Automotive Systems Group of Johnson Controls grew to US$3.1 billion automotive turnover in 1988, up from US$1.8 billion in 1985, chiefly by acquisition (Hoover Universal in 1985, Ferro Mfg Co. in 1985 and A.G. Simpson in 1988). The company supplies the Big Three, Toyota and Nissan, in the USA, and manufactures also in France and the UK, where it has joint ventures with Ikeda Bussan, a Nissan group supplier.

9 | Beyond Partnership: The Implications of Lean Supply

Analysis of the history of the automotive industry reveals that the craft manufacturers had something special, something of great value, that was lost during the development and dominance of mass production. That special something was collaboration: between workforce and management, between labour and capital, and between vehicle assembler and component supplier.

The pressures for change which we saw in the early chapters have led the industry back to collaboration – mostly involuntarily. The reasons for collaboration may be different from those in the craft production era but the needs and the results are very similar. The spirit of 'all hands to the pump' which was imposed upon the Japanese after the war, for example, was clearly a major factor in their subsequent economic success. The opposite attitude of 'You've never had it so good'[1] during the same period in the West appears to have contributed to the decline of the USA and parts of Europe. Above all, the jealous demarcation of duties and covetous ownership of the value chain (vertical integration), so stereotypical of mass production, have shown themselves to be out of step with modern, international, industrial dynamics.

We saw, in Chapter 6, how the relationships between vehicle assemblers and their component suppliers collapsed with the demise of mass production and how they are currently being reconceived in the light of lean production. We also saw that a new step – towards a relationship model which is right for global lean production – is currently under way. The renewed efforts of best practice manufacturers – from Japan – to organize their supply chains in new regions illustrates the incomplete nature of the present position: lean supply is still a goal, rather than a reality, for everyone.

Partnership in supply chain relationships is clearly a very powerful strategy. It encourages a joint approach to problems and it can lead to reductions in costs, improvements in quality, and so on. It appears, however, that partnership (or partnership sourcing) retains a traditional view of the supply chain – that it is the customer, the company which in mass production has accumulated most of the

238

control of the value chain, that 'owns' the whole process, whilst the suppliers are 'fitted in' by a procurement process still based upon buyer power. Partnership is seen by many suppliers, as just another way of appeasing the customer – perhaps with slightly less effort to win by guile. The essence of partnership is sound – it is cooperation – but the prevailing climate of ownership works against this ever developing into true collaboration.

This is where lean supply goes beyond partnership. For there to be a genuine rationalization of the supply chain, there has to be true collaboration between the companies jointly involved in providing the end product. This entails a great deal of change of ownership of the process – a disaggregation of the chain – and with it, a new honesty in supply chain relationships.

Lean supply, then, emerges as the state of business in which there is dynamic competition and collaboration of equals in the supply chain, aimed at adding value at minimum total cost, while maximizing end-customer service and product quality. Some organizations in the supply chain will inevitably control more of the value-adding process than others, but this sharing of technical, logistical and commercial responsibilities will be based upon value/cost calculations, not excessive concern for ownership.

In completing this account of the evolution of the lean supply concept, we should consider how it fits with relevant theories – because theoretical frameworks are an essential part of strategic thinking – and with practice (at both the operational and policy levels). Finally, we should look at some factors of the business environment which may affect, and be affected by, lean supply.

■ Lean supply in theory

The development of lean supply has implications for theories relating to interorganizational relationships, to strategic collaboration, and to innovation and technical change. In discussing each of these below, the links to practice will be identified in each case. This will show how the theoretical basis and practical applications are related.

Interorganizational relationships

We have seen that there is an identifiable progression through the five models of relationships. At any point a pair of firms or, perhaps, a national industry, may be described in terms of progress through the models – along a trajectory. As with any trajectory (see Figure 3.6) the firms within this development may be expected to try a variety of strategic directions in the search for best practice. At each point the reasons for existence of specific factors may be analyzed to understand the constraints upon individual firms or national industries.

This trajectory is not smooth however, and the stages are not strictly delineated. At any time a customer and supplier may be expected to be in transition from one state to another and their relationship may be observed to contain some features from one model type and some from another. This is also the case for national situations. For example, in the UK, the general situation on relationships with respect to quality may still be seen as 'aggressive campaigns: SQA etc.' – a stress model feature while the working pressure may still equate to a resolved model position (medium). In this case, the relationship still has to develop considerably before being seen as a case of partnership or lean supply. In addition, this snapshot reveals not one clear type of relationship, but an amalgam of two (or more).

The implication of this is that managing the development of relationships is a 'lumpy' process, requiring a concentration on specific factors. Thus the Japanese transplants in the USA have spent a great deal of effort in bringing their American suppliers up to speed on 'pressure', and are now focusing on developing cost reductions norms and *kaizen*. At the same time, the assembler's ability to give responsibility for technical matters to the supplier must develop (just as difficult a process for the customer as the bearing of that responsibility is for the supplier).

As a theoretical framework, the series of models is strengthened by this 'lumpiness' and contingency. It may be employed in practice to analyze complex relationships without demanding a 'force fit' – without trying to make the reality stretch to match the theoretical factors. Taken to a further stage, the models might be employed to describe a particular relationship as, say, 20 per cent stress, 60 per cent resolved, 20 per cent partnership. Using this 'factor analysis' method, specific targets for action may be identified by strategists.

It is quite possible that steps may be taken backwards, i.e. that some exogenous shock might 'worsen' relationships, say from the partnership (or something very close to it) to the stress model. In the early 1990s, for example, with an automotive industry hard hit by recession, there are many signs of relationships stretched to their limits and, in some cases, reshaped, by such forces.

We have seen how the Japanese model of relationships has developed through a prolonged period of growth. The firms with which it is associated have only recently faced declining markets. Exogenous shocks are thus a new factor for lean supply to combat. In recession, all the factors of the lean supply relationship are heightened in order for interdependent customers and suppliers to survive. The need for cost reduction (and with it transparency of data, etc.) and communications (for the control of processes, etc.) are both increased immensely. The effects of a market downturn will naturally cause pain throughout an industry: in lean supply the short-term expedients of irrational action by the customers towards the suppliers make no sense. At the same time, the onus upon suppliers, to find cost reductions and efficiency improvements, is great.

The progression from traditional to lean should not be seen as a simple one-way street, nor an inevitable path as some theorists have suggested. The implication is that modelling for relationships is contingent upon technical and economic environmental conditions. It does seem, however, that Lean Supply, once adopted as a *modus operandi*, replaces traditional contracting practice – there would be little point in readopting techniques which have been recognized as wasteful and inefficient. The development of lean supply may thus be seen as irreversible: while it may be expected to change further in future, an unravelling of the fabric of interdependence would have little benefit for suppliers or customers. A firm may choose not to adopt the principles of lean supply but once they have been chosen as a strategic direction, it is unlikely that traditional, adversarial and isolationist supply strategies could be resurrected profitably.

If we use the conventional terminology expression, vertical, to denote connections between manufacturers and their suppliers (e.g. vertical integration), then we might call lean supply 'vertical collaboration'. (The term vertical is probably inappropriate in the long run, however, if collaborators are seen as equals, as suggested above.)

This reinforces the importance of recognizing collaboration principally as a learning strategy. For horizontal collaborators, as seen in Chapter 4, there is the challenge of learning about a 'similar' business (that of the collaborator) and a new business (the joint venture). For vertical collaborators there is the need to learn about two new 'businesses' – that of the partner, a firm at a different point in the value chain, possibly grounded in an entirely different industry – and that of the joint venture, which, while it may not be a defined business entity in itself, demands the same degree of strategic conceptualization. In both cases the organizational learning required is double loop, culturally embedding learning as a feature of the firm (see Chapter 4).

The implication for practice here is that the management of lean supply chains may require both collaborators to view the relationship as a 'quasi-firm', with its own organizational structure and goals, communication mechanisms and culture. This is illustrated in Figure 9.1. In order to develop a 'quasi-firm' in the relationship, each company has to commit resources outside its organizational boundaries. The 'third partner' thus has its own resource base – people, equipment, premises – with which to operate. Its broad goals are to rationalize the part of the supply chain to which it relates and to provide added value at lowest cost. Its 'shareholders' – the customer and supplier – will watch its performance carefully. The cost of resourcing the quasi-firm must be justified by the value it adds, the cost and time savings it achieves, and the mutual competitive advantage which it provides.

The theoretical framework represented by the relationship models may be used as a method of analyzing historical developments and making reasonable predictions of future scenarios. It shows that the business relationship between a manufacturer and its component suppliers can be said to represent a case of strategic and technical collaboration. The contingency evident in this framework could also be considered as relevant to theories of collaboration.

The idea that the nature of collaboration is contingent upon many factors is further strengthened by the evidently finite life of specific joint ventures, as

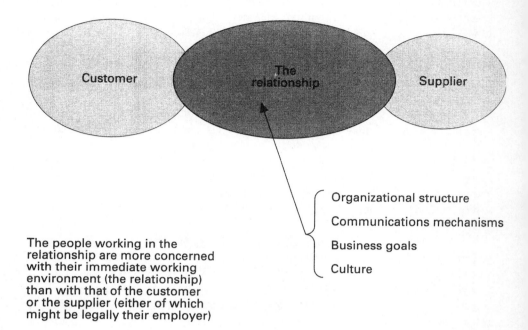

Organizational structure

Communications mechanisms

Business goals

Culture

The people working in the
relationship are more concerned
with their immediate working
environment (the relationship)
than with that of the customer
or the supplier (either of which
might be legally their employer)

Figure 9.1 The relationship takes on an identity of its own

discussed in Chapter 4. It is possible to envisage a sort of 'collaboration lifecycle'
(akin to the product lifecycle concept) to describe specific ventures. Similarly,
customer–vendor relationships might be seen in the lean supply model as having
finite lives, as a result of their contingent nature (as opposed to the Japanese model
in which it is implicit that specific relationships will last indefinitely). This clearly
has important implications for managing relationships – the concept of a
'relationship strategy' arises, perhaps with components as illustrated in Figure
9.2.[2]

A relationship strategy would clearly be linked to the structure of the network
of companies in which the assembler wishes to work: the types of supplier with
which collaborations must be formed, etc. Geographical, commercial, historical,
and technical factors would be involved in this consideration. Indeed, a
relationship strategy must be intrinsically linked to the technology strategy of the
firm, since technology is expected to flow into the organization via suppliers and
other collaborators.

From the strategy must come some imperatives for managing relationships –
including a plan for moving through stages of relationships (using some form of
framework, such as the models in Table 6.3 and Table 7.2, as a map for
monitoring and directing progress) and for implementation of the identified
concepts. Thus, for each supplier, the customer would have a planned development
of the relationship, based upon the practical limits of performance, the scope for

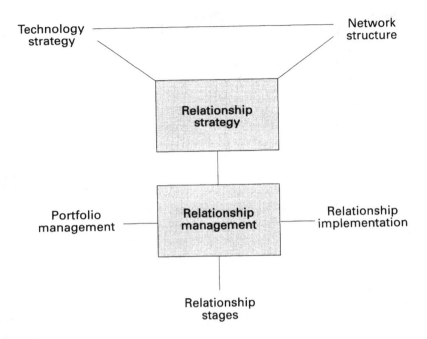

Source: From Ford *et al.* (1992).

Figure 9.2 A model of relationship strategy

improvement, useful life and so on. It is possible that some relationships will never need to reach a full lean supply state. It is also possible that the partnership stage may ·be a requisite step in the development towards lean supply.

This leads to the idea of a portfolio of relationships on the part of the customer. This is a strategic plan, to operate differing levels of developed relationships with various suppliers. The relationships interrelate and support one another on a continually reviewable basis. Thus, a critically important supplier might be part of a fully developed lean supply relationship, providing technological solutions through collaboration etc., whilst a source of commodity items might be run on a more arm's length basis – still with excellent service but without the need for such intimate working practices.

Strategic collaboration

Lean supply compares well with the concepts of strategic collaboration, which we saw in Chapter 4. It is possible, for example, to identify cases of risk reduction strategies in assemblers wishing to exploit product innovations, using the technical abilities of suppliers to do so, instances of vertical quasi-integration in which assembler and supplier remain legally independent but operate very closely towards mutual advantage and shared destiny and so on. The description of the European and American component industries provided many examples of collaboration between suppliers, aimed at enabling international expansion. It is also apparent from the research that collaboration between assemblers from one region (e.g. Japan) and suppliers from another (e.g. Europe) is often sought by the former in order to become established in the latter's region. The model exhibits most of the features of collaboration, as defined by the literature.

In short, lean supply is a framework for developing strategic collaboration – the basis for the relationships which have emerged as crucially important for the next phase of global business. The model also reflects the revealed strategies of progressive firms within the automotive industry, which are seeking to develop competitive positioning via vertical quasi-integration. Thus, we may conclude that the best practice business relationship between a manufacturer and its component suppliers may be said to represent a case of strategic and technical collaboration.

The first implication of this book for theories of collaboration is that vertical collaboration appears to have distinct similarities to horizontal collaboration. We can now go further and say that the resonance which the development of lean supply has found in the conclusions of other research in joint venturing between equals (including competitors) suggests strongly that vertical collaboration shares a common theoretical base with horizontal collaboration. It is interesting to note that the strategic developments necessary for both parties in vertical collaboration appear to lead towards equality in partnership: the sharing of responsibility and benefit, as a result of increased confidence and cooperation. This means that 'perfect' vertical collaboration develops towards horizontal collaboration.

The question remains: 'What ties the equals together in long-term commitment and collaboration?' The interdependence in technology may only count for one or two product cycles – lean supply may require a longer-term perspective that this. It is probable that equity exchanges will be required in some cases (not ownership, but shared destiny) and the exchange of personnel (discussed below). Both these practices will improve mutual concern for continued prosperity and understanding of value chain dynamics, potential for research and development responsibility, etc. Lean supply may thus challenge the observed finite life characteristics of strategic collaboration by introducing 'bonding' measures which extend the period of interdependence – perhaps indefinitely. In this way, a situation akin to the horizontal groupings in Japan (but not as tightly integrated as *keiretsu*) may arise: the key players and their customers, interlocked in this way, will operate as free agents, with an array of shared interests and a portfolio of relationships.

Innovation: shared technical change

The main theories of innovation between customers and suppliers are those put forward by Von Hippel and by Foxall, as we saw in Chapter 3. Von Hippel appears to favour the customer-active idea generation paradigm as a model for innovation across commercial boundaries, i.e. customers or users influence and even determine designs for new products. The alternative, manufacturer-active paradigm is credited in a few specific contexts.

We can now see that vertical collaboration relationships, as exemplified by lean supply, can blur the demarcation between customers' and vendors' roles, emphasizing the importance of joint development of new technologies, using complementary assets in the process. The commercial conditions necessary for such shared technical change are complex – perhaps corresponding to joint strategy formulation, which is a feature of lean supply.

The Rothwell and Zegveld model of innovation (Figure 3.5) appears to be very appropriate to technical change within vertical collaboration. Responsibility for the recognition of market needs (e.g. for the vehicle characteristics) will remain with the assembler, whilst the technology push will be shared by assembler and component supplier. The process of innovation, combining aspects of both push and pull equates to the manner in which lean supply deals with technology: assigning the development task to the part of the value chain best suited to it, on the basis of identified complementarity and specificity of tangible and intangible assets.

The networking of supplier firms in pursuit of technical change and innovation is reflected in the lean supply paradigm, as a natural result of assemblers relying increasingly upon suppliers for partnership. As supply bases are rationalized, so it is unlikely that the technical links discussed above would be formed with only a small proportion of suppliers: the more probable scenario would be that most, if not all, supply relationships (except those in the tail: Figure 7.2) would eventually operate in this manner (and the assembler would reconfigure the R&D function accordingly). Given this situation, the propensity for suppliers to form networks, either for specific supply arrangements, or for more general shared knowledge, might be expected to increase. This might lead to Crane's 'invisible college' of shared knowhow, to which the assembler and all the component suppliers in the supply base would contribute.

Finally, the application of Allen's technological gatekeeper concept (Figure 4.5), developed from research within an organization (a scientific laboratory), to the network of firms in a supply base (or, more generally, in the supply industry: Figure 7.7) appears to find resonance in the above conclusion. The implication for theory from this conclusion is that the technical roles of firms within networks may vary, with some taking on special functions, for the eventual good of all.

■ Implications for management: lean supply in practice

As we have seen during the discussions above, lean supply has many implications for management, in both customers and suppliers. For both, the main implication is that a fundamental shift in attitude is required. For the suppliers, this shift is towards a proactive and closely monitored approach to customer service, including self-imposed pressure to exceed expectation. For the customers, the new attitude must remove the traditional obsession with ownership of the process and short-term cost savings through coercion.

In lean supply, the challenge for management in the supplier is to achieve a position from which to influence the relationship to the mutual benefit of both partners; customer and supplier. For the customer, the challenge of lean supply is to recognize the benefits of accepting this influence and to learn new ways of formulating and operating strategies which are interdependent with those of the supplier.

The challenge, and the attitudinal shift, are not matters for purchasing and sales alone. The combination of factors (commercial, technical, logistical, legal, financial, etc.) in the relationship also requires collaboration internally, i.e. within the organizations. This means teamwork between purchasing, design and engineering, production, quality and commercial departments is essential for lean supply.[3] Similarly, such teams must be formed within the supplier organization. In this way, the problems and practicalities of supply, which are naturally multi-disciplinary, can be approached in a non-territorial manner.

For assemblers who reconfigure their technical capabilities and rely upon suppliers' collaboration to a greater extent, it is apparent that strategic planning can no longer be carried out in isolation: the unit of strategic planning is no longer the firm but rather a combination of the firm, parts of other firms, and the relationship between them. Thus it is necessary for assemblers to develop strategies which are interdependent with those of partner suppliers (key players and loyal collaborators) and to put in place systems and policies which enable such strategies to be operationalized.

At one end of this spectrum of strategic choice lies integration, e.g. Honda's decision to develop its own version of anti-lock braking systems. At the other might be the decision to subcontract all development, e.g. Epeda Bertrand Faure's design and build service for all Renault seating. It appears that these choices will be made on a system-specific basis, taking into account both engineering and manufacturing practicalities. One term for this is retention of core technology in house: the assembler decides what it is that gives the car competitive differentiation and may decide to control that technology personally. This suggests a limited acceptance of supplier collaboration: the notion is that there are limits to the security or confidentiality of shared technical matters. As the influence of key players grows, however, this may not always be a course of action open to assemblers.

Whilst it is likely that joint strategic planning (i.e. between customer and supplier) will be led by assemblers in the short, and possibly medium, term, it is possible to envisage a full lean supply scenario in which the supplier plays an equal part in most stages of the development and launch of new products. Figure 9.3 shows how this process might work.

Product/process development from the point of view of the customer

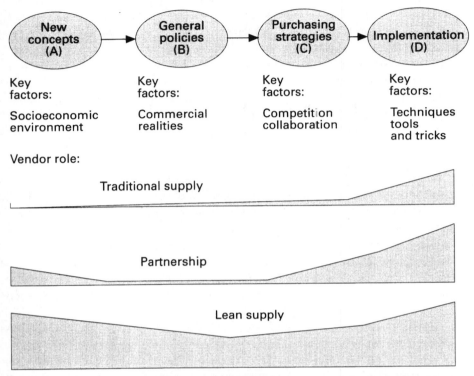

Key
factors:

Socioeconomic
environment

Key
factors:

Commercial
realities

Key
factors:

Competition
collaboration

Key
factors:

Techniques
tools
and tricks

Vendor role:

Traditional supply

Partnership

Lean supply

Note: [a] The three blocks at the bottom of the diagram represent the amount of involvement, or the significance of the role (of the supplier) in the development process over time and relate to the four process stages illustrated above. Letters A–D refer to discussion in the text.

Figure 9.3 Lean supply relationships in product and process development[a]

New Concepts (A) are introduced to the customer via a search and selection environment. In traditional supply, this search activity is carried out by the customer without the benefit of the abilities of the supplier. The socioeconomic environment (including technology) is the key factor here: the customer must be aware of all the developments which are likely to take place and choose a strategic response to each one. This includes identification of all the technology trajectories which might be relevant to the customer's products and services. This leads the customer to formulate policies (B), to address commercial realities. This is a private matter for the company, and one which does not traditionally require involvement of the suppliers.

One of the outcomes of this policy formulation is a purchasing strategy (C) for the customer, containing all sorts of plans and 'thrusts'. This strategy must be made in the light of the strengths of competitors and potential collaborators and is again something which the customer traditionally keeps secret. The strategic thrusts and plans give rise to a variety of tools and techniques (D) which require the full involvement of the suppliers in order to work. This is the point at which the supplier is traditionally brought into the picture – and required to assimilate all that has gone on before, while implementing the plans which the customer has made.

This process is clearly doomed to failure. The suppliers cannot adapt to the new plans fast enough and the customer is likely to miss the strategic target identified in the early part of the process. In addition to this, the supplier's potential for input has been wasted – some innovative ideas which could have provided both companies with shared competitive advantage have possibly been missed.

In partnership, the supplier has a greater role to play in the early stages. The customer involves the supplier in the identification of new concepts, and keeps communication open so that the implementation phase is more easily entered. The policy and strategy-forming stages are still carried out in isolation, however – again missing potentially important input from the suppliers. In lean supply, the supplier and customer share a common search and selection environment – neither could operate fully in the identification of relevant concepts without the other. The supplier is also involved in policy and strategy formulation, and probably provides the management for some of the implementation. Throughout, the identification–planning–implementation process is a joint collaboration of equals.

Such processes have usually been carried out in the traditional manner. As greater environmental pressures and new concepts provide increasing challenges to assemblers, so lean producers will turn to suppliers, in lean supply, for collaborative efforts such as that shown above. For example, supplier accreditation schemes have been (and still are) developed entirely by customers (responding to market environment needs, the activities of competitors, etc.), with the supplier becoming involved only at the implementation stage (or perhaps immediately prior to it in a pilot scheme). Such schemes might be more successful (especially as the criteria for performance monitoring become more sophisticated) if suppliers were involved from the beginning in setting up the framework and targets. It will be interesting to observe how the assemblers handle similar schemes aimed at the more complex matter of developing environmentally sound supply chains. It seems that a top-down approach, in which the customer tries to do all the environmental assessment and then set the rules, is unlikely to succeed. Pursuit of this objective (e.g. including BS7750 in the UK) clearly requires a lean supply approach, as illustrated in Figure 9.3.

The management concern in craft production was to bring together diverse resources, internal and external, with which to provide solutions to customers' needs. In mass production, this concern changed to one of comprehensive control, often manifested in vertical integration, to produce products which would then be aggressively sold to the customer.

In lean production, there is a development towards a management role similar to that in craft production: a very developed market orientation, based upon coordination of diverse resources. Control systems developed under mass production were based upon control from a distance – from arm's length. Lean production provides control of actual costs at the process level. Mass production attempted to enforce predictability on to the market from the manufacturer: lean production requires flexible responses to the market. For assemblers, the management task is at first complicated by the need to rely upon suppliers for responsibilities previously held in house, but subsequently simplified by the focusing of management attention on the assembly process and lean supply relationship communications (see below). The lean purchaser, as has been seen earlier, spends less time and effort in matters of detail – both in logistics and technology – relying upon the supplier to provide full service in these respects.

We have seen the principle of disaggregation in the supply chain, in order to reduce duplication and to lower the cost of adding value, primarily in the context of manufactured components for integration into the vehicle. The same principle of out-sourcing is also applicable to administrative and support functions within the organisation (e.g. personnel functions, financial accounting, maintenance, sales, etc.). It is likely that the lean enterprise will evaluate all its functions very carefully from the point of view of value for money. Current indications (from sectors other than the automotive industry) are that much of the administrative load could be out-sourced to the advantage of the company. In this way, the company can focus totally on core technology, devoting all its learning and expertise to this and to the development and management of relationships with its collaborators in lean supply.

The diagram in Figure 9.4 (from a non-automotive company) illustrates a profound and radical approach to identification of core technology. In this case the manufacturer (IBM Northern Europe) is considering out-sourcing everything which is not covered by a very strict definition of the company's core business. Note that in Figure 9.4, only non-strategic manufacturing is considered for out-sourcing: in fully developed lean supply, this restriction would almost certainly not apply. Indeed, much of the collaboration into which IBM is currently entering cannot be classed as non-strategic.

The retention of skills in-house in order to conduct discussions with the technology partner (the contractor) is a complex problem for firms in approaching a contracting out strategy. It is clearly necessary to be able to assess market trends, supplier suggestions, joint development programmes and so on, after the specialist role has been contracted out. This is akin to the concept of *adequatio* in philosophy – the ability to understand the environment is based upon adequate perception (see Schumacher, 1978). The individuals employed by the customer to provide this perception will be important team members for the customer–supplier relationship, but may become frustrated at not being required to develop the technologies for themselves (i.e. in-house).

Taken to a very advanced state, it is clear that lean supply has fundamental implications for purchasing. It is no longer sufficient to see this function – dealing with suppliers – as a matter of spending money, of buying parts and services. The suppliers are now parts of the extended organization of the assembler – intrinsic parts of the value-adding process. As such, they are external resources (with

Contracting out:
Make/do versus buy

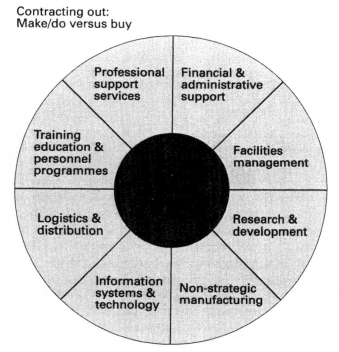

Reprinted with permission from a 1992 presentation by Mr. J. Gillett, IBM Northern Europe.

Figure 9.4 Identification of core business and out-sourcing strategy

complementary assets) – as important in the development and manufacture process as the customer's internal resources. Purchasing and supply thus becomes a matter of external resource management in lean supply, and a change of title for the function may well be necessary to focus strategic attention (and imagination) accordingly. This is illustrated in Figure 9.5.

Measuring the lean supply relationship

As we saw earlier, many sophisticated techniques have been developed for assessment of suppliers. All assemblers practise such schemes, which now incorporate assessment (by a team from the customer including purchasing and engineering personnel) of a supplier's strategy as well as traditional factors such as quality control procedures, house keeping and delivery performance. In 1988, for example, GM and Ford, introduced schemes in the USA which set the suppliers hurdles which seemed intentionally too high to clear – especially in terms of product development resources. Perhaps it was the assemblers' plan to sort out the key players: public statements at the time certainly made it clear that only a few suppliers were expected to achieve accreditation for the Targets for Excellence (GM) and Total Quality Excellence (Ford) award schemes.

As complementarity of assets in the internal and external
resource bases becomes the focus for optimization . . .

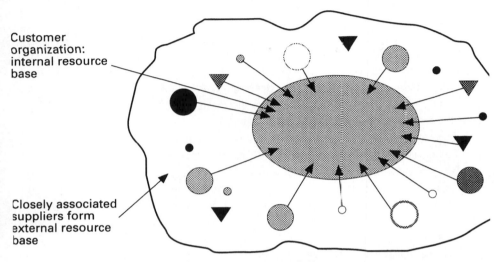

Customer
organization:
internal resource
base

Closely associated
suppliers form
external resource
base

. . . the responsibility of purchasing and supply bec
external resource management – a strategic functic

Figure 9.5   The development of external resource management

The Japanese assemblers abroad have had to develop such schemes anew, since the traditional approach in Japan has been very different. The close Japanese relationships have provided the basis for continual assessment of performance of the supplier by the customer, accompanied by pressure to perform (both junior–senior characteristics). In developing schemes for global application, a regional approach has been taken by the Japanese assemblers, with some interregional coordination managed on a personal network basis. This approach allows for the different levels of development in each region. Toyota in Australia, for example, has developed a scheme (the Toyota Supplier Assessment scheme: TSA) which rates the supplier's performance on quality, delivery, price, management and other (a mix of technical support, packaging, flexibility, warranty claims, etc.). TSA awards points in each category and presents the results visually as a target – the centre being a perfect score in each of the four categories. The Australian automotive parts industry, while it numbers many excellent suppliers amongst it (capable of developing to meet Toyota's tough requirements) depends upon a very small domestic assembly industry and thus has limited prospects for research and development (which might otherwise be given a higher priority in an assessment scheme).

Nissan in the UK has recently launched an initiative which places higher demands on the product-development side of the relationship, incorporating assessment of quality, management, design capability, delivery and cost performance. The QCDDM scheme (quality, cost, delivery, development and management) provides quarterly feedback to suppliers on their achievements level, and incorporates a business plan review, covering a broad range of management topics. The implementation of the scheme is coupled with renewed efforts by the assembler to develop lean supply in its local supply base.

Elsewhere in Europe such schemes are already in use. Peugeot and Renault have agreed to accept each other's accreditation of suppliers, and the link between the latter and Volvo has a similar objective. As noted earlier, the degree to which such assessment is linked to supplier development (see Chapter 8) varies and it is this, rather than the sophistication of the assessment scheme, which really contributes to the development of lean supply.

In strategically developed cases such as these, the role and responsibility of the buyer are greatly increased. A full assessment of the supplier's business prospects is required – something of which the traditional buyer would never have been capable. There are obvious implications for the higher education and management development needs of buyers and purchasing managers. The transfer of personnel (on a secondment basis) between suppliers and customers and the operation of a quasi-firm (Figure 9.1) would strengthen this process.

As external resource management (under a variety of titles) replaces the more narrowly defined purchasing function, so personal development paths must be redefined. A large proportion of responsibility within the function will be based upon technology – suggesting that the background of external resource managers should be technical. The need for understanding complementarity of assets is also clear – external resource managers should have experience of working in companies at different points in the value chain, in order to build comprehensive views. The narrow criteria traditionally used for assessing performance in purchasing will clearly be inadequate for external resource management. The external resource manager will be judged by the integrity of the collaborations which are set up – using some form of relationship assessment technique (see below).

Opinions vary on whether or not merit awards (coupled to accreditation and assessment schemes) should be given by the customer to the supplier. On the one hand, such schemes clearly provide the supplier with a goal for which to aim. On the other, the notion of the supplier remaining a junior partner is reinforced – possibly detracting from the progression to lean supply. For the equality of collaborators in Lean Supply, some less patronizing method of publicly recognizing joint progress and achievements may be needed.

Recently, tools have been designed to aid purchasers in judging suppliers in the light of partnership sourcing. Of these, the positioning tool of Macbeth *et al.* and the Vendor Management Model of Cousins (see Chapter 6) have found widespread application. Cousins's approach is especially interesting, employing a computer-based multi-criteria decision-making technique and a very large database from research in the UK. With these, Cousins constructs bespoke and general models of best practice in suppliers as a means for customers to evaluate potential partners.

At present, however, such techniques and tools are still based upon the individual assessment of the supplier (and, to an extent, of the customer). Lean supply calls for a technique of relationship assessment – a method for monitoring and developing the relationship itself, not either company. This has potential applications in the quasi-firm concept which we saw above, as a method of determining requirements and measuring joint progress. Such a technique has yet to be developed, and may require more implementation of lean supply before it is possible. Figure 9.6 uses the nine factors of the relationships models discussed in Chapters 6 and 7, to suggest a basis for some future measuring device.

Such a device should help in answering the question: 'How lean is our relationship and what needs to be done next to improve it?' For each relationship factor (none of which can be attributed to one company alone but only to the result of collaboration) minimum, maximum, actual and target levels can be established, so that the slider design may be used as a management tool. The method of attaching values to the factors is the subject of current research.

As noted earlier, in lean supply the concept of the customer constantly assessing the supplier is redundant. Supplier assessment schemes may thus be seen as necessary but transitory devices for rationalizing supply bases. When lean

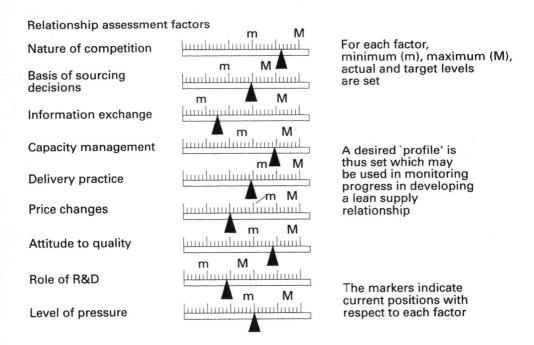

Figure 9.6 Relationship assessment using the nine-factor model

supply is achieved between two companies, the concept of relationship assessment is still required, and has the potential for stimulating the necessary pressure on (and within) each of the collaborators.

Communication in lean supply

Developments in electronic data interchange have changed the nature of communication in industry greatly over the past decade and look set to do so further for some time to come. In the automotive industry, suppliers have been required to have on-line connections to their customers for such purposes as delivery requirements since the late 1980s. GM Europe, for example, intends to have 100 per cent of its suppliers on EDI links for shipping schedules, actual delivery data and stock status data by 1994. (In 1990, its levels were 77 per cent, 23 per cent and 23 per cent respectively.) Development of more technical communications – design data, etc., has been slower, due to the greater complexity of such transmission, and the problems for customer and supplier of protecting intellectual property rights (an electronic 'drawing' sent down a computer line is more vulnerable to piracy than a traditional print).

For lean supply, communications must clearly be excellent – on both a personal level and automatically. The personal level is a matter of attitude and collaboration. The 'automatic' level relies upon interorganizational information systems to ensure that data and intelligence are transferred perfectly, as required.

In the same way that lean supply requires fundamental reassessment of business roles, so that development of information systems, within and between organizations, can be used to stimulate strategic change. For customers and suppliers, therefore, a review of information systems should be a central part of a strategy for 'going lean'.

In 1991 the MIT-based Management in the 1990s Research Program produced a five-layer model of 'business transformation as a result of information technology', which explains this strategic process. This is shown in Figure 9.7. The types of business transformation which the MIT 1990s authors classify as revolutionary are those which might be expected of lean supply – a redesign and redefinition of business process, networks and scope. The lean supplier is fundamentally concerned with these goals:

■ Process redesign – in order to rationalize the supply chain, and hence the value chain.
■ Business network redesign – to collaborate 'horizontally' perhaps in Allen's gatekeeper network.
■ Business scope redefinition – to recast the role of the supplier as an equal collaborator in lean supply.

There may also be a significant need to employ the first two levels of the MIT 1990s' model. For example, the Japanese *kanban* system was hailed as a model of simplicity by its observers in the early 1980s, but is now largely computerized.

254

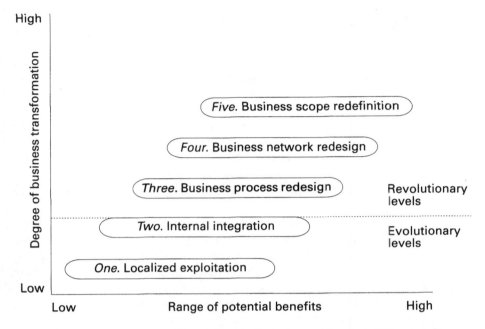

Source: From *The Corporation of the 1990s: Information Technology and Organizational Transformation,* edited by Michael S. Scott Morton. Copyright 1991 by Sloan School of Management. Reprinted by permission of Oxford University Press, Inc.

Figure 9.7 Five levels of IT-induced reconfiguration: the MIT Management in the 1990s Research Program

Another example is computer-aided production management (CAPM), which has brought benefits to the shopfloor control of many small firms, replacing the mountains of card and paper previously in use.

Moving to lean strategies: the independent suppliers

The major transition from traditional relationships to partnership demands a new way of working with suppliers. The move from partnership to lean supply requires a further step – giving up control over parts of the process which, it might be assumed, are the natural preserve of the customer. This, it might be feared, could expose the customer to abuse by suppliers. We have seen, however, that such moves are necessary in order to rationalize the value chain and reduce costs, etc.

Perhaps the greatest hurdle to be overcome for the assembler is gaining the confidence of suppliers. There are several ways in which this might be approached, two of which are discussed briefly below.

The first is to set up value analysis/engineering teams (as part of the target costing process, starting with the market price of the vehicle and working backwards to the cost of the components) which include the supplier as well as the assembler's staff. In some cases, the assembler's (external resource managers, engineers, etc.) staff may even be outnumbered by suppliers, especially if more than one component manufacturer is involved (i.e. collaborating to provide a major system). The team must be free to suggest solutions which appear at first unpalatable to the assembler, but which appeal on their own merits and logic. In other words, the assembler shows that the technical decisions are not always taken in house, especially when the supplier may have a smarter idea.

This may even involve strategic decisions on outsourcing and value chain rationalizing. The final decision to out-source will perhaps always remain with the assembler, but once again the logic of the multi-party team should be the prime factor. Unless the assembler is prepared to develop this type of technical liaison with suppliers, it is unlikely that their full cooperation (in lean supply mode) will ever be forthcoming.

The second way of making the transition from old-style supplier accreditation schemes to relationship assessment, is to set up a new scheme in which the suppliers decide upon the criteria for assessment. This would probably not depart much from existing schemes, but would certainly be seen in a different light by suppliers. Setting levels of performance (for operational factors such as delivery performance, and strategic challenges such as new technology development etc.) would stimulate competition within the supply industry and provide a chance for really innovative suppliers to shine. It would be necessary for suppliers to collaborate in competition – and to see themselves in some grouping (both factors of importance in developing a lean supply base). The risk for the assembler in this case is low: if the scheme did not work the previous programme could be reintroduced. The nature of this initiative is experimental and transitional – endorsing the need for continuous improvement and organization learning. In introducing such a scheme, the assembler would be indicating to suppliers that the success of the supply relationship is crucial to both parties – a genuinely lean concept.

■ Moving to lean strategies: breaking up vertical integration

The essential technology link in a lean supply relationship and the notion of equality between collaborators are effectively denied the wholly owned divisions of vertically integrated assemblers when it comes to other customers. Thus, GM may rely upon a component subsidiary for technology and the exchange of staff between divisions may help to remove inequalities, at least on a personal level; but that subsidiary component manufacturer will find it impossible in the long term to act as a lean partner to other assemblers. The logical result of this is that the vertically integrated assembler will be reliant upon non-lean suppliers.

It seems that some of the semi-detached but wholly owned suppliers (such as Magneti Marelli – part of Fiat) fare slightly better in business with other assemblers. It is unlikely, however, that the degree of technological interdependence, necessary for lean supply, which we have seen in this book, will be built up with such companies while an assembler holds a controlling stake.

There are several ways in which the restrictions of vertical integration (present in the Western and Japanese versions, as we have seen) may be lessened, some of which are noted below:

- A change of name for the subsidiary. Other assemblers are unlikely to enter into lean supply relationships with a division of Ford, for example, if it retains the company name. The location of new Ford component divisions in Europe during the past five years shows that the company is still developing its global ability, but such new companies are unlikely to become lean on Ford business alone.
- Selling some of the equity (possibly more than half). Component firms with equity links to more than one assembler, or to other, non-automotive customers, are more likely to sustain lean relationships than those wholly owned by one group. The Japanese version of vertical integration has shown that it is possible to have influence without total ownership.
- Genuine out-sourcing of technology. This would probably need to be accompanied by one or both of the above strategies – including some honeymoon period after the partial flotation. Until in-house divisions face true competition they are unlikely to progress towards lean production. The principle is not limited to the supply of production components – as illustrated in Figure 9.4.

■ The future

There is no sign of personalized transportation – the car – disappearing in future and investments in infrastructure in developing countries appear to be soundly in favour of roads.[4] The future may appear bright, therefore for those involved in the manufacture of automotive products. As Shoichiro Toyoda pointed out in the late 1980s, 75 per cent of the world's population have yet to own a motor car.

The vehicles themselves are about to change fundamentally in some ways, however, to eradicate the pollution of the atmosphere which they have traditionally caused, to enable total recycling of materials and to accommodate the massive control requirements for increased ownership (and therefore road congestion) which are forecast.

Such turbulence is not limited to automobiles. There are signs that the speed with which new products are introduced by the Japanese producers in several sectors will slow down in the future. Akio Morita of Sony has suggested that the product churning evident in consumer durable markets has reached its logical limit and must now give way to development towards meeting environmental concerns. Several observers of the automotive industry say that this applies to new vehicles also, although Toyota does not agree.[5] A slow down in new product development times, and an increase in product lifecycles might sound like a relief for hard-pressed component suppliers, but lean supply, with all its demands, will be just as necessary for the new competitive pressures which will surely follow.

The capability to introduce new products quickly will find new competitive outlets. For example, the steady upgrading of product image and refinement achieved by the Japanese assemblers over the 1970s and 1980s was a result of their ability to run short replacement cycles. The market demands for environmentally sound vehicles mean that no one currently has an accurate picture of the car of the future. Lean producers, able to develop improvements more quickly (via shorter product life-cycles) will clearly have major advantages. To complete this process they will rely upon their suppliers for product development. At present, this reliance is only evident in Japan – lean supply is necessary for it to be a reality globally.

Product changes will be matched by process changes. The emergence of new regions for manufacture (China, South America, Eastern Europe, Africa) in the medium to long term will provide new potential for expansion, including implementation of lean production *ab inititio*. The technology of the process, meanwhile, must undergo similar scrutiny to accommodate the tendency of people to move into and out of industrial employment (as illustrated in the 1990s by the disenchantment of young Japanese with jobs in manufacturing industry).[6] Lean production is developing at a time when the industry is going global: it is essentially a basis for genuine global operation. Lean supply mirrors this, posing immense challenges for its suitors.

It has been said that there will be three key management tasks in the future: the management of change or transformation, the management of processes, and the management of relationships.[7] The development of lean supply provides a strategic framework and a map for the third task: without it, industry cannot move forward.

■ Notes

1. British Prime Minister, Harold Macmillan, from a speech in 1957. The expression was also the US Democratic Party slogan in the 1952 election campaign.
2. This discussion is a brief summary of the Ford *et al.* (1992) paper, to which the reader is referred for a full explanation.
3. See the work of Clark and Fujimoto on product development teams: Clark *et al.* (1987, 1989 and 1991), and also the concept of 'mandate teams' in Carlisle and Parker (1989).
4. The discussions regarding a 'dry canal' road across Central America (Costa Rica), to join the Pacific and Atlantic oceans and compete with the Panama Canal, is perhaps the most interesting example of this.

5. See *The Financial Times*, 29 June 1992.
6. In 1990, the shortfall in manufacturing employees in Japan was estimated by several interviewees as almost 6 per cent. The strategic response, said one interviewee, was to automate processes to make up for the lack of people. In 1992 Honda Engineering's Vice President Ryuichi Tsukamoto estimated that to replace one worker with machinery costs between ¥10 million and ¥80 million (£42 000–£336 000). He further estimated that it was technically possible to raise the level of automation in final assembly of cars from the industry norm of about 5 to 30 per cent – including use of the Honda general assembly trucks' (GAT) system which replaces the continuous assembly line with a sequence of independent (but in-line) self propelled units (*The Financial Times*, 16 July 1992).
7. The quotation is from Daniel Jones's presentation on lean production, 1992.

Appendix 1

The International Motor

Vehicle Program

The International Vehicle Program (IMVP) was a major research project, conducted between 1986 and 1990, based within the Centre for Technology, Policy and Industrial Development (CTPID), at the Massachusetts Institute of Technology, Cambridge, MA, USA.

The IMVP was the second major international research project undertaken in the automotive industry by MIT in the 1980s: the first was the Future of the Automobile programme, conducted between 1980 and 1985.

The first programme identified the transformations which had taken place in the automotive industry, as discussed in Chapter 1 of this book, and concluded that the automobile would remain the prime source of personal transportation for the foreseeable future. It also suggested that there might be a new best practice in manufacturing vehicles.

The Future of the Automobile programme had been sponsored by major research foundations and the industry itself. The industry was impressed by the success of the research and asked MIT to repeat the exercise, focusing upon the possibility of identifying best practice within the industry.

The CTPID at MIT therefore set about restarting the work and formulated the IMVP.

Funding for the research was obtained from the following firms and organizations:

AKZO nz.
Australian Department of Industry, Technology and Commerce
Automotive Industry Authority of Australia
Canadian Department of Regional Industrial Expansion
Chrysler Motor Corporation
Commission of the European Communities
Committee of Common Market Automobile Constructors
Daimler-Benz AG
Du Pont de Nemours and Co. Automotive Products

Fiat Auto SpA
Ford Motor Company
General Motors Corporation
Japan Automobile Manufacturers Association
Japan Automotive Parts Industry Association
Mexican Association of the Automobile Industry
Mexican Autoparts National Industry Association
Montedison Automotive Corporate Group
Motor and Equipment Manufacturers Association (of the USA)
Motorola Inc.
Ontario Ministry of Industry, Trade, and Technology
Peugeot SA
Quebec Ministry of Industry and Commerce
Regie Nationale des Usines Renault
Robert Bosch GmbH
Rover Group
Saab Car Division
Swedish National Board for Technical Development
Taiwan Ministry of Economic Affairs
United Kingdom Department of Trade and Industry
United Kingdom Economic and Social Research Council
United States of America Department of Commerce
United States of America Department of Transportation: NHTSA
United States of America Office of Technology Assessment
Volkswagen AG
Volvo Car Corporation

In addition to these sponsors, many other firms gave their time to the project, including BMW AG, Jaguar Cars Ltd, Porsche KG, and many component firms. Other participants in the research forums included the Chinese National Automotive Council, and representatives from Korea, Brazil and Argentina. All the Japanese assemblers and component suppliers took part, via JAMA and JAPIA, through whom sponsorship was channelled.

The project employed the services of fifty-five researchers, drawn from academic establishments around the world. A small team, comprising the Director, Research Director, Coordinator and Secretary worked at MIT, in conjunction with the European Director, based in the UK.

The programme had researchers' meetings at MIT in the autumn of each year: 1986, 1987 and 1988, and sponsors' meetings at the International Policy Forums, held in Niagara on the lake, Canada (1987), Como, Italy (1988) and Acapulco, Mexico (1989). The final meeting of the IMVP was held in Tokyo in November 1990, at which the book *The Machine that Changed the World* was launched in English and Japanese. By 1992 the book had sold over 250 000 copies, worldwide, in seven languages.

The objectives of the IMVP were to identify best practice within the automobile industry. The research was divided into six parts:

- Strategy (for existing players and for new entrants).
- Assembly practice.
- Human factors (in assembly).
- Supply systems.
- New product development (R&D).
- Distribution and retailing.

Some 160 papers were written on these subjects throughout the programme, and are available from the CTPID at MIT. In addition, presentations were made to the forums by politicians, company chief executives and senior academics. Several spin-off research programmes grew from IMVP, both private (in company) and publicly available.

Techniques and methods varied across the research projects contained within the IMVP. Gradually some convergence was recognized and a final report was made possible by the efforts of the Research Director and the European Director, with the help and direct involvement of a small number of the researchers, closely concerned with the programme.

The generic name given by the IMVP to best practice was lean production – clearly explained in the book. IMVP found three areas within the industry in which best practice could be identified: assembly, global strategy and supply systems.

Appendix 2

Major Japanese Auto Parts Manufacturers' Presence in Europe (as of Summer 1990)

Company name in Japan	Country	Equity (%)	Established	Local partners (%)	Major business	OEM alliance
Asahi Glass	Netherlands	40	1981	Glaverbel (60)	Sheet glass	Independent
Calsonic	Netherlands	100	1984		Mufflers for replacement	Nissan
Calsonic	UK	100	1989		Radiators, mufflers	Nissan
Calsonic	UK	100	1986		Mufflers	Nissan
Clarion	France	51	1983	Besis Group (49)	Car radios/stereos	Independent
Clarion	Sweden	100	1979		Car radios/stereos	Independent
Hashimoto Forming Ind.	UK	—	1990		Mouldings, exterior parts	Nissan
Ikeda Bussan	UK	51	1986	Hoover Universal (49)	Car seats and interior parts	Nissan
Inoue MTP	W. Germany	49	1986	J.H. Benecke (51)	Instrument panels	Independent
Kanto Seiki	UK	50	1990		Meters	Nissan
Matsushita Communication Ind.	UK	40	1989		Car telephones	Independent
Koyo Seiki	France	35	1990	SMI (65)	Steering systems	Toyota
Mitsuboshi Belting	Austria	50	1981	Semperit (50)	Rubber V. belts	Independent
Nachi-Fujikoshi	Spain	38	1976	Banesto (62)	Ball, roller bearings	Independent

Appendix 2 continued

Company name in Japan	Country	Equity (%)	Established	Local partners (%)	Major business	OEM alliance
NHK Spring	Spain	40	1980	MBHA	Coil springs, stabilizers	Independent
Nippon Seiki	UK	100	1987		Meters	Honda
Nippon Seiko	UK	100	1964		Bearings	Independent
Nippondenso	UK	75	1990	Magneti Marelli (25)	Car air conditioners	Toyota
Nippondenso	Spain	50	1991	Valeo (50)	Ignition coils	Toyota
NTN	W. Germany.	100	1971		Bearings	Independent
Pioneer Electronic	Belgium	100	1976		Audio equipment	Independent
Sumitomo Rubber	Finland	20	1988		Tyres	Independent
Sumitomo Rubber	France	57.5	1984	Ohtsu Tyre (9)	Tyres, tubes, air-suspensions	Independent
Sumitomo Rubber	W. Germany	50.5	1984	Ohtsu Tyre (<1)	Tyres, tubes, air-suspensions	Independent
Sumitomo	UK	69.04	1987	Ohtsu Tyre (9)	Tyres, tubes rubber	Independent
Topy Industries	UK	15	1987	Dunlop (85)	Wheels	Independent
Toyoda Machine Works	France	50	1985	Toyota Tsusho (4)	Machine tools	Toyota
Yuasa Battery	UK	100	1981		Sealed lead batteries	Independent
Yuasa Battery	UK	100	1988		Lead acid storage batteries	Independent

Source: Chatterjee (The Technology Partnership) (1991).

Appendix 3

Major Japanese Auto Parts Suppliers' Sales
Companies in Europe (as of June 1990)

Company name in Japan	Country	Equity (%)	Local company name	Established	Employees	Major business
Aisin Seiki	Belgium	100	Aisin Europe	1971	45	Auto parts, home appliances
Akebono Brake	France	100	Akebono Europe	1985	4	Brakes
Alpine Electronics	Germany	100	Alpine Electronic	1978	30	Audio equipment
Alpine Electronics	UK	80	Alpine Electronics of UK	1986	17	Audio equipment
Asahi Glass	Belgium	100	Euro Safety Glass	1983	4	Auto Safety Glass
Bridgestone	Denmark	60	Bridgestone Tire A/S	1972	32	Tyres, tubes
Bridgestone	Germany	83.2	Bridgestone Reifen	1976	103	Tyres, tubes
Bridgestone	Switzerland	100	Bridgestone (Schweiz)	1965	25	Tyres, tubes

265

Appendix 3 continued

Company name in Japan	Country	Equity (%)	Local company name	Established	Employees	Major business
Bridgestone	UK	51	Bridgestone Tyre UK	1972	67	Tyres, tubes
Clarion	Germany	100	Clarion Deutschland	1968	23	Car radios/stereos
Clarion	UK	100	Clarion Shoji (UK)	1980	43	Car audio equipment
Hitachi Chemical	Germany	100	Hitachi Chemical Europe	1982	—	Chemical products
Inoue MTP	Germany	49	Benoac Fertigteil	1986	—	Instrument panels
Japan Storage	Germany	100	GS Battery (Europe)	1985	4	Batteries
Koyo Seiko	Germany	99.4	Deutsche Koyo Walzlager Verkaufs	1964	61	Bearings
Koyo Seiko	Netherlands	100	Europa-Koyo	1973	36	Bearings
Koyo Seiko	Spain	100	Koyo Espanola	1978	9	Bearings
Koyo Seiko	Sweden	100	Koyo Kullager Scandinavia	1977	8	Bearings
Koyo Seiko	UK	100	Koyo (UK)	1972	25	Bearings
Matsushita Communication Ind.	Germany	50	Matsushita Communication Deutschland	1985	30	Audio equipment
Minebea	Germany	100	NMB	1981	44	Bearings, precision equipment parts
Minebea	UK	100	NMB (UK)	1971	17	Bearings
Mitsubishi Electric	Germany	100	Mitsubishi Europe	1978	—	Electrical auto parts, home electrical appliances
Mitsubishi Electric	Netherlands	100	Mitsubishi Electric Netherlands	1972	—	Heavy electric machinery, electric/electronic parts
Mitsuboshi Belting	Netherlands	100	MBL (Europe)	1977	9	Conveyor belts, V-belts

Appendix 3 continued

Company name in Japan	Country	Equity (%)	Local company name	Established	Employees	Major business
Nachi-Fujikoshi	Germany	100	Nachi Germany (27% owned by Nachi America)	1967	19	Bearings
Nachi-Fujikoshi	UK	60	Nachi (UK)	1974	13	Bearings cutting tools
NGK Spark Plug	Germany	100	NGK Spark Plug (Deutschland)	1980	—	Spark plug, ceramic parts
Nippon Piston Ring	Germany	45	Schottle Motorenteile	1973	11	Piston rings, engine parts
Nippon Seiko	Italy	100	NSK Italia	1976	—	Bearings, machinery parts
Nippon Seiko	Netherlands	100	NSK Netherland	1975	—	Bearings, machine parts
Nippondenso	Netherlands	100	Nippondenso (Europe)	1973	58	Electrical auto parts, air-conditioners, compressors, plugs
NTN	France	99.97	NTN France	1976	57	Bearings
NTN	Germany	100	NTN Walzlager (Europe)	1961	124	Bearings
NTN	UK	100	NTN Bearings (UK)	1964	46	Bearings
Omron	Netherlands	100	Omron Electronics	1974	26	Electronic controller parts
Pioneer Electronic	Belgium	100	Pioneer Electronic (Europe)	1970	173	Audio equipment
Pioneer Electronic	Denmark	100	Pioneer Electronics Denmark	1978	26	Audio equipment
Pioneer Electronic	Germany	80	Pioneer Melchers	1978	134	Audio equipment
Pioneer Electronic	Italy	100	Pioneer Electronics (Italy)	1980	—	Audio equipment
Pioneer Electronic	Netherlands	100	Pioneer Electronics	1981	—	Audio equipment
Pioneer Electronic	Netherlands	100	Pioneer Electronics 1981 (Holland)	1981	56	Audio equipment
Pioneer Electronic	Spain	80	Pioneer Electronics Espana	1986	85	Audio equipment

Appendix 3 continued

Company name in Japan	Country	Equity (%)	Local company name	Established	Employees	Major business
Pioneer Electronic	UK	100	Pioneer High Fidelity	1978	149	Audio equipment
Riken Corp.	Germany	100	Euro-Riken	1983	2	Piston rings, engine parts
Toyo Tyre & Rubber	Germany	60	Toyo-Reifen	1975	22	Tyres, tubes
Tsubakimoto Chain	Netherlands	50	Tsubakimoto Europe	1972	18	Chains etc.
Yazaki Corp.	UK	100	Yazaki (UK)	1980	17	Wire harness
Yuasa Battery	Germany	100	Yuasa Battery (Europe)	1982	5	Batteries

Source: Technomic Consultants International (1990).

Appendix 4

Some Examples of Strategic Alliances between UK and Japanese Auto-Component Companies

	UK Company	Japanese Company	Type of Alliance	Products
1.	Automotive Products	Akebono	Technology imported	Composite system brakes
2.	Otter Controls	Murata	not known	not known
3.	ASE	Ashimori Kogyo	Technology imported	Seat belts
4.	BSRD	Ashimori Kogyo	Technology imported	Seat belts
5.	ICI	Dai Nippon Toryo	Technology imported	Multi-purpose millbases-paint
6.	Glacier Metal	Daido Metal	Technology exported	White metal
7.	Kangol Magnet	Fuji Kiko	Technology imported	Seat belt retractors
8.	Holset Engineering	Fukoku	Technology imported	Viscous dampers
9.	Lucas Industries	Hitachi Seisakusho	Technology exported	Electrical autoparts
10.	Hoover	Ikeda Bussan	Joint venture	Seats
11.	UGC (Unipart)	Yotaku-Giken	Joint venture	Exhausts/catalytic converters
12.	Marley	Kanto Seiki	Joint venture	not known
13.	Dowty Seals	Ishino Gasket	Technology imported	Dowprint gaskets
14.	Laystall Engineering	Izumi Kogyo	Technology imported	Chromium-plated cylinder lines
15.	Lucas Girling	Japan Brake Ind. (Nippon Brake Kogyo)	Technology imported	Drum brake assemblies

Appendix 4 continued

	UK Company	Japanese Company	Type of Alliance	Products
16.	Ferodo Ltd	Japan Brake Ind. (Nippon Brake Kogyo)	Technology exchange	Brakes and new materials
17.	Lucas Electrical	Jidosha Denki Kogyo	Technology exported	Windshield washer pumps
18.	Boalloy Ltd	Kato Shatai Kogyo	Technology imported	Curtain sided body
19.	George Angus	Keeper Co.	Technology imported	Oil seals
20.	Rist's Wire & Cables	Kyoritsu Hiparts	Technology imported	Wire harness
21.	Rota Belt	NHK Spring (Nippon Hatsujo)	Technology imported	Load monitoring sensors
22.	Unipart	Nikko Electric (Nikko Denki Kogyo)	Technology exported	Starters
23.	Associated Engineering	Nippon Piston Ring	Technology imported	Sintered alloy products
24.	Torrington	Nippon Seiko	Technology imported	Needle bearings
25.	Trico-Folberth	Nippon Wiper Blade	Technology imported	Wiper blades and arms
26.	Lucas Girling	Nisshinbo Ind. (Nisshin Boseki)	Technology imported	Disc brakes for commercial vehicles, control valves, drum brake assemblies
27.	Lucas Girling	Nissin Kogyo	Technology imported	Brake parts, brake servos and cylinders
28.	Hardy Spicer	NTN Corp.	Technology imported	Constant velocity universal
29.	Railko	Oiles Corp. Kogyo	Technology exported	Oil-less bearings
30.	Concentric Pump	Saitama Kiki	Technology imported	Oil pumps, fan clutches
31.	ICI	Shinto Paint (Shinto Toryo)	Technology imported	Automotive paints
32.	Lucas Girling	Sumitomo Electric (Sumitomo Denki Kogyo)	Technology imported	Disc brakes for auto/industrial use, anti-lock brake systems
33.	Multilastic Ltd	Tachi-S Co.	Technology imported	Springs, spring units
34.	Canning Brett	Togo Seisakusyo	Technology imported	Hose clips
35.	Lucas Girling	Tokico Ltd	Technology imported	Brake boosters, drum disc brakes
36.	BTR Dunlop	Topy Ind. (Topy Kogyo)	Technology exported	Wheels
37.	Air Cleaner Technical Services	Tsuchiya Manufacturing (Tsuchiya Seisakusho)	Technology exported	Filters

Appendix 4 continued

	UK Company	Japanese Company	Type of Alliance	Products
38.	Lucas Industries	Yuasa	Joint venture	Batteries
39.	Smiths Industries	Kanto Seiko	Technology cooperation	Speedometer cables
40.	Slumberland Group	Tachi-S Co.	Technical assistance	Seats
41.	Wagon-Industrial	Tri-Wall	Joint venture	Car roof linings
42.	Bristol Vending Services	Sanoh Industrial	Joint venture	Pipes for brake and fuel systems
43.	Torrington	Fuji Kiko	Technology exported	not known
44.	Cape Asbestos	Nichias Corp.	Technology exported	Ceramic fibres technology

Source: Technomic Consultants International (1990).

Appendix 5

Japanese–Japanese Joint Ventures in North America

Partners	%[a]	Local company	Product
Alps Electric Alpine Electronic of America	30 (70)	Alpine Electronics Manufacturing of America	Car radio/stereos Security systems
APM/Kasai Kogyo	55/45	M-TEK Inc.	Interior parts
C.Itoh & Co. Sumitomo Wiring System	60 40	Sumitomo Electric Wiring System	Wire harnesses
Calsonic/Sumitomo Corp. Yoruzu Manufacturing Corp.		Calsonic Yoruzu	Suspensions
Clarion/Clarion Shoji		Clarion Shoji USA	Stereos, radios
Daido Steel/Daido Kogyo	60/40	Daido Steel (America)	Steel, other material products
Enkei Corp./Mitsubishi Corp.	60/20	Enkei America	Aluminium wheels
Inoue MTP/Inoue Rubber	67/33	INOAC USA Inc.	Mouldings, air spoilers
Kikuchi Metal Stamping Takao Kinzoku Kogyo Honda Motor		Jefferson Ind.	Dashboard parts
Kikuchi Metal Stamping Takao Kinzoku Kogyo Hirata Press Industry Horgo Seiskusho Honda Motor	1.25 1.25 1.25 1.25 (95)	KTH Parts Industries	Pressed parts

Appendix 5 continued

Partners	%[a]	Local company	Product
Kuriyama/Mitsuboshi Belting	5/95	MBL (USA) Corp.	Rubber V-belts
Matsushita Comms Ltd Matsushita Elec. Ind.	50 50	Matsushita Comms Ind. Corp. of America	Car telephones, radios, stereos
Nachi-Fujikoshi Kanematsu Corp. Nissho Iwai Shima Trading Others	40 15 15 15 (15)	Nachi Bearing	Ball bearings
NGK Insulators Mitsubishi Corp.	85 15	NGK-Locke	Glass and ceramics
NHK Spring NHK Sales Nippon Gasket Topra	45 37.5 2.5 2.5	NHK International	Springs, gaskets, shafts, etc.
Nippon Pipe Manfg Sumitomo Metal Inds Mitsui & Co.	50 30 20		High precision steel pipes for shock absorbers and steering columns
Nippondenso Toyoda Automatic Loom Wks	50 50	Michigan Automatic Compressors	Compressors, magnetic clutches
Ogihara Iron Works Marubeni Corp.	80 20	Ogihara America	Auto parts
Press Kogyo/Mitsui & Co.	75/25	PK USA	Stamped parts, plastic parts
Sankei Giken Kogyo Toyo Seat Honda Motor	2 2 (96)		Seats, wheels
Sanoh Inds/Sanyo Electric	90/10	Sanoh Manufacturing	Brake tubes, fuel tubes
Showa Mfg/Honda Motor	65/ (35)	Sun Bury Components	Shock absorbers
Sumitomo Rubber/ Electric	(86)/ 11	Dunlop Tire Co.	Tyres
Stanley Electric Kyokuto Boeki	(70) 30	II Stanley	Electric products
Sumitomo Electric Sumitomo Wiring Systems	60/40	L-S Electro Galvanizing	Galvanized steel sheets

Appendix 5 continued

Partners	%[a]	Local company	Product
Tokyo Steel	58.81	ATR Wire & Cable	Steel codes for tyres
C.Itoh & Co.	20		
Misubishi Corp.	20		
Nippon Steel	1.19		
Toyoda Gosei/Misui & Co.	80/20	TG (USA)	Steering wheel resin gears
Toyota Motor	89.3	TABC Inc.	Catalytic converters
Cataler Corp.	10.7		
Yamakawa Industrial	60	Yamakawa Mnfg Corp. of America	Pressed body parts
Marubeni Corp.	40		
Yuasa Battery	50	Yuasa Battery (America)	Batteries
Yuasa Shoji	50		

Note: [a] ( ) indicates equity held through existing subsidiaries already established in the USA.
Source: Chatterjee, The Technology Partnership (1991).

Appendix 6

Japanese–American Joint Ventures in the USA

Date	Company	Partner	Japanese ownership (%)	Product
1971	Tsubakimoto Chain	Roger Lewan	94	Chains
1981	Ishikawajima Harima Heavy Inds	Borg Warner	50	Turbochargers
1983	Koito Manufacturing	Hella North America	39	Lighting
	Ichikoh Industries		10	
1984	Usui Kokusai Sangyo	Bundy Tubing	51	Brakes, fuel tubes, car telephones, stereos
	Manyasu Inds	Curtis Products	50	
1985	Inoue MTP	Woodbridge	49	Seats, arms, headrests
1986	Toyota Tsusho	Kelsey-Hayes	20	Wheels
	Central Motor Wheel		40	
	Namba Press Works	Douglas & Lomason	50	Seats
	NHK Spring	Barnes Group	55	Coil springs
	Sanoh Industrial	Higbie Manufacturing	50	Brake, fuel, electronic parts
	Sumitomo Metals	LTV	40	Galvanized steel sheets

Appendix 6 continued

Date	Company	Partner	Japanese ownership (%)	Product
1987	Asahi Glass	PPG Industry	51	Manufacture and sale of safety glass
	Bridgestone	Clevite	49	Rubber dampers
	Central Motor Wheel	FTC Int.	55	Auto parts
	Daikin Manufacturing	Rockwell Corporation	40	Clutches
	Fusukawa Electric	United Technologies	48	Wire harness
	Ohmi Electric Wire		1	
	Hashimoto Forming	Automotive Moulding	60	Interior/exterior parts
	Jidosha Kiki	Allied Signal	49	Power brakes
	Nifco	Illinois Tool Works	50	Plastic fasteners
	Nikon Tokushu Toyo	Globe Ind.	50	Soundproofing materials, anti-chipping paints
	Sango	Arvin Industries	50	Mufflers, exhaust pipes
	Sankei Giken Kogyo	Tailor Metal Products	70	Muffler parts, door sashes
	Tachi-S	Hoover Universal Inc.	49	Trim covers
	Yuasa Battery	Exide Battery	50	Batteries
1988	Honda Lock	All Rock	50	Locks
	Japan Storage Battery	GNB	50	Batteries
	Nippon Seiko	The Torrington	50	Steering wheels
	Nittan	Eaton Group	30	Engine valves
	Ohio Seisakusho	Atwood	50	Window regulators, doors
	Shiroki Corporation	Wickes	50	Auto parts
	Tachi-S	Hoover Universal Inc.	51	Seats
	Duramax	Tokai Rubber Inds	70	Rubber dampers, hoses
	Yokohama Rubber	Morton	50	Shielding materials
1989	Asahi Tec	Motor Wheel	40	Manufacture of aluminium wheels
	Toyo Menka Kaisha		10	
	Central Glass	Ford Motor	51	Automotive glass
	Ikeda Bussan	Johnson Control	50	Seats

Appendix 6 continued

Date	Company	Partner	Japanese ownership (%)	Product
	Ishino Gasket Mfg	Dana Corp	49	Engine gaskets
	Mitsubishi Kasei	A. Schulman	30	Vinyl chloride compounds
	NHK Spring	Lear Siegler Seating	65	Seats
	Nippon Steel	Inland Steel Ind.	not known	Sheet steel coating
	Nippondenso	Facet of the US	50	Filters
	Sansei Tosei	Larry Campbell	1	Die cast parts
	Yohshin	Orscheln	50	Switches, keys
1989/90	Calsonic	General Motors Delco Electronics Divn	not known	Electronics
1990	Marugo Rubber Inds Mitsubishi Corp.	Plumley Rubber	41 9	Rubber parts
1991	Kawasaki Steel Saga Tekkosho	Armco Inc. Ring Screw Works	40 50	Surface-treated steel Air-conditioners, compressors
not known	Mitsubishi Rayon Sanko Senzai Kogyo	Network Polymers Peterson American	35 50	ABS resin Power train parts

Source: Chatterjee (1991).

Appendix 7

Other Japanese Greenfield Sites in USA

Date	Company	Products
1958	Koyo Seiko	Ball bearings
1962/69	Nachi-Fujikoshi	Radial ball bearings
1966	NGK Spark Plug	Coil springs
1968	NOK	Rubber parts
1970/88	Aisin Seiki	Pressed body parts
1971/85	NTN	Bearings
1973	Mitsuboshi Belting	Polyurethane belts
	Nippon Seiko	Bearings
1974	Minebea	Control-use electrical equipment
1974/89	Kayaba Industries	Shock absorbers
	Sanden	Air conditioners and compressors
1976	Oiles Industry	Oiless bearings
1977/86/90	Tokyo Seat	Seats and interior parts
1978/81/82	Pioneer Electronic	Audio equipment
1979	Central Glass	Safety glass
1980	Musashi Seimitsu	Ball joints and suspensions
	Nipon Sheet Glass	Optical fibres
1981/88	Mitsui Metal Mining	Car doors and lock parts R&D
1982/88	Riken Corp.	Seal rings
1983	Daikin Manufacturing	Clutches
	Mikuni	R&D
	Sumitomo Electric Industries	Optical fibre cables
1984	Mitsubishi Metal	R&D
1984/87	Diesel Kiki	Air-conditioner components, heat exchangers
1985	Hitachi Ltd	Electronic/electrical parts
	Hiratu Kogyo	Pressed parts
	Sumitomo Metal Industries	Exhaust and stabilizer tubes
1986	Fujitsu Ten	Stereos/radios
	Kasai Kogyo	Trim boards, sun visors
	Tokai Rika	Switches
	Tokai Rubber Industries	Rubber dampers

Appendix 7 continued

Date	Company	Products
1986/87	Tsuchiya Manufacturing	Weather strips, carbon canisters, oil coolers and filters, etc.
1986/89	Clarion	Car stereos/radios, portable telephones for cars
	Kato Hatsujo Kaisha	Spring fasteners
1987	Japan EWI	Exterior pressed parts
	Mitsubishi Electric	Electric products and stereos
	NHK Spring	Sale of stabilizers
1988	Hitachi Cable	Hoses
	Hitachi Chemical	Printed circuit board
	Ichikoh Industries	Rearview mirrors
	NGK Insulators	Catalytic converters
	Omron	Electronic controllers
	Togo Seisakusho	Springs
	Ikeda Bussan	Interior parts
1989	Arai Seiskusho	Oil seals
	Nanjo Sobi Kogyo	Door trims
	Nissei Sangyo	Brake systems
	Pacific Industrial	R&D, tyre valves and valve cores
	Yamada Seisakusho	Rack and pinion, steering gears
	Yanagwa Seiki	Front limbs, bearing caps, brackets
	Yokohama Aeroquip	Hoses and fittings
	Central Motor Wheel	Aluminium wheels
1990	Nippon Cable System	Control cables and power window regulators
	Nippon Zeon	'Zet Pol' nitrile hydro-rubber
1991	Diamond Electric	Ignition coils
N/K	Keioisha Manufacturing	Pressed parts

Source: Chatterjee (1991), Technomic Consultants International (1990).

Glossary

ANFIA: Associazione Nazionale fra Industrie Automobilistiche, Italy
Assembler: A company whose principal activity is manufacturing (assembling) vehicles
Big Three: (In the USA) General Motors, Ford and Chrysler
BMW: Bayerishe Motoren Werke
CCMC: Confederation of Common Market Automobile Constructors
CEO: Chief Executive Officer
CLEPA: Confederation Les Europeannes Produits Automotive, EEC
CNAC: China National Auto Industry Council, China
Dual sourcing: The purchasing practice of buying an item from two separate suppliers, splitting the business between them
EC: European Community
EDI: Electronic Data Interchange
FAPM: Federation of Automotive Parts Manufacturers, Australia
FIEV: Fédération Industries Equipements Vehicules, France
FMEA: Failure mode and effect analysis
GM: General Motors
Greenfield site: A new industrial (manufacturing) plant, built on a site not previously used for such purposes, possibly in a geographical region not traditionally associated with manufacturing
INA: Industria Nacional Autopartes, Mexico
JAPIA: Japan Auto Parts Industry Association, Japan
JAMA: Japan Automotive Manufacturers Association
Just-in-time (JIT): The philosophy associated with reduction of waste and improvement in product and service quality and personal motivation through a reduction of inventory and buffers (contingency allowance for errors). The term was invented (in English) in Japan to describe a system in which materials and parts are made available just at the point at which they are required
Logistics: The management of physical resources within the supply chain to ensure timely provision of requirements. The term is used synonymously with materials management, and is loosely used to incorporate purchasing and supply, etc.
MCI: Ministry for Commerce and Industry (Japanese: forerunner of MITI)
MIT: Massachusetts Institute of Technology
MITI: (Japanese) Ministry of International Trade and Industry
MEMA: Motor & Equipment Manufacturers Association, USA
Multi-market: Pertaining to more than one sales market, identified by technology and product/service type

Multi-sourcing: As dual sourcing, but with more than two sources of supply

MVMA: Motor Vehicle Manufacturers Association (USA)

NUMMI: New United Motor Manufacturing Inc. (the Toyota/GM joint venture assembly plant in Fremont California)

OE: Original equipment (i.e. as fitted to the vehicle in the assembly plant)

OECD: Organisation for Economic Co-operation and Development

OEM: Original equipment manufacturer (peculiarly used in the automobile industry to refer to the vehicle assembler)

Purpose-built plant: Factory designed and constructed specifically for the manufacture of a product (e.g. a type of component, or a vehicle)

SMMT: Society of Motor Manufacturers and Traders, UK

SQA: Supplier quality assurance

SPC: Statistical process control

Sub-assembly: Group of components which are fitted together and identified as a unit for subsequent fitting into a system

System: Group of components which together form the physical means of effecting a specific function within the vehicle

TQC: Total quality control

TQM: Total quality management

Transplant: Assembly or manufacturing plant (factory) built in one country by a firm based in another country. Applies especially to best practice manufacturers setting up new facilities to manufacture in a sub-best practice country

UAW: United Auto Workers (Union: USA)

VDA: Verbandes Der Automobilindustrie, Germany

Bibliography

Abernathy, W.J. (1978) *The Productivity Dilemma: Roadblock to innovation in the automobile industry,* Johns Hopkins University Press: Baltimore MD.

Abernathy, W.J. and Hayes, R. (1980) 'Managing our way to economic decline', *Harvard Business Review.* July–August pp. 67–77.

Abernathy, W.J., Clark, K.B. and Kantrow, A.M. (1983) *Industrial Renaissance: Producing a competitive future for America,* Basic Books: New York.

Abernathy, W.J. and Utterback, J. (1978) 'Patterns of industrial innovation', *Technology Review,* vol. 80, no. 7, pp. 40–7.

Abernathy, W.J. and Clark, K. (1985) 'Mapping the winds of creative destruction'. *Research Policy,* vol. 14, pp. 3–22.

Allen, T. J. (1977) *Managing the Flow of Technology,* MIT Press: Cambridge, MA.

Altshuler, A., Anderson, M., Jones, D.T., Roos, D. and Womack, J.P. (1984) *The Future of the Automobile: The Report of MIT's International Automobile Program,* MIT Press. Cambridge, MA.

Argyris, C. and Schon, D. (1978) *Organisational Learning,* Addison Wesley: London.

Arrow, K.J. (1962) 'Economic welfare and the allocation of resources for invention', in *The Rate and Direction of Inventive Activity,* Princeton University Press for the National Bureau of Economic Research: Princeton, NJ.

Automotive Industry Authority [of Australia] (1991) *Report on the State of the Automotive Industry 1990,* Australian Government Publishing Service: Canberra.

Axelrod, R. (1984) *The Evolution of Co-operation,* Penguin: London.

Baily P.J.H. (1987) *Purchasing and Supply Management, 5th edn,* Chapman and Hall: London.

Baily, P. and Farmer, D. (1990) *Purchasing Principles and Management,* 6th edn, Pitman: London

Baker, N.R., Siegman, J. and Rubenstein, A.H. (1967) 'The effects of perceived needs and means on the generation of ideas for industrial research and development projects', N.R. Baker, J. Siegman and A.H. Ruberstein, *IEEE Transactions on Engineering Management,* December. pp. 156–63.

Baker, N.R., Siegman, J. and Larson, J. (1971) 'The relationship between certain characteristics of industrial research projects and their subsequent disposition', *IEEE Transactions on Engineering Management,* November, pp. 118–23.

Barras R. (1986) 'Towards a theory of innovation in services', *Research Policy,* vol. 15, pp. 161–73.

Baughan, C. and Osborn, R. (1990) 'The role of technology in the formation of multinational cooperative arrangements', *Journal of High Technology Management Research,* vol. 1, no. 2.

Bessant, J.R., Jones, D.T., Lamming, R.C. and Pollard, A. (1984) *Recent Changes and*

Future Prospects: The West Midlands automobile components industry, West Midlands County Council, Economic Development Unit, Sector Report No. 4: Birmingham.

Bessant, J.R. and Lamming, R.C. (1985) *Jaguar Cars Ltd: Impacts on employment and implications of privatisation,* West Midlands County Council, Economic Development Unit, unpublished internal report.

Bessant, J.R. and Grunt, M. (1985) *Management and Manufacturing Innovation in the United Kingdom and West Germany,* Gower: Aldershot, UK.

Bessant, J.R. (1988) 'Pushing boxes or solving problems? Some marketing issues in the diffusion of computer-integrated manufacturing innovations', *Journal of Marketing Management,* vol. 3, no. 3, Spring.

Bessant, J.R. (1991) *Managing Advanced Manufacturing Technology: the challenge of the fifth wave,* NCC Blackwell: Oxford.

Blois, K.J. (1972) 'Vertical quasi integration', *Journal of Industrial Economics (UK),* vol. 20, no. 3, July, pp. 253–71.

Blois, K.J. (1975) 'Supply contracts in the Galbraithian planning system', *Journal of Industrial Economics (UK),* vol. 24, no. 1, September, pp. 29–39.

Boston Consulting Group (BCG) (1991) *The Competitive Challenge Facing the European Automotive Components Industry,* Report compiled for DGIII of the European Commission (Executive Summary): Brussels.

Bund Jackson, B. (1985) 'Build customer relationships that last', *Harvard Business Review,* vol. 63, no. 6, Nov–Dec, pp. 120–8.

Burns, T. and Stalker, G. (1961) *The Management of Innovation,* Tavistock: London.

Cammish, R. and Keough, M. (1991) 'A strategic role for purchasing', *McKinsey Quarterly,* November.

Campbell, N.C.G. (1985) 'Buyer/seller relationships in Japan and Germany: an interaction approach', *European Journal of Marketing,* vol. 19, no. 3, pp. 57–66.

Carlisle, J. and Parker, R. (1989) *Beyond Negotiation: Redeeming customer–supplier relationships,* Wiley: Chichester.

Carr, C. (1990) *Britain's Competitiveness: The management of the vehicle component industry,* Routledge: London.

CBI (Confederation of British Industry, UK) (1991) *Partnership Sourcing,* CBI: London.

CBI (Confederation of British Industry, UK) (1992) *Making Partnership Sourcing Happen,* CBI: London.

Chandler, A. (1962) *Strategy and Structure.* MIT Press: Cambridge, MA.

Chandler, A. (ed.) (1964) *Giant Enterprise: Ford, General Motors, and the automobile industry,* Harcourt Brace and World: New York.

Chandler, A.D. (1977) *The Visible Hand: The managerial revolution in American business* Harvard University Press: Cambridge, MA.

Chatterjee, J. (1991) Unpublished consultancy working papers, The Technology Partnership Ltd, Melbourn, Royston, UK.

Clark, K.B. (1985a) *Managing Technology in International Competition: The case of product development in response to foreign entry.* Harvard Business School Working Paper: Boston, MA.

Clark, K.B. (1985b) 'The interaction of design hierarchies and market concepts in technological evolution', *Research Policy,* vol. 14, pp. 235–51.

Clark, K.B. (1989a) 'Project scope and project performance: the effects of parts strategy and supplier involvement on product development', *Management Science,* vol. 35, no. 10, October, pp. 1247–63.

Clark, K.B. (1989b) 'High performance product development in the world auto industry', Paper presented at the International Forum on Technology Management, La Hulpe, Belgium, July.

Clark, K.B. and Fujimoto T. (1987) *Overlapping Problem Solving in Product Development,* Harvard Business School Working Paper No. 87–048, Cambridge, MA.

Clark, K.B. and Fujimoto T. (1988a) 'The European model of product development: challenge and opportunity', *Proceedings of MIT International Motor Vehicle Program 2nd Annual Policy Forum*, MIT: Cambridge, MA.

Clark, K.B. and Fujimoto T. (1988b) *Lead Time in Automobile Product Development: Explaining the Japanese Advantage*, Harvard Business School Working Paper No. 89–033: Cambridge, MA.

Clark, K.B. and Fujimoto, T. (1989) 'Product development and competitiveness', Paper presented at the OECD International Seminar on Science Technology and Economic Growth, Paris, June.

Clark, K.B. and Fujimoto, T. (1991) *Product Development Performance*, Harvard Business School Press: Boston, MA.

Clark, K.B., Chew, W.B. and Fujimoto, T. (1987) 'Product development in the world auto industry: strategy, organisation and performance', *Brookings Papers in Economic Activity*, vol. 3, pp. 729–71.

Clark, K.B., Hayes, R.H. and Lorenz, C. (eds) (1985) *The Uneasy Alliance: Managing the productivity dilemma*, Harvard Business School: Cambridge, MA.

Clark, P. and Starkey, K. (1987) *Organisation Transition and Innovation Design*, Frances Pinter: London.

Clark, P. and Staunton, N. (1989) *Innovation and Technology in Organisation*, Routledge: London.

Coase, R.H. (1937) 'The nature of the firm' *Economica* (NS), vol. 4, pp. 386–405.

Cole, R. and Yakushiji, T. (eds) (1984). *The American and Japanese Auto Industries in Transition*, Center for Japanese Studies, University of Michigan: Ann Arbor.

Collins, T.M., Doorley, T.L. and Connell, D. (1991) *Teaming Up for the 90s: A guide to international joint ventures and strategic alliances*, Business One Irwin: Homewood, IL.

Contractor, F.J. (1986) 'An alternative view of international business', *International Marketing Review*, Spring. MCB University Press Limited: Bradford, UK.

Contractor F.J. and Lorange P. (1988) *Co-operative Strategies in International Business: Joint ventures and technology partnerships between firms*, Lexington Books: Lexington, MA.

Cooper, R.G. (1984) 'The performance impact of product innovation strategies', *European Journal of Marketing*, vol. 18, no. 5, pp. 1–54.

Corey, E.R. (1976) *Industrial Marketing: Cases and Concepts*, 2nd edn, Prentice Hall: Engelwood Cliffs, NJ.

Cousins, P. (1992) 'Choosing the right partner', *Purchasing and Supply Management Journal*, March, Institute of Purchasing and Supply: Stamford, UK.

Crane, D. (1972) *Invisible Colleges: Diffusion of knowledge in scientific communities*, University of Chicago Press: Chicago, IL.

Crandall, Robert W. (1968) *Vertical Integration in the US Automobile Industry*, PhD thesis, Northwestern University, Chicago.

Cusumano, M.A. (1985) *The Japanese Automobile Industry: Technology and management at Nissan and Toyota*, Harvard University Press: Cambridge, MA.

Cusumano, M.A. (1988) 'Manufacturing innovation: lessons for the Japanese auto industry', *Sloan Management Review*, Fall, pp. 29–39.

Dankbaar, B. (1990) 'International competition and national institutions: the case of the automobile', in Freeman, C. and Soete, L. (eds) *New Explorations in the Economics of Technical Change*, Frances Pinter: London.

Dasgupta, P. and Stiglitz, J. (1980) 'Uncertainty, industrial structure, and the speed of R&D', *Bell Journal of Economics*, vol. 11, no. 1, Spring, pp. 1–28.

Davis, W. (1987) *The Innovators*, Ebury Press: London.

Davies, S. (1979) *The Diffusion of Process Innovations*, Cambridge University Press: Cambridge.

DeBresson, C. and Amesse, F. (1991) 'Networks of innovators: a review and introduction to the issue', *Research Policy*, vol. 20, no. 5, pp. 363–79.

Department of Trade and Industry (DTI) (1992) *Supplier Innovation: The role of strategic partnerships in the UK automotive components sector*, DTI/SMMT: London.

Dobler, D.W., Burt, D.N. and Lamar, L.J. (1990) *Purchasing and Materials Management: Text and Cases* 5th edn, McGraw Hill: New York.

Dodgson, M. (1991a) *The Management of Technological Collaboration*, SPRU/Centre for Exploitation of Science and Technology: UK.

Dodgson, M. (1991b) *Technological Collaboration and Organisational Learning: A preliminary view of some key issues*, DRC Discussion Paper, Science Policy Research Unit: University of Sussex, UK.

Dodwell Marketing Consultants (1986) *The Structure of the Japanese Auto Parts Industry*, 3rd edn, Dodwell: Tokyo.

Dodwell Marketing Consultants (1990a) *The Structure of the Japanese Auto Parts Industry*, 4th edn, Dodwell: Tokyo.

Dodwell Marketing Consultants (1990b) *Industrial Groupings in Japan*, 9th edn, Dodwell: Tokyo.

Dore, R.P. (1987) *Taking Japan Seriously*, Stanford University Press: Stanford, CT.

Dosi, G. (1982) 'Technological paradigms and technological trajectories: a suggested interpretation of the determinants and directions of technical change', *Research Policy*, vol. 11, no. 3, pp. 147–62. Elsevier: Amsterdam.

Dosi, G., Freeman, C., Nelson, R., Silverberg, G. and Soete, L. (eds) (1988) *Technical Change and Economic Theory*, Frances Pinter: London.

Doz, Y. (1988) 'Technology partnerships between larger and smaller firms: some critical issues', in Contractor, F. and Lorange, P. (eds) *Cooperative Strategies in International Business*, Lexington Books: Lexington, MA.

Doz, Y. and Shuen, A (1988) 'From intent to outcome: a process framework for partnership', Paper presented at the Prince Bertil Symposium Corporate and Industry Strategies for Europe, Stockholm, 9–11 November.

Data Research International Europe (1991) *World Automotive Forecast Report*, Wimbledon, UK.

Drucker, P. (1946) *The Concept of the Corporation*, John Day: New York.

Drucker, P. (1967) *Managing for Results*, Pan Piper: London.

Dumbleton, J.H. (1986) *Management of High Technology R&D*, Elsevier: Amsterdam.

Eckhard, E. (1984) 'Alternative vertical structures: the case of the Japanese auto industry', *Business Economics*, October, pp. 57–61.

Economist Intelligence Unit (EIU) (1989) *The European Automotive Components Industry: A Review of Eighty Leading Manufacturers*, Business International Special Report No. 1186, April.

EIU (Economist Intelligence Unit) (1991) *The European Automotive Components Industry 1991: A Review of Eighty Leading Manufacturers*, Business International Special Report No. 2107.

ELM International (1989a) *The ELM Guide to US Automotive Sourcing*, 2nd edn, ELM International: Detroit.

ELM International (1989b) *The ELM Guide to Japanese Transplant Suppliers*, ELM International: Detroit.

ELM International (1992a) *The ELM Guide to Japanese Transplant Suppliers*, 3rd edn, ELM International: Detroit.

ELM International (1992b) *The ELM Guide to Mexican Automotive Sourcing*, ELM International: Detroit.

England, W. (1970) *Modern Procurement Management: Principles and cases*, 5th edn, Irwin: Homewood, IL.

Epstein, R.C. (1928) *The Automobile Industry: Its economic and commercial development*, Shaw: Chicago, IL.

Euromotor Reports Ltd (1991a) *Euromotor Financial Yearbook 1991*, London.

Euromotor Reports Ltd (1991b) *The World Vehicle Market Strategic Review and Data Book*, London.

Farmer, D.H. and MacMillan, K. (1976) 'Voluntary collaboration vs. "Disloyalty" to suppliers', *Journal of Purchasing and Materials Management*, Winter, pp. 3–8.

Farmer, D.H. and Ploos van Amstel, R. (1990) *Effective Pipeline Management: How to manage integrated logistics*, Gower: Aldershot.

Flaherty, T. (1981) 'Prices versus quantities and vertical financial integration', *Bell Journal of Economics*, vol. 12, Autumn, pp. 507–25. Rand: Santa Monica, CA.

Flink, J.F. (1970) *America Adopts the Automobile, 1895–1910*, MIT Press: Cambridge, MA.

Ford, H. (1922) *My Life and Work*, Heinemann: London.

Ford, I.D. (1978) 'Stability factors in industrial marketing channels', *Industrial Marketing Management*, vol. 7, pp. 410–22.

Ford, I.D. (1980) 'The developments of buyer–seller relationships in industrial markets', in Ford, I.D. *European Journal of Marketing*, vol. 14, nos. 5/6, pp. 339–53.

Ford, I.D. (1984) 'Buyer–seller relationships in international industrial markets', *Industrial Marketing Management*, vol. 13, no. 2, May, pp. 101–12.

Ford, I.D (ed.) (1990) *Understanding Business Markets: Interaction, relationships, networks*, Academic Press: UK.

Ford, I.D., Lamming, R.C. and Thomas, R. (1992) 'Relationship strategy, development and purchasing practice', *Proceedings of the 8th IMP Conference*, E.S.C.: Lyon, France.

Foxall, G.R. and Johnston, B. (1986) 'Strategies of user-initiated product innovation', *Technovation*, vol. 6, no. 187, p. 80.

Foxall, G.R. (1987) 'Strategic implications of user-initiated innovation', in Rothwell, R. and Bessant, J.R. (eds), *Innovation, adaptation and growth: An international perspective*, Elsevier: Amsterdam.

Fransman, M. (1990) *The Market and Beyond: Cooperation and competition in information technology development in the Japanese system*, Cambridge University Press: Cambridge.

Freeman C. (1969) 'National science policy', *Physics Bulletin*, vol. 20, pp. 265–70.

Freeman C. (1982) *The Economics of Industrial Innovation*, 2nd edn, Frances Pinter: London.

Freeman C. (1987) *Technology Policy and Economic Performance: Lessons from Japan*, Frances Pinter: London.

Freeman, C. and Perez, C. (1989) 'Structural crises of adjustment, business cycles and investment behaviour', Dosi, G. (ed), *Technical Change and Economic Theory*, Frances Pinter: London.

Freeman, C. (1991) 'Networks of innovators: a synthesis of research issues', *Research Policy*, vol. 20, no. 5, pp. 499–514.

Freidman, D. (1983) 'Beyond the age of Ford: the strategic basis of the Japanese success in automobiles', in Zyzsman J. and Tyson, L. (eds), *American Industry in International Competition*, Cornell University Press: Ithaca, NY.

Fujimoto, T. (1989) *Organisations for Effective Product Development: The case of the global motor industry*, PhD Thesis, Harvard Business School.

Fujita, K. (1965) *Nihon Sangyo Kozo to Chusho Kigyo (Japanese Industrial Structure and Small and Medium Enterprises)*, Iwanami Shoten: Tokyo.

Fusfeld, H. and Haklisch, C. (1987) 'Collaborative industrial research in the US', *Technovation*, vol. 5, pp. 305–15.

Galbraith, J.K. (1972) *The New Industrial State*, 2nd edn, Penguin: Harmondsworth.

Gardiner, P. (1984) 'Design trajectories for airplanes and automobiles during the past fifty years', in C. Freeman (ed), *Design, Innovation and Long Cycles in Economic Development*, Design Research Publications, Royal College of Art: London.

Georghiou, L., Metcalfe, J.S., Gibbons, M., Ray, T. and Evans, J. (1986) *Post-Innovation Performance: Technological development and competition*, Macmillan: London.

Gibbons, M. and Johnston, R. (1974) 'The roles of science in technological innovation', *Research Policy*, vol. 3, pp. 220–42.

Globerman, S. (1980) 'Markets, hierarchies and innovation', *Journal of Economic Issues*, vol. 14, December, pp. 977–98.

Granstrand, O. and Sjolander, S. (1990) 'Managing innovation in multi technology corporations', *Research Policy*, vol. 19, no. 2.

Graves, A.P. (1987) *Comparative trends in automotive research and development*, International Motor Vehicle Program, MIT: Cambridge, MA.

Graves, A.P. (1991) *International Competitiveness and Technology Development in the World Automobile Industry*, DPhil Thesis University of Sussex, Science Policy Research Unit, UK.

Gross, A., Banting, P., Meredith, L. and Ford, I.D. (1992) *Business Marketing: an international perspective*, Houghton Mifflin: Boston, MA.

Hakansson, H., Johanson, J. and Wootz, B. (1976) 'Influence tactics in buyer–seller processes', *Industrial Marketing Management*, vol. 4, no. 6, pp. 319–32.

Hakansson, H. (ed) (1982) *International Marketing and Purchasing of Industrial Goods: An Interaction Approach*, Wiley: Chichester.

Hakansson, H. (1987) *Product Development in Networks in Industrial Technological Development: A network approach*, Croom Helm: London.

Haklisch, C.S., Fusfeld, H.I. and Levenson, A.D. (1985) *Trends in Collective Industrial Research*, Centre for Science and Technology Policy, New York Graduate School of Business Administration: New York.

Hagedoorn, J. and Schakenraad, J. (1991) 'Interfirm partnerships and co-operative strategies in core technologies', in Freeman, C. *New Explorations in the Economics of Technical Change*, Frances Pinter: London.

Halberstam, D. (1986) *The Reckoning*, Morrow: New York.

Hamel G., Doz, Y. and Prahalad, C. (1989) 'Collaborate with your competitors – and win' *Harvard Business Review*, Jan–Feb.

Hardwick, R. and Ford, D. (1986) 'Industrial buyer resources and responsibilities and the buyer–seller relationship', *Industrial Marketing and Purchasing*, vol. 1, no. 3, pp. 3–26.

Harry, M.J. (1986) *The nature of six sigma quality*, Internal paper, Government Electronics Group, Motorola Inc.: Schaumberg, IL.

Hayes, R.H. and Abernathy, W. (1980) 'Managing our way to economic decline', *Harvard Business Review*, vol. 58, July–August, pp. 67–77.

Hayes, R.H. and Wheelright, S. (1984) *Restoring Our Competitive Edge: Competing through manufacturing*. Wiley: New York.

Hayes, R.H., Wheelright, S.C. and Clark, K.B. (1988) *Dynamic Manufacturing: Creating the learning organization*, The Free Press: New York.

Hegert, M. and Morris, D. (1988) 'Trends in international collaborative agreements', in Contractor, F. and Lorange, P. *Co-operative Strategies in International Business*, Lexington Books: Lexington, MA.

Helper, S.R. (1987) *Supplier Relations and Technical Change: Theory and application to the US automobile industry*, Unpublished PhD Thesis, Harvard University.

Helper, S.R. (1991) 'How much has really changed between US automakers and their suppliers?', *Sloan Management Review*, Summer, pp. 15–28.

Hessen, B. (1931) 'The social and economic roots of Newtons's principle', in Bukharin, N. (ed), *Science at the Crossroads: Papers from the Second International Congress of the History and Science of Technology, 1931*, (Revised edn), Frank Cass: London.

Heywood, J.B. and Wong, V. (1986) *A Study of How New Product Technologies are Adopted by Automobile Companies in the United States, Europe and Japan*, International Motor Vehicle Program, MIT: Cambridge, MA.

Hines, P. (1992) 'How should the purchasing profession learn from and develop present world best practice?' *Proceedings of the First Conference of the Purchasing and Supply Education and Research Group*, Strathclyde University, April.

Hirschman, A.O. (1970) *Exit, Voice, and Loyalty: Responses to decline in firms, organisations and states*, Harvard University Press: Cambridge, MA.

Horsley, W. and Buckley, R. (1990) *Nippon: New superpower*, BBC Books: London.

Hounshell, D. (1984) *From the American System to Mass Production, 1800–1932*, Johns Hopkins University Press: Baltimore, MD.

House of Commons (1987) *The UK Motor Components Industry, Report, Proceedings of the Committee, Minutes of Evidence and Appendices: Third Report from the Trade and Industry Committee*, Session 1986–87, HC 407.

Hout, T., Porter, M.E. and Rudden, E. (1982) 'How global companies win out', *Harvard Business Review*, September–October, pp. 98–108.

Hurley, N.P. (1959) 'The automotive industry: a study in industrial location', *Land Economics*, vol. 35.

Iacocca L. (1984) *Iacocca: An autobiography*, Bantam.

Ikeda, M. (1987) *An International Comparison of Subcontracting Systems in the Automotive Component Manufacturing Industry*, International Motor Vehicle Program, MIT: Cambridge, MA.

Ikeda, M., Sei, S. and Nishiguchi, T. (1988) *U-Line Auto Parts Production*, International Motor Vehicle Program, MIT: Cambridge, MA.

Imai, K.-I., Nonaka, I. and Takeuchi, H. (1985) 'Managing the new product development process: how Japanese companies learn and unlearn', in Clark, K., Hayes, R. and Lorenz, C. (eds) *The Uneasy Alliance: Managing the productivity–technology dilemma*, Harvard Business School Press: Cambridge, MA.

Imai, K. (1989) 'Evolution of Japan's corporate and industrial networks', in Carlsson, B. (ed) *Industrial Dynamics: Technological, organisational and structural changes in industries and firms*, Kluwer: Dordrecht.

Jewkes, J., Sawers, D. and Stillerman, R. (1958) *The Sources of Invention*, Macmillan: London.

JAMA (1991a) *The Motor Industry of Japan*, Japan Automotive Manufacturer's Association: Tokyo.

JAMA (1991b) *Information Update: Localization*, July, Japan Automotive Manufacturer's Association: Tokyo.

Johnson, C. (1982) *MITI and the Japanese Miracle: The growth of industrial policy, 1925–1975*, Stanford University Press: Stanford, CA.

Jones, D.T. (1985) 'Vehicles', in Freeman, C. (ed), *Technological Trends and Employment, No. 4: Engineering and Vehicles*, Gower: Aldershot.

Jones, D. T. (1988) *Measuring Technological Advantage in the Motor Vehicle Industry*, International Motor Vehicle Program, MIT: Cambridge MA.

Jones, D.T. (1989) 'Corporate strategy and technology in the automobile industry', in Dodgson, M. (ed), *Technology Strategy and the Firm: Managment and public policy*, Longman: London.

Kanter, R.M. (1985) *The Change Masters*, Counterpoint: London.

Kanter, R.M. (1989) *When Giants Learn to Dance*, Simon and Schuster: London.

Katz, H. (1977) *The Decline of Competition in the Automotive Industry, 1920–1940*, Arno Press: New York.

Klein, B., Crawford, R. and Alchian A. (1978) 'Vertical integration, appropriable quasi-rents, and the competitive contracting process', *Journal of Law and Economics*, p. 297.

Kogut, B. (1988) 'A study of the life cycle of joint ventures', in Contractor, F. and Lorange, P. *Cooperative Strategies in International Business*, Lexington Books: Lexington, MA.

Kotler, P. (1976) *Marketing Management, Analysis, Planning and Control*, 3rd edn, Prentice Hall: Englewood Cliffs, NJ.

Krafcik, J.F. (1986) *Learning from NUMMI*, International Motor Vehicle Program, MIT: Cambridge, MA.

Krafcik, J.F. and MacDuffie, J.P. (1989) *Explaining High Performance Manufacturing: The International Automotive Assembly Plant Study*, International Motor Vehicle Program, MIT: Cambrige, MA.

Kuhn, T. (1962) *The Structure of Scientific Revolutions*, University of Chicago Press: Chicago, IL.

Lamming R.C. (1975) *The Purchasing Procedures Involved in the Introduction of a New Motor Car*, Unpublished Bachelor's degree project report, University of Aston in Birmingham, UK.

Lamming, R.C. (1986) 'For better or for worse – impacts of technical change upon the UK automotive components sector', in Voss, C. (ed), *Managing Advanced Manufacturing Technology*, Proceedings of the first UK Operations Management Association conference, IFS: Bedford, UK.

Lamming, R.C. (1987a) 'Strategic approaches to just in time purchasing and supply in the automotive and electronics industries (UK, USA and Canada)', *Proceedings of the 2nd International Conference on Just-in-Time Manufacture*, IFS: Bedford, UK.

Lamming, R.C. (1987b) *Towards Best Practice: A Report on Components Supply in the UK Automotive Components Industry*, Brighton Business School (IRG Report No.4)/SPRU and International Motor Vehicle Program, MIT: Cambridge, MA.

Lamming, R.C. (1988) *The Post Japanese Model for International Automotive Components Supply*, International Motor Vehicle Program, MIT: Cambridge, MA.

Lamming, R.C. (1989a) *The Causes and Effects of Structural Change in the European Automotive Components Industry*, International Motor Vehicle Program, MIT: Cambridge, MA.

Lamming, R.C. (1989b) *The International Automotive Components Supply Industry: The Next 'Best Practice' for Suppliers*, International Motor Vehicle Program, MIT: Cambridge, MA.

Lamming, R.C. (1990) *Strategic Trends in the Global Automotive Components Industry: The implications for Australia*, Federation of Automotive Parts Manufacturers: Canberra.

Langlois, R. (1989) 'Economic change and the boundaries of the firm' in Carlsson, B. (ed) *Industrial Dynamics*, Kluwer: Berlin.

Langrish, J., Gibbons, M., Evans, W.J. and Jevons, F.R. (1972) *Wealth From Knowledge*, Macmillan: UK.

Lee, L. Jr and Dobler, D.W. (1971) *Purchasing and Materials Management: Text and cases*, 2nd edn, McGraw Hill: New York.

Levy, J. and Samuels, R. (1991) 'Institutions and innovation: research collaboration as technology strategy in Japan', in Mytelka, L. (ed) (1991) *Strategic Partnerships in the World Economy*, Frances Pinter: London.

Lewchuk, W. (1987) *American Technology and the British Vehicle Industry*, Cambridge University Press: Cambridge.

Lievegoed, B.C.J. (1973) *The Developing Organisation*, Tavistock: London.

Lievegoed, B.C.J. (1979) *Towards the 21st Century: Doing the good*, Steiner Book Centre: Vancouver.

Macaulay, S. (1963) 'Non-contractual relations in business: a preliminary study', *American Sociological Review*, vol. 28, no. 1, pp. 55–66.

Macbeth, D.K., Baxter, L.F., Ferguson, N. and Neil, G.C. (1989a) 'Buyer/supplier relationships: making it work', in *Competitive Sourcing: The Battleground of the 1990s*, IFS: Bedford, UK.

Macbeth, D.K., Baxter, L.F., Ferguson, N. and Neil, G.C. (1989b) 'Not purchasing but supply chain management', *Purchasing and Supply Management*, November, pp. 30–2.

Macbeth, D.K. and Ferguson, N. (1990) 'Strategic aspects of supply chain management', Paper presented at OMA-UK Conference on Manufacturing Strategy, Theory and Practice, University of Warwick.

Macdonald, S. (1991) 'Formal collaboration and informal information flow', *International Journal of Technology Management*, October.

Mansfield, E. (1961) 'Technical change and the rate of imitation', *Econometrics*, vol. 29, no. 4, pp. 741–66.

Mansfield, E. (1971) *Research and Innovation in the Modern Corporation*, Norton: New York.

Mansfield, E. and Wagner, S. (1975) 'Organizational and strategic factors associated with probabilities of success in industrial R&D', *Journal of Business*, vol. 48, no. 2, April, pp. 179–98.

Mansfield, E. (1977) *The Production and Application of New Industrial Technology*, Norton: New York.

Mansfield, E. (1985) 'How quickly does new industrial technology leak out?' *Journal of Industrial Economics*, vol. 34, no. 2, December, pp. 217–23.

Marler, D. L. (1989) *The Post-Japanese Model of Automotive Component Supply: Selected North American case studies*, International Motoral Vehicle Program, MIT: Cambridge, MA.

Masten, S. (1984) 'The organisation of production: evidence from the aerospace industry', *Journal of Law and Economics*, vol. 27, October, pp. 403–18.

McCarthy, E.J. (1978) *Basic Marketing*, 6th edn, Irwin: Homewood, IL.

McKinsey & Co. Inc. (1991) *Succeeding at Cross-Border Alliances: Lessons from winners*, Working Paper, London.

Mensch, G. (1979) *Stalemate in Technology*, Ballinger: New York.

Metcalfe, J.S. (1981) 'Impulse and diffusion in the study of technical change', *Futures*, vol. 13, no. 5 pp. 347–59.

Miles, R. and Snow, C. (1986) 'Organisations: new concepts for new forms', *California Management Review*, vol. 27, no. 3.

Miller, R. (1989) *The New Locational Dynamics in the Automobile Industry: Assembly facilities, parts plants and R&D centers*, International Motor Vehicle Program, MIT: Cambridge, MA.

Monden, Y. (1983) *Toyota Production System*, Industrial Engineering and Management Press: Atlanta, CA.

Monteverde, K. and Teece, D.J. (1982a) 'Supplier switching costs and vertical integration in the automobile industry', *Bell Journal of Economics*, vol. 13, no. 1, Spring, pp. 206–13.

Monteverde, K. and Teece, D.J. (1982b) 'Appropriable rents and quasi-vertical integration', *Journal of Law and Economics*, vol. 25, October, pp. 321–8.

Morishima, M. (1982) *Why Has Japan Succeeded? Western technology and the Japanese ethos*, Cambridge University Press: Cambridge.

Morita, A. and Reingold, E.M. (1986) *Made in Japan*, Dutton, New American Library, Penguin Books: New York.

Mowery, D. and Nelson, R. (1979) 'The influence of market demand upon innovation: a critical review of some recent empirical studies', *Research Policy*, vol. 8, p. 102.

Mowery, D.C. (ed) (1988) *International Collaborative Ventures in US Manufacturing*, Ballinger: Cambridge, MA.

Mowery, D.C. and Rosenberg, N. (1979) 'The influence of market demand upon innovation: a critical review of some recent empirical studies', *Research Policy*, April, pp. 103–53.

MVMA (1988) *Motor Vehicle Manufacturers' Association Yearbook*, MVMA: New Jersey.

Myers, S. and Marquis, D.G. (1969) *Successful Industrial Innovations*, National Science Foundation: London.

National Economic Development Council (NEDC) (1991) *The Experience of Nissan Suppliers: Lessons for the United Kingdom engineering industry*, London.

Nelson, R. and Winter, S. (1977) 'In search of a useful theory of innovation', *Research Policy*, vol. 6, no. 1, pp. 36–76.

Nelson, R. and Winter, S. (1983) *An Evolutionary Theory of Economic Change*, Harvard University Press: Cambridge, MA.

Nevins, A. and Hill, F. (1954a) *Ford: Expansion and challenge, 1915–1933*, Charles Scribner & Sons: New York.

Nevins, A. and Hill, F. (1954b) *Ford: The times, the man, the company*, Charles Scribner & Sons: New York.

Nishiguchi T. (1987) *Competing Systems of Automotive Component Supply: An examination of the Japanese 'clustered control' model and the 'Alps' structure*, International Motor Vehicle Program, MIT: Cambridge, MA.

Nishiguchi, T. (1989) *Strategic Dualism: An alternative in industrial societies*, Unpublished DPhil Thesis, Oxford University.

Nishiguchi, T. (1993) *Strategic Industrial Sourcing: The Japanese advantage*, Oxford Univerisity Press: New York.

Ohmae, K. (1985) *Triad Power: The coming shape of global competition*, Macmillan: London.

Ohmae, K. (1989) 'The global logic of strategic alliances', *Harvard Business Review*, Mar–Apr.

Ohmae, K. (1990) *The Borderless World*, Collins: London.

Oliver, N. and Wilkinson, B. (1988) *The Japanisation of British Industry*, Blackwell: Oxford.

Ordover, J.A. and Willig, R.D. (1985) 'Antitrust for high technology industries: assessing research joint ventures and mergers', *Journal of Law and Economics*, vol. 28, no. 2, May, pp. 311–33.

Pavitt, K. (1988) 'International patterns of technological accumulations', in Hood, N. and Vahlne, J.E. (eds) *Strategies in Global Competition*, Croom Helm:

Pavitt, K., Robson, M. and Townsend, J. (1989) 'Accumulation, diversification and organisation of technological activities in UK Companies, 1945–83', in Dodgson, M. (ed) *Technology Strategy and the Firm*, Longman: Harlow.

Pavitt, K. (1991) 'Key characteristics of the large innovating firm', *British Journal of Management*, vol. 2, pp. 41–50.

Piore M.J. and Sabel C.F. (1984) *The Second Industrial Divide*, Basic Books: New York.

Philips, A. (1971) *Technology and Market Structure*, Lexington Books: Lexington, MA.

Pisano, G., Shan, W. and Teece, D. (1988) 'Joint ventures and collaboration in the biotechnology industry', in Mowery, D. (ed) *International Collaborative Ventures in US Manufacturing*, Ballinger: Cambridge, MA.

Pisano, G., Teece, D. and Schuen A. (1990) *Firm Capabilities, Resources and the Concept of Strategies*, University of California: Los Angeles.

Polyani, M. (1962) *Personal Knowledge: Towards a post-critical philosophy*, Harper and Row: New York.

Porter, M. (1980) *Competitive Strategy: Techniques for analyzing industries and competitors*, The Free Press: New York.

Porter, M. (1983) 'The technological dimension of competitive strategy', in Rosenbloom R.S. (ed), *Research on Technological Innovation, Management and Policy*, vol. 1, JAI Press: Greenwich, CT and London.

Porter, M. (1985) *Competitive Advantage: Creating and sustaining superior performance*, The Free Press: New York.

Porter, M. and Fuller, K. (1986) 'Coalitions and corporate strategy', in Porter, M. *Competition in Global Industries*, Harvard Business School, Boston Press: Boston, MA.

Prahalad, C. and Hamel, G. (1990) 'The core competences ot the corporation', *Harvard Business Review*, May–June.

Riordan, M.H. and O.E. Williamson (1985) 'Asset specificity and economic organisation', *International Journal of Industrial Organisation*, vol. 3, pp. 365–78.

Robertson, P.L. and Langlois, R.N. (1988) 'Innovation and vertical integration in the

American automobile industry, 1900–1940', Paper presented at the (American) Economic History Association Annual Meeting, 24 September, Detroit.

Robson, M., Townsend, J. and Pavitt, K. (1988) 'Sectoral patterns of production and use of innovations in the UK: 1945–1983', *Research Policy* vol. 17, no. 1, February.

Rogers, E. and Shoemaker F. (1971) *Communications of Innovation*, The Free Press: New York.

Rogers, E. (1983) *Diffusion of Innovation*, 3rd edn, The Free Press: New York.

Rohlen, T. and Pascale, A. (1983) 'The Mazda turnaround', *Journal of Japanese Studies*, vol. 9, no. 2, Summer, pp. 219–64.

Rosenberg, N. (1976) *Perspectives on Technology*, Cambridge University Press: Cambridge.

Rosenberg, N. (1982) *Inside the Black Box: Technology and economics*, Cambridge University Press: Cambridge.

Rothwell, R. (1974) 'SAPPHO updated – Project SAPPHO phase 2', *Research Policy*, vol. 3, pp. 258–91.

Rothwell, R. (1977) 'The characteristics of successful innovations and technically progressive firms', *R and D Management*, vol. 7, no. 3.

Rothwell, R. (1981) *Industrial Innovation and Public Policy*, Frances Pinter: London.

Rothwell, R. (1983) *Information and Successful Innovation*, British Library Report No 5782: London.

Rothwell, R. (1989) 'Small firms, innovation and industrial change', *Small Business Economics*, vol. 1, pp. 51–64.

Rothwell, R. (1991) 'External networking and innovation in small and medium-sized manufacturing firms in Europe', *Technovation*, vol. 11, no. 2, pp. 93–112.

Rothwell, R. and Gardiner, P. (1984) 'Design and competition in engineering', *Long Range Planning*, vol. 17, no. 3, June, pp. 78–91.

Rothwell, R. and Gardiner, P. (1985) 'Invention, innovation, re-innovation and the role of the user: a case study of the British hovercraft development', *Technovation*, vol. 3, pp. 167–87.

Rothwell, R. and Gardiner, P. (1989) 'The strategic management of re-innovation', *R&D Management*, vol. 19, no. 2, April.

Rothwell, R. and Zegveld, W. (1985) *Reindustrialisation and Technology*, Longman: Harlow, UK.

Rothwell, R. and Bessant J.R. (eds) (1987) *Innovation, adaptation and growth: An international perspective*, Elsevier: Amsterdam.

Ruttan V. and Hayami, Y. (1971) *Agricultural Development*, Johns Hopkins University Press: Baltimore, MD.

Sakiya, T. (1987) *Honda Motor: The men, the management, the machines*, Kodansha International: Tokyo.

Sako, M. (1992) *Prices, Quality and Trust: Inter-firm relations in Britain and Japan*, Cambridge University Press: Cambridge.

Scherer, F. (1980) 'Demand pull and technological invention: Smookler revisited', *Journal of Industrial Economics*, vol. 30.

Schmookler, J. (1966) *Invention and Economic Growth*, Harvard University Press: Cambridge, MA.

Schonberger R.J. (1982) *Japanese Manufacturing Techniques: Nine hidden lessons in simplicity*, The Free Press: New York.

Schonberger R.J. (1987) *World Class Manufacturing: The lessons of simplicity applied*, The Free Press: New York.

Schumacher, E.F. (1978) *A Guide for the Perplexed*, Abacus Sphere: London.

Schumpeter, J. (1934) *The Theory of Economic Development*, Oxford University Press: New York.

Schumpeter, J. (1935) 'The analysis of economic change', *The Review of Economic Statistics*, May reprinted in 1944, *Readings in Business Cycle Theory*, Blaikston: Philadelphia.

Schumpeter, J. (1942), Translated (1950) *Capitalism, Socialism and Democracy*, Harper and Row: New York.

Scott Morton, M.S. (ed) (1991) *The Corporation of the 1990s: Information technology and organisational transformation*, Oxford University Press: New York.

Seltzer L.E (1928) *A Financial History of the American Automobile Industry*, Houghton-Mifflin: Boston, MA.

Shapiro, R.D. (1986) *Towards Effective Supplier Management: International comparisons*, Harvard Business School Working Paper.

Shapiro, B.P. (1988) *Close Encounters of the Four Kinds: Managing Customers in a Rapidly Changing Environment*, Harvard Business School Working Paper, No. 9-598-015, August.

Shaw, B. (1987) 'Strategies for user–producer interaction', in R. Rothwell and J.R. Bessant (eds) (1987) *Innovation, Adaptation and Growth: An international perspective*, Elsevier: Amsterdam.

Sheriff, A. (1988) *The Competitive Product Position of Automobile Manufacturers: Performance and strategies*, International Motor Vehicle Program, MIT: Cambridge, MA.

Sheth, J.N. (1973) 'A model of industrial buyer behaviour', *Journal of Marketing*, vol. 37, pp. 50–6.

Slack, N. (1991) *The Manufacturing Advantage*, Mercury Business Books: London.

Sloan, A. (1964) *My Years with General Motors*, Doubleday & Co.: Garden City, NY.

Smitka, M.J. (1991) *Competitive Ties: Subcontracting in the Japanese automotive industry*, Columbia University Press: New York.

Sorensen, C.E. (1956) *My Forty Years with Ford*, Norton: New York.

Stoneman, P. (1976) *Technological Diffusion and the Computer Revolution: The UK experience*, University of Cambridge, Department of Applied Economics Monograph No. 25, Cambridge University Press: Cambridge.

Syson, R. (1992) *Improving Purchase Performance*, Pitman: London.

Technomic Consultants International (1990) *The Japanese in the European Automotive Market: Scenarios for the 1990s*, Consultancy Report for multiclient study, No. 90–5466R: Epsom, Surrey, UK.

Teece, D. J. (1982) 'Towards an economic theory of the multiproduct firm', *Journal of Economic Behaviour and Organisation*, vol. 2, pp. 39–63.

Teece, D.J. (1986) 'Profiting from technological innovation: implications for integration, collaboration, licensing and public policy', *Research Policy*, vol. 15, pp. 285–305.

Teece, D.J., (1987) *The Competitive Challenge: Strategies for industrial innovation and renewal*, Ballinger: Cambridge, MA.

Teece, D. and Mowery, D. (1988) *International Collaboration Ventures in US Manufacturing*, Ballinger: Cambridge, MA.

Teece, D.J., Pisano, G. and Schuen, A. (1990) *Firm Capabilities, Resources and the Concept of Strategy*, Working Paper No. 90–8, University of Berkeley; Berkeley, CA.

Thomas, R.P. (1977) *An Analysis of the Pattern of Growth of the Automobile Industry, 1895–1929*, Arno Press: New York.

Uhlenbruch, W.W.J. (1986) *Australian Motor Vehicles and Parts: A study of an industry shaped by government*, CEDA Occasional Paper No 27, October, Committee for Economic Development of Australia: Melbourne.

Van de Ven, A.H., Emmit, D.C., and Koenig, R. (1975) 'Frameworks for interorganisational analysis', in Negandhi, A.R. (ed) *Interorganisational Theory*, Kent State University Press: Kent, OH.

Veblen, T. (1899) *The Theory of the Leisure Class: An economic study of institutions*, Viking Press: New York.

Von Hippel, E. (1976) 'The dominant role of users in the scientific instrument innovation process', *Research Policy*, vol. 5, pp. 212–39. Elsevier: Amsterdam.

Von Hippel, E. (1978) 'A customer-active paradigm for industrial product idea generation', *Research Policy*, vol. 7, pp. 240–66. Elsevier: Amsterdam.

Von Hippel, E. (1982) 'Get new products from customers', *Harvard Business Review*, vol. 60, no. 2, March–April, pp. 117–22. Elsevier: Amsterdam.

Von Hippel, E. (1988) *The Sources of Innovation*, Oxford University Press: New York.

Voss, C.A. (1984) 'Multiple independent invention and the process of technological innovation', *Technovation*, vol. 2, pp. 169–84.

Voss, C.A. (ed) (1987) *Just in Time Manufacture*, IFS: Bedford, UK.

Voss, C.A. and Robinson, S. (1987) 'The application of just-in-time techniques', *The International Journal of Operations and Production Management*, vol. 7, no. 4, pp. 46–52.

Walker, G. and Weber, D. (1984a) 'A transaction cost approach to make or buy decisions', *Admin Science Quarterly*, vol. 29, September, pp. 373–91.

Walker, G. and Weber, D. (1984b) *Supplier Competition, Uncertainty, and Make or Buy Decisions*, Working Paper, MIT Sloan School: Cambridge, MA.

Walsh, V., Townsend, J., Achilladelism, B.G. and Freeman, C. (1979) *Trends in Invention and Innovation in the Chemical Industry*, mimeo, Science Policy Research Unit, University of Sussex.

Webster, Jr, F.E. and Wind, Y. (1972) 'A general model for understanding organisational buyer behaviour', *Journal of Marketing*, vol. 36, pp. 12–19.

Westing, J.H., Fine, I.V., and Zenz, G.J. (1976) *Purchasing Management: Materials in motion*, John Wiley: New York.

Whipp, R. and Clark, P. (1986) *Innovation and the Auto Industry: Product, process and work organisation*, Frances Pinter: London.

White, L.J. (1971) *The Automobile Industry since 1945*, Harvard University Press: Cambridge, MA.

Williamson, O.E. (1975) *Markets and Hierarchies*, The Free Press: New York.

Williamson, O.E. (1985) *The Economic Institutions of Capitalism*, The Free Press: New York.

Williamson, O.E. (1986) *Economic Organization: Firms, markets and policy control*, Wheatsheaf: Brighton, UK.

Willman, P. (1986) *Innovation and Industrial Relations*, Oxford University Press: Oxford.

Womack J.P., Jones, D.T, and Roos, D. (1990) *The Machine that Changed the World*, Rawson Ass.: New York.

Womack, J.P. (1988) 'Multinational joint ventures in motor vehicles', in D.C. Mowery (ed), *International Collaborative Ventures in U.S. Manufacturing*, Ballinger: Cambridge, MA.

Zeitlin J. and Hirst, P. (1988) *Reversing Industrial Decline*, Berg: Oxford.

Index